Sexual Revolutions

The ideas of psychoanalyst Otto Gross (1877–1920) have had a seminal influence on the development of psychoanalytic theory and clinical practice and yet his work has been largely overlooked. For Freud, he was one of only two analysts 'capable of making an original contribution' (Jung was the other), and Jung called Gross 'my twin brother' in the course of their mutual analysis.

This is a major interdisciplinary enquiry into the history, nature and plausibility of the idea of a 'sexual revolution', drawing also on the related fields of history, law, criminology, literature, sociology and philosophy. Divided into four parts and offering an interdisciplinary and international range of contributors, areas of discussion include:

- a contemporary perspective on sexual revolutions
- the broad influence of Otto Gross
- the father–son conflict
- a Jungian perspective on history

Sexual Revolutions introduces Gross's work to the academic and clinical fields of psychoanalysis and Jungian Analysis. Although most people associate the term with the 1960s, its foundations lie in the long-neglected but sensational work of the early psychoanalyst Otto Gross. This book will be essential reading for all psychoanalysts and Jungian analysts with an interest in learning more about his work.

Gottfried Heuer is a Jungian Training Analyst and Supervisor, and a Body psychotherapist, with over 35 years' private practice in West London. He is an independent scholar with over 60 published papers on the links between analysis, radical politics, body psychotherapy and spirituality, and on the history of analysis. He is co-founder and Chair of the International Otto Gross Society, for which he (co-)edited seven volumes of *Congress proceedings*, and editor of *Sacral Revolutions Reflecting on the Work of Andrew Samuels – Cutting Edges in Psychoanalysis and Jungian Analysis*, Routledge.

Revolution

Otto Gross
1877 - 1920

Psycho-Analyst
Psycho-Anarchist

Sexual Revolutions

Psychoanalysis, History and the Father

Edited by Gottfried Heuer

LONDON AND NEW YORK

First published 2011 by Routledge
27 Church Road, Hove, East Sussex BN3 2FA

Simultaneously published in the USA and Canada
by Routledge
270 Madison Avenue, New York, NY 10016

Routledge is an imprint of the Taylor & Francis Group, an Informa business

Typeset in Times by Garfield Morgan, Swansea, West Glamorgan
Printed and bound in Great Britain by TJ International Ltd, Padstow, Cornwall
Paperback cover design, 'Father Time, Eros and Essential Feminine', by Gottfried Heuer

This publication has been produced with paper manufactured to strict environmental standards and with pulp derived from sustainable forests.

British Library Cataloguing in Publication Data
A catalogue record for this book is available from the British Library

Library of Congress Cataloging-in-Publication Data
Sexual revolutions : psychoanalysis, history and the father / edited by Gottfried Heuer.
p. cm.
Includes bibliographical references.
ISBN 978-0-415-57043-5 (hardback) – ISBN 978-0-415-57044-2 (pbk.)
1. Gross, Otto, 1877-1920. 2. Psychoanalysis. 3. Jungian psychology.
4. Psychology, Pathological. I. Heuer, Gottfried, 1944–
BF175.S48 2010
150.19'52092–dc22

2010019575

ISBN: 978-0-415-57043-5 (hbk)
ISBN: 978-0-415-57044-2 (pbk)

For Birgit
With gratitude, in love

'Create new heavens and a new earth' (Isaiah 65: 17)

Otto Gross's 1919 call to replace the 'will to power' with the 'will to relating' as 'the highest, the essential goal of all revolutions' re-emerged in the 1960s as 'make love, not war!': *Now*, if God *is* love, then making love is to invoke the sacred – 'two bodies, one flesh' – and 'in our flesh we shall see God' (Job 19: 26).

Gottfried M. Heuer

Contents

Figures

Contributors

David Bennett teaches English and Cultural Theory at the University of Melbourne and is a visiting professor in the Department of History, Classics and Archaeology at Birkbeck College, University of London. He has published around 90 scholarly articles in the fields of literary, musical and cultural history, including a dozen on the political and economic histories of psychoanalysis and sexology in such journals as *New Literary History*, *Public Culture* and *Textual Practice*. His books include *Cultural Studies: Pluralism and Theory* (1993), *Multicultural States: Rethinking Difference and Identity* (1998), *Sounding Postmodernism* (2009) and *Postmodernism, Music and Cultural Theory* (2009).

Dr. Gerhard M. Dienes, born in Graz, Austria, read History and was appointed curator at the Museum of the City of Graz in 1980. He was the museum's director from 1990 to 2004 and has worked for the Universalmuseum Joanneum, Styria, since 2005. From 1985 to 1994 he lectured at the University of Graz and he is a member of the Advisory Committee on the Promotion of Culture in Styria, currently based in Graz. He has curated more than 70 exhibitions in Austria and abroad and has authored about 150 publications on the history of transport and on local, social, economic and industrial history. Further fields of interest include suburbs, cultural history, the history of mentalities and the history of the Alps-Adriatic region.

Sander L. Gilman is a distinguished professor of the Liberal Arts and Sciences and Professor of Psychiatry at Emory University, Atlanta, USA (Director of the Program in Psychoanalysis and the Health Sciences Humanities Initiative). A cultural and literary historian, he is the author or editor of over 80 books. He is the editor of *Race and Contemporary Medicine: Biological Facts and Fictions* (2008) and the author of *Diseases and Diagnoses: The Second Age of Biology* (2010); the basic study of the visual stereotyping of the mentally ill, *Seeing the Insane* (1982, reprinted 1996); and the standard study of *Jewish Self-Hatred* (1986).

Albrecht Götz von Olenhusen, Dr. Jur., Freiburg i. Br., is a lawyer, law historian and lecturer at the University of Düsseldorf. His works include publications on Walter Benjamin, Siegfried Kracauer, Louis Blanc, Proudhon, Karl May, Johannes Nohl, Erich Mühsam, Franz Jung, and Hans and Otto Gross. He co-edited two Congress Proceedings of the International Otto Gross Society (*Die Gesetze des Vaters, Graz 2003*, Marburg, 2003; *Psychoanalyse und Expressionismus, Dresden 2008*, Marburg, 2010). List of publications: www.drgoetzvonolenhusen.de

Jungian Analyst **Birgit Heuer** is a senior practitioner with 30 years of clinical experience. She is also trained in body-oriented psychotherapy and – informally as a personal pupil of the late Rose Gladden – in healing. She has served on the training committee of the British Association of Psychotherapists and was clinical supervisor at Kingston University Health Centre, London, for a number of years. She has written and lectured internationally on the psychodynamics of the healing process, on the body in psychotherapy and on forgiveness. At present she is engaged in doctoral research on *sanatology*, her term for a psychotherapeutic theory of health and healing.

Dr. Gottfried M. Heuer is a Jungian training analyst and supervisor with the Association of Jungian Analysts, London and a Neo-Reichian body psychotherapist. He has been in clinical practice for over 35 years and is also an independent scholar, graphic artist, photographer, sculptor and poet. He has written over 60 published papers on the links between analysis, radical politics, body psychotherapy and spirituality, as well as on the history of analytic ideas, in journals including *Spring*, *the International Journal of Psychoanalysis*, *the Journal of Analytical Psychology*, *the International Journal of Jungian Studies*, *Harvest*, *Psychotherapy and Politics International*. He is (co-) editor of seven congress and symposium proceedings for the International Otto Gross Society (www.ottogross.org/), which he co-founded, and editor of *Sacral Revolutions: Reflecting on the Work of Andrew Samuels: Cutting Edges in Psychoanalysis and Jungian Analysis*, Routledge (2010). He is author of 'In My Flesh I Shall See God' – Body and Psyche in Analysis (2009), available as a podcast at http://www.guildofpastoral psychology.org.uk/index.php?option=com_content&view=article&id= 215&Itemid=102

Amanda Hon, MA, Adv Dip, is a psychotherapist registered with the United Kingdom Council for Psychotherapy and has a private practice in West London. She trained at the Centre for Transpersonal Psychology, London and holds a Masters degree in Jungian and Post-Jungian Studies from the Centre for Psychoanalytic Studies, University of Essex, UK. She is a Director/Trustee of FreshStart Psychotherapy, a charity that provides low-cost psychotherapy to members of the Greater London community.

Professor Brett Kahr is Senior Clinical Research Fellow in Psychotherapy and Mental Health at the Centre for Child Mental Health in London, and Honorary Visiting Professor in the School of Arts at Roehampton University, London. He also serves as Consultant Psychologist to the Bowlby Centre, and as the Chair of the British Society of Couple Psychotherapists and Counsellors, the Professional Association of the Tavistock Centre for Couple Relationships, at the Tavistock Institute of Medical Psychology. He is a Registered Psychotherapist with the Council for Psychoanalysis and Jungian Analysis, the United Kingdom Council for Psychotherapy and the British Psychoanalytic Council. His many books include *Sex and the Psyche* (2007).

Kevin Lu is a PhD candidate and lecturer in psychoanalytic studies at the University of Essex, UK. He is the Director of the MA in Jungian and Post-Jungian Studies and a member of the Executive Committee of the International Association for Jungian Studies. He holds degrees from New College, University of Toronto (BA Hons) and Heythrop College, University of London (MA in Psychology of Religion). His doctoral thesis explores the possibility of a distinctly Jungian approach to psychoanalytic history.

Jennifer E. Michaels is Samuel R. and Marie-Louise Rosenthal Professor of Humanities and Professor of German at Grinnell College in Iowa, USA. She received her MA degree in German from Edinburgh University and an MA and a PhD in German from McGill University in Montreal, Canada. She has published four books and numerous articles about twentieth-century German and Austrian literature and culture, which is her main teaching and research interest, and has served as president of the German Studies Association and the Rocky Mountain Modern Language Association.

Thomas Mühlbacher, Dr. Jur., graduated from the University of Graz, Austria, in 1986 and was appointed as a judge in 1990. Since 2010 he has been chief prosecutor of the Public Prosecution Service Graz/Austria and vice president of the Association of Austrian Prosecutors. He has written several publications on criminal law and proceedings, the history of criminology and Hans Gross.

Susie Orbach is a psychoanalyst and writer whose interests have centred around feminism and psychoanalysis; the construction of femininity and gender; globalisation and body image; emotional literacy and psychoanalysis; and the public sphere. She co-founded The Women's Therapy Centre in London in 1976 and The Women's Therapy Centre Institute, New York, in 1981. Her numerous publications include the classic *Fat is* *a Feminist Issue*, along with other such influential texts as *Hunger Strike*, *The Impossibility of Sex* and the recently published *Bodies*. Susie is a founder member of Antidote (working for emotional literacy) and Psychotherapists and Counsellors for Social Responsibility and is convener of Anybody (www.any-body.org), an organisation campaigning for body diversity. She is currently chair of the Relational School in the UK and has a clinical practice, seeing individuals and couples.

Andrew Samuels is Professor of Analytical Psychology at the University of Essex and holds visiting chairs at London, Roehampton and New York Universities. He is a Training Analyst for the Society of Analytical Psychology and is in clinical practice in London. He works internationally as a political consultant and is co-founder of Psychotherapists and Counsellors for Social Responsibility and chair of the United Kingdom Council for Psychotherapy. His books have been translated into 19 languages and include *Jung and the Post-Jungians*, *The Father*, *A Critical Dictionary of Jungian Analysis*, *The Plural Psyche*, *Psychopathology*, *The Political Psyche* and *Politics on the Couch* (www.andrew samuels.com).

Alfred Springer, MD, is a professor in Psychiatry at the Medical University of Vienna and a psychoanalyst (VPA). He is director emeritus of the Ludwig Boltzmann Institute for Addiction research and editor of *Wiener Zeitschrift für Suchtforschung*. Books include *Kokain: Mythos und Realität*; *Pathologie der geschlechtlichen Identitität*; *Homosexualität und Transsexualismus*; and *Die Wiener Drogenszene*. He has published widely on drug addiction and sexuality (with a focus on gender dysphoria); the history of psychoanalysis; the political discourse on psychoanalysis; literature and psychoanalysis; fetishism and the visual arts; movies and psychoanalysis; the cultural aspects of psychoanalysis and the cultural and political involvement of psychoanalysts (with a focus on Otto Gross and German expressionism); and the history of psychiatry (with a focus on national socialism). On the occasion of Freud's 150th birthday, he lectured in Vienna, Toronto and Istanbul.

Nick Totton is a therapist and trainer in private practice. Originally a Reichian body therapist, he currently teaches and practises his own synthesis, Embodied-Relational Therapy. He holds an MA in Psychoanalytic Studies, and has also worked with Process Oriented Psychology and trained as a craniosacral therapist. He is currently immersed in ecopsychology. His books include *The Water in the Glass: Body and Mind in Psychoanalysis*; *Body Psychotherapy: An Introduction*; *Psychotherapy and Politics*; and *Press When Illuminated: New and Selected Poems*. There is an extensive website at www.erthworks.co.uk. Nick lives in Yorkshire with his partner and grows vegetables.

John Turner was formerly a senior lecturer in English at Swansea University, South Wales. He has written books on Wordsworth and *Macbeth*, co-authored two books on Shakespeare and written over 20 essays on D. H. Lawrence as well as an as yet unpublished book on D. H. Lawrence and the history of psychoanalysis. Together with Gottfried Heuer, he is currently preparing an English edition of the complete psychoanalytic writings of Otto Gross.

Sam Whimster is professor of social economics at the Global Policy Institute, London Metropolitan University. He is the editor of the international journal *Max Weber Studies* and is currently involved in a new edition and translation of Weber's *Wirtschaft und Gesellschaft*, to be published by Routledge. He is a founder member of the Otto Gross Gesellschaft and his *Max Weber and the Culture of Anarchy* was published by Macmillan in 1998. He is currently putting together a database of Max Weber's letters.

Acknowledgements

For the exhibition entitled The Laws of the Father: Freud/Gross/Kafka and the accompanying symposia on which the present volume is based, support of the following organisations is gratefully acknowledged: The Anna Freud Centre, London; the Austrian Cultural Forum, London; Brühl, Austria; the City of Graz Culture and the Federal State of Styria Culture, Austria; the Freud Museum, London; the International Otto Gross Society, Hannover/London; Pischler Engineering; University of Graz, Austria; and the Universalmuseum Johanneum, Graz.

The front and back cover compositions are both variations on a theme by Agnolo Bronzino: *Allegory with Saturn, Cupid and Venus* (ca. 1550). Sadly, high copyright costs make a reproduction – even on the smallest scale – an impossibility, but the image is available on numerous internet sites: just Google 'Bronzino Allegory of Venus and Cupid'.

In gratitude to the contributors and my editors at Routledge, Kate Hawes, Erasmis Kidd and Sarah Gibson, and to Sally Mesner Lyons for her careful and caring copy-editing. Many thanks also to Brendan O'Brien for his meticulous work on compiling the index, and to Kristin Susser of the production team.

Gottfried M. Heuer
London, June 2010

Introduction

'The angel of history'[1]

'The past and the present are entwined like lovers in an embrace'[2]

Gottfried M. Heuer

> We create the meaning of events. [. . .] The meaning of events is the way to salvation you create. The meaning of events comes from the possibility of life in this world that you create. [. . . It] is not in events, and not in the soul, but is the God standing between events and the soul, the mediator of life, the way, the bridge, and the going across.
>
> C. G. Jung (2009: 239)

This volume presents a multi-faceted, interdisciplinary and international approach by authors from six countries and three continents to the theme of *Psychoanalysis, History and the Father* and the ways in which each of these impacts on the other with the explicit aim of furthering individual and collective growth and healing. As each is seen in the alive fluidity of its changing reality, a pluralistic approach is required. Unavoidably, this creates certain overlaps, yet within the context of the individual text, each contributes to a unique perspective and thus fulfils an important function. Taken together as a whole, these individual voices of the different authors collectively are 'looking back towards the future', as it were, in the way the philosopher Walter Benjamin spoke of 'the angel of history':

> His face is turned towards the past. [. . .] The angel would like to stay, awaken the dead, and make whole what has been smashed. But a storm is blowing from Paradise, it has got caught in his wings [. . .] that the angel can no longer close them. The storm irresistibly propels him into the future to which his back is turned.
>
> (Benjamin 1940: 259–260)

In this respect there is an important parallel with analytic clinical work. The continuation of the psychoanalytic revolution which Otto Gross started by sowing the seeds of change from a hierarchical – I might also say 'patriarchal' – and authoritarian analyst–patient relationship of the traditional medical model towards a relational concept in theory and practice can be understood as one aspect of his rebellion against 'The Law of the Father'. When, in 1913, Gross writes, 'The coming revolution is the revolution for matriarchy' (387), we may understand this with hindsight from the vantage point of today as a statement regarding the feminist revolution that has since then changed the world we live in, and is continuing to do so. Values that can traditionally be regarded as masculine are losing their monolithic power to be replaced by those traditionally regarded as feminine, such as relatedness, feeling, subjectivity, tolerance of not knowing, etc. – in the widest sense a sexual revolution. This is also reflected in the pluralistic way of dealing with the subject matter from many different angles in order to arrive at a more realistic picture.

When Barack Obama speaks of the necessity to 'beat back the politics of fear, and doubt, and cynicism' (2008: 216) and of 'choosing hope over fear' (ibid.: 214), we see the same teleological attitude in politics, especially when he defines this hope as 'this thing inside us that insists, despite all evidence to the contrary, that something better awaits us if we have the courage to reach for it' (ibid.: 216). Jonathan Lear calls this *Radical Hope: Ethics in the Face of Cultural Devastation* (2006).

The previous century has shown – possibly more than any other before – that, 'The dream of reason produces monsters', as Goya illustrated over 200 years ago. An important part of this 'dream of reason' is the dream of a science that in certain areas still insists on the delusion of being capable of an 'objective' view of reality: originally from the Latin word for knowledge, since the 'enlightenment' science has come to be used as implying 'hard', 'objective'. Yet, some 100 years after Goya, Nietzsche wrote, 'However far man may extend himself with his knowledge, however objective he may appear to himself – ultimately he reaps nothing but his own biography' (1878: 513). Since then, another spectre is haunting not just Europe – the spectre of relativity, uncertainty. The literal meaning of the German term *Wissenschaft* may be helpful in this context, as it just means 'that which creates knowledge', leaving the door more open for those traditional feminine values mentioned above. This means incorporating previously discarded aspects of reality, as in, for example, Sally Vickers boldly stating that 'a myth is a fiction that gives us the facts' (2007). Some cutting-edge historians therefore speak of *Mythistory* (Mali 2003), no longer necessarily trying to distinguish what 'really' happened and what people believe happened. This may well mean reconciling apparent contradictions.

The cause of Otto Gross's death may serve as an example to illustrate this point: Sander Gilman (cf. Chapter 4) writes that he committed suicide. Yet the official death certificate states 'pneumonia' – seemingly a contradiction. Only a wider perspective that takes into account the surrounding circumstances of decades of a severe cocaine addiction that ultimately led to Gross roaming half-starved through a wintry Berlin in February 1920, until he was found collapsed in a doorway, allows an approach where both 'suicide' *as well as* 'pneumonia' are different aspects of a historical 'truth'.

The scientific revolutions of the last century – I am particularly thinking of relativity, uncertainty and quantum theory in the realm of physics – have continued to help us wake up from the nightmare of reason. Psychoanalysis has played an important part in this, as Freud noted in 1917, when he spoke of the three severe blows to what he called man's narcissistic self-love (142ff.): the dethroning of man by Copernicus (the earth not being the centre of the universe); Darwin (man's descent from animal life): and Freud himself, who made us aware that we are not master in our home but ruled from and by our unconscious. And Freud also wrote about science in 1933: 'What we give out as being scientific truth is only the product of our needs as they are bound to find utterance under changing external conditions: once again, they are illusion' (175). In a very similar vein, C. G. Jung echoed Nietzsche, stating that 'every psychological theory [is] in the first instance [. . . a] subjective confession' (Jung 1934: 540). Let us assume, then, that the same is true for scientific theories in general – which is what Nietzsche might well have meant, and Freud explicitly said – especially the science of history, which is, in fact, so similar to psychoanalysis. Without directly linking these two, in *Composing Useful Pasts: History as Contemporary Politics* (2000), the American historian Edmund Jacobitti argues that every historical exploration starts with the desire to heal an issue in the present. *Composing Useful Pasts* implies a fluid notion: the past is not static, it can change, and indeed it changes according to the subjective perspective. Jacobitti's take on the collective past corresponds to the way psychoanalysis works with an individual's past.

Adding to this the way Otto Gross introduced the concept of mutually relating as equals into psychoanalysis in the way Jung later elaborated further, takes us to Robert Romanyshyn's (2000) application of these ideas to the relationship between the researcher and his/her subject: he postulates that both are changed by the work. If we take yet another step and consider the implications of the statement made by Peter Ackroyd that I have chosen as the title for my introduction, we may also see past and present as conceiving the future. In addition, in lovingly embracing each other, each of the partners is contained in the other *as* an other. From a Grossian perspective, which Jung later found confirmed by the alchemists he studied, *making love* also invokes the numinous (cf. Chapter 16). It follows that historical research, the way I understand it, is 'research with soul in mind' (Romanyshyn 2000). In a further parallel to the analytic couple, this way of mutual relating furthermore also invokes the numinous, which is also considered in this volume.

Concerning the sexual revolution, the psychoanalyst Reimut Reiche has suggested that its 'attraction [. . .] lies not least in the compulsion to deny again and again guilt and depression linked with parenticide' (Reiche 1988:

68). This is a fight that seems to have been predominantly fought in the male arena between fathers and sons – the oedipal realm. Correspondingly, nearly all of the known sexual revolutions – from the millenarian sects of the Middle Ages, the Adamites, Anabaptists and others, through to Charles Fourier at the turning from the eighteenth to the nineteenth century, to John Humphrey Noyes in the nineteenth century and Otto Gross at the turning from the nineteenth to the twentieth century, right through the efforts in this direction of the 1960s – have as a common link the ruling male perspective. They were, as David Bennett appropriately calls them, 'masculinist sexual revolutions' (cf. Chapter 2). From this perspective we have to understand them as ultimately not much more than more or less pornographic male fantasies, because, as Gross himself observed, 'the revolutionary of yesterday carried the authoritarian [we might call it patriarchal] structure within himself' (Gross 1913: 386). Accordingly, and by definition, in patriarchal historiography, woman's voice remains unheard, is 'persecuted speech' (Kuhn 2002: 344). Only in the year 2000 could Tirzah Miller's heart-wrenching 'intimate memoir' of life in Noyes's Oneida commune in the mid-nineteenth century be published (and it remains unmentioned in Bennett's account). Only recently have Frieda Gross's letters to her lifelong friend Else Jaffé been published, which movingly speak of how painful life was with the sexual revolutionary Otto Gross – to the extent that she contemplated suicide more than once (Bertschinger-Joos 2005; 2006). From this perspective, the feminine voices of Jennifer Michaels, Amanda Hon, Birgit Heuer and Susie Orbach in the present volume are of particular importance in the way they point to a possible future.

Focusing our considerations on Otto Gross means seeing him in his relation to *Psychoanalysis, History and the Father* as paradigmatically standing for 'the revolution of the impossibility of revolution', as Sam Whimster beautifully puts it (cf. Chapter 12), at the very centre of the storm of the cultural revolution we call modernism, yet with his ideas reaching far beyond the postmodern present.

Outline

I have divided the book into four parts. As well as a general outlook, the introductory *Part I: History* offers, with Kevin Lu's Chapter 1, a continuation and deepening of the ideas on history presented in the introduction – with a specifically Jungian perspective. In Chapter 2 David Bennett places the concept of sexual revolution into a historical context.

Part II: Fathers and sons, broadly speaking, gathers aspects of the father–son conflict – touching upon the oedipal fighting of men over women – by first focusing, in Thomas Mühlbacher's Chapter 3, on the father Hans Gross. Sander Gilman, in Chapter 4, speaks of Kafka's relationship to the same father figure, and how this relationship shaped his sexuality. In

Figure 0.2 Otto Gross, 1877–1920.

Chapter 5, Gerhard Dienes continues with detailing the paradigmatic generational conflict between Gross father and son. Albrecht Götz von Olenhusen, in Chapter 6, broadens out the issue to include Otto Gross's conflicting relationships with other-than-biological father figures in his life: Sigmund Freud and Max Weber.

Part III: Psychoanalysis, literature and sociology is concerned with the history of ideas and deals with wide-reaching influences Otto Gross had on psychoanalysis (in the first three chapters), literature (in the following two) and sociology (in the final chapter). In Chapter 7 Alfred Springer looks at the exchange of ideas between Gross and Freud. Gottfried Heuer, in Chapter 8, writes about the revolutionary innovations some of Gross's ideas brought to the theory and clinical practice of psychoanalysis. In Chapter 9, Nick Totton speaks of the continuation of the sexual revolution through the work of Wilhelm Reich, who introduced the body into 'the talking cure'. Based on her 1983 book *Anarchy and Eros* – a seminal work in the field of Gross studies – Jennifer Michaels in Chapter 10 charts the impact of Otto Gross on German Expressionist writers. In Chapter 11, John Turner focuses on the way Gross's ideas impacted on D. H. Lawrence and thus also on Anglo-American literature. Sam Whimster, in Chapter 12, presents Otto Gross's relationship to the members of the Heidelberg circle – the brothers Alfred and Max Weber and the latter's wife, Marianne; Edgar Jaffé and the von Richthofen sisters, Else and Frieda, and their friend Frieda Schloffer, Otto Gross's wife.

Part IV: Sexual revolutions concentrates on the present facing the future, starting with Chapter 13, Susie Orbach and Brett Kahr in conversation considering the sexual revolutions of the past 50 years with a view towards the future. In Chapter 14, Andrew Samuels takes a multi-faceted view on promiscuities – usually implied in the term 'sexual revolution'. Amanda Hon, in Chapter 15, contributes a perspective from the vitally important feminine position that has usually been overlooked in the past as men lived out their sexual fantasies and called them 'revolution'. In Chapter 16, Birgit Heuer speaks of the advent of post-postmodernism and forgiveness as the healing agent of relating. Gottfried Heuer, in the concluding Chapter 17, describes how seminal concepts of Otto Gross are being confirmed by cutting-edge findings in physics, biology, psychoanalysis and philosophy, completing the arc of history from the past to the future.

'The continuing life of an exhibition'[3]

It is the intrinsic character of an exhibition to be a temporary event. However, it can still achieve sustainability and act as a catalyst for subsequent projects. This is particularly true of the exhibition '*Die Gesetze des Vaters: Hans und Otto Gross, Sigmund Freud and Franz Kafka*' (The Laws of the Father: Hans and Otto Gross, Sigmund Freud and Franz Kafka), devised and curated by Dr. Gerhard Dienes and Dr. Ralf Rother for Graz, Cultural Capital 2003.

The exhibition modelled encounters between the four people and their discussions of law and penalty, the father figure, patriarchy and the (father) state: four people in a biographical, reflective, literary and disputative relational network between criminology and revolution, father and son.

The response was great and extremely positive. Events in Prague, Trieste, Zagreb and other cities followed, until, eventually, in 2007, '*FatherState–MotherSon*' opened at the Croatian seaport of Rijeka, an exhibition that dealt with Hans and Otto Gross and their relations with the Adriatic coast. Then, on 27 November, 2008, the Styrian Universalmuseum Joanneum in collaboration with the Austrian Cultural Forum, London and the Freud Museum, London presented, in the historic ambiance of Sigmund Freud's own home, '*The Laws of the Father: Freud/Gross/Kafka*' in a contemporary staging. In a series of presentations accompanying the exhibition and in concluding symposia at the end of January 2009 at the Freud Museum/ Anna Freud Centre, scholars from Great Britain, Germany, Austria, the United States and Australia presented and discussed the themes of 'Fathers and Sons' and 'Sexual Revolutions'.

The present volume unites the revised proceedings of these symposia. In addition I have invited contributions from other scholars to give the themes a wider scope.

London, 17 March, 2010
(on the anniversary of Otto Gross's birth, 1877).

Bibliography

Benjamin, W. (1940) Theses on the Philosophy of History. In *Illuminations*. London: Fontana (1970).

Bertschinger-Joos, E. (2005) Frieda Gross – Briefe aus Graz 1882–1906. Ein Beitrag zur Biographie. In Götz von Olenhusen, A. and G. Heuer (eds.) *Die Gesetze des Vaters. 4. Internationaler Otto Gross Kongress, Graz*. Marburg: LiteraturWissenschaft.de (pp. 310–319).

Bertschinger-Joos, E. (2006) Frieda Gross-Schloffer – ihr Leben mit Otto Gross 1906–1920. In G. Heuer (ed.) *Utopie und Eros. Der Traum von der Moderne. 5. Internationaler Otto Gross Kongress, cabaret voltaire / Dada-Haus, Zürich*. Marburg: LiteraturWissenschaft.de (pp. 277–310).

Dienes, G. and Heuer, G. M. (2010) The laws of the father. Hans and Otto Gross, Sigmund Freud and Franz Kafka. The continuing life of an exhibition. In W. Felber, A. Götz von Olenhusen, G. M. Heuer and B. Nitzschke (eds.), *Psychoanalyse & Expressionismus. 7. Internationaler Otto Gross Kongress Dresden*. Marburg: LiteraturWissenschaft.de (pp. 540–541).

Freud, S. (1917) *A Difficulty in the Path of Psycho-Analysis. Standard Edition*, Vol. XVII. London: Hogarth.

Freud, S. (1933) *New Introductory Lectures on Psycho-Analysis. Standard Edition*, Vol. XXII. London: Hogarth.

Gross, O. (1913) Zur Ueberwindung der kulturellen Krise. *Die Aktion*, Vol. III, No. 14 (pp. 384–387).

Jacobitti, E. E. (2000) Introduction: The role of the past in contemporary political life. In E. E. Jacobitti (ed.) *Composing Useful Pasts: History as Contemporary Politics*. Albany, NY: State University of New York Press (pp. 1–51).

Jung, C. G. (1934) A Rejoinder to Dr. Bally. *CW* 10. London: Routledge & Kegan Paul.

Jung, C. G. (2009) *The Red Book: Liber Novus*. London and New York, NY: Norton.

Kuhn, P. (2002) 'Romancing with a wealth of detail': Narratives of Ernest Jones's 1906 trial for indecent assault. *Studies in Gender and Sexuality*, *3*(4), 344–378.

Lear, J. (2006) *Radical Hope: Ethics in the Face of Cultural Devastation*. Cambridge, MA and London: Harvard University Press.

Lowenstein, C. (dir.) (2007) *Building Britain*. London: Juniper Productions for BBC (TV documentary).

Mali, J. (2003) *Mythistory: The Making of Modern Historiography*. Chicago, IL and London: University of Chicago Press.

Michaels, J. (1983) *Anarchy and Eros: Otto Gross' Impact on German Expressionist Writers*. New York, NY: Lang.

Miller, T. (2000) *Desire and Duty at Oneida*. Bloomington, IL and Indianapolis, IN: Indiana University Press.

Nietzsche, F. (1878) *Human, All-Too-Human*. Retrieved from http://nietzsche.holtof.com/Nietzsche_human_all_too_human/sect9_Man_Alone_with_Himself.htm

Obama, B. (2008) *Change We Can Believe In*. London: Canongate.

Reiche, R. (1988) Sexuelle Revolution: Erinnerung an einen Mythos. In L. Baier, W. Gottschalch, R. Reiche, T. Schmidt, J. Schmierer, B. Sichtermann and A. Sofri (eds.), *Die Früchte der Revolte. Über die Veränderung der politischen Kultur durch die Studentenbewegung*. Berlin: Wagenbach (pp. 45–71).

Romanyshyn, R. D. (2000) *The Wounded Researcher: Research with Soul in Mind*. New Orleans, LA: Spring.

Vickers, S. (2007) Blind to the truth. *The Guardian, Satuday Review*, 15 December, 22.

Notes

1 Benjamin, 1940: 259.
2 Peter Ackroyd in Lowenstein, 2007.
3 This concluding part of the introduction is based on a text by Gerhard Dienes.

Part I

History

Chapter 1

Jung and history

Adumbrations of a post-Jungian approach to psychoanalytic history

Kevin Lu

Introduction

The problems plaguing psychohistory[1] have been well documented (Barzun 1974; Stannard 1980), so any attempt to view history from a depth psychological perspective requires an awareness of the pitfalls and critiques, as well as how the theory would approach telling, interpreting and imaging the past. This accordingly entails a critical analysis of the primary sources, which has not been extensively pursued by Jung scholars. To date, no one has systematically distilled what Jung actually said and thought about history. This chapter aims to remedy this gap in Jungian studies. It is only with this crucial work in place that a critical assessment of post-Jungian approaches to history can be pursued.

Some academics have considered the relationship between analytical psychology and history. The most noteworthy contributions are from Sonu Shamdasani (2003/2004) and J. J. Clarke (1994; 1992), who have studied the intellectual precursors – including historians – shaping Jung's thought and how he in turn mobilised history and the historical method when defining central analytical psychological concepts. Along with Saul Friedländer (Friedländer 1978: 11, 17) and William Langer (1958: 290), Clarke is the only scholar in recent memory to suggest the possibility of a Jungian psychohistory (1994: 161). Other scholars who have examined the critical points of convergence between Jungian thought, history and contemporary events include: Ira Progoff (1953/1985), Arnold J. Toynbee[2] (1954; 1956), Marvin Goldwert (1983), Joseph Henderson (1990), Thomas Singer and Samuel Kimbles (2004), Murray Stein (1987), Roderick Main (2006), Susan Rowland (2005) and Ruth Meyer[3] (2007). There are, further, Jungian psychobiographies (Kirsch 1973; Jung 1963/1989; Hayao 1992; El Saffar 1994; Smith 1996/1997; von Franz 1975/1998; Reid 2001), though these remain unaware of the impact they could have on psychohistorical methodology.[4]

It is beyond the scope of this chapter to cover all of Jung's statements on history.[5] However, three major themes frequently arise: Jung's consistently inconsistent evaluation of history's place in both individual and collective development; his distinction between 'objective' and 'natural' history which, I suggest, can be better understood as a tension between *conscious history* and *archetypal history*; and the significant role exceptional individuals play in history. Although these initial thoughts do not exhaust the complexity of Jung's approach to history, they do provide a taste of what his philosophy of history might be.

Contradictory statements on the value of history

The tension between Jung's romantic view of history and the overall empirical ethos governing his psychological method crystallises in his contradictory statements on history's value. An examination of these discrepancies further shows the uniqueness of a Jungian psychohistorical approach, and the lengths to which historians would need to stretch if Jungian tools are to be utilised. Stated succinctly, what Jung means by 'history' and being 'historical' is opposed to more conventional conceptions held by western historians (Carr, 1961/90; Elton, 1969/87; Evans, 1997; Marwick, 2001; Tosh, 1984/2010).

The negative aspects of history and tradition

In his paper Woman in Europe, Jung depicts history and tradition as forces hindering individual progress. He asserts that feminine love defies all masculine constructs of traditional marriage, which brings into question the vow of fidelity. 'Tradition' incapacitates the potential for true feeling. Yielding to collective expectations only perpetuates the donning of a fraudulent persona (CW10: 265).[6] Modern women realise that only in the state of love can they achieve everything of which they are capable.[7] Yet this acknowledgement brings about psychological conflict, for as soon as they apprehend the redemptive and liberating functions of love, 'a sort of conscience' or, as I understand it, a misogynistic and patriarchal voice, holds them in check (CW10: 266). Coming face to face with public opinion, a woman's initial intuition and willingness to be guided by feeling are crushed. Jung interprets this as being in 'conflict with history' (ibid.). As long as women '[live] the life of the past [they] can never come into conflict with history' (CW10: 267). As soon as they deviate from this well-worn path, they encounter 'the full weight of historical inertia', which could have fatal psychic effects (ibid.). Jung thus implies that history and tradition are outdated relics stifling progress, mitigating an individual's urge to follow her inner voice.

The problem of 'historical inertia', Jung continues, becomes a question of personal fulfillment, of whether an individual desires to make history, thus realising a sense of vocation so pivotal to Jung's theory of individuation. 'In the end,' he comments, 'it boils down to this: is one prepared to break with tradition, to be "unhistorical" in order to make history, or not?' (CW10: 268) In other words, history cannot be made without first breaking away from tradition. He continues: 'No one can make history who is not willing to risk everything for it, to carry the experiment with his own life through to the bitter end, and to declare that his life is not a continuation of the past, but a new beginning' (ibid.). Jung reiterates the importance of being 'unhistorical' in The Spiritual Problem of Modern Man.

Jung comments that a truly modern man must break free from the shackles of the past. 'Every step forward,' he writes, 'means tearing oneself loose from the maternal womb of unconsciousness in which the mass of men dwells' (CW10: 150). If aspects of the collective psyche remain unexamined, a collective malaise or herd mentality will result. The individual who sheds the shackles of the past, thereby breaking free from the herd, will transcend that which prevents every other ordinary person from realising true fulfillment. This gifted individual is described as becoming '"unhistorical" in the deepest sense' and 'estrang[ing] himself from the mass of men who live entirely within the bounds of tradition' (ibid.). The truly modern individual 'must [leave] behind him all that has been discarded and outgrown, and acknowledging that he stands before the Nothing out of which All may grow' (ibid.). Though in the eyes of the collective, the one who strays too far from the accepted viewpoint should be ostracised, the sin of being unhistorical is a promethean transgression required for the attainment of higher consciousness (CW10: 152). Only by outgrowing 'the stages of consciousness belonging to the past [. . .] can [one] achieve full consciousness of the present' (ibid.).[8]

The positive aspects of history

History as the ideal container

Jung's antagonistic assessment of history and tradition contradict his other statements on the subject. In his Commentary on *The Secret of the Golden Flower*, he contends that the West's knowledge of history and science prevents a childish engagement with the psyche, which is characteristic of eastern approaches. These disciplines serve as necessary containers effectively mediating the West's interaction with the unconscious. Subsequently, the combination of history and science finds its teleological climax in psychology. In Jung's opinion, this is the only subject that equally values both introspection and scientific rigour (CW13: 63). Psychology can extract the same knowledge the East has attained while simultaneously protecting the western ego from exposure to abnormal psychic states (ibid.). Jung's recognition of history, however, is tempered with a criticism of its overt rationality. '[K]nowledge of the external world,' he reflects, 'is the greatest obstacle to introspection' (ibid.). If I am reading Jung correctly, history, in an unmediated form, is a hindrance. But when combined with science to spawn psychology, it serves a useful purpose. Ultimately, Jung is not commending history *per se*, but recognising its role in the then burgeoning study of psychology. This ambivalence, however, is a doorway to exploring his more positive evaluations of history.

Jung's thoughts on psychology and history outlined above – placed in the context of discussing the East – raise a number of issues. To reiterate Jung's position, the West can extract more from the unconscious and do so more effectively than the East because it is equipped with disciplines serving as sufficient containers, mediating an encounter with the unconscious. The respective downfalls of history and science – being overtly rational approaches – are adequately addressed with the perfection of psychology as a branch of knowledge. Jung applauds the East for engaging the unconscious on the one hand, but criticises it for how it gets there on the other. Jung ultimately insists that a western perspective (steeped in rationality) is better than an eastern one (which is essentially backward) when engaging the unconscious. He thus expresses a Eurocentric model based on binary thinking – the West is best and progressive, the East is backward and regressive. Even in its positive form – where Jung praises eastern philosophies, or when he calls the 'mystical', introverted East the unconscious complement of the rational, extraverted West – he is employing simplistic divisions that fail to appreciate the East for its difference from and independence of the West. If Jung is endorsing certain eastern tenets because they prove his own psychological insights, the East then becomes 'acceptable' only because it resembles the West in some way. Rather than promoting the unity of the human race – a ramification implicit in his theory of the collective unconscious – Jung may be perpetuating division. Though Clarke makes a strong case that Jung's dialogue with the East aims to build bridges of understanding (1994: 189), his Eurocentric mindset (ibid.: 160–61) and, by extension, the Eurocentrism woven into the fabric of analytical psychology, still needs to be acknowledged when applying analytical psychology to history.

A 'living sense of history'

In Basic Postulates of Analytical Psychology, Jung advocates fostering a 'living sense of history' by recognising the reality of historical continuity (CW8: 655). By only prizing conscious knowledge, the West has grown in many respects, but not in others. Mainly, its knowledge of the unconscious remains limited. If individuals were aware of its presence and its influence, they would comprehend that change in the present only mimics transformations that have occurred in the past. The 'continuity of history' forwarded by Jung here is different from what he perceives to be an outmoded traditional history. The importance of realising the 'continuity of history' is intrinsically bound to recognising the unconscious operating in history. An awareness of one's personal and impersonal link to the past serves as a grounding mechanism and reference point – a firm foundation fostering the development of a healthy personality. At the collective level, society is inherently linked to an ancient past, and knowledge of this connection is integral to deciphering the psychological effects the unconscious has had on cultural and intellectual progress.

Jung explicitly supports the study of history in his essay The Gifted Child. Knowledge of the past plays an integral part in the cultivation of the gifted. Jung writes: 'And it seems to me especially important for any broad-based culture to have a regard for history *in the widest sense of the word*. Important as it is to pay attention to what is practical and useful, and to consider the future, that backward glance at the past is just as important' (CW17: 250, emphasis added). Jung, however, is not referring to the discipline of history, but a form of metahistory. This perspective stresses continuity with, and being entrenched in, the roots of humanity's history, i.e. the unconscious. As children are by nature closer to the unconscious, an early understanding of it, and the history of which it is comprised, could prevent a deleterious separation from the unconscious in adult life. This specific explanation – emphasising a form of history wedded to the unconscious – suggests a particular perception of history moving beyond its more familiar definitions (Carr, 1961/90; Elton, 1969/87; Evans, 1997; Marwick, 2001; Tosh, 1984/2010). Jung's contradictory thoughts on history outlined in this section, moreover, ultimately attest to the fact that for him, history operates at two distinct levels.

A philosophy of history: Conscious history vs archetypal history

'Objective history' and 'natural history'

Jung's central distinction is established in his essay The Role of the Unconscious. He begins by noting the drawbacks of only understanding the unconscious in light of one's personal experiences. Admittedly, a large portion of the analysand's material can be traced back to his individual case history, but certain fantasies have roots in mythology. 'They are,' Jung writes, 'elements which do not correspond to any events or experiences of personal life, but only to myths' (CW10: 11). He continues:

> We receive along with our body a highly differentiated brain which brings with it its entire history, and when it becomes creative it creates out of this history – out of the history of mankind. By 'history' we usually mean the history which we 'make', and we call this 'objective history.' The truly creative fantasy activity of the brain has nothing to

> do with this kind of history, but solely with that age-old natural history which has been transmitted in living form since the remotest times, namely, the history of the brain-structure. And this structure tells its own story, which is the story of mankind: the unending myth of death and rebirth, and of the multitudinous figures who weave in and out of this mystery.
>
> (CW10: 12)

Jung thus distinguishes between 'objective history' and 'natural history'[9], a form of the past transmitted along with the brain-structure. Humanity inherits 'natural history' and from it creatively reproduces new forms of universal, mythic motifs, such as death and rebirth. 'Natural history' resides in, and emanates from, the collective unconscious and only discloses its living presence 'through the medium of creative fantasy' (CW10: 13). 'Natural history' transcends 'objective history', which is bound by space and time. Underlying recorded history is a greater historical process imbedded in the collective unconscious.

What Jung calls 'objective history', I suggest, could be more usefully referred to as *conscious history*. The term denotes that form of history which is, for him, a product of the conscious mind, further expressing the rationality with which historians usually engage the past. What Jung terms 'natural history' could be designated *archetypal history*. Not only would this prevent confusing Jung's employment of 'natural history' with the way it was used – denoting psychology as a discipline – in the nineteenth century (Dallas 1860), but it captures what Jung actually meant by it. This form of history dwells in the unconscious, and only becomes partially distinguishable through its manifestations as conscious history.[10]

The value of archetypal history and the denigration of conscious history

In The Meaning of Psychology for Modern Man, Jung provides a description of the relationship between conscious and archetypal history. He undeniably attributes, moreover, greater value to the latter:

> When we look at human history, we see only what happens on the surface, and even this is distorted in the faded mirror of tradition. But what has really been happening eludes the inquiring eye of the historian, for the true historical event lies deeply buried, experienced by all and observed by none. It is the most private and most subjective of psychic experiences. Wars, dynasties, social upheavals, conquests, and religions are but the superficial symptoms of a secret psychic attitude unknown even to the individual himself, and transmitted by no historian; perhaps the founders of religions give us the most information

in this regard. The great events of world history are, at bottom, profoundly unimportant.

(CW10: 315)

According to Jung, 'history' occurring on 'the surface' is not the real form of history. True history exists *a priori* in the unconscious, in seed form. It merely awaits the right opportunity or psychic situation allowing for the content's movement into consciousness. Historical events are subsequently trivialised and deemed inconsequential. This controversial perspective is further asserted in Jung's statements on historical change.

Jung on historical change

In The Psychological Foundations of Belief in Spirits, Jung proposes that the blueprint for historical change exists *a priori* in the unconscious: 'Incisive changes in history are generally attributed exclusively to external causes. It seems to me, however, that external circumstances often serve merely as occasions for a new attitude to life and the world, long prepared in the unconscious, to become manifest' (CW8: 594). Not only does this confirm his view that another form of history operates at an unconscious level, but further reveals an additional quality of archetypal history, which may in turn be considered a crucial pitfall. The archetype underpinning events predetermines the outcome of its conscious materialization. A pattern 'long prepared in the unconscious' merely awaits the appropriate situation that will express the compensatory messages complementing a myopic, conscious viewpoint. The event becomes a container or shell which is, in and of itself, meaningless. An occurrence is meaningful only when the psychological process – i.e. the constellation of an archetypal pattern in history – underlying it is discerned.

External change in historical time, according to Jung, is ultimately an erroneous conception. Authentic historical change occurs in 'unconscious time', for the unconscious *is* the true reality. (Jung 1963/1989: 323–25; 341; 348–49) Conscious experiences and historical events are, by extension, merely images of the true reality (ibid.: 324). Contrary to popular belief, historians are not dealing with 'actual facts' – the data produced by the unconscious parts of our psyches – but meandering in abstraction.

Critical assessment

Upon reading the above quotations, many historians would be justifiably cautious of a Jungian approach to telling psychoanalytic history. To assume that events are immaterial, and placing emphasis instead on the 'objective truth' emanating from the depths of the unconscious, contravenes most forms of historical investigation.[11] What is important for Jung is grasping the underlying blueprint, as its conscious manifestations are but mere repetitions of a pivotal pattern. The denigration of the conscious occurrence and the staunch advocacy of archetypes leave little room for appreciating the event for what it truly is – an integral instance never to be repeated in human history. Further, suggesting the immateriality of external events implies that they should be studied less, with concentration instead being focused on the greater patterns governing their outcome. This consequently sidesteps the moral responsibility and obligation we should have to the outside world, nullifying the compassion felt for all those affected by the all too *real* events of the past. To say that external happenings are ultimately unimportant and to myopically concentrate on internal images means that Jungian history is not really history at all.

A Jungian narrative of history – if it uncompromisingly adheres to archetypal theory – is one of repetition, rejecting the possibility that new things can occur. Stagnation – not development – is the result. That is not to say the alternative – a myth of historical progress – is any less problematic. However, if Jung's brand of history is one of repetition – thus rendering historical events predictable – we still need to study this. This exploration would be valuable for the history of ideas, but it would contribute little to the viability of applying analytical psychology to elucidate any aspect of the historical enterprise.

From the historian's vantage point, two interrelated issues remain, which I will touch on briefly here. First is the extermination of human agency implicit in postulating the reality of archetypal history. Second, is the question of change, and whether or not Jung provides space for its existence in his approach.

Saying that a greater pattern governs and thus predetermines historical outcomes inevitably takes human agency out of the historical equation. This is something most historians – and most people – would be unwilling to relinquish. Jung's interpretation of the meaning of history – assuming there is one – could thus provide a way of avoiding both collective and individual responsibility. For instance, archetypal history could narrate contemporary rivalries between two groups – such as the Chinese and Japanese – as a lineage of historical clashes that are ultimately insurmountable due to how deeply they have been entrenched in the group psyche. Stated another way, if we argue that China's animosity towards Japan is *intrinsic*, *unchanging, inherited, patterned* and archetypal, then hatred will continually be the result. The argument for archetypicality potentially stifles the possibility for change, denying the fact that communities can repair antagonisms of the past simply because their origins are identifiable, not hard-wired or imbedded into our very beings. We are not doomed to repeat the mistakes of the past, however hard it may be to escape from it. Consequently, Jung's preference for archetypal history fails to see events and disputes contextually, historically and politically. If we assume the archetypal nature of

Chinese hatred towards different groups, we unavoidably give licence to perpetual retaliation, accepting it as an automatic and expected response being governed by some psychological meta-pattern. Stated simply, archetypal history could inflict a repetition of potentially harmful discourses, unwillingly justifying the recourse to violence and legitimising destruction and intellectual passivity. Hatred thus becomes a cycle that cannot be broken; vengeance becomes the norm, not the anomaly.

The problematic nature of Jung's philosophy of history which would surely be classified as *speculative*[12] needs to be dealt with proactively, and can neither be sidestepped nor brushed under a rug of psychological determinism, failing to attach itself to some real-world context. The downfall of an archetypal reading of history is that it assigns simple causes to complex historical events. In light of its defects, any reading of history needs to be contextual in the first instance, and not archetypal. History needs to be seen for its complexity, and not forced to fit theoretical structures that deny it a multiplicity of potential meanings. Further issues arise in the third major attribute of Jung's approach to history – the prominence placed on exceptional individuals.

The role of the individual in history

Jung places individuals (in the Jungian sense) at the centre of history though ultimately, they are merely the vehicles for historical change. In The Meaning of Psychology for Modern Man, Jung comments:

> In the last analysis, the essential thing is the life of the individual. This alone makes history, here alone do the great transformations first take place, and the whole future, the whole history of the world, ultimately springs as a gigantic summation from these hidden sources in individuals. In our most private and most subjective lives we are not only the passive witness of our age, and its sufferers, but also its makers. We make our own epoch.
>
> (CW10: 315)

Jung's emphasis on individuals can be framed not only within the 'great man' narrative of history which was still prominent when Jung was writing, but in view of his theory of individuation, a teleological process of personality development (CW7: 266). The duty of the exceptional individual in history is not simply to foster his own individuation, but to mobilise that process for the entire culture. By consciously following his own path of psychological development, he also changes society. Effecting larger alterations at the collective level is a mere consequence of the more important task of realising the Self (Jung 1963/1989: 3–5). This consequently leads to a methodological concern beyond the scope of this chapter: how can we comprehend the past events of our external world through a psychological lens which affirms the veracity of the inner life over and above an engagement with concrete reality?

Jung's paper The Gifted Child outlines the ideal education exceptional children should receive. Because their temperament should never be stifled, lessons must not deviate 'from the humanities into over-specialised fields' (CW17: 250). To cultivate an open mind, it is 'especially important for any broad-based culture to have a regard for history in the widest sense of the word' (ibid.). Based on my examination of Jung's other statements on history – especially those concerning 'objective' and 'natural' history – the type of history to which he refers here is archetypal history. Respecting history and learning from the past – what Jung calls fostering a sense of continuity (ibid.) – balances the psyches of gifted children. As they are typically one-sided, another aspect is inescapably vulnerable and underdeveloped. By directing them to history 'in the widest sense of the word', Jung aims to reconnect them to their psychic heritage, which in turn is built upon the historical experiences of humanity. As children are by nature closer to the unconscious, making them aware of this realm of psychic activity reinforces a connection to it, before maturity and bitterness lead them astray. Jung writes:

> Childhood [. . .] is a state of the past. Just as the developing embryo recapitulates, in a sense, our phylogenetic history, so the child-psyche relives 'the lesson of earlier humanity' [. . .] The child lives in a pre-rational and above all in a pre-scientific world, the world of the men who existed before us. Our roots lie in that world and every child grows from those roots. Maturity bears him away from his roots and immaturity binds him to them. Knowledge of the universal origins builds the bridge between the lost and abandoned world of the past and the still largely inconceivable world of the future.
>
> (CW17: 250)

Fostering a connection with the unconscious entrenches children in the experiences and wisdom gained from those coming before them. Any novelty can prove to be a potential danger, which is why the gifted need to be capable of 'well-balanced judgment' (CW17: 251). History facilitates this, providing a 'firm standpoint' stemming from 'sound knowledge of what has been' (ibid.). 'The man who is unconscious of the historical context,' Jung argues, 'and lets slip his link with the past is in constant danger of succumbing to the crazes and delusions engendered by all novelties' (ibid.). True individuality is only achieved by anchoring oneself in the 'wider' history of the collective, thereby distancing oneself from mass movements and trends. A purely technical and practical education, Jung continues, '[lacks] the culture whose innermost law is the continuity of history, the long procession of man's *more than individual* consciousness' (ibid., emphasis added). It is this continuity which 'reconciles all opposites' and 'heals the conflicts that threaten the gifted child' (ibid.). For Jung, history needs to serve a psychological function. A purely conscious approach to history, therefore, is not enough. A more comprehensive history needs to factor in the unconscious.

Individuals and historical change

Gifted children or exceptional individuals, capable of acknowledging the unconscious and its compensatory messages whilst withstanding its overwhelming power, are chosen to change the course of history as they are able to perceive this 'abandoned world of the past' (CW17: 251). They help ensure a collective future by combating widespread mass-mindedness (ibid.). Jung argues this on two other occasions (CW10: 315; CW8: 314) and although these statements do, in some ways, conflict with his other remarks on historical change (CW8: 594; CW10: 315), I argue that for him, historical change fundamentally springs from the unconscious, and not from individual agents.

After arguing that historical change is the expression of unconscious processes in The Psychological Foundations of Belief in Spirits, Jung writes: 'Certain individuals gifted with particularly strong intuition then become aware of the changes going on in it [the unconscious] and translate these changes into communicable ideas' (CW8: 594). These sentiments are repeated in 'The Meaning of Psychology for Modern Man.' As the great events of world history are 'profoundly unimportant', the 'essential thing is the life of the individual' (CW10: 315). 'This alone,' Jung remarks, 'makes history, here alone do the great transformations first take place, and the whole future, the whole history of the world, ultimately spring as a gigantic summation from these hidden sources in individuals' (ibid.). At the outset of this quotation, individuals are described not as passive bystanders, but the key to historical change. Upon closer examination, however, and in light of his other statements (CW8: 594), exceptional individuals are simply the 'lucky' and appointed hosts with the ability to intuit the process of historical change occurring in the unconscious. The whole history of the world emanates from the hidden sources found *within* individuals. Accordingly, they are the translators of change, but not its agents. In summary, the elite do possess a degree of autonomy – to decipher and interpret historical change – but they too must bow before the power of the unconscious.

Jung's view of the individual in history raises some issues. It buttresses the 'great man' narrative, where historical change (or, in Jung's case, knowledge of its source) is attributed to the choices and actions of one individual. Although there is no doubt that individuals do contribute to historical change, their intervention in world affairs is never isolated. There is a context to every historical outcome, as well as other individuals and groups who shape the unfolding of events. Any historian interested in telling history from the 'bottom up' rather than the 'top down' would find Jung's emphasis on the individual problematic, providing as it does only one perspective that inevitably stifles the voices of other historical agents.

Conclusion

Jung possesses contrasting opinions of history, and a tension subsequently arises in his writings. Ultimately, he distinguishes between two types of history, which I have termed conscious and archetypal history. Jung was vague about the value of conscious history, sometimes seeing it as a vessel serving a containing function, and at others conflating it with his negative evaluation of tradition. It is clear, however, that he bestowed greater value upon archetypal history. All history and the seeds of historical change are to be found, preformed, in the unconscious. Telling the history stemming from the unconscious is the true task of historians, not the recounting of minute facts that are ultimately meaningless.

In attempting to extract Jung's philosophy of history, my interest has not been in his telling of history per se, but how we can use Jungian psychology to tell history. In other words, based on his psychological model specifically and his understanding of history more generally, can we illuminate the nature of historical events or an historical period? Can we mobilise analytical psychology to intelligently and responsibly comment on different times and places neither contingent to, nor directly considered by, Jung? Or is the real contribution limited to historiography? Teasing out Jung's thoughts on history is the crucial, preliminary step that needs to precede any forays into telling Jungian psychoanalytic history. Post-Jungians interested in this area of study need to be aware of the pitfalls and arguments against Jung's reading of history so that his mistakes may be avoided and, if possible, corrected.

Future studies need to apply analytical psychology to various spectrums – not just biography – within the historical enterprise, seeing if the theoretical tension evident in Jung's thinking on history can be resolved. Moreover, the question needs to be asked: 'Do the Jungian and Post-Jungian lenses yield fruitful results that cannot be achieved via other viewpoints, and do they *add value* to historical analysis?' Jung certainly saw history through the lens of his psychology, which led to an underestimation of the principles of historical investigation. Yet can we uncover more open Jungian and Post-Jungian approaches to history, rendering the endeavour a more viable form of psychohistorical – and indeed, historical – research? It is clear, however, from the history of psychohistory that depth psychological perspectives – evidenced by the strong work of Lyndal Roper (1994) and Daniel Pick (2005) – are to be used as supplements to, and not replacements for, good historical research. Historical facts should not be trumped by psychological ones. Concrete connections – and not psychological coincidences – are the building blocks of history, and any decent research refusing to denigrate the historical record must be founded upon the former.

Bibliography

Banner, L. (2009) Biography as history. *American Historical Review*, *114*(3), 579–86.

Barzun, J. (1974) *Clio and the Doctors*. Chicago, IL and London: University of Chicago Press.

Caine, B. (2010) *Biography and History*. Basingstoke : Palgrave Macmillan.

Carr, E. H. (1961/1990) *What is History?*, 2nd edn. London: Penguin Books.

Clarke, J. J. (1992) *In Search of Jung*. London and New York, NY: Routledge.

—— (1994) *Jung and Eastern Thought*. London and New York, NY: Routledge.

Dallas, E. S. (1860) Student Life in Scotland. *Cornhill Magazine*, *1*, 366–79.

Dray, W. H. (1964) *Philosophy of History*. Englewood Cliffs, NJ: Prentice-Hall.

El Saffar, R. (1994) *Rapture Encaged*. London and New York, NY: Routledge.

Elton, G. R. (1969/1987) *The Practice of History*. London: Fontana Press.

Evans, R. J. (1997) *In Defence of History*. London: Granta Books.

Friedlander, S. (1978). *History and Psychoanalysis: An Inquiry into the Possibilities and Limits of Psychohistory*. S. Suleiman (Trans). New York and London: Holmes & Meier.

Goldwert, M. (1983) Toynbee and Jung: The historian and analytical psychology. *Journal of Analytical Psychology*, *28*, 363–66.

Hayao, K. (1992) *The Buddhist Priest Myōe: A Life of Dreams*. Venice, CA: Lapis.

Henderson, J. L. (1990) The cultural unconscious. In *Shadow and Self*. Wilmette, IL: Chiron (pp. 103–13).

Jordanova, L. (2000/2006) *History in Practice*, 2nd edn. London: Hodder Arnold.

Jung, C. G. (1953–83) *The Collected Works*, 20 vols. London: Routledge & Kegan Paul.

—— (1963/1989) *Memories, Dreams, Reflections*. New York, NY: Vintage.

—— (1974) *Gesammelte Werke Zehnter Band*. Olten, Freiburg i. Br: Walter.

Kessler-Harris, A. (2009) Why biography?, *American Historical Review*, *114*(3), 625–30.

Kirsch, J. (1973) *The Reluctant Prophet*. Los Angeles, CA: Sherbourne.

Langer, W. L. (1958) The next assignment. *The American Historical Review*, *63*(2), 283–304.

Lu, K. (2008) Book review of *Clio's Circle: Entering the Imaginal World of Historians* by Meyer, Ruth. *Journal of Analytical Psychology*, *53*(5), 722–23.

Main, R. (2006) The social significance of synchronicity. *Psychoanalysis, Culture and Society*, *11*, 36–53.

Marwick, Q. (2001) *The New Nature of History: Knowledge, Evidence, Language*. Basingstoke: Palgrave Macmillan.

Meyer, R. (2007) *Clio's Circle*. New Orleans, LA: Spring.

Nasaw, D. (2009) AHR roundtable, historians and biography: Introduction. *American Historical Review*, *114*(3), 573–78.

Pick, D. (2005) *Rome or Death*. London: Jonathan Cape.
Progoff, I. (1953/1985) *Jung's Psychology and its Social Meaning*. New York, NY: Dialogue House.
Reid, J. (2001) *Jung, My Mother and I: The Analytic Diaries of Catherine Rush Cabot*. Einsiedeln: Daimon.
Roper, L. (1994) *Oedipus and the Devil*. London and New York, NY: Routledge.
Rowland, S. (2005) *Jung as a Writer*. London and New York, NY: Routledge.
Shamdasani, S. (2003/2004) *Jung and the Making of Modern Psychology*. Cambridge: Cambridge University.
Singer, T. and Kimbles, S. (2004) The emerging theory of cultural complexes. In J. Cambray and L. Carter (eds.), *Analytical Psychology: Contemporary Perspectives in Jungian Analysis*. Hove and New York, NY: Brunner-Routledge (pp. 176–203).
Smith, R. C. (1996/1997) *The Wounded Jung*. Evanston, IL: Northwestern University.
Stannard, D. E. (1980) *Shrinking History*. Oxford and New York, NY: Oxford University Press.
Stein, M. (1987) Looking backward: Archetypes in reconstruction. In N. Schwartz-Salant and M. Stein (eds.), *Archetyapl Processes in Psychotherapy*. Wilmette, IL: Chiron (pp. 51–74).
Tosh, J. (1984/2010) *The Pursuit of History*, 5th edn. London: Longman.
Toynbee, A. J. (1956) The value of C. G. Jung's work for historians. *Journal of Analytical Psychology*, *1*(2), 193–94.
——. (1954) *A Study of History, Volume VII*. London, New York, NY, Toronto: Oxford University Press.
von Franz, M. L. (1975/1998) *C. G. Jung: His Myth in our Time*. Toronto: Inner City.

Notes

1 In this chapter, I distinguish between *psychohistory*, which refers to reductive studies championing the psychoanalytic lens with little regard for historical method, and *psychoanalytic history*, which utilizes depth psychology only when appropriate, as one perspective out of many upon which the historian can draw. The latter emphasizes responsible history, rather than advancing one particular approach to it.
2 Toynbee was one of the first to utilise Jungian psychology (typology) to explicate some aspect of history (his concept of *higher religions*). This study can be found as an Appendix to Vol 7 of *A Study of History* (Toynbee 1954).
3 For a critique of Meyer's text, see my review (Lu 2008).
4 Regarding the relationship between biography and history, see: Barbara Caine (2010); Ludmilla Jordanova (2000/2006); David Nasaw (2009); Lois Banner (2009) and Alice Kessler-Harris (2009).
5 The chart in the Appendix outlines some of Jung's statements on history as found in his *Collected Works*.
6 For its simplicity, I follow J. J. Clarke's format for citing the *Collected Works*. CW10 points to *Collected Works* Volume 10, and 265 refers to the paragraph.
7 In this instance, Jung wrongly assumes that all women are governed by feeling and emotion, an erroneous presumption highlighting his tendency to essentialise.

8 Jung takes a similar stance in Psychotherapists or the Clergy, arguing that modern man – insisting on living 'with every side of himself' – must cast history aside (CW11: 528).
9 In the nineteenth century, the phrase 'natural history of the human mind' referred to psychology (Dallas 1860). Accordingly, it is possible that Jung is not introducing a distinctive form of history, but referring to psychology as a discipline. Thus, a comparison with the original German and R. F. C. Hull's translation was required. I am indebted to Rev. Dr. Ann Jeffers for aiding me in the translation, and confirming that Jung's use of 'natürlichen Geschichte' – in light of an analysis of the paragraph specifically and the chapter more generally – is indeed referring to a separate form of history opposed to 'objektive Geschichte' (CW12: 10; Jung 1974: 22). Arguably, Jung's way of combating Rankean-style history – in the same vein as Jacob Burckhardt's response – was to aim to tell a more subjective history by utilising what he knew best: the notion of a dynamic unconscious (Jeffers, personal communication, 15 June 2009).
10 I avoid the term *unconscious history*, for it implies a general unawareness of the past which, I believe, is neither advocated by historians, nor would it have been by Jung himself.
11 See Carr's comments, (1961/90: 48–9).
12 Regarding the distinction between *critical* and *speculative* philosophy of history, see William Dray's *Philosophy of History* (1949).

Appendix

Jung's statements on history as found in his *Collected Works*[1]

Location of reference in *Collected Works*	Title of work	Year of publication	Year of lecture	Topic of reference to history	Critical point made
1) (CW5: 1; p. 3) *Symbols of Transformation*	Introduction to *Symbols of Transformation* (First published in 1912)	German publication: **1952** – Translation of the Fourth Swiss Edition	–	Continuity of history	History working at a deeper, unconscious level.
2) (CW5: 3; p. 5) *Symbols of Transformation*	Introduction to *Symbols of Transformation* (First published in 1912)	German publication: **1952** – Translation of the Fourth Swiss Edition	–	Historical material; Comparative study of history	Jung encourages the application of analytical psychology to history.
3) (CW6: 8–100; pp. 8–66) *Psychological Types*	The Problem of Types in the History of Classical Medieval Thought in *Psychological Types*	German publication: 1921; English publication: **1923**	–	History (in title)	Jung embarks upon a typological analysis of the Gnostics and a psychobiographical commentary of Tertullian and Origen. In Part II, he argues that religious schisms and heresies can be understood in terms of typological differences.
4) (CW6: 231–32; pp. 141–42) *Psychological Types*	The Apollonian and the Dionysian in *Psychological Types*	German publication: 1921; English publication: **1923**	–	Historical approach	Jung uses the term 'history' as exemplifying an overtly rational, conscious, and thus one-sided approach to knowledge.

5) (CW7: 159; pp. 96–7) *Two Essays on Analytical Psychology*	*The Psychology of the Unconscious* (Loosely based on the 1912 essay New Paths in Psychology)	Translation based on the Fifth Edition, **1943**; First Edition: 1917; Second Edition: 1918; Third Edition: 1926	–	Racial history	Jung describes the archetypes of the collective unconscious as 'residues of our racial history'.
6) (CW8: 594; p. 314) *The Structure and Dynamics of the Psyche*	*The Psychological Foundations of Belief in Spirits*	German publication: 1928; English publication: 1928; Revised and Expanded Edition: **1948**	4 July 1919. Read at a General meeting of the Society for Psychical Research	Changes in history	Jung contends that history is 'long prepared in the unconscious'.
7) (CW8: 655; p. 341) *The Structure and Dynamics of the Psyche*	*Basic Postulates of Analytical Psychology*	German publication: 1931; English publication: **1933** in *Modern Man in Search of a Soul* (on which the present translation is based); Revision of original: 1934	–	History	Jung advocates the cultivation of a 'living sense of history'. Acknowledging the unconscious and realising the continuity of history – that society is still linked to its ancient past – is crucial to deciphering the psychological effects the unconscious has had on cultural development.
8) (CW9ii: 162–180; pp. 103–117) *Aion: Researches into the Phenomenology of the Self*	The Historical Significance of the Fish in *Aion: Researches into the Phenomenology of the Self*	First five chapters, translated into English, were published in **1958**; Jung dates the Foreword to the entire text as being written in 1950	–	History (in title)	Jung explores the historical manifestations of the archetypal image of wholeness. More specifically, he examines the dual nature of the fish symbol, which is representative of both Attis and Christ.

Location of reference in *Collected Works*	Title of work	Year of publication	Year of lecture	Topic of reference to history	Critical point made
9) (CW9ii: pp. ix–xi)	Foreword to *Aion: Researches into the Phenomenology of the Self*	**1950**	–	Jung's inadequacy as a historian	In his Foreword to *Aion*, written in 1950, Jung outlines the historical nature of the work as well as noting his own inadequacies as a historian. He sees his individual work as 'contributing to the historical process of assimilation'. He is aware of the dangers of using historical examples to buttress his psychological contentions. Jung further states, however, his unwillingness to be constrained within safe and rigid academic boundaries.
10) (CW10: 617; pp. 324–25) *Civilization in Transition*	*Flying Saucers: A Modern Myth of Things Seen in the Skies*	German publication: 1958; English publication: **1959**	–	Historians; psychological factors and history	In light of The Second World War, humanity's psychic equilibrium has been affected, resulting in an increased vulnerability to psychic disturbances. Even historians – quintessential representatives of rational knowledge – cannot fully explain the events which have unfolded in Europe. It must be admitted that 'psychological and psychopathological factors are beginning to widen the horizons of historiography [. . .]'.
11) (CW10: 265–68; pp. 129–30) *Civilization in Transition*	*Woman in Europe*	German publication: Oct. 1927, republished in 1929, 1932, 1948 and 1959; English publication: **1928**	–	Conflict with history/ historical inertia/ unhistorical	Women come into conflict with 'history' (by which he means tradition) when they choose to 'go against the grain'. History is here conveyed as something hindering progress, what Jung terms *historical inertia*. Paradoxically, in order to make history, one must break with history (tradition), thus

					becoming 'unhistorical'. 'Making history' is not about continuity with the past, but a separation from it.
12) (CW10; pp. 177–78) *Civilization in Transition*	Preface to *Essays on Contemporary Events*	German publication: 1946; English publication: **1947**	–	Contemporary therapist and history	Psychologists must be in tune with contemporary history in order to best serve their analysands. What happens in the outer world has a huge impact on the inner life of the individual.
13) (CW10: 985–86; pp. 517–180) *Civilization in Transition*	The Dreamlike World of India	English publication: **1939**	–	Indian attitude to history	India, because it is closer to the unconscious, has no need of history, which is a western invention. History gives shape and form to the chaotic experiences of Europe.
14) (CW10: 315; pp. 148–490) *Civilization in Transition*	*The Meaning of Psychology for Modern Man*	German publication: 1933; Revised and Expanded German edition: **1934**	February 1933; Given as a lecture in Cologne and Essen	Subjective in history	The 'history' that occurs on the surface is not the real history. True history occurs in the unconscious, or is pre-formed in the unconscious, 'experienced by all and observed by none'. Jung notes the connection between the individual and collective levels, for what occurs at the individual level is a microcosmic reflection of what is occurring at the macrocosmic level (ontogeny recapitulates phylogeny – *recapitulation theory*). Historical events are merely the vehicle for the expression of the unconscious. Historical events are ultimately unimportant. The individual is the harbinger for historical change.

Location of reference in *Collected Works*	Title of work	Year of publication	Year of lecture	Topic of reference to history	Critical point made
15) (CW10: 11–14; pp. 9–11) *Civilization in Transition*	*The Role of the Unconscious*	German publication: 1918; English publication: **1964**	–	'Objective history' v. 'natural history'	**para. 12:** Humanity inherits, along with a highly differentiated brain, its entire history. The brain creates out of, or draws from, the foundation provided by the history of mankind. The history which is of humanity's making, and to which one usually refers, Jung terms *objective history*. Jung does not favour this form of history. The creative fantasy activity of the brain is connected to another form of history – 'an age-old *natural history* which has been transmitted in living form since the remotest times [. . .]'. This inherent brain structure tells the stories of mankind, expressing themselves as myths. **para. 14:** Ideas themselves are not inherited, but, rather the innate possibility of those ideas. This is the difference between *archetypes* and *archetypal images*. By extension, historical events are archetypal images expressing *a priori* archetypal structures. In this light, the pattern of historical events is pre-determined.
16) (CW10: 22; p. 16) *Civilization in Transition*	*The Role of the Unconscious*	German publication: 1918; English publication: **1964**	–	Analytical psychology in its historical setting	Jung displays an understanding of history that is characteristically teleological. He contextualises and charts the role of significant events, as well as the contribution

					of historical figures, to the rising, general interest in the unconscious. In his immediate context, Jung notes that humanity is in danger of suffering a bursting forth of the unconscious.
17) (CW10: 47; pp. 27–8) *Civilization in Transition*	*The Role of the Unconscious*	German publication: 1918; English publication: **1964**	–	History	The question of the relation between consciousness and the unconscious is inextricably intertwined with the history of humanity. Knowledge of the unconscious cannot be gained by exploring contemporary problems alone, but must be done in tandem with an inquiry into the history of humanity.
18) (CW10: 150–52; p. 75) *Civilization in Transition*	*The Spiritual Problem of Modern Man*	German publication: 1928; Revised and Expanded Edition: 1931; English publication in *Modern Man in Search of a Soul* (which was consulted in this translation): **1933**	–	Unhistorical	For Jung, a truly modern man must break free of the past – thus becoming 'unhistorical' – in order to attain higher levels of consciousness.
19) (CW10: 431; pp. 210–12) *Civilization in Transition*	*After the Catastrophe*	German publication: 1945; Reprinted in German: 1946; English publication: **1947**	–	Contemporary history	Jung refers to the history of the previous 12 years (1933–45) as reminiscent of the case chart of a hysterical patient.

Location of reference in *Collected Works*	Title of work	Year of publication	Year of lecture	Topic of reference to history	Critical point made
20) (CW11: 528; p. 342) *Psychology and Religion: West and East*	*Psychotherapists or the Clergy*	German publication: 1932; English publication: **1933** in *Modern Man in Search of a Soul*	May 1932. Given as a lecture before the Alsatian Pastoral Conference at Strasbourg	Modern man and history	Modern man casts history aside, wanting to break with tradition in order to find meaning and value for himself.
21) (CW13: 63; p. 43) *Alchemical Studies*	Commentary on *The Secret of the Golden Flower*	German publication: 1929; English publication: 1931; Revised German Edition: 1938; Fifth Edition (from which this translation is derived): **1957**	–	History	History is a necessary, intellectual container which will mediate humanity's engagement with the unconscious – an approach to the unconscious contrasting the entirely intuitive nature of the East's engagement. At the same time, Jung seems to be criticising overtly rational attempts to gain knowledge of the external world. By extension, the type of history of which Jung speaks integrates introspection and, more specifically, a psychology of the unconscious.
22) (CW13: 252; pp. 204–05) *Alchemical Studies*	*The Spirit Mercurius*	German publication: 1943; Revised and Expanded German Edition: 1948; English publication (from which this translation is derived): **1953**	1942: Given as two lectures at the Eranos Conference, Ascona, Switzerland	History of religion	Jung promotes a symbolic, psychological interpretation of the history of alchemy. Studying the history of alchemy from this perspective inevitably leads to a consideration of the history of religion, hence the inadequacy of a purely scientific approach which is unwilling to cross the disciplinary boundary into more symbolic considerations.

23) (CW13: 352; p. 273) *Alchemical Studies*	*The Philosophical Tree*	German publication: 1945; Revised and Expanded Edition (upon which this translation is based): **1954**		Human history	For Jung, there is a definite link between archetypes, myth and history. An image can be considered archetypal if it can be found to exist in the records of human history, identical in form (but not necessarily content), and conveying the same meaning.
24) (CW13: 470; p. 344) *Alchemical Studies*	*The Philosophical Tree*	German publication: 1945; Revised and Expanded Edition (upon which this translation is based): **1954**	–	History of symbols	Jung is against a reductive approach to interpreting dreams (i.e. claiming that dream image x = y in reality). Rather, he advocates working with the image, which necessitates a consideration of the symbol's history or historical manifestations (i.e. studying its historical variations [*archetypal images*] in order to gain knowledge of its inherent structure [*archetype*]; Jung is promoting a psychological interpretation of the history of symbols.
25) (CW15: 44–59; pp. 33–59) *The Spirit in Man, Art and Literature*	*Sigmund Freud in his Historical Setting*	Published in both German and English simultaneously: **1932**; Essay reprinted in 1934	–	History (in title)	Jung criticises Freud for failing to note the debt owed to intellectual predecessors of psychoanalysis. Jung thus embarks upon a contextualisation of Freud's theories. Freud's theory of sexuality is an expression of, and reaction against, the historical context in which it developed.
26) (CW17: 250–52; pp. 144–45) *The Development of the Personality*	*The Gifted Child*	German publication: 1943 and 1946; (English translation based on the **1946** edition)	December 1942 Paper delivered at the annual meeting of the Basel School Council	History	**para 250:** Studying history is integral to the intellectual cultivation of the gifted child. Jung is speaking of an appreciation of history 'in the widest sense of the word'. He uses the term 'history' to denote an acknowledgement of a link to a shared, collective past which has contributed to the development of each individual's psychic disposition.

Location of reference in *Collected Works*	Title of work	Year of publication	Year of lecture	Topic of reference to history	Critical point made
					para 251: History provides a 'firm standpoint' or strong-enough container to withstand the danger of succumbing to mass trends and thus is essential to true individuality. To resist the dangers of collectivity one must be entrenched in the lessons stemming from the history of the collective. **para 252:** The individual can potentially influence and change the path of history.
27) (CW17: 250; pp. 144–45) *The Development of the Personality*	*The Gifted Child*	German publication: 1943 and 1946; (English translation based on the **1946** edition)	December 1942. Paper delivered at the annual meeting of the Basel School Council	Continuity of history	Jung argues for the continuity of history, which points to a potential, teleological element in his thinking. The unconscious simultaneously directs and reconciles the experiences of humanity. The continuity that regulates opposites in history at the macro level also moderates the personal fluctuations and conflicts of the gifted child at the micro level (*archetypal history*). The unconscious operates at both the individual and collective levels and thus its effects should be studied at both stratums.

Note

1 These do not include references to history made in the context of discussing the figure of Christ.

Chapter 2

Sexual revolutions

Towards a brief history, from the Fall of Man to the present[1]

David Bennett

Numerous books and innumerable articles have been written on the topic of this volume, three of the best known being John Heidenry's *What Wild Ecstasy: The Rise and Fall of the Sexual Revolution* (1977), Linda Grant's *Sexing the Millennium: A Political History of the Sexual Revolution* (1993) and David Allyn's *Make Love, Not War: The Sexual Revolution: An Unfettered History* (2001). Note the recurring formula in the subtitles of these books, with its misleading definite article: 'the sexual revolution'. Writers on our topic often ask whether 'the sexual revolution' ever really happened. ('So, *has* there been a sexual revolution?' asks Grant, by way of introducing *Sexing the Millennium* [op. cit.: 18], a book that confines its ambit almost exclusively to the two decades between *Time* magazine's 1964 heralding of a 'World Sexual Revolution' and its 1984 announcement: 'the revolution is over'.) A better question, if an unanswerable and hence purely rhetorical one, would be: *how many* sexual revolutions have there been? The history of radical shifts in the kinds and conditions of human sexual relating is almost unimaginably long, and there can be no justification for limiting the historical and cultural reference of the term 'sexual revolution' to that notoriously elastic decade, the 1960s, or to the western edge of Europe and North America. Judaeo-Christian myth *begins* with a story of sexual revolution, the Temptation and Fall of Man – at least as the *Book of Genesis* was read in the 1830s by the heretical Perfectionist preacher and sexual liberationist, John Humphrey Noyes (of whom more in a moment). Modern ethnography posits a no less mythical, originary revolution in its story of how patriarchy must have overturned the 'primitive matriarchal societies' – the gynocracies and free-love regimes – that Bronislaw Malinowski postulated were pervasive features of the Neolithic era, and which such twentieth-century sexual radicals as Otto Gross, Wilhelm Reich and Georges Bataille (all readers of Malinowski's *Argonauts of the Western Pacific* [1922]) imagined as blueprints for sexually liberated societies of the future.

In short, history inherits the very notion of sexual revolution from prehistory, and fitting a chronicle of sexual revolutions – from the Fall to, say, pornography-dot-com – into the scope of a brief essay such as this would be beyond even a sexological Stephen Hawking. In the interests of economy, then, and in deference to the many writers who have already documented the distinctive features of '*the* (sic) sexual revolution', this essay will have relatively little to say about the rhetorics and rationales of sexual liberation during the 1960s (an era tellingly revisited by two other contributors to this volume, the distinguished psychotherapists and authors Susie Orbach and Brett Kahr).

Whether or not Noyes was right to interpret the biblical Fall as a story of transgressive sexual desire, it did have four specific consequences that all utopian-socialist sexual revolutions have been trying to put right ever since: namely, the curses of shame, toil, the pains of motherhood, and woman's subservience to male desire – God's four curses on Adam and Eve for tasting the fruit of knowledge (Genesis 3: 6–24).

Like other millenarians, the eighteenth-century Shakers solved the problem of toil by abolishing private property, collectivising their wealth, and instituting gender-equality in the division of labour, and they eliminated sexual shame and the pains of motherhood by practising a strict code of celibacy – a solution revealed in a vision to their founder, Ann Lee (regarded by the Shakers as God's second and female incarnation), following her own harrowing experience of four traumatic deliveries and four infant deaths. The Shakers' consequent reliance on recruitment, not reproduction, to maintain their community (children were recruited into its communal 'families' through adoption or conversion) has not stopped it lasting some 260 years – the most successful countercultural movement in American history. The Shakers' putatively matriarchal model has been invoked by many radical-feminist historians since the eighteenth century as a prototype for women seeking gender equality and prepared to practise chastity, or the withdrawal of sexual labour, to achieve it. Most recently, Kenya's Federation of Women Lawyers famously organised a nationwide boycott of heterosexual intercourse by Kenyan women in April 2009, taking a leaf out of Aristophanes's comedy, *Lysistrata*, (411 BC) to force resolution of a factional impasse in Kenya's male-dominated government. But the strategy has also been advocated as a genuinely revolutionary one, never more sincerely than by the radical lesbian feminist activist Sheila Jeffreys in her verdict on the 1960s sexual revolution as 'anticlimactic' for women. In 1990 Jeffreys concluded her book, *Anticlimax: A Feminist Perspective on the Sexual Revolution*, by arguing that the only way for women to dismantle male privilege and power was to practise lesbianism as a political choice, withdrawing their 'most valuable energies' from men (Jeffreys 1990: 291, 293). By the 1970s, many straight women who were sexually active in the 1960s were arriving at a similar conclusion: better that eroticism be put on hold till gender and class relations are overhauled than that women become the tea-makers, typists and bedmates of another masculinist sexual revolution.

Celibacy and sublimation have figured large in other revolutions, but the founder of the second most celebrated countercultural experiment in early American history took the opposite view to Mother Ann Lee's, arguing that the Shakers had freed women from the burden of motherhood at unnecessary cost: the cost of the sexual pleasure for which God created Eve as companion to Adam before banishing them from Eden with the curse of parenthood ('in sorrow thou shalt bring forth children'). This was the heretical theologian and Owenite socialist John Humphrey Noyes, coiner of the term 'free love' in the 1840s and founder of what would become the 300-strong Oneida Community, which successfully practised sexual and economic communism for some 40 years in New York State before disbanding in 1881 and turning itself into a joint-stock company that became the multinational Oneida corporation, known today as a tableware brand. The Oneida experiment has been an inspiration for countercultural communes and sexual-liberation movements ever since.

As Perfectionists, the Oneida Communists believed themselves reconciled with God and freed from sin and shame. They combined gender equality in all aspects of community life, work and governance with a principle of collective ownership that extended from wealth to persons to sexual desire, or libido itself. As a utopian-socialist, Noyes argued that monogamy both contradicted the natural law of desire and institutionalised property in persons and sexual pleasure, breeding jealousy, shame and inhibition. Abolishing the nuclear family was a precondition for recovering the prelapsarian state of innocence, to which end the Oneidans practised what they called 'complex marriage' – meaning that every (post-pubescent) member of the community was married to every other ('Communism of property goes with Communism of persons', they argued [Noyes 1870: 639]). Exclusive couple-relationships were not permitted, children were raised communally and privacy was abolished along with private property: the sexes shared common sleeping as well as living and working quarters, and sexual desire was supposed to be exchanged or circulated as freely and equally, or undiscriminatingly, as possible. The sexes were encouraged to mingle pleasurably in work as well as play, breaking down the dichotomy between labour and pleasure in ways that directly anticipated Herbert Marcuse's vision of unalienated work and the 're-sexualised body' a century later (Noyes 1870: 636; Marcuse 1966: 20–54).

Here is a taste of Noyes's 'Bible Communism', illustrating how his arguments for the pleasure principle of spending energy in sexual intercourse, and not investing it in production or reproduction, rely uncannily on the very language of profit and loss that 'free love' and Bible Communism were meant to transcend. Noyes distinguished the 'profitable' parts of sexual intercourse – meaning its yield of pleasure – from the 'expensive' parts, meaning the costs in energy that child bearing and child rearing levy on women and the community:

> *PROPOSITION XIX.*—The propagative part of the sexual relation is in its nature the *expensive* department. 1. While amativeness keeps the capital stock of life circulating between two, propagation introduces a third partner. 2. The propagative act, i.e. the emission of the seed, is a drain on the life of man, and when habitual, produces disease. 3. The infirmities and vital expenses of woman during the long period of pregnancy waste her constitution. 4. The awful agonies of childbirth heavily tax the life of woman. 5. The cares of the nursing period bear heavily on woman. 6. The cares of both parents, through the period of the childhood of their offspring, are many and burdensome. 7. The labor of man is greatly increased by the necessity of providing for children. A portion of these expenses would undoubtedly have been curtailed if human nature had remained in its original integrity [i.e. in Eden], and will, when it is restored. But it is still self-evident that the birth of children, viewed either as a vital or a mechanical operation, is in its nature expensive; and the fact that multiplied conception was imposed as a curse, indicates that it was so regarded by the Creator.
>
> *Note 1.*—Amativeness being the profitable part, and propagation the expensive part of the sexual relation, it is evident that a true balance between them is essential to the interests of the vital economy. If expenses exceed income, bankruptcy ensues. After the Fall, sin and shame curtailed amativeness, thus diminishing the profitable department; and the curse increased propagation, thus enlarging the expensive department. Death, i.e. vital bankruptcy, is the law of the race in its fallen condition; and it results more from this derangement of the sexual economy than from any other cause, except the disruption from God. It is the expression of the disproportion of amativeness to propagation – or of life to its expenses; each generation dies in giving life to its successor . . .
>
> *Note 3.*—The grand problem which must be solved before redemption can be carried forward to immortality is this: *How can the benefits of amativeness be secured and increased, and the expenses of propagation be reduced to such limits as life can afford?*
>
> (Noyes 1853: 45–46)

To maximise pleasure and minimise its libidinal costs, the Oneidans combined free love with the practice of what Noyes called 'male continence', or *coitus reservatus*, which prolonged and intensified erotic pleasure for both sexes while preventing conception, thus eliminating the drain on the community's energy of constant child bearing and rearing. (Some 40 years later, Edward Carpenter, the gay, utopian-socialist sexual revolutionary, would press the same argument on readers of his book, *Love's Coming of Age* (1906[1896]). Noting that 'woman objects to being a mere machine for perpetual reproduction', Carpenter recommended the practice of *karezza*, or non-orgasmic sexual intercourse, in which, 'given abundant time and mutual reciprocity, the interchange becomes satisfactory and complete without emission or crisis by either party' and 'gives to the sexual relation an office entirely distinct from the propagative act – it is a union on the affectional plane' [ibid.: 172–73].) For the Oneida Community, 'male continence' (a century and a quarter before the contraceptive pill would become definitive of 1960s sexual revolution) meant that decisions about when and by whom children were conceived could be made rationally and collectively, a principle Noyes called 'scientific breeding' or 'stirpiculture'.

As John Levi Martin has noted, two themes have invariably converged in the rhetoric of modern sexual revolution: vitalism and scientism (Martin 1996: 107). Calls for a return to nature and spontaneity in sexuality, for an eros undistorted by a repressive culture, have converged with calls for a modern, scientific attitude towards sex and its rational organisation according to 'Darwinian' principles of selective breeding, or 'race hygiene', and Malthusian calculations of economically sustainable birth rates and optimal population sizes.

If the language of capitalism returned uncannily to haunt the very doctrines of free love and Bible Communism that were meant to end the commodification and exploitation of bodies, labour and love at Oneida, it also haunts the Freudo-Marxist tradition of libidinal economy and what Wilhelm Reich called his 'sex-economic' theory, to which so many twentieth-century sexual radicals would look for inspiration. If the Freudian self was an economy of libido that could be variously saved, profitably invested, spent in sexual pleasure or locked up unproductively in neurosis, like a sleeping asset (Bennett 1999: 269–72), then it seemed to Reich that the free and unreserved spending of this libidinal currency by adolescents, women and men alike constituted a radical rejection of the capitalist ethos of acquisition, accumulation and productive investment.

There are two basic models of the libidinal economy of revolution, which could be called the Freudian and Reichian, or petit-bourgeois and socialist, or Puritan and Keynesian models – the first based on a vision of spending as depletion or loss, the second on a vision of spending as *generating* wealth. Mahatma Gandhi adopted the petit-bourgeois or Puritan theory of libidinal economy in his 1930 treatise *Self-restraint or Self-indulgence*. Addressing fellow Indians and would-be revolutionaries in the chapter entitled 'On the Necessity of Continence' (and stressing that 'no other chapter [of his treatise] is nearly as important as this'), Gandhi insisted that the doctrine of 'free love' was fundamentally misconceived and that 'the true sexual emancipation' consists in 'perpetual restraint', or life-long chastity. Citing personal experience and scientific precedent, Gandhi argued that the expenditure 'of vital energy' in orgasm is 'positively injurious to health' and that conserving such energy is crucial to the 'economic progress and success' of any society. Thus, unless Indians learned to conserve their libidinal energies and invest them in industry and politics, instead of squandering them in their habitual promiscuity (the Indian people's 'almost incurable disease' of sexual 'merry-making') and consequent unplanned pregnancies, they would never throw off the yoke of British imperialism. Gandhi claimed that it was the high proportion of celibates and nuns in Western European populations that had enabled them to accumulate the vital energy to subjugate the lascivious Indians. As for Sigmund Freud, so for the Mahatma, libido spent in erotic pleasure becomes unavailable for sublimation and hence civilisation – or for the revolutionary struggle for Indian self-rule (ibid.: 32–33, 66–76).

Much to Wilhelm Reich's dismay, it was this same view of libidinal economy that the Bolsheviks would adopt when they started rolling back the sexual revolution they had introduced in Russia in the early 1920s with a raft of progressive laws on sexual freedom, gender equality, women's rights, divorce, abortion, state-provided childcare and the decriminalisation of homosexuality. Intent on overcoming gender inequality and dismantling the traditional patriarchal nuclear family, the Bolshevik reformers were progressive, not least, in formulating their policies on sexual and gender issues in social terms, rather than medicalising or biologising them and thus handing them over to a scientific elite for deliberation. Treating the sexual as permeated by the social and hence as available to political transformation, the Bolsheviks were being true to Engels's analysis of the superstructural dependence of gender relations and sexual morality on property relations in his *The Origin of the Family, Private Property and the State* (1902[1884]). But this approach could also turn into a politically convenient, 'vulgar' economic determinism, according to which the state had no real need to concern itself with sexual reforms and freedoms as such, since the 'new sexuality', like the 'New Man' and 'New Woman' (reconstructed as 'socialised' subjects), was supposed to follow automatically from the abolition of private property. Already over-stretched by the task of managing the simultaneous economic, educational and cultural modernisation of Russia, the Soviet authorities decided they could shelve the issue of sexual revolution for Soviet youth, since sexual problems would simply wither away in the transformed conditions of revolutionary society. This view was compounded by what has been called 'Stalinist sexophobia', an important strand of Stalin's 'cultural revolution' or counterrevolution in the early 1930s, which 'aimed at liquidating social and cultural diversity and at establishing total control over the personality' (Kon 1995: 266). By the mid 1920s, Bolshevik moralists such as Aron Zalkind were stigmatising 'free love' as a decadent bourgeois doctrine, deploring the degeneracy of Soviet university students, and blaming the remnants of the bourgeois class for injecting 'the laboring masses with a sexual narcotic' (Carleton 2005: 57). Ironically, party-line Soviet sexual ideology began to echo the most conservative Victorian marriage-advice manuals in maintaining that sexual intimacy had no other purpose than the 'creation of healthy, robust descendants', as Dr. A. L. Berkovich argued in his plan for the complete 'rationalisation of sex', published in *The Young Guard* in 1923 (ibid.: 62). Stalin's sexual counterrevolution included the recriminalising of homosexuality and culminated in 1945 in his prohibition of abortion (Martin 1996: 124). Gregory Carleton cites as 'the crowning statement of Bolshevik asceticism' in the 1930s a sentiment voiced by a newly converted communist character in Nikolai Ostrovsky's classic socialist-realist novel, *How the Steel Was Tempered* (1973[1932]): 'Mama, I've sworn to myself not to chase girls until we've knocked off the bourgeoisie in the whole world' (Carleton 2005: 222).

While the Western press demonised the Bolshevik's free-love regime for desecrating the sanctity of marriage and the dignity of womanhood, then, the Bolsheviks themselves succumbed to the view that the libidinal costs of civil war and revolution required Soviet youth to stop squandering its energies in sexual experimentation, and instead they started offering youth the examples of celibate great men – Leonardo, Newton, Beethoven and Kant – as models of productive sublimation. Driving sex underground, Soviet asceticism ensured that sex of any kind became, in Igor Kon's words, 'a sign of social protest and a refuge for individuals from the totalitarian state. Forbidden erotica became a strong anti-Soviet and anti-Communist symbol, pressing the people to make their choice' (Kon 1995: 266–67). One outcome of the Communist Party's systematic suppression of all things sexual – sex research, sex education, 'erotic' art and literature – would be Russia's second abortive sexual revolution in the twentieth century, the one that followed perestroika in the late 1980s, when rigid government control gave way to a deregulated market in unclassified pornography and commoditised sex, which delivered the long-desired sexual liberation in the form of deromanticised and commercialised, anarchic and alienated, obscene and trivialised sex.

Wilhelm Reich keenly followed the Bolshevik experiment with sexual revolution and he returned from a lecture tour in Russia in 1929 impressed by progressive institutions such as the State Psychoanalytic Orphanage-Laboratory, in which children of Party members (including Joseph Stalin's son) were raised without guilt-inducing judgement or punishment for sexual behaviour, with a view to obviating all sexually derived problems in their later lives (Etkind 1997: 203). At the same time, Reich was depressed by the early signs of the Soviet retreat from sexual liberalisation (Sharaf 1984: 142–43). Though not the coiner of the term 'sexual revolution', Reich is now inextricably linked to it. (J. L. Martin has traced the first usage of the term to Wilhelm Heinrich Dreuw's 1921 book, *Die Sexual-Revolution*, which advocated a 'revolution' in legal thinking about prostitution and venereal disease [Martin 1996: 107].) Reich authored several mutating editions of a two-part study entitled, in 1936, *Die Sexualität im Kulturkampf: zur sozialistischen Umstrukturierung des Menschen* (sexuality in the culture struggle:

For the socialist restructuring of humans) and retitled, from the 1945 English edition onwards, *The Sexual Revolution: Toward a Self-Governing Character Structure* (1949). Reich devoted Part I of his book to analysing the failure of attempted sexual reforms in bourgeois society to overhaul the institutions of monogamy and the patriarchal family that sustained capitalism, and Part II to tracking the rise and fall of the Soviet sexual revolution. His career as an ideologue of sexual liberation spanned both of the decades popularly identified with sexual revolutions in the West – the so-called 'Roaring Twenties' and the 1960s – but it was the early Marxist Reich whose thinking would shape the revolutionary calls to arms issued by 1960s theorists of sexual liberation such as Marcuse and Norman O. Brown, rather than the cloud-busting exponent of orgone theory that Reich became during the McCarthy era (Reich 1973: 368–93).

Like his fellow psychoanalyst and would-be revolutionary, Otto Gross, Reich was a classical Freudian to the extent that he based his revolutionary theory on the 'hydraulic' model of liberation, positing that 'natural', 'healthy', 'instinctual' erotic drives were psychically repressed by introjected 'foreign' authorities, in the form of the superego, with pathological consequences – and that exorcising the most pathogenic of those introjected authorities, using psychoanalytic techniques, was the only route to salvation. The sadistic conscience or superego was the internalised representative of the patriarchal head of the bourgeois nuclear family and the authoritarian state, institutions that propped up class society and its exploitative divisions of labour and wealth. (According to Max Weber, who rejected an article Gross sent to his journal for publication, Gross insisted that '*every* suppression of emotion-laden desires and drives leads to "repression" and therefore calls for revolution' – a naive and dangerous view, in Weber's judgement, making no allowance for the fact that the ethical life always entails some repression [Zaretsky 2004: 86; cf. Whimster, Chapter 12, this volume].)

In *The Sexual Revolution* Reich insisted that individual neurosis and 'pathological' or 'irrational mass behaviour' can invariably be traced to the same source, namely, sexual repression, which he explained as an unconscious conflict between instinctual drives for sexual gratification and 'the moral pressure which is needed to keep the dammed-up energies under control' (Reich 1949: 3–4). The consequence of this conflict is that 'the natural capacity for sexual gratification' is thwarted, 'entirely destroyed' or displaced into 'sadistic concepts of the sexual act, rape phantasies, etc.' (ibid.: 4). As the ego arms 'itself against the instinct as well as the outer world', libidinal energy congeals into a form of 'character armour', which functions as a prison to the instinctual drive to release or spend libido in orgasm (ibid.). Only by 'eliminat[ing] the genital inhibitions and genital anxiety' that are instilled in individuals by the ages of four or five through the taboos against masturbation, incest and infantile polymorphous sexuality, and reinforced by the institutions of the patriarchal family, premarital chastity and life-long monogamy, could both individual neurosis and mass pathology be cured (ibid.: 116–49). Carolyn Dean summarises Reich's logic: 'healthy sexuality leads to democracy and perverted sexuality leads to fascism' (Dean 1996: 60). Nor was Freud correct in positing that 'culture always owes its existence to instinctual repression and renunciation. . . . that cultural achievements are the result of sublimated sexual energy'; for 'there is historical evidence', Reich insisted vaguely, 'of the incorrectness of this formulation':

> there are in existence highly cultured societies without any sexual suppression and a completely free sex life. What is correct in this theory is only that sexual suppression forms the mass-psychological basis for a *certain* culture, namely, the *patriarchal authoritarian* one, in all of its forms.
>
> (Reich 1949: 10)

Marcuse would refine this challenge to Freud's pessimistic, ahistorical, universalist conception of repression with his theory of 'surplus repression', developed in what became one of the key philosophical handbooks for sexual revolutionaries in the 1960s, *Eros and Civilization* (1966[1955]). Oedipalisation was the disciplinary process by which the body and its senses became organised around work or utility, rather than around instinctual gratification or sensual pleasure, and it necessitated a contraction of the erotogenic zones of the body to the single zone of the genitals, thereby 'freeing' the rest of the body for labour. Marcuse described this process as 'the desexualization of the organism required by its social utilization as an instrument of labour' (Marcuse 1966: 39); but he argued that the material abundance that the Industrial Revolution had delivered to first-world societies in the form of labour-saving technology should have rendered much of traditional work – and hence the repression and sublimation by which libidinal energy is channelled into work – redundant. If such repression was still being exacted by civilisation, Marcuse argued, it was only because of the exploitative division of labour in class society, which demands 'surplus repression' from the so-called 'working', or 'dominated', classes. Marcuse's utopian vision was of a non-repressive society of material abundance, in which the body would be fully restored to its 'natural' potential for unsublimated erotic pleasure diffused across all its surfaces, senses and organs (Marcuse 1966: 34–35).

Construing repression as a blockage of the body's instinctual drive to expend libidinal energy, then, Reich advocated its antithesis, which he called 'orgastic potency', meaning the capacity for 'complete' orgasm, for spending all one's hoarded libidinal energy without reserve – such unreserved spending being (*pace* Freud) the key to both the psychic health and the collective wealth of any society (Bennett 2010: 102–104). What Reich called 'compulsive [i.e. compulsory] sexual morality' compromised the natural human 'right' to orgastic potency, withholding it from adolescents, the unmarried and even married women, and went hand in hand with patriarchal power structures, reserving a monopoly on free sexual spending for the head of the bourgeois 'patriarchal-authoritarian family', which in turn was the nucleus of the fascist state (Reich 1972 and 1930). Only the unreserved spending by all, which keeps libido in continual circulation or exchange, could guarantee socio-economic health, obviating the depressions or recessions that result from the unequal distribution and hoarding of libido in capitalist society (Mairowitz 1986).

Under the auspices of the German Communist Party in the early 1930s, Reich's Sex-Pol movement claimed a following of some thirty thousand German youth and workers, committed to providing the sex education, law reform, free contraception and abortions that would make 'orgastic potency' accessible to all, thus realising the libidinal revolution that Reich saw as the promise of Bolshevism in the 1920s (Reich 1975: 11). It was his campaigning for the orgasmic rights of children and workers that got Reich expelled from the Austrian, German and Danish communist parties, and his socialist activism that got him expelled from the International Psychoanalytic Association in 1934 (Freud himself was a classical liberal, pessimistic about all radical or utopian political programmes, anxious to dissociate psychoanalysis from any political ideology that might compromise its claims to 'scientific' objectivity, and quick to excommunicate analysts who – like Reich, Gross or Alfred Adler – insisted otherwise). By the time Reich issued the fourth edition of *The Sexual Revolution* (1949), he was stressing that he had given up any affiliation with political movements and parties in 1932; he was now looking to consumer-capitalist America, in the 1940s and 1950s, to realise the sexual revolution that had failed to materialise in Austria, Germany or Russia during the 1920s (Reich 1949: xiv–xv).

As we have already seen, Reich was not the first socialist sexual revolutionary to advocate libidinal spending, rather than hoarding and investment, as the key to common wealth. When Noyes came to publish his 600-page *History of American Socialisms* in 1870, he would review the economic, sexual and governmental policies and practices of more than 50 experiments in utopian socialist living, ranging from the early Fourierist and Owenite settlements through to his own Oneida Community, tabulating all the available figures on their annual economic productivity and communal wealth (Noyes 1870). What his analysis showed, contrary to the Freudian or petit-bourgeois model of libidinal economy and civilisation's discontents, was that the economically most successful communist experiment could also be the sexually least repressed, the one that practised the 'freest' love. Such was the Oneida Community's 'complex marriage', in which all members of the collective 'family' were expected to engage in pleasure-yielding (normally non-procreative) sexual intercourse with all others, and to permeate their everyday lives, at work as well as at play, with a generalised eroticism. (For all its rhetoric of sexual liberation, Noyes's vision of revolution was no less strictly heterosexual or heterosexist than Reich's would be.) Intermixing vitalism, scientism and heretical theology, Noyes argued that love, both divine and human, is a form of electrical energy or current, sometimes called animal magnetism, which flows between men and women, as between the poles of an electrical battery, most intensely during sexual intercourse (Noyes 1847: 65–78). It was this same galvanising current, 'fluid energy' or life force that the Creator transmitted to the first human, Adam; that the miraculous healers of the Bible transmitted by their laying on of hands; and that animates all living creatures. The more frequently or protractedly the Oneida Communists engaged in pleasure-yielding sexual intercourse, the more of this vital energy they would generate and, since vital energy is work-power, the more economically productive the commune would become (Noyes 1870: 636). Noyes envisaged a properly scientific future understanding and harnessing of this vital currency becoming an insurance against not only disease but even death. ('In vital society, strength will be increased and the necessity of labor diminished, till work will become sport, as it would have been in the original Eden state . . . We can now see our way to victory over death. . . . Vital society increases strength, diminishes work, and makes labor attractive, thus removing the antecedents of death' [Noyes 1870: 635–36].) His economic vision of the erotic 'mingling of the sexes' as generating, rather than squandering, libidinal energy seemed vindicated by the fact that the Oneida Communists were renowned for producing large economic surpluses (excess to their own requirements) while reducing their work hours to a minimum. Combining productive work with erotic play in a manner that broke down the dichotomy between pleasure and labour proved 'economically as well as spiritually profitable' (Noyes 1870: 636). By the time the community disbanded in 1881, under the pressure of internal rivalries and external opposition to its practice of 'complex marriage', its assets were valued at $600,000.

The Oneidans, then, were Keynesians or Reichians in libidinal economy *avant la lettre*, believing that the more freely desire was circulated or exchanged between bodies, the more of it would be generated, and the richer in energy the community would become. A century later, the Friedrichshof commune, founded by the Viennese Actionist leader Otto Muehl in Burgenland, Austria, instituted an even more radical version of libidinal Keynesianism than the Bible Communists had, but without their economic success. Described by the *Guardian* newspaper as being 'for a halcyon period between the early 70s and the beginning of the 90s . . . the world's most famous sex commune', the Friedrichshof 'family' had 600 members at its height, and saw itself as building on millenarian experiments like Oneida, but exchanging their theology for a heady mix of Marxism, anarchism and Reichian psychoanalysis. The Friedrichshof communards pooled their resources and established a kind of anti-society based on the abolition of money, property, careers, romantic love, and the nuclear family. Muehl proclaimed 'group marriage' in 1973, couple relationships were dissolved, and private space and intimacy were abolished, with a view to producing a completely communal or collective sexuality.

Just as Oneida had its daily group therapy sessions, known as 'mutual criticism', in which individuals' thoughts and feelings became common property, as it were, so Friedrichshof had its *Selbstdarstellung*, or 'self-presentation' sessions, in which individuals cleared out all the nuclear-familial furniture from their psyches in Muehl's version of Reichian body therapy, laced with Janov's primal scream therapy, undertaking a process of regression and rebirthing as fully liberated (de-oedipalised) and 'socialised' subjects. The process was known as *Aktionsanalyse* or *AA* (action-analysis). The aim was to become what Muehl called an 'exemplary energeticist', freely and pleasurably circulating or exchanging libido, maintaining the circuitry by which the currency flowed through and around the community. To optimise the libidinal energy in circulation, communards were required to make love as often as Muslims bow to Mecca – five times a day – with the maximum number of different partners and a minimum of romantic fore-play, in order to discourage the forming of exclusive couple relationships that would result in libidinal disinvestment from the group. The ideal was a totally non-repetitive copulation that would eventually recruit the whole world's population to the libidinal economy that the communards were pioneering, while their withdrawal from the global capitalist economy would precipitate its collapse (Schlothauer 1975). As the commune's population expanded, it had recourse to the notorious computer-generated *ficklisten* ('fuck-lists' or 'fuck-registers'), issued daily, indicating who should make love to whom and when, formalising what was initially supposed to be a spontaneous arrangement and transforming a free-love commune into an authoritarian biopolitical regime (Altenberg 2001). The Friedrichshof commune lasted some 20 years and, during the late 1970s, associated *AA* communes were established in Frankfurt, Krefeld and Berlin, living according to the six *AA* principles established at Friedrichshof: (1) Self-Expression (2) Free Sexuality (3) Common Property (4) Common Work and Production (5) Common Child Rearing (6) Direct Democracy.

In contrast to the economically successful Oneida Community, the Friedrichshof commune teetered on the brink of bankruptcy and could only survive through regular injections of capital from new members and the communards' earnings in the Austrian business economy. Despite their economic differences, however, the Oneida Community and the Friedrichshof commune would fail for similar reasons. Sooner or later, practice began to contradict revolutionary theory, some animals on their farms became more equal than others, and their charismatic leaders betrayed their own doctrines by hoarding sexual pleasure and partners for themselves, prompting oedipal challenges that eventually broke apart the communities. Both leaders were also charged with statutory rape (and, in Muehl's case, incest[2]) under laws that their communes had abolished and in relation to which they were in a revolutionary 'state of exception'.

But the chief irony of the Oneida and Friedrichshof experiments, I would suggest, is not that capitalism's *Homo oeconomicus* reappeared to practise private enterprise where there was supposed to be libidinal socialism. Rather, the irony is that their ostensibly free libidinal economies turned out to be rigidly, even baroquely, ordered, no less rule-bound than bourgeois sexuality is by its codes of incest, courtship, modesty, marriage, filiation and so on. As one Friedrichshof communard put it: the principle of absolute fidelity was replaced by one of absolute promiscuity, and the demands of monogamy on the bourgeois couple were as nothing compared to the commune's demands on its members. As our fiscal policy makers kept rediscovering during the recent 'global financial crisis', there is an uncanny convergence between Keynesian policies of unconstrained spending and central state control of the institutions that keep the currency of desire circulating. What the Oneida and Friedrichshof experiments in collectivising desire suggest is that there is no such thing as a 'free' or un-rule-bound sexual desire, merely different regimes of sexuality by which desire is defined and generated.

There is also an uncanny resemblance between the sexual liberationists' calls for disinhibited libidinal spending and consumer culture's summons to instant gratification through guilt-free spending – as if utopian sexual-revolutionary movements, despite themselves, have been in the ideological vanguard of the transition from liberal capitalism's producer ethic to late capitalism's consumer ethic. Along with Reich and Marcuse, another straight, male Freudian, Norman O. Brown, proved to be an influential ideologue of sexual revolution and libidinal spending in the 1960s. Though Brown's vision of sexual liberation would turn out, disappointingly for many of his readers, to be more poetical than carnal when he published *Love's Body* in 1966, the revolutionary rhetoric of his *Life Against Death: The Psychoanalytical Meaning of History* (1968[1959]) seemed to dismiss even the need for a 'basic' repression such as Marcuse acknowledged. In *Life Against Death* Brown mustered canonical Romantic poets, Christian and oriental mystics, Marx and Nietzsche to critique the classical Freudian hypothesis of repression as indispensable to civilisation and, like Reich in the 1944 edition of *The Sexual Revolution*, announced, under the banner of 'The Resurrection of the Body', an imminent apocalyptic ending to millennia of sublimation (Brown 1968: 269). In Brown's version of Freudianism, repression and sublimation were primary agents of the death instinct, which 'the friends of the life instinct' were combating with their vision of life as 'play', not work, for the 'resurrected' body, 'based not on anxiety and aggression but on narcissism and erotic exuberance' (Brown 1968: 269). Like Noyes, Reich and Marcuse before him, Brown argued that 'the abolition of repression would abolish the unnatural concentrations of libido in certain bodily organs' (the genitalia), permitting all the senses of the human body to be developed and intensified to their full potential, affording a 'consciousness which *does not negate any more*' (Brown 1968: 270). Brown's 'resurrected' body, like Reich's and Marcuse's 're-sexualised body', was the 'polymorphously perverse' one of Freud's pre-oedipal infant, blissfully innocent of both work and shame, in a psychic Eden. Brown argued that in Jacob Boehme's concept of life as 'love-play' and his vision of 'the spiritual or paradisiacal body of Adam before the Fall', we can recognise 'the potent demand in our unconscious both for an androgynous mode of being and for a narcissistic mode of self-expression, as well as the corruption in our current use of the oral, anal, and genital functions' (Brown 1968: 272).

Such calls to 'narcissistic' hedonism and polymorphous pleasures *as liberation*, and hence as a political duty to oneself and society at large, were potent rhetoric for a generation of post-war Western baby boomers growing accustomed, in the 1960s, to healthcare and higher education provided by the welfare state, the promise of full employment should it ever be wanted, and a booming consumerist culture.

Within the socialist tradition from the outset, the question of sex has been treated as a question of property, as institutionalised in monogamy, in which the patriarchal male claims a monopoly on the body, labour power and libido of the female (and parents can claim ownership of the child's). It is this private property-relation that utopian sexual revolutionaries have sought to 'socialise' or collectivise. While classical liberalism of John Locke's kind posits the individual as owner of his/her body as a form of private property, which can be used, traded (as in marriage), sold (as in prostitution) or refashioned (cosmetically, athletically, transsexually) by a subject as ideally 'free' as the market should be, socialism set out to abolish the property-relation altogether, thereby throwing open the question of what new kinds of freedom – and, indeed, subjectivity or selfhood – a 'sexual liberation' movement might entertain.

One of the powerful theses advanced by the minority liberation movements of the 1960s sexual revolution was the 'sexual preference' model of sexuality. From the emergence of sexology as a discipline in the late nineteenth century through to its grappling with gender-role confusion during and after the Second World War, sexologists had pathologised sexual 'deviance', attributing divergences from normative definitions of 'healthy', 'natural' sexuality to psychological damage or disease. Such pathologising of homosexuality, lesbianism, sadomasochism, transvestism and so forth had the dubious virtue of freeing the 'deviant' subject from a discourse of moral opprobrium while defining him or her as a suitable case for treatment. The 'sexual preference' model reversed this logic: while seeking 'tolerance' of a minority's right to exercise its sexual preference, it represented sexuality as a matter of choice or taste, at once voluntary and cultivated, and not of innate predisposition, insisting that anyone is potentially capable of choosing heterodox sexual practices and relationships. In doing so, the 'sexual preference' model de-naturalised what would come to be called 'heteronormativity' and de-pathologised its alternatives. The charge of pathology was pinned, instead, on the heteronormative police: it was the disease of 'homophobia' that now needed diagnosis and cure.

The Reichian stress on 'natural', 'healthy' sexuality, freed from neuroses (civilisation's discontents), had driven sex out into the open – into the countercultural Californian sun, where, for example, an invariably naked Fredrick 'Fritz' Perls offered free love and gestalt therapy at the Esalen Institute to anyone seeking a back-to-nature refuge from consumer capitalism. But the 'sexual preference' model shifted the ground from nature to choice, and hence from determinism to liberalism. Sexuality became the stuff of self-fashioning. And it was a short step from the notion of sexual identity as a self-fashioning choice or taste to the idea of the consumer as sovereign in a free market of sexual pleasures, lifestyles and identities. Sexuality thus came to seem as susceptible to manipulation by commercial fashion cycles as any other kind of consumer choice. As Sheila Jeffreys puts it: 'Heterosexuality and homosexuality are seen as sexual preferences or choices, defined by sexual activities and feelings or even "lifestyles", but having no more to do with politics than a preference for peas or cabbage' (Jeffreys 1990: 289).

Conclusion

To summarise: For the Freudo-Marxist tradition, sexual repression (and its secret agent, the superego) is a mechanism of capitalist domination, operating through the patriarchal family; and the more naive liberation campaigns – like *Oz* magazine's in the 1960s, with its slogan, 'The destruction of all inhibition is our aim' – view the pursuit of sexual pleasure and license *per se* as a means of resisting capitalist domination. But, as Marcuse pointed out, some kinds of sexual liberalisation operate as 'repressive desublimation', complicit with the system they oppose (Marcuse 1968: 69). And when the postmodern superego is heard issuing the command, 'Enjoy!', instead of 'Don't!', how can we be sure that obeying it will mean emancipation?

With the advent of 1980s identity politics, we saw a shift from a politics of liberation to a politics of representation – of subaltern groups and minority subcultures demanding 'recognition', 'respect' and representation. Queer theory signalled another shift, in some (university-related) quarters, from a politics of representation to a politics of deconstruction. The postmodern deconstruction of representations – re-casting sexuality as a realm of plurality, ambiguity and fluidity, rather than of identities – has been seen *both* as a site of radical change today *and* as complicit with a mainstream consumer culture whose ever changing fashion cycles interpellate the consumer as the self-fashioning subject of an always mobile, polymorphous and insatiable desire. Queer theory here meets Madison Avenue. In Viagra culture, desire itself is sold back to us as a desirable commodity, and the question of what might constitute an un-alienated or liberated sexuality today seems no easier to answer than it was for the nineteenth-century utopian-socialists who finally admitted defeat by turning their commune into a joint stock company.

Bibliography

Allyn, D. (2001) *Make Love, Not War: The Sexual Revolution: An Unfettered History*. New York, NY: Routledge.

Altenberg, T. (2001) *Das Paradies Experiment: Die Utopie der freien Sexulität Kommune Friedrichshof 1973–1978*. Wien: Triton.

Bennett, D. (1999) Burghers, burglars and masturbators: The sovereign spender in the age of consumerism. *New Literary History*, *30*(2), 269–94.

Bennett, D. (2010) Libidinal economy, prostitution and consumer culture. *Textual Practice*, *26*(1), 93–122.

Brown, N. O. (1966) *Love's Body*. New York, NY: Random House.

Brown, N. O. (1968[1959]) *Life Against Death: The Psychoanalytical Meaning of History*. London: Sphere.

Carleton, G. (2005) *Sexual Revolution in Bolshevik Russia*. Pittsburgh: University of Pittsburgh.

Carpenter, E. (1906[1896]) *Love's Coming Of Age: A Series of Papers on the Relations of the Sexes*. London: Swan Schonnenheim.

Dean, C. J. (1996) *Sexuality and Modern Western Culture*. New York, NY: Twayne.

Dreuw, W. H. (1921) *Die Sexual-Revolution: Der kampf um die staatliche. Bekämpfung der Geschlechtskrankheiten*. Leipzig: Ernst Bircher Verlag.

Engels, F. (1902[1884]) *The Origin of the Family, Private Property and the State* (Trans. E. Untermann). Chicago, IL: C. H. Kerr.

Etkind, A. (1997) *Eros of the Impossible: The History of Psychoanalysis in Russia*. Boulder, CO: Westview.

Gandhi, M. (1930) On the Necessity of Continence (1927). In *Self-restraint or Self-indulgence*. Ahmedabad: Navajivan (pp. 66–76).

Grant, L. (1993) *Sexing the Millennium: A Political History of the Sexual Revolution*. London: HarperCollins.

Heidenry, J. (1977) *What Wild Ecstasy: The Rise and Fall of the Sexual Revolution*. New York, NY: Simon and Schuster.

Jeffreys, S. (1990) *Anticlimax: A Feminist Perspective on the Sexual Revolution*. London: Women's Press.

Kon, I. S. (1995) *The Sexual Revolution in Russia: From the Age of the Czars to Today* (Trans. James Riordan). New York, NY: Free Press.

Marcuse, H. (1966[1955]) *Eros and Civilization*. Boston, MA: Beacon Press.

Marcuse, H. (1968) *One-Dimensional Man*. London: Sphere.
Mairowitz, D. Z. (1986) *Reich for Beginners*. London: Unwin.
Malinowski, B. (1922) *Argonauts of the Western Pacific*. New York, NY: Dutton & Co.
Martin, J. L. (1996) Structuring the Sexual Revolution. *Theory and Society, 25*, 105–51.
Noyes, J. H. (1847) *The Berean: A Manual for the Help of Those Who Seek the Faith of the Primitive Church*. Putney, VT: Office of the Spiritual Magazine.
Noyes, J. H. (1853) *Bible Communism: A Compilation from the Annual Reports and Other Publications of the Oneida Association and Its Branches: Presenting, in Connection with their History, a Summary View of their Religious and Social Thoughts*. Brooklyn, NY: The Circular.
Noyes, J. H. (1870) *History of American Socialisms*. Philadelphia, PA: Lippincott.
Ostrovsky, N. (1973[1932]) *How the Steel was Tempered*. London: Central Books.
Reich, W. (1930) *Geschlechtsreife, Enthaltsamkeit, Ehemoral* (Sexual Maturity, Abstinence and Marital Fidelity). Vienna: Muenster.
Reich, W. (1949) *The Sexual Revolution: Toward a Self-Governing Character Structure*. London: Vision.
Reich, W. (1972) The Problem of Sexual Economy. In L. Baxandall (ed.) *Sex-Pol: Essays 1929–1934*. New York, NY: Random House (pp. 226–49).
Reich, W. (1973) *The Function of the Orgasm*. New York, NY: Farrar, Straus and Giroux.
Reich, W. (1975) *Wilhelm Reich Speaks of Freud*. Harmondsworth: Penguin.
Schlothauer, A. (1975) *Die Diktatur der freien Sexualitaet – AAO, Muehl Kommune, Friedrichshof*. Retrieved from http://www.agpf.de/Schlothauer-AAO-Muehl.htm
Sharaf, M. (1984) *Fury on Earth: A Biography of Wilhelm Reich*. London: Hutchinson.
Zaretsky, E. (2004) *Secrets of the Soul: A Social and Cultural History of Psychoanalysis*. New York, NY: Knopf.

Note

1 Research for this chapter was supported by an Australian Research Council Discovery Project Grant.
2 Convicted of sexual abuse of minors and rape in 1991, Muehl spent seven years in prison. A 1999 BBC program about the Friedrichshof commune was aptly titled *Slaves in Paradise* (editor's note).

Part II

Fathers and sons

Chapter 3

Elementary my dear Holmes

Hans Gross, the father of Criminology, and Arthur Conan Doyle

Thomas Mühlbacher

According to Lois Madison (Gross 2000: 8), who devoted many years to research on the background of Otto Gross's ideas and the correlation of his work to modern theories of the mind, the universal myth of Sherlock Holmes is that he was a modern hero of criminal investigation – someone who had, by study and genius, become the first and only criminal investigator in the late nineteenth century to approach the crime scene scientifically, specialising in the deductive method and applying psychology to the interrogation of witnesses and the apperception of the criminal mind. Dispelling the Sherlock Holmes myth, Hans Gross's handbook of criminal investigation, which was written at about the same time as Arthur Conan Doyle began to publish his Holmes stories, taught principles of detective work that were, as he acknowledged, the fruits of years of his and others' own experiences. In point of fact, the introduction of the investigative techniques for which Holmes is celebrated was long since a *fait accompli* by the time Doyle created his dashing detective for the satisfaction of a public hungry for stories about modern criminal investigation.

In contrast to Doyle, Gross was important not for his introduction of new types of evidence nor for being the first to take a scientific approach, but rather for his instruction and advice, as well as for the thoroughness and comprehensiveness with which he covered the subject of criminology. Gross's handbook of investigation, published in virtually all the major languages, quickly became a bible for the criminal investigator. Commenting on the scope and intent of the handbook, Hans Gross summed up not only his own dedication to his field but the basis for the potential impact of his work for decades to come.

Doyle delighted audiences by unravelling stories out of details ignored by the average individual, reflecting the novelty and appeal of the concept of deduction at the turn of the century. Regularly trumping Scotland Yard's inspectors, Holmes employs a wealth of investigative methods: the smallest, indeed to the untrained eye virtually invisible, shreds of fibre are gleaned from sofas or articles of clothing and serve as clues to the identity of the

Figure 3.1 Hans Gross, 1847–1915. Painting after a photograph, artist unknown.

perpetrator of a crime; names are teased from burned paper in a fire, etc. But these were in fact the very methods used and prescribed by Hans Gross.

So we see that Holmes – however great we may think him to be, a foremost representative of the field of criminal investigation around 1890 – was not the only innovative or modern investigator alive. Compared with the true genius of Hans Gross, Holmes's greatness inevitably pales, and his methods take on the very note of dilettantism for which his arrogance appears to habitually compensate.

Can we assent this opinion? Let us have a glance at the state of development of criminology in the nineteenth century.

In those days forensic science was largely a function of the medical profession. Physicians had changed the focus of anatomical dissection, not only searching for an understanding of the structure of the human body, but also trying to match the changes in the cadaver to the clinical symptoms of disease reported before death. From there it was a short step to the idea of dissecting bodies to look for changes caused by criminal acts.

Incidentally, this is how Sherlock Holmes is introduced in *A Study in Scarlet*, when Stamford tells Watson:

> He is a little too scientific for my tastes – it approaches to cold-bloodedness. I could imagine his giving a friend a little pinch of the latest vegetable alkaloid [. . .] simply out of a spirit of inquiry in order to have an accurate idea of the effects [. . .] He appears to have a passion for definite and exact knowledge [. . .] but it may be pushed to excess. When it comes to beating the subjects in the dissecting room with a stick – to verify how far bruises may be produced after death – it is certainly taking rather a bizarre shape.
>
> (Doyle 1981: 12)

E. J. Wagner (2006: 8) tells us that initially there was little public support for forensic medicine in Britain. This began to change in the mid nineteenth century when Alfred Swaine Taylor, a young British pathologist who had trained in Paris, was appointed to teach forensic medicine in London. He brought with him a new perspective of examining violent death and presented his ideas in a carefully reasoned text full of detailed examples. Taylor's seminal work on pathology and toxicology had enormous influence on criminal investigation in the days of Holmes and Watson. We should remember in this connection that Arthur Conan Doyle was a physician by profession. Consider Watson's vivid description in *A Study in Scarlet* of Holmes examining not only the corpse but everything else at the crime scene: 'his nimble fingers were flying here, there and everywhere, feeling, pressing, unbuttoning, examining' (Doyle 1981: 33). It is clearly an echo of Taylor's exhortation in the 1873 edition of *A Manual of Medical Jurisprudence*:

> The first duty of a medical jurist is to cultivate a faculty of minute observation [. . .] A medical man, when he sees a dead body, should notice everything. He should observe everything which could throw a light on the production of wounds or other injuries found upon it. It should not be left to a policeman to say whether there were any marks of blood on the dress or on the hands of the deceased, or on the furniture of the room. The dress of the deceased as well as the body should always be closely examined on the spot by the medical man.
>
> (in Wagner 2006: 8)

There being no forensic medical specialist at the scene, Holmes simply fills the role himself. He takes what he likes from the new science and improvises the rest. Hans Gross, on the contrary, would consider this a blunder. Nothing could be more harmful than such advice, he says, nothing could so expose the investigator to mistakes as such fancied independence (Gross 1893). But there is a vast gulf between permitting an investigating officer to undertake work beyond his sphere and instructing him in how to realise when he ought to resort to experts, what experts should be chosen, and what questions must be submitted to them.

Indeed the first half of Part II of Gross's handbook, entitled Knowledge Special to the Investigating Officer, deals with the assistance to be expected from experts. Apart from forensic medicine it comprises the subjects of microscopy, chemistry, physics, mineralogy, zoology, botany and anthropometry. But there are also cases, Gross says, and they are not even extremely rare, where the investigating officer must himself play the role of the expert, especially in all cases where no real expert exists and where a little reflection alone is required. He has to solve problems relating to every branch of human knowledge. He has to be as conversant with the dodges of the poacher as with the wiles of the stockjobber; as acquainted with the method of fabricating a will as with the cause of a railway accident; he must know the tricks of card sharpers, why boilers explode, how a horse-coper can turn an old screw into a young hunter. He should be able to pick his way through account books, understand slang and read ciphers, and be familiar with the processes and tools of all classes of workmen.

In all of these areas, apart from descriptions of cases, there was no criminological research deserving the name 'scientific' until the late nineteenth century.

Hans Gross, the son of an army administration officer, was born on 26 December 1847 in Graz, today the second largest city of Austria. On concluding his studies at the law faculty of the university in his home town, he took up court practice in 1869 and graduated as Doctor iuris in the following year. In October 1871 Gross turned to the legal profession and spent the following four years as an aspirant in a solicitor's office. At this time he began to publish his first minor scientific pieces on legal matters, which came to the attention of the creator of the Austrian code of criminal procedure, Julius Glaser, who was minister of justice at that time. Hence Hans Gross was appointed as a judge at the county court in Feldbach, a small town about 50 kilometres southeast of Graz, in November 1875.

The Austrian Criminologist Roland Grassberger tells us of personal experiences Hans Gross had in those days:

> So far he had only known the criminals by the few types of juridical abstraction but now in the small towns and villages he found a life rich in individual varieties he had never thought of. Due to a great number of problems offered by the practice Hans Gross was shocked to realize that during all the years he spent at the university he had learned almost nothing about how to establish the facts on which he had to base his legal judgement.
>
> (Grassberger 1956: 379)

This impression certainly hardened when he was appointed as an examining justice at the district court in Graz (1880) and as a public prosecutor in Leoben (1884) and Graz (1885).

On one occasion he had to expose an impostor who by pretending to be a respectable nobleman had fraudulently obtained a loan and some jewellery from a well-to-do citizen; at another time he had to reveal the tricks of a fortune teller. On other occasions he even had to solve a murder case or – what is much more difficult than that – to find out by whom or by what a fire had been caused.

In Austria the task of crime detection since 1850 had been almost entirely in the hands of specially appointed judges (so-called examining justices), who had to solve any criminal case to the best of their ability without those technical aids and appliances that today appear to be indispensable. The police forces in both town and country were composed of ex-soldiers who had proven their moral reliability and physical vigour. They knew very well how to keep peace and order by simply applying mother wit and common sense supported by the imperial uniform, but they certainly were not well-trained criminal investigators. So all the examining justices could use was the juridical knowledge gained at the university.

Being aware of the insufficient practical training the student had received at the university, Hans Gross, owing to his industrious character, immediately began to work hard on filling this educational gap. In doing so he was greatly assisted by his capability for concrete reasoning and careful description. From the very beginning he was convinced that the purpose of his task was not only to obtain the necessary knowledge for himself, but to make up a deficiency concerning every law student once and for all. During many years of devoted groundwork he checked each case he had to investigate with regards to its aptitude for supplying results of general importance. With the same zeal he made each interrogation of a witness or an accused person the subject of a delicate psychological study.

As a result of his activity his *Handbuch für Untersuchungsrichter* (Manual for the Examining Justice) was published in 1893. Although it was soon translated into nearly all the major languages of the continent, it took a further 13 years until it came to Britain. In 1906 John Adam, who was then crown and public prosectuor in Madras, India, with the help of his son, J. Collyer Adam, published the first English adaptation there, primarily for the benefit of Indian and colonial magistrates, lawyers and police officers.

Introducing his classic work, Gross writes:

> The Examining Justice must know something more than what is set out in the Codes. No doubt the investigating officer can find much of the requisite information in a mass of books, yet some is to be found nowhere; as to the books themselves, they are not always to his hand, and when he has them at his disposition, he speedily realises that a man without some knowledge of a subject cannot intelligently use a scientific manual. It is impossible for him to find the notions he is in need of, united in one systematic whole; and he has often neither time nor opportunity to question anyone in a position to give him information. . . . In fact he wants a book of 'First Aid'. The present volume is intended to be such an auxiliary.
>
> (Gross 1893: Introduction)

The systematic clarity was at first hampered by the huge amount of material presented: gradually Gross worked out the term 'Criminalistics', using it the first time as a subheading in the third edition of his manual, which he called the 'System of Criminalistics'. The term comprised two fields of science which are nowadays considered to be different from each other. It included the phenomenology of crime on the one hand, and police science on the other. Within the latter he differentiated between 'Criminal Tactics' and 'Criminalistic Technology'.

Gross soon realised that a further subject needed special attention. As the second great result of his scientific work, *Criminal Psychology* was published in 1898. His basis in this instance was not a certain theory, and he therefore defined Criminal Psychology as a summary of all subjects of psychology that are necessary for the criminal investigator's work. In his opinion the same general procedure must be applied to studies in Criminal Psychology as to Criminalistics in the strict sense. The criterion of any progress is careful observation and description of facts and not a daring interpretation of them. In spite of all the modern methods of material evidence even nowadays we should not underestimate the great importance of evidence given by witnesses. Hans Gross did not intend to eliminate this kind of evidence from modern proceedings, but tried to clearly explain its limits and weaknesses. Statements of witnesses must be used with great care, and even the statement of an honest witness may be untrue. And very often, Hans Gross pointed out, the failure of a witness is not due to his inability but to unskilful questioning.

In September 1898 Hans Gross introduced his *Archiv für Kriminalanthropologie und Kriminalistik* (Archives for Criminal Anthropology and Criminalistics). The most important task of this new journal was – and still is, now in its 113th year – to report on observations and to collect material, sort it out and check it if it can be utilised for forensic research.

In December 1898 Hans Gross was appointed a professor for Criminal Law at the University of Czernowitz, which at that time was part of Austria. Five years later he was called to the University of Prague, finally returning to Graz in 1905 to hold the chair at the university of his home town. His lifelong work was crowned when he succeeded in opening a Criminalistic Institute at the University of Graz in 1912. For the first time a university centre for teaching and research had been founded, at which all problems raised by crime and the necessity for its prosecution were scientifically administered.

On 9 December 1915 Hans Gross died of pneumonia, leaving behind a new scientific discipline he undoubtedly had created.

From a chronological point of view, we can hardly say that Hans Gross influenced Sir Arthur Conan Doyle's early work. When the first Sherlock Holmes mystery, *A Study in Scarlet*, was published in the 1887 issue of *Beeton's Christmas Annual*, Hans Gross was a man of 40 serving as a public prosecutor in Graz. When his handbook was published in 1893, Holmes had already solved his 'Final Problem' and was believed to lie dead in the Reichenbach falls. Hence we can say that Sir Arthur Conan Doyle did not know the work of Hans Gross when he wrote his first Holmes novels and therefore Gross certainly is not the model for the great detective. Whenever Arthur Conan Doyle was asked if there was a real Sherlock Holmes, his answer was that he was inspired by Dr Joseph Bell, who was his teacher at the Edinburgh Royal Infirmary and noted there for drawing large conclusions from the smallest observations. He never mentioned Hans Gross, who on the other hand definitely knew at least some of Conan Doyle's stories, which he recommended to students as a surrogate for real cases.

Although they never met and – as far as we know – never got in touch with each other in any way, both lived in a period when everybody trusted in science and scientific solutions for any problem. That might explain why Gross and Sherlock Holmes seem to resemble each other at first glance – although they are as different as chalk and cheese on further examination. To Holmes – convinced of his superiority not only to Watson but also to his earlier fictional colleagues, Dupin and Lecoq (in *A Study in Scarlet* Holmes tells Watson that in his opinion the former was an inferior fellow using showy tricks and that the latter was a miserable bungler) – solutions seemed to be self-explanatory and often 'simplicity itself'. By contrast, Gross's books are not written by a pedantic schoolmaster but rather by a 'fatherly friend', at every possible opportunity illustrated by interesting examples.

According to David Stuart Davies, the writer and playwright who has written extensively about Sherlock Holmes, and is the editor of *Red Herrings*, the monthly in-house publication of the Crime Writer's Associaton, the inspiration for Conan Doyle's *The Problem of Thor Bridge* (first published in 1922) came from a real-life German case, which the editor of the *Strand Magazine* had brought to Conan Doyle's attention. I am convinced that it concerns one of Gross's examples. This is how Hans Gross describes it:

> Early one morning the authorities were informed that the corpse of a murdered man had been found. At the spot indicated, in the middle of a bridge crossing a rather deep stream, the body was found of a grain merchant, A. M., supposed to be a well-to-do man, face downwards with a gunshot wound behind the ear. The bullet, after passing through the brain, had lodged in the frontal bone above the left eye. His pocket book was missing and the seam of the inside pocket in which it usually was carried was ripped up, as if the pocket book had been rapidly and violently snatched out. His watch and chain were also missing; of the latter the ring attaching it to the waistcoat button was left.
>
> A policeman stated that A. M. had been seen the evening before in a spirit shop, where he drank with moderation and left about 10.30 p.m. To reach his house he had to pass the bridge where he was found dead. In the spirit shop there was at the same time as A. M. an unknown, wretched-looking man, who throughout the evening drank but a single glass of spirits and left shortly after A. M. The latter had several times taken out his pocket book, which appeared well-filled, though no one could say whether he had any money or how much. The supposition was therefore natural that the unknown had followed A. M., murdered him on the bridge, and robbed him; he was accordingly searched for, arrested and brought to the spot. He denied all knowledge of the crime and said he had passed the night in a barn, which however he could not point out to the police.
>
> Just when the inquiry was concluding and the corpse was about to be removed after the post-mortem, the investigating officer observed quite by chance that on the decayed wooden parapet of the bridge, almost opposite the spot where the corpse lay, there was a small but perfectly fresh damage which appeared to have been caused by a violent blow on the upper end of the parapet of a hard and angular body. He immediately suspected that this damage had some connection with the murder. Examination with a magnifying glass showed nothing important, but it

was impossible to avoid the impression that the murderer had thrown something into the water and thus damaged the parapet. Accordingly, the investigating officer determined to drag the bed of the stream below the bridge, and almost immediately there was picked up a strong cord about 14 feet long with a large stone at one end and at the other a discharged pistol, the barrel of which fitted exactly the bullet extracted from the head of A. M.

The case then was thus evidently one of suicide; A. M. had hung the stone over the parapet of the bridge and discharged the pistol behind his ear. The moment he fired he let go of the pistol, which the weight of the stone dragged over the parapet and into the water, but the pistol had struck violently against the parapet in passing over and so caused the damage observed. Experiments showed the trick to be quite easy and the parapet was damaged every time. Subsequent inquiries disclosed that the pistol actually belonged to A. M., that his affairs were hopelessly involved, and that he had just effected an insurance on his life for the benefit of his family for a large sum. As the company did not pay in cases of suicide, A. M. had adopted this means to conceal the suicide and lead to the belief that he had been murdered.

(Gross 1896: 602f.)

And now this is what Sir Arthur Conan Doyle tells us in *The Problem of Thor Bridge*:

Maria Gibson, the wife of the 'Gold King' Neil Gibson, was found lying in a pool of blood on Thor Bridge with a bullet through the head and a note from the governess Grace Dunbar, agreeing to a meeting at that location, in her hand. A recently discharged pistol with one shot fired was found in Miss Dunbar's wardrobe. Holmes observed some rather odd things about the case. How could Miss Dunbar so coolly and rationally have planned and carried out the murder and then carelessly tossed the murder weapon into her wardrobe? If it was one of a matching pair, why couldn't the other one be found in Mr. Gibson's collection? And most of all, what was the strange chip on the underside of the bridge's stone balustrade?

(Retrieved from http://en-wikisource.org/wiki/The_Problem_of_Thor_Bridge)

The plot is quite simple: no murder was committed here, either. Mrs Gibson, like the grain merchant A. M., committed suicide. A stone connected to a rope pulled the pistol over the balustrade into the water. For this reason the weapon could not be found and suspicion of murder arose. Whereas the bankrupt grain merchant had to simulate a crime because of the life insurance, Mrs Gibson defamed the governess, whom she suspected of having a love affair with her husband.

In Nicholas Meyer's 1974 novel *The Seven-Per-Cent Solution*, Holmes and Watson meet Sigmund Freud in Vienna. Maybe some day another 'lost manuscript' of the late John H. Watson, M. D. will be discovered, from which we will learn about a meeting of the great detective and Hans Gross. What matters would they have talked over? I will leave it to your imagination, but there is a good chance that in the end Watson will exclaim in response to Gross's explanations: 'Excellent!' And Holmes would add: 'Elementary, my dear Watson.'

Bibliography

Doyle, A. C. (1981) *A Study in Scarlet*. London: Penguin.

Grassberger, R. (1956) Pioneers in Criminology. *The Journal of Criminal Law, Criminology and Police Science*, *47*, 397–405.

Gross, H. (1873) *Entwurf einer Rechtsentwicklung*. Graz: Leykam-Josefsthal.

Gross, H. (1874) *Über die Ehrenfolgen bei strafrechtlichen Verurteilungen*. Graz: Leykam-Josefsthal.

Gross, H. (1893) *Handbuch für Untersuchungsrichter*. Graz: Leuscher & Lubensky.

Gross, H. (1896) *Handbuch für Untersuchungsrichter. 2nd Edition*. Graz: Leuscher & Lubensky.

Gross, H. (1898) *Kriminalpsychologie* (Criminal Psychology). Graz: Leuscher & Lubensky.

Gross, O. (2000) *Collected Works: The Graz Years* (L. Madison, Ed.). Hamilton, NY: Mindpiece.

Meyer, N. (1974) *The Seven-Per-Cent Solution*. New York, NY: Ballantine.

Wagner, E. J. (2006) *The Science of Sherlock Holmes*. Hoboken, NJ: Wiley & Sons.

Chapter 4

Kafka, sex and the Jews

Sander L. Gilman

Recently, the Kafka study by James Hawes, *Excavating Kafka* (2008), made headlines in the UK. His image of Kafka as a sex fiend and fan of expensive pornography appealed to the prurient interest of the newspapers. Kafka was, according to the *Daily Telegraph*, 'also a man of the world, who enjoyed the city's more fashionable nightclubs, visited brothels and had an impressive stash of pornography – which, as Hawes says (and the book illustrates), certainly wasn't quaintly "naughty"' (Walton 2008).

Hawes's argument is rather simple: Kafka was a person just like you and me. He had the same needs, desires, and demands. Sure he wrote really interesting things but he was a 'modern' man and modern man is a universal type. So Hawes's fascination with Kafka's pornography is proof that he is just like us. Well, not 'just' like us really: we download porn from the internet and store it on our computers; he bought expensive literary journals with dirty pictures and locked them in his closet. But that is merely a change of technology – we know Kafka because Kafka is 'us'. And 'we' are not bound by time or place; 'we' are universal, unchanging. Sex becomes the common denominator.

But sex can be read differently from different positions in history. In Kafka's world the anti-Semites had the cliché of the Jew compulsively seducing Christian girls or the Viennese commonplace of the Jewish pornographer, which led to the murder of the Jewish-identified writer-publisher Hugo Bettauer in Vienna in 1925. Being Jewish in a world of sexual metaphor and reality shapes what sexuality means. Thus there are the myths that separate Hawes's Kafka from being 'just like you and me'. These are not only the image of Kafka as a suffering artist, as a tormented asexual being driven by his desire for and fear of women, but, more concretely, Kafka as the exemplary Jewish figure of modernity. Is Kafka's Jewish identity (which shifts radically over his own lifetime) central or peripheral to our understanding of his work and of his own understanding of his and his figures' sexuality?

The Romantic image of the suffering artist and that of the asexual Kafka were purposeful creations of Kafka, who 'sold' this image as part of his own sense of what a writer and intellectual should be in turn-of-the-century Central Europe. At the core of this deracinated image of the intellectual and writer was a self-conscious attempt by Kafka (as well as a wide range of his Jewish contemporaries in the German-speaking world) to distance himself (and themselves) from the allegations which he read virtually every day on the front pages of his newspapers and heard shouted regularly at him on the street, at university, in the work place, about the sexualised, devious, corrupt, clever but superficial and thus inherently different nature of the Jew from that of the Teuton (or indeed the Slav). 'Being Jewish' colored every aspect of Kafka's identity – including 'class' and 'gender'. Being a Jew of the middle class or being a Jewish male was understood at that time as inherently different from being 'middle class' or 'male'.

It was impossible for *fin de siècle* 'Jews' (even those such as Kafka's contemporary Hugo von Hofmannsthal who were raised Christian and upper class in Vienna) to escape dealing on a conscious or a subconscious level with the implications of these charges of Jewish creative inferiority. 'Being Jewish' for Kafka had to do with the Jew as a member of a 'race' (not a religion) and the claimed permanent nature of the Jews' racial markers (from the nose to the psyche to sexuality) became one of the central aspects with which Kafka struggled. Being a Jewish male was different from being a 'man'. It signified a radically different relationship to masculinity, to health, to the body, to gender roles. One could repress this – as I have argued in my 2005 biography of Kafka – one could flaunt this – as Daniel Boyarin argued in his *Unheroic Conduct: The Rise of Heterosexuality and the Invention of the Jewish Man* (1997) – or one could deny this – as the German-Jewish novelist Jacob Wassermann (1933) said in his autobiography written in the the 1920s – but this did not mean that it could be ignored. Kafka obsessively inscribed these struggles in his writing, stripping them of the overt anti-Semitic rhetoric of his time, and universalised them. These anxieties about 'being different' became, then, attributed to the 'modern' condition. Kafka scrubbed clean all of the contemporary references to race, leaving only the deracinated image of the Jew now as 'modern man'. It is an old cliché that being Jewish in the modern age is simply being modern and that being modern is simply being a Jew: that all of the anxieties that modern man experiences – from alienation from the world to the sense of impotence of action – simultaneously defines both states.

Kafka's is an image so brilliantly polished that it reflects back only the reality of the readers and biographers – as Hawes shows all too well in his book. Thus I made an argument in *Franz Kafka: The Jewish Patient* (1995) that Kafka's mistrust of his own body was that of the Jew whose body was seen as inherently and 'racially' different, deformed, weaker, ill, degenerate. Hawes dismisses this as merely Kafka's anxiety about being an over-stimulated 'intellectual' hyper concerned about looking 'too intellectual':

'To see this fashionable (and eventually for Europe almost fatal) *intellectual self-hatred* only through the eyes of Jewishness does not help open up Kafka's writing, but puts blinkers on it' (2008: 123). This is a reduction to the autobiographical well worth noting. Being Jewish is not central to this.

Yet by the time Franz Kafka attended the Prague German-language Ferdinand-Karls University for eight semesters beginning in November 1901, he was moving in a typical trajectory for secularised Jews in Central Europe – from the rural or ghetto environment of the grandparents to the small shopkeeper or manufacturer of the parents to the status of the professional: Freud, Einstein, Kafka and thousands of others followed this upwardly mobile trajectory. The University was the engine for that final stage of Jewish social mobility. The struggle over admittance of Jews to the various faculties (colleges) of the universities was an ongoing one. It was only in the 1860s that Jews were regularly admitted to the medical faculty in Vienna and then only if they agreed to have only Jewish patients. The Prague university had split into a German and a Czech section in 1882, the year before Kafka was born. There were clear limits to the number of Jews who could be admitted to any one of the faculties whether German- or Czech-speaking.

Kafka decided initially to become a chemist as there was said to be jobs for Jews in the chemical industry, but he quickly detested the physical nature of laboratory work. (One is reminded that Primo Levi [1919–1987] maintained his fascination with chemistry, earning his doctorate in 1942 at Turin. This profession saved his life when he was sent to Auschwitz and was able to work as a chemist there: 'I write because I am a chemist. My trade has provided my raw material, the nucleus to which things join . . . Chemistry is a struggle with matter, a masterpiece of rationality, an existential parable . . . Chemistry teaches vigilance combined with reason' [in Anissimov 1999: 316].) Kafka's friend and fellow chemist-in-waiting Hugo Bergmann stated that Kafka had abandoned the study of chemistry 'because our hands were too clumsy to cope with the glassware.' It is always his body that seems to betray young Franz. After two weeks, he switched to law as a profession that would enable him to earn a living. Bergmann remained in the laboratory of Professor Goldschmied, a converted Jew (which is how you received a professorship in Prague as a Jew) for another year.

By the next semester he was also auditing lectures in German Literature, which, as it was taught in Prague by August Sauer, stressed the racial determinism of German 'tribal' culture that would have excluded him and all Jews. Kafka joined the Reading and Lecture Hall for German Students (*Lesehalle*), a heavily Jewish discussion group, to engage the intellectual world of letters. It was the organisation that attracted those Jews who did not join the Zionist Bar Kochba Society – and that was the majority. Kafka eventually, in 1904, became the secretary of the Literature and Art section.

For Kafka had been writing even in high school, if only for his own amusement. Kafka describes in his diary of 19 January 1911 his output of hundreds of pages including a novel about two brothers, one of whom goes to prison while the other escapes to a fabled America. America – not the America of history but of German myth – fascinated him, just as it did his older contemporary Karl May (1842–1912), whose novels about mythic America, such as his *Winnetou* (1893–1910), paralleled Kafka's own later work and shaped the Germans' image of America to this day. Kafka destroys all of this after his uncle reads a page of the novel and dismisses it as 'the usual stuff'. Childish aspirations to thinking of himself as a writer ('I did it mostly out of vanity, and by shifting the paper about on the tablecloth, tapping with my pencil, looking around under the lamp, wanted to tempt someone to take what I had written from me, look at it, and admire me' [in Gilman 1995]) give way to a sense of writing as not pursuing the 'usual stuff'. Now writing became more than a vocation – it was a sign that he could belong to a world of culture that wished to exclude him because he was a Jew. But the pressure on him, from his family and his world, was that he also had to be able to function economically in this world.

Kafka dedicated himself full-time to the study of law, which he said he picked so it would not interfere with his creative life. But the study of law in Prague had shifted shortly before Kafka arrived from the rote memorisation of legal codes to the study of how the 'law' constructed worlds of meaning using the cutting-edge biological sciences as the basis for law. Among his teachers was the criminologist Hans Gross, who taught that racial typologies were one of the best indicators of real or potential criminality. He was particularly fascinated with the Jewish body as revealing the true nature of Jewish difference. Hans Gross in 1908 noted that ritual murder should be defined as a crime under the new category of 'psychopathological superstition' (in Gilman 1995). Gross attacks a colleague, A. Nussbaum, who believes that accepting ritual murder as a legal concept would support the reality of the charge, which would then cause a persecution of the Jews. For Gross, 'ritual murder' is a sign of the madness of the accuser and of the accuser's culture, and does not reflect on the Jews as the accused at all. Later one of Kafka's most critical comments, in 1922, dealt with the by then anti-Freudian Hans Blüher's pamphlet, *Secessio Judaica* (1922), which advocated the view that the Jews were unable to truly be assimilated into German society. Blüher (1888–1955) had been a one-time advocate of Freud, with whom he had broken over Freud's Jewishness, and had been a strong advocate of the German Youth Movement. He was by the 1920s an implacable anti-Semite. One of Blüher's markers of the male Jew was 'the way *his* fingers grow from *his* hand' (in Gilman 1995).

Further, Hans Gross's views on deportation, which are echoed in Kafka's tale *In the Penal Colony*, are closely connected to conjectures about degenerative illness and disease. One exiles the degenerate from society and places him or her into a penal colony. But degeneration is not manifested simply in crime, although the literature of the period insists that those predisposed to tuberculosis also manifest a higher rate of sociopathic acts. Degeneration is more than the 'morbid deviation from the type', to use the classic definition of the mid nineteenth century. By the close of the nineteenth century, it also means the inheritance of negative acquired characteristics. In sheltering them, society spares these individuals the struggle for life, enabling them to develop and grow. Then they merely degenerate, and commit sociopathic acts. The degenerate criminal should be permanently exiled, recommends Gross, as he can no more be 'cured' of his criminality than an amputee can be cured of a missing limb. Like the Jew?

Kafka studied with Hans Gross for three semesters. He also studied with Horaz Krasnopolski, perhaps the most conservative figure at the law school. Franz's cousin, Bruno Kafka (1881–1931), served as Krasnopolski's 'assistant' and worked his way up the academic ladder to eventually serve as the *Rektor* (President) of the university. When Kafka joined the Reading and Lecture Hall for German Students (*Lesehalle*), he found his cousin Bruno a prominent member, even reading a paper in Franz's section of literature. Of course, the study of literature – central to European notions of education (*Bildung*) – provides a cultural veneer for the bourgeoisie, especially those Jews now entering the middle class for the first time. It enabled them to sound 'like every one else'. But it was not a 'serious' occupation, merely the amassing of cultural capital. Like his teacher, Bruno was strongly a German nationalist and was involved in some of the violent confrontations with Czech students when he was a law student. Kafka not only looked down on his politics but also on his attitude toward literature as well as his choice of profession – the law.

Studying law is, oddly, closely associated with Kafka's sense of his first initiation into the 'mysteries' of the body. When Kafka was 20 and studying for the State examinations after his university studies, he found himself memorising 'disgusting Roman law' while walking the streets of Prague. He sees a 'shop girl' through a window and, according to a much later letter to Milena Jesenská in 1920, arranges an assignation. The experience is much less awful than he had imagined: 'I was in fact happy, but happy at finally having some peace from my ever complaining body; happy, above all, that the whole experience hadn't been filthier and more disgusting' (in Gilman 1995). His response to this unnamed woman eventually is disgust and 'she had become my bitter enemy', perhaps because she showed him that his anxieties about his body could be suspended. He concentrated on a misplaced gesture and a rudely-spoken word to explain his seeing her as his enemy (as his father had called his Czech employees). In truth Kafka saw his sexuality in terms of his sexual difference, encompassed in the reality of his own circumcised penis. Sexuality, he recounts, 'had in it something of the eternal Jew, being senselessly drawn, wandering senselessly through a senselessly obscene world' (Kafka 1990: 198). But without these associations, he could never be Kafka.

At the university, Kafka met another student, a year younger than he was, at the Reading and Lecture Hall for German Students after he read a paper on Nietzsche in October 1902. Max Brod (1884–1968) was already a writer of some note and had his own literary circle. His talk, in which he dismissed Nietzsche as a fraud, engaged Kafka, who had already learned the value of Nietzsche as a means of both enlightenment and to seduction in his own life. Brod had come from a much 'higher' social class in Prague, having attended, as did the Jewish poet Franz Werfel, the Catholic Piarist School of the *Heilige Kreuzkirche* along with Rilke. The two would become intimate friends for the rest of their lives. The irony is that the tall, stylish, ever youthful Kafka dressed in elegant blue suits was the handsome one of the pair; Brod was pigeon-breasted and hunchbacked, his huge head out of proportion to his body. Kafka, however, sees Brod as the epitome of health as opposed to his own 'self-enamored hypochondria' (Kafka 1973: 27). Even at the end of his life, when he writes to Brod, admiring how he had come to terms with his disability, Kafka could not even come to terms with his earlier health (ibid.: 254).

In June 1906, Kafka graduated with his doctorate in law, a guarantee of how he could earn his living without impinging on his true love, the cultural world that he and his friends were joining. And yet Kafka never leaves the world of work – until he is truly too ill to fulfill its claims on him. Work, a job, provides a structure, like his family, that he needs to have, if just to rebel against. Of course, he never rebels as radically as does his teacher Hans Gross's son, Otto – whom his father has committed to an asylum because of his radical, psychoanalytically inspired actions, such as providing his patients with the means to commit suicide – but just enough, and in his writing, to play at rebellion. The anarchist and psychoanalyst Otto Gross, whose work Kafka knew and admired, having met him in July 1917, committed suicide in 1920. For Gross, 'The psychology of the unconscious is the philosophy of the revolution [. . .] It is called upon to enable an inner freedom, called upon as preparation for the revolution' (Gross 1913: 384).

In the age of psychoanalysis, the psychosomatic model offers a cure of the body by way of a cure of the psyche. Kafka's reading of Freud and his introduction to psychoanalysis through his friend Otto Gross meant that (even though he comes to doubt the efficacy of the method) he has an escape clause from the 'merely' physical. On the other hand, he can also claim *not* to be suffering from mental illness. 'My mind is clear,' he seems to say, 'for all my symptoms are "merely" physical.' But health, according to Kafka, is illusion: all is illness. The ghost-in-the-machine here stems from Kafka's understanding that his illness is the result of a Jewish, materialistic mindset.

Kafka's 'exile' was self-imposed when in 1903 he went for the first time for a 'rest cure' at a sanatorium in Dresden 'where you drink air instead of beer and bathe in air instead of water' (Kafka 1990). He leaves, as he writes to his friend Oskar Pollak, healthier and stronger and able to speak with women.

For Kafka had a lively and engaged circle of friends, all of whom saw themselves as the next generation to dominate German culture. This group, in addition to Bergmann, Pollak and especially Brod, was part of the extended German-speaking literary world of Prague, most of whom were Jews: the blind novelist Oskar Baum, Johannes Urzidil, Robert and Felix Weltsch (all of whom wrote about their friend Kafka), the syphilitic and half mad Paul Leppin, and the German-language inventor of modern muckraking journalism, Hans Egon Kisch, as well as his brother Paul. To their ranks came writers such as the German Jew Carl Einstein, whose monograph on African sculpture, *Negerplastik* (1915), began a modernist fascination with the 'primitive', and Gustav Meyrink, the non-Jewish author of the most famous of all novels about Jewish Prague, *The Golem* (1915). Meyrink was a favorite writer of Max Brod; Kafka found him 'far-fetched and much too blatant. [Kafka] rejected anything that seemed contrived for effect, intellectual, synthetic . . .' In other words, too Prague. Unlike the view in the German department at the Charles University, these young Jews – and virtually all of them were Jews – saw themselves as the next best hope for German culture not only in Prague but also in Central Europe. Between 1902 and 1904 Kafka had begun to write *Description of a Struggle*, the surreal account of, among other things, a conflict between a very thin and a very fat man. It is written in a language quite different from the overblown and very popular novels of Meyrink. Cool, distant and descriptive rather than evocative, it is shorn of the excesses not only of the Prague writers of his time but of the entire *fin de siècle* love of verbal ornament. With it Kafka ironically turned to a seemingly transparent language that hid much more than it revealed.

Up the street from the Sixt House, where Kafka had lived as a child from 1888 to 1889, was the Unicorn Apothecary building, adorned with a sculpture of a child with a unicorn on its facade. Here Kafka, often accompanied by Brod and Werfel, attended Prague's only German-language literary salon, which was hosted by arts patron (and one of the first women to attend the Prague University) Berta Fanta, whose husband owned the pharmacy downstairs. In 1911, Albert Einstein was also a salon regular for the year he was 'in exile' as a young physics professor in Prague. At the salon the work of the banned former priest Franz Brentano (1838–1917), with whom Sigmund Freud had also studied in Vienna, was hotly discussed. Brentano provided an empirical and scientific foundation to both philosophy and psychology through his doctrine of intentionality, developing a theory that saw the fundamental acts of one's mental processes, sensations, as linked to consciousness. Brentano's importance for late nineteenth and early twentieth-century thinkers was, however, as much in his anti-authoritarian stance as in his philosophy. He became the philosopher of choice for many in Kafka's salon. Eventually he abandoned Sixt's salon because of its unbridled pretentiousness. Kafka moved his allegiance to the Prague Café Arco (among the so-called Arconauts) where in addition to intellectual exchange the circle would regularly adjourn to one of the neighborhood bordellos, where Kafka, no longer shy and distant, regularly engaged with young women such as the 'twenty-three-year-old girl who provided me with a miracle of a Sunday' (Kafka 1988b: 24). He would sit with his friends, including Max Brod, in the local bars, such as the Trocadero and the Eldorado, not drinking alcohol, but inspecting the available women. With all of his anxieties about sex, with his father's admonition to visit the whores filed away as an example of his crudeness, Kafka can still write that 'I passed by the brothel as though past the house of a beloved' (Kafka 1988a: 11). At least in the brothel there was no anxiety about rejection, even if there was a substantial fear of infection.

Life at the university was demanding and Kafka did what virtually everyone in his generation did when exhausted – he went to a sanatorium. In 1905 he went to Zuckmantel in Silesia, run by Ludwig Schweinburg, for another rest cure and met there yet another unnamed 'love'. She was 'a woman, and I was a boy [. . .] sick in every sense conceivable.' Kafka devoted his time in such sanatoria to seduction. Indeed he writes to Brod in the fall of 1905 that he comes there 'to mingle with people and womenfolk.' Illness and desire are self-consciously linked throughout his life, but it is at this point still a playing with illness, a use of hypochondria as a means of seduction. That fall Kafka took his written examinations at the law school, barely passing them, indeed so anxious about them that he contemplates asking for a medical postponement, and receives his law degree from the Dean, Alfred Weber, Max Weber's equally renowned sociologist brother, on 18 June 1906. He manages a pass of three out of five votes deeming his performance acceptable.

From the beginning of April to the beginning of October 1906 Kafka served an apprenticeship (*Advokaturs-Concipient*) at the law office of Richard Löwy. He then worked for a year as a 'law probationer' at the Prague Courts. At that moment he also received an official clearance from the police, which testified to Kafka's being 'unmarried, of Jewish faith and good behaviour'. His earlier interest in socialist thought had not marked his scrupulously clean, middle class record. He began to sense that law, as a 'calling', would not be his career: he writes on 9 March 1914 in his diary that in no way could he be seen as 'an Austrian lawyer, which, speaking seriously, I of course am not.' In the summer of 1907 he was in Triebsch, swimming and sunbathing with a 19-year-old language student, Hedwig Therese Weiler, whose 'plump little legs' feature in his dreams. After she returned to Vienna and he to Prague he bombarded her with letters over the next two years, trying to get her to visit him. She of course did not.

And this then shaped all of his encounters – all failures, all dramas, all performances of sexuality – echoing Otto Gross's anxieties and demands for a revolutionary sexuality.

It culminated in Kafka's meeting on 13 August 1912 with Felice Bauer (1887–1960), a secretarial assistant, when he arrived to discuss the tales in *Observations* with Max Brod at the home of Brod's father. On 20 September, Kafka began writing a stream of about 350 of the most extraordinary letters and more than 150 postcards to this most ordinary of young women. The first of these letters was written two days before Kafka wrote *The Judgment*. As the German-language Jewish Nobel Prize winner Elias Canetti notes in his reading of Kafka's letters to Felice Bauer, *Kafka's Other Trial: The Letters to Felice* (1974), the most 'authentic' line in the correspondence is Kafka's claim that 'I am a mendacious creature; for me it is the only way to maintain an even keel; my boat is fragile.'

Felice had, according to Kafka's first impressions, a 'bony, empty face, which wore its emptiness openly. Bare throat. Blouse tossed over. . . . Almost broken nose. Blonde, rather stiff unalluring hair, strong chin.' She was a serious professional woman, the office manager of the Berlin firm Carl Lindström A. G., which produced recording machines and record players. She represented the firm in numerous public presentations. Indeed we have a short advertising film of her using the 'Parlograph', a new dictating machine. Kafka writes to her on 11 November 1912 of his intense desire, but couches it in terms of physical discomfort:

> Write to me only once a week, so that your letter arrives on Sunday – for I cannot endure your daily letters, I am incapable of enduring them. For instance, I answer one of your letters, then lie in bed in apparent calm, but my heart beats through my entire body and is conscious only of you. I belong to you; there is really no other way of expressing it, and that is not strong enough. But for this very reason I don't want to know what you are wearing; it confuses me so much that I cannot deal with life; and that's why I don't want to know that you are fond of me. If I did, how could I, fool that I am, go on sitting in my office, or here at home, instead of leaping onto a train with my eyes shut and opening them only when I am with you? Oh, there is a sad, sad reason for not doing so. To make it short: My health is only just good enough for myself alone, not good enough for marriage, let alone fatherhood.

Oh, that beating, weak heart – the heart of the Kafkas – that stands between Franz and the fulfillment of his desire! Sex is for him the punishment for his desire – not its reward.

It was not until Easter of 1913 that Kafka met twice – nicely chaperoned – with Felice in Berlin and by May 1914 (a pace quite normal for the time) they announced their engagement in Berlin. Kafka feels his engagement as a 'torture'. Two months later, after a meeting with Felice in Berlin, Kafka ends it quite precipitously. The scene again is in Berlin:

> 23 July 1914. The tribunal in the hotel. Trip in the cab. F[elice]'s face. She patted her hair with her hand, wiped her nose, yawned. Suddenly she gathered herself together and said very studied, hostile things she had long been saving up. The trip back with Miss Bl[och]. The room in the hotel; heat reflected from the wall across the street. Afternoon sun, in addition. Energetic waiter, almost an Eastern Jew in his manner. The courtyard noisy as a boiler factory. Bad smells. Bedbug. Crushing is a difficult decision. Chambermaid astonished: There are no bedbugs anywhere; once only did a guest find one in the corridor. At her parents'. Her mother's occasional tears. I recited my lesson. Her father understood the thing from every side. Made a special trip from Malmö to meet me, traveled all night; sat there in his shirt sleeves. They agreed that I was right, there was nothing, or not much, that could be said against me. Devilish in my innocence. Miss Bl[och]'s apparent guilt. Evening alone on a bench on Unter den Linden. Stomach ache.

Everything is here: the guilt, the confrontation, the truths told, the parents, the friend who loves too well, the innocent lover who is not innocent at all, the eastern Jew, the pain of nausea – and the bed bug. One single bed bug never before seen in a room in the hotel.

Kafka had moved out of his parents' home in 1914, leaving them for the first time, into a furnished room in the Bilekgasse. His sister Elli needed his space as her husband had been drafted at the beginning of the war. Again it was not unusual that unmarried children remained in their parents' dwellings until they were married – but for Kafka the link of this space to his sexual life became a literary obsession. Place, and a quiet place at that, becomes one of the set themes in his life and work. He needs, he writes in his diary on 9 March 1914, only 'a room and a vegetarian diet, almost nothing more.' But he thinks too that he cannot marry because, in answer to Felice's imagined question: '"Are you healthy?" "No – heart, sleep, digestion."' Having his own place he again begins in October 1914 to court the abandoned Felice. His letters are seductive and clearly manipulative. In January 1915 he sees her again and then moves into a new room in the Lange Gasse. They take a vacation together in 1916, visiting Marienbad, and Kafka then moves into a new room in the Alchimistengasse. With his move into the rooms in the Schönborn Palace in 1917, Kafka again asks Felice to marry him, an engagement that lasts until the end of that year. When Felice finally does get married in 1919, it is not to Franz Kafka.

It is not as if Kafka's actual interest in women during this time only focused on Felice. On 30 October 1913 he evokes his desire to write in the context of quite another woman:

> I would gladly write fairy tales (why do I hate the word so?) that could please W. [Gerti Wasner, the girl he met in Riva] and that she might sometimes keep a book under the table at meals, read between courses, and blush fearfully when she noticed that the sanatorium doctor has been standing behind her for a little while now and watching her. Her excitement sometimes – or really all of the time – when she hears stories.

There is also evidence of a close friendship with Grete Bloch, a friend of Felice Bauer.

But it was Felice whom Kafka had turned into the object of his desire. The line between his experienced world and his literary one was non-existent. Everything became the stuff for his writing, as he noted in his diary:

> 11 February [1913]. While I read the proofs of *The Judgment*, I'll write down all the relationships, which have become clear to me in the story as far as I now remember them. This is necessary because the story came out of me like a real birth, covered with filth and slime, and only I have the hand that can reach to the body itself and the strength of desire to do so:
>
> The friend is the link between father and son, he is their strongest common bond [. . .]. In the course of the story the father, with the strengthened position that the other, lesser things they share in common give him – love, devotion to the mother, loyalty to her memory, the clientele that he (the father) had been the first to acquire for the business – uses the common bond of the friend to set himself up as Georg's antagonist. Georg is left with nothing; the bride, who lives in the story only in relation to the friend, that is, to what father and son have in common, is easily driven away by the father since no marriage has yet taken place, and so she cannot penetrate the circle of blood relationship that is drawn around father and son. What they have in common is built up entirely around the father, Georg can feel it only as something foreign, something that has become independent, that he has never given enough protection, that is exposed to Russian revolutions, and only because he himself has lost everything except his awareness of the father does the judgment, which closes off his father from him completely, have so strong an effect on him.

Now Kafka knew his Freud and he knows his Kafka. He provides a detailed 'reading' of his own tale to reveal the mechanisms by which he (or his unconscious now made quite conscious) writes his texts. Law and anxiety bubble to the surface of this text but all sexuality is tinged with Kafka's sense of self.

Kafka's sexuality is that of the turn of the century and shapes his sense of his adult possibilities. To echo Zionist contemporary Theodor Zlocisti's *About the Path Home: Verses of a Jew*:

> Over my childhood
> Hung a threatening fist.
> All my peaceful pleasures
> Were shrouded in a mist.
>
> The wounds this left were deep,
> Like a dagger, stabbing me,
> I could forget them, or dream them away . . .
> But healed – they never shall be.
>
> (Zlocisti 1903: 24)

As the reader's introduction to the struggles of Kafka to learn to be a man, this poem reflects the author's sense of a trauma beyond healing. Repression perhaps; but reconstitution never. The poem clearly refers to the actual author's Jewish identity in the Diaspora. The transformation of the politics of race into gender was part and parcel of Kafka's Jewish struggle.

References

Anissimov, M. (1999) *Primo Levi: The Tragedy of an Optimist*. New York, NY: Overlook.

Boyarin, D. (1997) *Unheroic Conduct: The Rise of Heterosexuality and the Invention of the Jewish Man*. Berkeley, CA and London: University of California Press.

Gilman, S. (1995) *Franz Kafka: The Jewish Patient*. New York, NY: Routledge.

Gilman, S. (2005) *Franz Kafka*. London: Reaktion Press.

Gross, O. (1913) Zur Ueberwindung der kulturellen Krise. *Die Aktion*, Vol. III, No. 14: 384–387.

Hawes, J. (2008) *Excavating Kafka*. London: Quercus.

Kafka, F. (1973) *Letters to Felice* (Trans., J. Stern and E. Duckworth). New York, NY: Schocken.

Kafka, F. (1988a) *The Diaries, 1910–1913* (Trans., J. Kresh). New York: Schocken.

Kafka, F. (1988b) *The Diaries, 1914–1923* (Trans., M. Greenberg). New York, NY: Schocken.

Kafka, F. (1990) *Letters to Milena* (Trans., P. Boehm). New York, NY: Schocken.

May, K. (1977) *Winnetou*. New York: Seabury Press.

Walton, J. (2008) The monstrous vermin as an ordinary man: Kafka was no tortured soul, argues a new book – he was a clubber with a penchant for porn. *The Daily Telegraph*, 16 August.

Wasserman, J. (1933) *My Life as a German and Jew*. New York, NY: Coward-McCann, Inc.

Zlocisti, T. (1903) *Vom Heimweg. Verse eines Juden*. Brünn: Jüdische Volksstimme.

Chapter 5

Gross v. Gross

Gerhard M. Dienes

Otto Gross, born 1877, was the only child of Hans Gross, coroner, criminal law reformer and later world-famous criminologist in Graz, and his wife, Adele Gross, née Raymann (Dienes 2005: 12).

According to Else Jaffé, both parents spoiled their son, whom they treated like a little prince and regarded as a kind of child prodigy. In that family realm, with its humid incestuous atmosphere, law and order belonged to daily life (Nitzschke 2000: 112f.). According to Otto Gross himself, his father, who had received his formal education from the monks of the Benedictine Order in the strict Roman Catholic atmosphere of a 'thousand year old school discipline', dominated family life (Dienes 2003: 16). The mother of Otto Gross did not seem to exist. Emotions were hidden behind a façade of restraint and respectability. The traditional patriarchal order was strictly observed without the participants ever realising to what extent that outward regime would internalise itself as 'chaos' inside the family members. Apparent freedom turned out to be the opposite. Proximity almost led to suffocation. Instead of becoming a home, the family was a place of torture (Nitzschke 2000: 112).

It seems certain that, in his innermost being, Otto Gross fought a desperate, lifelong battle that ended fatally; he struggled between the self and the other, between his will to self-assertion and his parents' will, to which he was expected to submit. Otto Gross did not, like Franz Kafka, merely write a letter to his father (Dienes 2007: 16).

At the beginning of the twentieth century, the Gross case caused an international public outcry and for artists like Franz Werfel, his fate attained a certain motive function (Jungk 1987: 88, 118, 137, 140, 143; Anz 2002: 81f.). According to Werfel, Otto Gross hated Moses and the Prophets, Socrates and Plato, not to mention those so-called perpetrators. He regarded those people as hellish demons who had supplied the moral basis for the concept of power and the urge to rape.

Werfel wrote in one of his novels about Otto Gross, alias Dr. Gebhardt:

> Father, was the name of the arch-enemy, the hateful link in the chain, who passed the smurky torch of the original sin rape from generation to generation. His father was indeed an extreme case, who not only represented the implacable authority of patriarchal right in life, but had also been appointed by the state as a teacher to provide it with a supporting structure and armour as a science.
>
> (Werfel 2000: 556)

As a consequence of his own family experience of an omnipotent and authoritarian father and a subordinate mother, Gross came to the early conclusion that the roots of emotional suffering lie in the structure of the core family (Heuer 2007: 47).

Therefore he analysed:

> Matriarchy guarantees the economic and thus sexual and human independence of the woman from the individual man and places the mother, as the bearer of interest in the future, into a relationship of direct responsibility towards society. The mythology of all peoples preserves the memory of the prehistoric status of free matriarchy within the idea of a righteous golden age and paradise of primordial times.
>
> (Gross 1980: 30)

Gross pleaded for the emancipation and equality of women and propagated free partner selection as well as unconventional partnerships, which he envisaged as free of force and violence. And he saw connections between those issues and hierarchic structures in a broader societal context, thus he considered personal agony as a part of the agony of mankind: Gross said, 'the psychoanalyst's clinic itself embraces the entire agony of mankind' (Gross 1914: 529).

In his struggle against all forms of patriarchy, Gross was most fascinated by Bachofen's concepts of matriarchy. 'The coming revolution is a revolution in favour of matriarchy,' he wrote in 1913 (Gross 1913: 387; Jung 1980: 121).

Although he was inclined to concentrate on the phenomenon of sexuality, Gross nevertheless questioned Freud's emphasis on sexuality as the sole origin of neuroses (Hurwitz 2001: 145). In opposition to Freud's approach to the limits set to human motivation by the subconscious, Gross believed that pathologies were rooted in a more positive and even creative area of the subconscious. He wrote about homosexuality of both sexes and pleaded for its decriminalisation. Gross wanted psychoanalysis to become a weapon in a revolution of alternative culture aimed at bringing about the collapse of the existing order, instead of being a tool to force people into even greater conformity (Heuer 2007: 47). He wrote, 'The psychology of the unconscious is the philosophy of the revolution [. . .] it is destined to prepare the innermost for liberty and to prepare the revolution itself' (Gross 1913: col. 384).

Otto Gross came into even further conflict with his father, not only because of his attitudes, but also because of his way of life. The once subaltern son had changed into an enfant terrible; the erstwhile ascetic had mutated into an eccentric addicted to an excessive consumption of sex and drugs (Nitzschke 2000: 114). Arnold Zweig described the situation:

> When father Gross wrote a book about methods of detecting criminals [. . .] Gross junior would immediately publish a brochure addressed to those in question, explicitly naming those psychological methods in a battle against the art of jurisprudence.
>
> (Zweig 1996: 26)

With regard to a lost essay about the analysis of sadism as part of a coroner's societal function with definite associations to his father, which Hans Gross discovered before it was printed, Otto Gross said that from time to time he couldn't help thinking that his father scrutinised criminals like interesting insects, who would, after he had camphorated and classified them by means of an underlying kind of sadistic curiosity in a scientific disguise, forever disappear in the darkness of criminological depots (Buchner 1993: 49).

In contradiction to his father's theory of degeneration – he is known to have supported deportation to penal colonies – the son praised decadence, and in 1906, when Hans Gross was lecturing in Graz on the nature of prisons and imprisonment, Otto Gross travelled to Monte Verità near Ascona, Switzerland, a venue for famous dropouts. There, he developed a plan to establish a 'free academy, from where he planned to attack the values of western civilisation' (Jung 1972: 72; Hurwitz 1980: 115). In Ascona, some mysterious suicides happened, in which Otto Gross was involved. Two of his lovers and patients respectively died of an overdose of cocaine, which Gross had supplied. He was an apparent supporter of euthanasia (Müller 2008: 467).

The police searched for him, but due to his father's international reputation, criminal proceedings were never instigated. However, Otto Gross continued to mix in anarchist circles and even stepped up his erratic excessive life. Franz Jung remembers that Hans Gross was obsessed by the idea of leading his son back into the safety of a bourgeois existence as a private tutor.

'Somebody must have denounced Josef K., because one morning he was arrested for no apparent reasons at all.' So sober and stringent begins Franz Kafka's depressing document of growing fear. Kafka, who was instructed by Hans Gross as a law student, did not solely refer to the legal term *Proceß* in his depiction of *The Trial*, but rather to the vacuum of ever increasing dependency on social institutions and anonymous state power, to which we all succumb in the end (Stach 2002: 467).

'Somebody must have denounced Otto Gross', it could be argued; we could interpret the following incident, which happened in Berlin in the autumn of 1913, just as in Kafka's novel:

> Hans Gross hired three strong men to abduct his son from his home and bring him across the border to Austria where he was detained against his will in an asylum in Tulln, Lower Austria. This triggered a widespread press campaign in favour of his son's release.
>
> (Jung 2002: 161)

Ludwig Rubiner, a revolutionary writer and theatre founder, commented:

> The silencing of Dr Otto Gross is a typical thing [. . .] we, the mentally stable, we sub-proletarians are all good and strong – the professor in Graz is only anxious. The minders of the mentally sick, administrative curators and state officials stick together. We, the ones who have nothing to lose, also stick together.
>
> (Revolution, No. 5, 20 December 1913, in Hurwitz 1980: 108)

And Franz Pfemfert, editor of the expressionist magazine *Die Aktion*, reported,

> Gross has been dragged into a mental asylum, not because he was mad; not because he was mistakenly regarded as being crazy, no. It was because he had taken morphium. And what conclusion should a liberal publisher draw? Should he now demand that all aristocrats who take morphium (and there are quite a few of them) be sent to lunatic asylums?
>
> (Jung and Anz 2002: 105)

Erich Mühsam, writer and anarchist and one of Otto Gross's friends, wrote,

> That the professor from Graz acted in good faith and was convinced that only by an act of violence he could safeguard his son's interests seems understandable to me. But what I cannot understand is the behaviour of the Berlin-Schoeneberg police officers: Since when is a human being a nuisance because he takes drugs? Since when is it permitted to arrest and deport someone without notifying anyone and turn him over to foreign asylum staff? Since when does a father's wish suffice (even if he is a famous criminalist) to ruin the existence of those

> who may be regarded as 'inconvenient' without any consideration of customs or traditions? Whatever happened to Dr Groß today could happen to anyone else tomorrow. Especially those who create spiritual and intellectual values are endangered by the police. Can we tolerate this in silence? The entire German press certainly does.
>
> (in Hirte 2000: 3; in Jung and Anz 2002: 109)

Finally, the expressionist writer, Arnold Zweig, had his say:

> Why did the police deport Doctor Gross? Not because he took morphium, they now say, but because he did not have papers. It is a fact that Otto Gross did not have his identity papers; these were kept by his father, the criminalist Professor Hans Gross in Graz, and whenever he wrote to his father requesting them, he received the reply that he did not need them because the police in Berlin could refer to the father in Graz sparing the son any inconvenience. This because the police in all countries are a single large family.
>
> (in Dienes and Balluch 2005: 194)

Hans Gross responded to the press campaign:

> In one of the [. . .] papers, I was accused of having deprived my son of his papers; I sent him five copies of his doctor diploma and his certification of residence. He must have either mislaid or lent them to somebody, or they were confiscated or stolen. Other people travelled with his papers and were perhaps punished in lieu of him, and in at least one case, someone withdrew money by producing his papers.
>
> (in Jung and Anz 2002: 125; in Dienes and Balluch 2005: 194)

Otto Gross also put his views forward:

> The issue held against me is that I am dissatisfied with the present social order. I doubt if one can regard that as proof of a mental disorder, because this would depend on how we determine standards of mental health.
>
> (in Hurwitz 1980: 109)

Franz Kafka had been observing the campaign and the father–son conflict very closely: There are numerous analogies – the synthesis of fatherhood and bureaucracy, the patriarchal alliance of father figures, court authorities or lords of the castle – between the real case of 'Gross against Gross' and the fictitious case of Josef K. in *The Trial*. These prove that Kafka's literary punishment, guilt and terror fantasies were by no means departures from reality (Anz 1984: 27).

Back at the asylum in Tulln, Otto Gross underwent a medical examination and questioning. Here are some parts of his statement:

> My attitude is well known in Germany and in Switzerland, my circle of friends consists of anarchists and I believe in anarchy. My experience as a psychoanalyst suggests to me that the existing family model is all wrong. In fact, authority within the family as the source of authority will have to change; the conflict within a personality is that of one between the born entity and its own will. We are all victims of suggestion known as education. I believe in natural laws and their connection to natural sexuality, that this natural sexuality is other than the one forced upon us. [. . .] At the age of four I already had sexual feelings; I had daydreams in connection with the Atlas of Greek Art History. In my dreams I imagined humanity in a quite different state of liberty than it is today. For instance in warm climates where people can be in the nude. Even at that early age, my excitement culminated in an erection. I even felt superior to other people and loved animals only, because I thought their sexuality was innocent. My parents' sexuality disgusted me awfully; when I was about five years old, I used to imagine it being like killing chickens and thought it must be rape. My only thought was not to become like them, to refuse any suggestion. I felt terribly lonely at the time and stayed asexual until I was 24 [. . .] during my earliest childhood I experienced the pressure of parental authority, the feeling of not being able to break free; people need something to overcome inhibitions, so I took cocaine. I can't consume alcohol any more because it gets into my fists. When I took cocaine, I could think freely and had words at my disposal that were expressible. The inhibition lies in language coordination: I never ever want to give up taking cocaine, because I own nothing else but my thoughts [. . .] I intend to commit suicide when I am no longer able-bodied; I do not live for the sake of it, but for my thoughts and my work, which I like, because I am convinced of what I am doing [. . .] I came to Graz with my parents when I was four, because my father had been transferred there. During those early years in Graz, I recall having suffered from sudden panic attacks and that I was frightened every night, so that I sometimes felt the urge to jump out of the window. It was diagnosed as 'nostalgia' by our doctors. When I was six, my father was sent to Leoben [a city in the Austrian province of Styria] as a deputy coroner and ever since then, those panic attacks ceased. [. . .] My whole life was focused on overthrowing authorities, for example that of the fathers; for me, only matriarchy, the law of the horde, existed. That is why I was always fighting against the rules, against today's society.
>
> (in Götz von Olenhusen 2003b: Document 2; in Dienes and Balluch 2005: 107)

Responding to the doctors, Hans Gross described his son as follows:

> From early childhood onwards, he was very difficult to handle, because he revolted against authority in general which, unfortunately, had to be emphasized, because he never wanted to comply with the requirements of a normal life. He neither showed any interest in playing with other children nor did he wish to mix with children to whom he was either intellectually superior, or whose certitude in things of daily life attracted him. The normal kind of love other children feel for animals became a scientific pastime for him [. . .] his lack of restraint always drove his teachers up the wall, but they were fond of him just the same. It was impossible to overcome the irrevocable principle he soon made out of his rebellion against parents, teachers and all the usual conventions. All our endeavours to bring him up properly – after all, he was our only child – were to no avail, because he was never willing to listen to the advice of his elders; later on, he claimed that it had been his greatest luck that, whilst having had to put up with family oppression, he had never surrendered to it.
>
> From an early age he had numerous peculiarities; for example, he never learned how to deal with money [. . .] his vegetarianism seems to be inherent [. . .] his jolting gait is also very striking, his unpleasantness – that admittedly comes from my side of the family – and his effeminate ways that made him become a pioneer of women's emancipation and their rights; he also elevates women above men.
>
> What also struck me was his lack of sense of time from childhood on [. . .] he was also terribly irritable and violent, especially when he thought one wanted to oppress him [. . .] but the most alarming and devastating of all were those appalling, excruciating depressions from which he suffered from 15 to 16 onwards; when he went to university, he tried to alleviate them by taking drugs like morphia, opium and cocaine, to which he now had access. We only discovered all these things when it was already too late [. . .] a fact that added to the difficulties was his inclination toward anarchy. That undoubtedly stemmed from his love for animals which made him an enemy of all animal oppressors. As a consequence, he developed an oppositional attitude to all oppressors of human beings; then his advocacy for servants and the poor, his confusing sexual views – that is how altruism turned into anarchy.
>
> (Götz von Olenhusen 2003b: Document 2; Dienes and Balluch 2005: 185)

The doctors in Tulln found that 'the patient Dr Otto Gross suffers from a mental disorder legally defined as insanity and is therefore unable to attend to his personal affairs' (Götz von Olenhusen 2003b: Document 3). The decision of the provincial court in Graz was: On account of insanity, Otto Gross shall be put under tutelage and his civil rights be withdrawn. His guardian shall be Hans Gross, the father. Otto Gross was moved to the provincial asylum in Troppau in Upper Silesia for fear his friends should attempt to free him by use of force (Götz von Olenhusen 2003a: 135). After his recovery, he was discharged in July 1914; the outpatient treatment was then continued by Dr. Wilhelm Stekel, who diagnosed the following:

> He is a pioneer of matriarchy and believes that all social problems could be easily solved by introducing the matriarchal system. His books – mostly grossly dimensioned theories – are dedicated to the triumph and final emancipation of women. If anybody offended a lady, he would immediately challenge that person to a duel in spite of the fact that he is against duels and otherwise worships anarchist ideas. He demands freedom in every form. But that does not apply to all people and then only in an individual form, for he nurtures a burning hatred towards all homosexuals, as far as they are pederasts. If he were a king, he would lock them away, burn them and exterminate them. So, it is an odd kind of freedom that only applies to people who fit into his regime. To him, homosexuals are atrocious, because they despise women, thus rendering them superfluous.
>
> (in Michaels 2002: 114)

After putting Otto Gross under tutelage, his father commenced legal proceedings against his son's wife, Frieda Gross, for he wanted to take custody of his grandson Peter. During the course of the legal proceedings Hans Gross had instigated to wrest custody of the child. Frieda Gross's lawyer stated that Otto Gross had been kept in his parents' bedroom for many years. As a consequence, the unconscious perception of their intimacies, although of a completely harmless nature, had sparked off the child's nervous fantasies and excitability. In the end, Hans Gross lost the case because Frieda Gross was supported by prominent people such as Marianne, Max and Alfred Weber.

In October 1914, Otto Gross enlisted voluntarily for military service where he worked as a doctor in various epidemic hospitals. According to Franz Werfel, 'the power of the legal establishment was still so overwhelming, that the son cowardly avoided any talks his father called for' (Götz von Olenhusen 2005: 90f.).

Filled with bitterness, the father died on 9 December 1915 in Graz.

In 1914 Franz Jung summed up the conflict of Gross versus Gross in the following words:

> That man [Hans Gross] was lucky enough to have a son who was equal in genius to him. But the urge to 'possess' ended in a tragedy. The

> father exerted force upon the son and thus the genius son revolted in fury against his father. He then carried on destroying himself as long as the 'father was alive'.
>
> (Hurwitz 1988: 244)

Jung came to the conclusion that from that point in time onwards, Otto Gross abandoned all his work and was 'outwardly hardly able to act independently' (ibid.). Indeed, the son had lost his father as an enemy, but he had also lost his material and financial footing.

In 1917, he was to meet Franz Kafka (Alt 2005: 449; Dienes 2009: 321f.). Gross planned to publish a journal. It would discuss cultural problems from a psychoanalytic point of view, develop new principles and provide a forum for revolutionary methods of overcoming patriarchal forms of rule. Kafka was willing to join Gross 'in the struggle against the fathers of this world' as Martin Green put it (Green 1974: 94).

The journal, which bore the title *Papers Against the Will for Power*, was dedicated to the problem of authorities. From Kafka's point of view, it was not so much a matter of rebelling against one's own father, but rather a matter of comprehending that the rival living in one's innermost self was the culprit (Stach 2008: 332). Thence originated the peculiar paralysis that prevented Kafka's protagonists from fleeing from the scene and beginning something new.

Kafka was very enthusiastic about the project and told Max Brod:

> If there was one journal that would have seemed attractive to me over a longer period of time (as would any journal for a moment), then it was certainly that of Dr Groß; for it appeared to me, at least on that particular evening, that it was born by the ardency of a certain personal bond. Perhaps a journal can never be more than a sign of mutual ambition anyway.
>
> (Stach 2008: 194f.; Dienes 2003: 27)

In the end, however, the *Papers Against the Will for Power* were never published. The end of the First World War put an end to 'patriarchs'. In his essay *On the Psychoanalysis of Revolution: The Fatherless Society*, published in 1919, Paul Federn revealed that the sons, after spending four years in trenches, no longer trusted their fathers enough to allow them to take over rule again (Johnston 1974: 259).

Now Otto Gross thought the time had come to take action. He left Vienna, which he had planned to blow up, for Berlin (Heuer 2005: 223–239), where signs of radicalism flared up temporarily in artists' circles. It seemed as if the tide had turned in favour of Otto Gross, but his days were numbered. Physically and mentally at an end, he was found half-starved and frozen in a courtyard entrance. A few days later, on 13 February 1920,

Otto Gross died in an asylum for emotionally disturbed persons in Pankow, Berlin (Jung 1980: 155).

He had become one of those people whom his father would have had deported, a drug addict and psychopath; a degenerate. In her obituary for Gross, Kafka's girlfriend, Milena Jesenska, described him as being an 'interesting contemporary' with 'an odd mixture of naïve utopian and revolutionary fanatic ideas' (*Prager Tagblatt*, No. 45, 22 February 1920: 5).

And Otto Kaus concluded: 'As a final consequence of his own life principles, he was doomed to starve in the bourgeois world against whose social order he had fought all his life' (*Sowjet*, No. 8/9, 8 May 1920: 55).

References

Alt, P.-A. (2005) *Franz Kafka. Der ewige Sohn.* München: Beck.

Anz, T. (1984) Jemand musste Otto G. verleumndet haben . . . Kafka, Werfel, Otto Gross und eine 'psychiatrische Geschichte'. In C. Jung and T. Anz (eds.) (2002), *Der Fall Otto Gross. Eine Pressekampagne deutscher Intellektueller im Winter 1913/14.* Marburg/Lahn: LiterturWissenschaft.de (pp. 23–33).

Anz, T. (2002) *Literatur des Expressionismus.* Stuttgart/Weimar: Metzler.

Buchner, W. (1993) Hans Gross (1847–1915). Die Spuren des Bösen. In G. M. Dienes and G. Melzer (eds.), *Urstadtkult.* Graz: Grazer Stadtmuseum.

Dienes, G. M. (2003) Der Mann Moses und die Folter der Maschine. In G. M. Dienes and R. Rother (eds.), *Die Gesetze des Vaters. Hans Gross, Otto Gross, Sigmund Freud, Franz Kafka.* Wien: Böhlau (pp. 14–35).

Dienes, G. M. (2005) Hans Gross: Sherlock Holmes und Verfolger des Bösen. In G. M. Dienes, A. Götz von Olenhusen, G. Heuer and G. Kocher (eds.), *Gross gegen Gross. Hans & Otto Gross. Ein paradigmatischer Generationskonflikt.* Marburg/Lahn: LiteraturWissenschaft.de (pp. 11–24).

Dienes, G. M. (2007) Väter und Söhne. Hans und Otto Gross, Sigmund Freud und Franz Kafka. In *Očeva država – majčin sin. Vaterstaat-Muttersohn.* Rijeka: Muzej Grada (pp. 9–19).

Dienes, G. M. (2009) Die Hand aus dem 'Lächerlichen' – Hans und Otto Gross, zwei Grazer, die Franz Kafka beeinflussten. In *Historisches Jahrbuch der Stadt Graz*, Vol. 38/39. Graz: Stadt Graz (pp. 315–328).

Dienes, G. M. and Balluch, G. (2005) Gross gegen Gross. Ein schicksalshafter Vater-Sohn-Konflikt. In G. M. Dienes, A. Götz von Olenhusen, G. Heuer and G. Kocher (eds.), *Gross gegen Gross. Hans & Otto Gross. Ein paradigmatischer Generationskonflikt.* Marburg/Lahn: LiteraturWissenschaft.de (pp. 173–200).

Götz von Olenhusen, A. (2003a) Die Internierung und Entmündigung des Dr. med. Otto Gross und die Befreiungskampagne 1913/1914. In G. M. Dienes and R. Rother (eds.), *Die Gesetze des Vaters. Hans Gross, Otto Gross, Sigmund Freud, Franz Kafka.* Wien: Boehlau (pp. 126–139).

Götz von Olenhusen, A. (2003b) *Hans Gross gegen Otto Gross. Die Geschichte eines Prozesses 1913/1914. Berichte. Dokumente. Bibliographie.* Freiburg: A. Götz von Olenhusen (CD-ROM).

Götz von Olenhusen, A. (2005) Wahnsinn in den Zeiten des Krieges. Otto Gross,

Franz Jung und das Kriegsrecht. In G. M. Dienes, A. Götz von Olenhusen, G. Heuer and G. Kocher (eds.), *Gross gegen Gross. Hans & Otto Gross. Ein paradigmatischer Generationskonflikt*. Marburg/Lahn: LiteraturWissenschaft.de (pp. 82–128).
Green, M. (1974) *Else und Frieda. Die Richthofen-Schwestern*. München: Piper.
Gross, O. (1913) Zur Üeberwindung der kulturellen Krise. *Die Aktion*, Vol. 3(14), col. 384–387.
Gross, O. (1914) Über Destruktionssymbolik. *Zentralblatt für Psychoanalyse und Psychotherapie*, *4*, 11–12.
Gross, O. (1980) Vom Konflikt des Eigenen und Fremden. In K. Kreiler (ed.), *Von geschlechtlicher Not zur sozialen Katastrophe*. Frankfurt/Main: Robinson.
Heuer, G. (2005) 'Ganz Wien in die Luft sprengen? . . . Das wäre ja wunderbar!' Otto Gross und der Anarchismus. In A. Götz von Olenhusen and G. Heuer (eds.), *Die Gesetze des Vaters. 4. Internationaler Otto Gross Kongress Graz 2003*. Marburg/Lahn: LiteraturWissenschaft.de (pp. 223–239).
Heuer, G. (2007) Otto Gross, 1877–1920, Leben, Werk und Wirkung. In *Očeva država – majčin sin. Vaterstaat-Muttersohn*. Rijeka: Muzej Grada (pp. 45–49).
Hirte, C. (2000) Erich Mühsam und Otto Gross: Rekonstruktion einer Begegnung. In R. Dehmlow & G. Heuer (eds.), *1. Internationaler Otto Gross Kongress Bauhaus-Archiv, Berlin 1999*. Marburg/Lahn: Wissenschaft.de; Hannover: Laurentius (pp. 14–38).
Hurwitz, E. (1980) Otto Gross Von der Psychoanalyse zum Paradies. In H. Szeemann (ed.), *Monte Verità. Berg der Wahrheit. Lokale Anthropologie als Beitrag zur Wiederentdeckung einer neuzeitlichen sakralen Topographie*. Milano: Electra (pp. 107–116).
Hurwitz, E. (1988) *Otto Gross. Paradies-Sucher zwischen Freud und Jung*. Frankfurt/Main: Suhrkamp.
Hurwitz, E. (2001) Konflikt oder Wahrheit. Die politische Dimension der Psychoanalyse bei Otto Gross. In A. Schwab and C. Lanfranchi (eds.), *Sinnsuche und Sonnenbad. Experimente in Kunst und Leben auf dem Monte Verità*. Zürich: Limmat (pp. 143–155).
Johnston, W. M. (1974) *Österreichische Kultur- und Geistesgeschichte. Gesellschaft und Ideen im Donauraum 1848 bis 1938*. Wien/Köln/Graz: Boehlaus Nachf.
Jung, C. (2002) 'Aber wir wollen Otto Gross wiederhaben.' Eine Pressekampagne. In G. Heuer (ed.), *2. Internationaler Otto Gross Kongress Burghölzli Zuerich*. Marburg/Lahn: Literatur Wissenschaft.de (pp. 161–181).
Jung, C. and Anz, T. (eds.) (2002) *Der Fall Otto Gross. Eine Pressekampagne deutscher Intellektueller im Winter 1913/1914*. Marburg/Lahn: Literatur Wissenschaft.de.
Jung, F. (1972) *Der Torpedokäfer*. Neuwied/Berlin: Luchterhand.
Jung, F. (1980) Dr. med. Otto Gross. Von geschlechtlicher Not zur sozialen Katastrophe. In G. Bose and E. Brinkmann (eds.), *Grosz/Jung/Grosz*. Berlin: Brinckmann & Bose (pp. 103–155).
Jungk, P. S. (1987) *Franz Werfel*. Frankfurt/Main: Fischer.
Michaels, J. (2002) Otto Gross und das Konzept des Matriarchats. In G. Heuer (ed.), *2. Internationaler Otto Gross Kongress Burghölzli Zürich 2000*. Marburg/Lahn: LiteraturWissenschaft.de (pp. 105–115).
Müller, H. (2008) Woran starb Sofie Benz? Vom Matriarchat im Zeitalter der

Maschine. In R. Dehmlow, R. Rother and A. Springer (eds.), *". . . Da liegt der riesige Schatten Freuds jetzt nicht mehr auf meinem Weg." Die Rebellion des Otto Gross. 6. Internationaler Otto Gross Kongress Wien 2006*. Marburg/Lahn: LiteraturWissenschaft.de (pp. 438–482).

Nitzschke, B. (2000) *Das Ich als Experiment*. Göttingen: Vandenhoeck & Ruprecht.

Stach, R. (2002) *Kafka. Die Jahre der Entscheidungen*. Frankfurt/Main: Fischer.

Stach, R. (2008) *Kafka. Die Jahre der Erkenntnis*. Frankfurt/Main: Fischer.

Werfel, F. (2000) *Barbara oder Die Frömmigkeit*. Frankfurt/Main: Fischer.

Zweig, A. (1996) *Freundschaft mit Freud*. Berlin: Aufbau.

Chapter 6

Sigmund Freud, Max Weber and the sexual revolution

Albrecht Götz von Olenhusen

For Gottfried Heuer

The anarchistic movement around and after 1900 addressed to some extent the question of sexual liberation and with it the idea of sexual revolution. There are apparent links between intellectuals, bohemians and anarchism. Sigmund Freud wrote about anarchism in 1933 in one of his lectures on psychoanalysis and *Weltanschauung*:

> According to the anarchist theory there is no such thing as truth, no assured knowledge of the external world. What we give out as being scientific truth is only the product of our needs as they are bound to find utterance under changing external conditions: once again, they are illusion. [. . .] All I can say is that the anarchist theory sounds wonderfully superior so long as it relates to opinions about abstract things: it breaks down with its first step into practical life.
>
> (1933: 175–176)

In a very similar way anarchism and its doctrines were criticised by Max Weber. We therefore see Sigmund Freud and Max Weber united in their criticism of the sexual political anarchism of Otto Gross, especially in his individual/anarchistic/utopian theories to free the individual of all the terrible inhibiting forces imposed by early education. We will not try to discuss whether Sigmund Freud intended to paint a caricature of political anarchism. But in the historical view it is a fact and a strange contrast that Freud at the beginning of the last century had rather close contacts with three leading protagonists of anarchism: with Otto Gross, then an ardent student of Freud and praised by Freud as a highly gifted researcher and in the eyes of Ernest Jones a kind of genius; with Erich Mühsam, the well-known anarchistic writer and poet; and – in those days better known but rather neglected today – with Johannes Nohl, an early essayist and writer from Berlin, later living in Ascona until 1920. (Incidentally, the latter muddled through the 'Third Reich' and ended up, curiously enough, as a devoted communist comrade and member of the SED party of the German Democratic Republic in Weimar in the Sixties.)

Max Weber's keen interest in fundamental movements such as anarchism in its combination with the erotic movement is well known. His attitude in relation to anarchistic beliefs and attitudes can be shown best when – after discussions with pacifists and later revolutionaries like Ernst Toller – he came to the rigid conclusion that anarchism seemed to him no model for responsible ethics (*Verantwortungsethik*) but for *Gesinnungsethik* (an ethic of ultimate ends – 'the aim is nothing to me, the movement everything'), which he viewed as 'not from this world'. In Weber's opinion, Leo Tolstoi gave the best example of a consequent ethics of this kind. And, from Weber's perspective, the sexual liberation in the assumed new version of Otto Gross was, as he called it, '*Nerven-Ethik*' or '*psychiatrische Ethik*', an altogether pure, idealistic, 'average' ethic which took the normal nature of man as measure without any implication of responsibility.

Apart from this we find in Sigmund Freud and Max Weber two patriarchs, patriarchal figures who themselves represented strong father figures. And it is well known that in those and future days and years Freud also had his own severe conflicts with 'sons' – C. G. Jung, Alfred Adler and Wilhelm Stekel, for instance, dissidents and deserters from 'the cause' like Otto Gross. There are no similar personal events or effects known in the biography of Max Weber. But he, to some extent, was also involved in the father–son conflict of the expressionist generation between 1910 and 1920 and in the epochal conflict of the younger generation with their parents and *Kaiser* Wilhelm's state.

From a historical and biographical point of view I would like to present Freud's views as a person and according to his theories in relation to several protagonists of that group or generation involved with the sexual revolution and with the paradigmatic conflict between Hans Gross and his son Otto. I shall present in brief Erich Mühsam and Johannes Nohl, and I may also refer to some protagonists among male and female followers of Otto Gross and the anarchistic beliefs, at least in the version of Freud's theories, by Otto Gross. It may also be noted that the relationships among these and the differences in theory and practice are of some relevance.

In 1907 Erich Mühsam wrote an enthusiastic letter to Sigmund Freud about his own successful experience in a six-week analysis by Otto Gross. It sounds like a success report of a very profound analysis. Otto Gross, who had recently deserted from Freud and who in the beginning was highly estimated by Freud and C. G. Jung, had now fallen into deep disgrace mainly because of his drug addiction and because of his claim for the importance of psychoanalysis for society. Freud did not accept Otto Gross's basis and aims, his wide social and political scope and its consequences. This is illustrated by his short, sharp and well-known remark: 'We are doctors and doctors we should remain.'

The letter by Erich Mühsam to Freud seems rather strange as Mühsam did not know Freud personally and there was no real reason for it. One may see it as a kind of support for a controversial figure like Otto Gross and in his favour. But it seems that Mühsam's analysis may not have been so successful in the sense of Freud's concept as he made out – at least in view of his diaries, where he follows Otto Gross's solemnly outspoken aim to change people into sexual immoralists and polygamists.

Johannes Nohl reckoned himself to be a profound follower of Sigmund Freud, whom he praised in articles as 'the great conquerer' – but on the other hand, he very soon in his psychological practice and publications came out as a devotee of Otto Gross's theories. Johannes Nohl, as we now know, was perhaps the first analyst of the German writer Hermann Hesse. Nohl himself underwent an analysis with Otto Gross in Munich. And he then turned to make a living as an essayist, partly living on regular contributions from his friend Erich Mühsam and other friendly financial sponsors, mainly following the convictions and beliefs of Gustav Landauer, in those years the chief protagonist of anarchism in Germany and Switzerland. Nohl was the one who tried to combine Freud, Gross, psychoanalysis and the anarchism of Landauer and thought that psychoanalysis fitted in with his belief in religion and in the importance of prayers. This eclectic mixture of Nohl's had in fact in the beginning great impact on Hermann Hesse in Ascona and in his work. Hesse's later analysts were the Swiss psychiatrist Lang and C. G. Jung.

Otto Gross, his views about individual psychoanalysis and his social value and revolutionary importance had great impact on a series of German writers and artists before the First World War. Arnold Zweig, Johannes R. Becher, Leonhard Frank and Franz Jung, among others, were analysed or at least strongly influenced by Otto Gross, and he as a kind of cult figure and charismatic personality had great effects on the life and works of artists, too (although he seems to have been a kind of contested figure in Dadaism), such as Georg Schrimpf, Raoul Hausmann, Hannah Hoech and others. The direct and indirect influence of Otto Gross's theories on the work of D. H. Lawrence, via Frieda Weekley, is well known. Less well known is the fact that Otto's wife, Frieda Gross, had a short affair with Freud's later biographer Ernest Jones, and Jones himself underwent his analysis with Otto Gross in Munich. Frieda Gross – with a keen and sensible understanding of psychoanalysis herself – was one of the very few 'Teutonic women' who were accepted by Sigmund Freud. he liked Frieda, it seems, much more than he liked Otto, and it seems that he developed the idea that Frieda rather than Otto should come into analysis with him, transferring Otto to C. G. Jung in Zürich.

Otto Gross's convictions and theories turned into a great and somehow even dangerous influence on the relationships between the 'group', and seem to have affected him also. Frieda's love affair with Erich Mühsam in

Munich had the dangerous effect of making Johannes Nohl, in his own sessions on the couch with Otto Gross, make such cunning and deceitful remarks that the psychoanalytic guru himself became so jealous in the café Stefanie in Munich (his favourite analytical playground) that he came to the conclusion that he must murder his friend Erich Mühsam. From this perspective, Otto's version of psychoanalysis was not only an instrument of freeing the group members of indidual neuroses or social inhibitions but part of new and fascinating instruments and developments in the personal relationships of the avant-garde. The German psychoanalyst Johannes Cremerius some years ago called those years, somewhat euphemistically and ironically, the 'bucolic days of psychoanalysis'. Otto Gross's own analysis of the artist Sophie Benz, former girlfriend of the writer Leonhard Frank, turned out in such a way that Sophie left Leonard and moved to Ascona with Otto while Frieda, with outspoken consent and urging by Otto, had to change her life and loves and from then on lived with Otto's friend, the artist Ernst Frick, in Ascona.

Psychoanalysis seen from these perspectives was not only part of the permanent discussions in the bohemian milieus of Ascona, Munich, Berlin and Heidelberg, but developed strong and very often extreme and dubious effects on personal lives and destinies. The Swiss writer Friedrich Glauser reports a revealing and slightly satirical description of the scene in Ascona:

> Over there, near the castello [in Ascona] there live the analysts. Their leader's name is Nohl. He is surrounded by some friends and their wives. Every morning between coffee and buttered toast the dreams of the last night are thoroughly inspected and investigated in respect of complexes, the inhibitions identified and the direction of the libido controlled.
>
> (Glauser 1976: 75)

This view of Glauser, drug addict and at times inhabitant of Swiss asylums like Otto Gross, and of his local guru Goetz, an experienced Asconian writer, paint a kind of caricature. An echo can be found in John Kerr's book, *A Most Dangerous Method*:

> In the realm of enacted psychoanalytical fantasy, Otto Gross was proudly living out his antipatriarchal daydream, and his call for 'polygamy' amounted to nothing more or less than winning away from the fathers all the mothers and daughters who were brave enough to come.
>
> (Kerr 1994: 226–227)

If Gross took his cue from Freud, Bachofen and Nietzsche, Erich Mühsam took his from Freud, Gross and Landauer, and his close friend of many years Johannes Nohl added Franz von Baader, thus linking the romantic philosophy of the nineteenth century with the myth of a former and future state under the reign of mothers instead of fathers – matriarchy as the utopian structure of the state.

Among the anarchistic 'Tat' group in Munich after about 1908, Freud and his theories – mainly Otto Gross's version of them – soon led to a severe split (for some of its important members, see the Appendix). This group was mainly influenced and led by Erich Mühsam as a follower of Gustav Landauer and his anarchistic 'Socialist Federation' (*Sozialistischer Bund*), and it was soon quickly divided. Landauer was convinced that psychoanalysis led directly to homosexuality and destroyed family and marriage. He held Otto Gross responsible. As the leading German figure of the Socialist *Bund* and an eminent protagonist in the fight against the monarchy, Landauer was a kind of patriarch himself. And Landauer (here we observe another father–son conflict) was not amused when his comrades in the Tat group began partly leaning toward Otto Gross, and his (in the eyes of Landauer) very dubious methods of psychoanalysis, and the liberation of bourgois sexual morality. So we must always be aware of the differences within the milieu and movement between bohemians, anarchists, sexual liberationists and supporters of Landauer, Mühsam and Otto Gross in the progessive intelligentsia.

One of the main figures in the Tat group of 1911 was the young and upcoming writer Franz Jung, soon to become notorious as a kind of public figure in the Munich milieu as he acted out permanent public neurotic fights with his wife Margot in coffee houses and restaurants. Franz Jung had quickly fallen for his new friend Otto Gross, for whom, as he wrote decades later, he would have sacrificed his life. Jung was no drug addict like Otto or many other writers – such as Johannes R. Becher – but, apart from quickly grasping the essence and relevance of psychoanalysis for personal relations, literary work and political activities, devoted much of his time to heavy drinking. In Munich and later in Berlin he made his name – not only in the perspective of his reviewer Robert Musil – as the most interesting expressionistic and experimental writer of a new genre – 'psychoanalytic novels'.

One cannot deny that the individual and political impact of psychoanalysis can be seen only too clearly in these small groups, such as Tat, and in the bohemian milieus of Munich, Heidelberg and Berlin. It was Franz Jung, together with Otto Gross, who prepared the ground for a more social and political understanding of psychoanalysis. The new orientation may also be seen clearly in the influence of the 'erotic movement' in Max and Marianne Weber's Heidelberg. Otto Gross's version of psychoanalysis, together with Franz Jung's literary and soon political impetus, would thus be changed into an instrument for new 'relations' (*Beziehungen*) and the so-called preparatory work (*Vorarbeit*) of small groups for the coming revolution.

It is difficult today to name all those who were analysed and more or less influenced in those years, after about 1907, by Otto Gross or who belonged to his followers in Munich, Berlin and Ascona before the First World War and in Vienna after it. I have tried to make up a by no means complete or in every aspect reliable but merely approximate list, which is preliminary and not in every case based on secure information and covers the periods between about 1907 and 1913 in Munich and Berlin, and 1917 and 1920 in Vienna and Berlin.

Analysands/followers

Erich Mühsam
Johannes Nohl
Johannes R. Becher
Regina Ullmann
Leonhard Frank
Franz Jung
Margot Jung
Beatrice Zweig
Arnold Zweig
Sophie Benz
Karl Otten
Ernst Frick
Margarete Faas-Hardegger
Oskar Maria Graf
Georg Schrimpf
Frieda Gross
Frieda Weekley, neé von Richthofen
Else Jaffé, neé von Richthofen
Carlo Holzer
Raoul Hausmann
Hannah Hoech
Heinrich Goesch
Paul Goesch
Mizzi Kuh
Nina Kuh
Anton Kuh
Franz Werfel
Gina Kaus
Otto Kaus

This by no means complete circle, or in-group as we may call it, influenced other circles. Erich Mühsam seems to have been the link to various literary and artistic bohemian circles in Munich. One of these existed around

Figure 6.1 Frieda Gross, 1876–1950, with her and Otto Gross's son Peter, 1907–1946.

Franziska zu Reventlow. She proudly declined to be analysed by Otto Gross. But it is well known that she was one of the outstanding figures to practise a kind of personal sexual revolution as a role model for independent women (Whimster 1999: 13).

The special political side of the scenery is represented by the Tat group mentioned above, the Munich branch of Gustav Landauer's '*Sozialistischer Bund*'. This anarchistic group existed from 1909 and included workers and intellectuals who believed in the revolutionary potentialities of drop-outs, of the so-called '*Lumpenproletariat*'. The key figures here were Erich Mühsam, Johannes Nohl, Otto Gross, Franz Jung and another 20 or so figures, including the likes of Oskar Maria Graf, Georg Schrimpf, Karl Otten and Eduard Schiemann, most of whom were part of the bohemian literary and artistic scenery and several of whom one could see as drop-outs or even 'petty criminals'. This group had its political and very public climax in 1911 when the Bavarian state tried to convict some of them in a trial called the Soller trial. The aim was to publicly expose the anarchistic Tat group as terrorists – with not much effect by law but with an enormous public propaganda impact. The question of sexual liberation led to intensive internal discussions in periodicals such as *Der Sozialist* and *Die Aktion*. This discourse shows the differences between the older, socialist- and anarchist-influenced, generation and the younger generation, which was more inclined to a new erotic and sexual orientation if not revolution. While Munich and Heidelberg were the main locations until 1912, the scene changed to Berlin when Franz Jung and some time later Otto Gross, moving from Ascona to Berlin, founded a new centre around Franz Pfemfert's Berlin journal *Die Aktion* with its radical political and revolutionary implications. In Berlin we can find the influence of Otto Gross as a revolutionary in this field in a somewhat smaller circle. This included mainly those who had had some therapeutic experiments with him in a kind of short analysis. We can see his nonetheless relevant and rising influence when we look at the following lists of people, who published articles after Otto Gross's forced departure from Berlin to Austria, and of papers and periodicals, whose authors and editors were willing to publish something about the *cause célèbre* or in favour of Otto Gross:

People

Franz Pfemfert
Ludwig Rubiner
Blaise Cendrars
Erich Mühsam
Simon G(h)uttmann
Guillaume Apollinaire
Arnold Zweig

Bess Brenck Kalischer
Oskar Kanehl
Else Lasker-Schüler
Maximilian Harden
Alfred Kerr
Claire Oehring
Richard Oehring
Hans von Weber

Papers and periodicals

Die Aktion, Berlin
Revolution, Munich
Wilmersdorfer Zeitung, Berlin
L'Intransigeant, Paris
Prager Tagblatt, Prague
Neues Wiener Journal, Vienna
Mercure de France, Paris
Die Welt am Montag, Berlin
Die Schaubühne, Berlin
März, Munich
Kain, Munich
Neues Wiener Abendblatt, Vienna
Die Zukunft, Berlin
Wiecker Bote
Bohemia, Prague
Der Zwiebelfisch, Munich

These lists are not complete, but the public scandal may show the influence of Otto Gross on the expressionist generation, and the press campaign of his supporters for his liberation, mainly organised by Franz Jung and Simon Guttmann in Berlin and Munich, shows how they claimed his cause as their own: Otto Gross was symbolically fighting the cause of a complete generation against the fathers and the state. Hans Gross, the famous patriarchal father in Graz, and Otto Gross, the notoriously rebellious and contested son in Berlin, can then be seen in their personal, private and public struggle as of European importance, both eager to use their different networks (see the Appendix).

The case of the individual sexual and erotic revolution – among other subjects of changes in the social and legal field – became now a part of the legal battles in different courts, especially in Austria between 1913 and 1918. In these Max Weber counselled and supported Frieda Gross. The campaign by his friends and sympathisers (Max Weber as a lawyer was strongly opposed to it) did not lead to Otto's release from asylums in Tulln and Troppau, but according to Franz Jung had great impact on the struggles in the years to come. Otto Gross was treated between November 1913 and July 1914 in Tulln and Troppau. It must have been the outcome of a compromise with his father when Otto was released as 'cured' in July 1914 under the condition that he agreed to follow-up treatment with Wilhelm Stekel – in those years already dissident from Freud, too, but well acquainted with Hans Gross and also well paid by him in the famous and fashionable Austrian holiday resort Bad Ischl, where the *Kaiser* also used to spend his summer holidays. But the Austrian courts in which, in November 1913, several cases began were by no means interested in questions of libertarian ideas or fights against the authoritarian state.

The cultural significance of the theory of a former and future 'matriarchy' as a modern myth played a signicant role in these counter-communities and anarchistic groups fighting against the patriarchal generation. (The matriarchal ideology, incidentally, strongly interested a young jurist named Carl Schmitt in Munich during and after the First World War in various discussions, and he in these early days realised the importance of Otto Gross's theories.) Nevertheless it must be noted that the relevant circles were mainly formed as *Männerbunde*. And we may compare these with similar contemporary *Männerbünde* in the youth movement and the circle around Stefan George. It can also be noted that the idea of an ahistoric matriarchal past and a utopian future had already been part of the discourse in the esoteric Klages-Schuler circle in Munich – a couple of years before Otto Gross's impressive appearance on the Munich stage.

Otto Gross's version of Freud's theories and thoughts celebrated sexuality, sexual revolution as a necessary basis for social transformation and femininity as a counter part of the authoritarian patriarchal social structures. Max Weber's attitude to the fundamentalist thoughts of people like Otto Gross, Frieda Gross, Ernst Frick and Erich Mühsam slowly changed his personal view into a somewhat different political attitude and theory. It seems he may have developed a deeper understanding of the anarchist ideology, especially in his discussions with Frieda Gross and Ernst Frick in Ascona in 1913/1914. One or two years later it was – apart from Otto Gross – now Ernst Toller who influenced his theories about the politically charismatic personality. The change of his attitude may be found in his well-known '*Zwischenbetrachtung*'. Weber did not accept Otto Gross's theories, which he claimed he plagiarised from Nietzsche, and he did not in the least accept the views of Prof. Hans Gross on child education or his attitude in the conflict with Frieda Gross about her and Otto's children. In the eyes of Max Weber the group of writers, artists and intellectuals around Otto Gross (the crème de la crème of the German expressionists) were sad dimwits and anarchist riffraff, spineless characters, fools and windbags who soiled the good name of revolution with their bragging heroics on paper and concern for their own advancement only. Weber therefore tried to convince Emil Lask, a philosopher in Heidelberg and a mutual friend of the Webers and Frieda Gross, and Erich Mühsam 'to get that lot to keep their gobs shut'. He never decided to take sides in public with Otto Gross and his sympathisers although he argued that his deportation from Prussia to Austria was a violation of the law.

Otto Gross for some time acted or was esteemed as a central figure of those years before the First World War, first as one of Freud's early followers, and soon as a dissident anticipating the views and theories of Wilhelm Reich. His ideas were mediated by small circles of devoted followers including bohemian writers and artists experimenting with Expressionism and Dadaism, and we can find him as a figurehead and protagonist of his ideas in different positive or negative perspective in the works of D. H. Lawrence and Franz Werfel. The movement to which all this belongs is German Expressionism but it is also a part of a wider and deeper social and political movement, not only restricted to a smaller rebellious underground subculture. When Otto Gross died it was his follower, the revolutionary Franz Jung, who transformed his theories into an instrument of class struggle. Franz Jung wrote in 1919:

> The history of this class struggle dates from the collapse of matriarchy, i.e. from the usurpation, from the property seizure of the family by the husband, which came to expression in the programation of patriarchy and suppression of matriarchy.
>
> (Jung 1919: 428f.)

At the same time Max Weber had given up his strict rejection of the adherents to an erotic-emotional lifestyle – in his own life in the end also. He showed understanding but still held up moral demands in interpersonal relations. The themes of sexuality and eroticism and the developments in the background of cultural history and political movements as far as Max Weber is concerned seem to have had more relevance in his life and work than has been generally acknowledged until now. Marianne Weber wrote in her biography of Weber that 'Weber was greatly interested in the effects of a norm-free eroticism upon the total personality, for the latter now seemed to him what was important in the final analysis' (Weber 1926/1984: 391).

References

Die Erde (1919) Walther Rilla (ed.). Vols. 1–2 (1919–1920). Rpt. Nendeln: Kraus (1970).

Freud, S. (1933) *New Introductory Lectures on Psycho-Analysis. SE*, Vol. XXII. London: Hogarth.

Glauser, F. (1976) *Dada, Ascona und andere Erinnerungen*. Zürich: Arche.
Götz von Olenhusen, A. (2005) Die heißen und die kalten Klaviere der Macht. Die Prozesse des Hans Gross. In G. Dienes, A. Götz von Olenhusen, G. Heuer and G. Kocher (eds.), *Gross gegen Gross. Hans & Otto Gross. Ein paradigmatischer Generationenkonflikt*. Marburg: LiteraturWissenschaft.de (pp. 111–171).
Jung, F. (1919) Zweck und Mittel im Klassenkampf. *Die Erde* Vol. 1, Nr. 14/15(1–8).
Kerr, J. (1994) *A Most Dangerous Method. The Story of Jung, Freud, and Sabina Spielrein*. New York: Random House.
Weber, M. (1926/1984) *Max Weber. Ein Lebensbild*. München: Piper
Whimster, S. (ed.) (1999) *Max Weber and the Culture of Anarchy*. London: Macmillan.

Appendix

Note: The networks and field structures set out here are intended as a preliminary structural analysis and survey of the private and public political and social conflict between Hans Gross and Otto Gross and its different levels, stages and instances, especially before and during the court cases of 1913/1914. There should be added the special and somewhat different network and field of Frieda Gross, in Munich/Ascona, in her struggle with Hans Gross, in Graz, and his successors 1913–1918 (cf. Götz von Olenhusen 2005). During the First World War the transfer of the conflict from the original fight against patriachalism and state onto the legal battlefield meant a fundamental change in measures and coordinates. *In nuce* the courts did not treat the original issues and fundamental social, political and psychological questions and claims of the sympathisers and supporters of Otto Gross but followed mainly traditional legal patterns and procedures, albeit during a time when the respective laws about legal guardians, protective custody, and public and private asylums since 1900 were widely discussed between lawyers and psychiatrists in Germany and Austria and – reluctantly, slowly and only partly – were reformed.

The complicated court cases brought by Hans Gross against his son and daughter-in-law were meant to have Otto Gross certified insane, to make Hans Gross legal guardian of Otto and his grandson Peter, and Hans Gross tried to keep Frieda and Eva out of inheritance. According to Hans Gross's will the cases had to be carried through even after his death in 1915. So it happened. Max Weber's participation in Frieda's – and to some extent indirectly Otto's – cases against Hans Gross may throw another and interesting light on the scenery seen through the eyes of the learned jurist and eminent sociologist and friend or acquaintance of many members of the milieu and campaign. In these cases the question of sexual revolution and anarchism played a role not so much with Otto Gross, although the authorities knew his close connections to it, but with Frieda Gross and her anarchist lover and companion Ernst Frick (Ascona) in the legal debate about legal guardianship of her children.

Network I and Fields (Prof. Hans Gross, Graz)

Medical/psychiatric field (Austria/Germany/Switzerland)

Lunatic asylums/clinical hospitals/sanatoriums:	Mendrisio, Am Steinhof, Burghölzli, Tulln, Troppau, Bad Ischl
Psychiatrist/psychoanalysts:	Berze, Birnbaum, Freud, Eugen Bleuler, C. G. Jung, Näcke, Wilhelm Stekel, Steltzer, Bonvicini (Tulln), Boeck (Troppau)
Locations:	Graz, Vienna, Munich, Ascona, Berlin, Tulln, Troppau

Field of police/prosecutors (Germany/Switzerland)

Police Berlin
Kronauer General Prosecutor (Bern, Zürich)
Irreninspektor
Police Munich
Police Zurich
Glättli (prosecutor, Zürich)

Field of courts of law (Austrian courts)

District Court (Bezirksgericht Tulln), Graz
Bezirksgericht, Graz
Landesgericht, Graz
Oberlandesgericht, Graz

Medical experts:	Berze, Steltzer, [Prof. Wagner-Jauregg]
Witnesses:	Hempt, Höller
Attorneys/barristers:	Anton and Carl Rintelen

Fields of general public

The University
The Press (incl. periodical of Hans Gross)
Newspapers (Graz, Vienna)

Network II and Fields (Dr. Otto Gross)

Private/professional field (Austria/Germany/Switzerland/Italy/France)

Wife/surroundings:	Frieda Gross-Schloffer, Marianne Weber, Max Weber (Frieda Weekley, Else Jaffé)
Friends/sympathisers:	Franz Jung, Simon G(h)uttmann, Erich Mühsam, Carl Einstein, Ludwig Rubiner, Franz Pfemfert, Blaise Cendrars, Arnold Zweig, Oskar Kanehl, Guillaume Apollinaire, Maximilian Harden, Richard Oehring, Alfred Kerr, Bess Brenck Kalischer, Emmy Hennings, Hugo Ball, Karl Otten, Otto Schrimpf, Oskar Maria Graf, Franziska zu Reventlow, Else Lasker-Schüler, René Schickele, Friedrich Hardekopf, Johannes R. Becher, Hans von Weber
Locations:	Graz, Munich, Ascona, Berlin

Medical/psychiatric field (Austria/Germany/Switzerland)

Analysts/therapists:	Dr. Berze, Sigmund Freud, C. G. Jung, Eugen Bleuler, Dr. Bonvicini, Dr. Boeck, Dr. Wilhelm Stekel

Field of courts and law

District courts:	Tulln and Graz, Landesgericht Graz, Oberlandesgericht Graz
Witnesses/experts:	Erich Mühsam, Franz Jung, Beatrice Zweig, Richard Oehring, Prof. Wagner-v. Jauregg [Wiener Medizinische Fakultät]
Attorneys/barristers:	Dr. Fischl [Dr. Otto Pellech], Dr. Veik, Dr. Schur

Field of general public

Newspapers:	*Wilmersdorfer Zeitung*, *Prager Tagblatt*, *Neues Wiener Journal*, *Neues*

	Wiener Abendblatt, *Die Welt am Montag*, *Bohemia*, *Mercure de France*, *L'Intransigeant*
Periodicals:	*Die Aktion*, *Revolution*, *Die Schaubühne*, *Kain*, *Die Zukunft*, *Wiecker Bote*, *Pan*, *Der Zwiebelfisch*
Acting persons:	Franz Pfemfert, Franz Jung, Simon G(h)uttmann, Arnold Zweig, Erich Mühsam, Maximilian Harden, Frieda Gross [Max Weber], Emil Lask

[Max Weber, Committee of Professors]
[Liberal Papers]
[*Reichstag*]

Part III

Psychoanalysis, literature and sociology

Chapter 7

Freud, Gross, sexual revolution

Alfred Springer

Introduction

The term 'sexual revolution' in the context of this chapter needs clarification. Since we will be concerned with constructs of ideas from the late nineteenth and the early twentieth century, the concept of sexual revolution that we are talking about needs as a cultural frame the standards of bourgeois morality prevalent during that epoch. It is based therefore also on a critique of some features of that set of moral rules, such as double moral standards or surplus repression of sexual acting out, as well as on the commitment to free women from the restraints of double moral standards. It seems clear that simple acting out of sexual desires is not a revolutionary issue. On the part of the male gender, that kind of lifestyle was rather usual during the late nineteenth century, as has been vividly depicted by the great novelists of that period. But we know that moral standards reigning at the same time led to a markedly different situation for men and women. Even if in Schnitzler's play *Reigen* (a remarkable document of the sexual – and seemingly liberal – mores of that time) *libertinage* is not restricted to men, there can be no doubt that female sexuality was kept down through the means of the taboo of virginity, and that transgressions of the rules of monogamy committed by women were sanctioned and eventually became both pathologised and criminalised. Unrestricted satisfaction of sexual needs alone therefore does not signify sexual freedom either on the social or on the psychic level and 'sexual revolution' must be something other than a call for erotic acting out. On a conceptual level it has to target attitudes and values and most importantly has to focus on the eradication of gender-related discrimination.

A process that included such issues and therefore can indeed be called 'sexual revolution' started in the late nineteenth century in bohemian circles in many places and it also occurred in Vienna within the small group of early psychoanalysts.

Already in one of the very first documents of the psychoanalytic movement the tension between the aim of sexual living-out and another type of erotic liberation shows up. On the occasion of the meeting of the

Wednesday Society on 16 December 1908, Freud pointed out that psychoanalysis aims at the liberation of sexuality; but that did not mean that after analysis sexuality would be lived-out in unrestricted freedom, rather it would have to be brought under a new kind of rational control, since the human being never should be dominated by his sexual impulses. In this contribution Freud turned against the bohemian approach, common in Viennese society at that time, especially pointing at Karl Kraus: 'The *Fackel* [The *Torch*, the famous journal Kraus edited] accompanies us on a certain stretch of the way, proposing that sexual repression causes damage. [. . .] But the *Fackel* is proposing living-out' (in Nunberg 1977: 81).

It may be surprising that in an article about sexual revolutions I am starting with Freud. In the history of psychoanalysis the term 'sexual revolution' is usually linked to Wilhelm Reich. But I would like to draw attention to the early days of psychoanalysis and even the time before the concept of psychoanalysis became formulated. This archaeological journey through the caves of the antiquity of modernism will show that ideas concerning the necessity of radical change within traditional structures of moral control and sexual behaviour are a vital part of psychoanalysis and that they have been expressed by Sigmund Freud from the start. Another personality that took part in the early psychoanalytic movement and is more often linked to the term 'sexual revolution' was Otto Gross. He possibly was the first one to use the term consciously in the psychoanalytically based social discourse on politics and sexuality as Franz Werfel implies in his novel *Barbara* (1990: 349; cf. also Heuer 2003; 2005).

Freud's critical position and the work and life of his most infamous pupil, Otto Gross, therefore will be used to outline the involvement of Psychoanalysis in the development of a radical change in sexual attitudes and the relationship between the sexes. Following some ideas which evolved within the early psychoanalytical discourse, some discrepancies and congruencies between Freud and Gross will be explored to show that psychoanalysis had a strong impact on the development of the ideology of sexual revolutions.

Furthermore I will try to outline that these developments of radical thinking took place within a broader discourse in accordance with endeavours from different intellectual influences.

Concerning the methodology of the study it could be said that it represents 'archaeological work in psychoanalysis' with the objective of raising some buried aspects, ideas and discourses to the surface. A further objective is to hint at repressed ideas and to redefine the importance of psychoanalysis for modernity. Last but not least the procedure shall show that psychoanalysis is much more than a kind of psychotherapy using a special technique.

Especially in his later years, when he wished for a 'Psychoanalytic academy', Freud understood treatment as just one special kind of application of the overall theories and conceptualisations of psychoanalysis. At a time when psychoanalytic discourse is increasingly restricted to treatment issues, and economical considerations and control mechanisms over treatment prevail, that part of Freud's work that constitutes a radical humanistic philosophy of change is in danger of vanishing and therefore deserves to be reassessed. Some reflections are nevertheless necessary concerning the tension that is inherent in our work, between psychoanalysis as a radical theory that challenges cultural mechanisms and restrictions, and a therapeutic practice that takes place inside that given society and has to conform with some rules of that same society, which, in theory, it puts in question.

Freud as a radical thinker

In my opinion the first, and perhaps the most radical, statement given by Freud concerning an issue that is related to 'sexual revolution' can be detected as early as 1895 in his conclusions concerning the hysteric case Elisabeth:

> In spring 1894 I heard that she was going to a private ball for which I was able to get an invitation. I was able to get an invitation, and I did not allow the opportunity to escape me of seeing my former patient whirl past me in a lively dance. Since then, by her own inclination, she has married someone unknown to me.
>
> (in Breuer and Freud 1895: 160)

This sentence, which gives the case history a 'fairy-tale ending', is a very early example of the concept of 'free love', which defines love and sexuality as natural psychic and somatic needs which should be lived out freely, independent from social pressure and social regulations. Naturally it includes the proposition that women should be able to choose their erotic partners according to their own desires. Freud's statement adds a new quality to the concept: free love is a healing force. To understand how remarkably early Freud expressed his opinion we have to be aware that Madelains Vernet's *On Free Love* (*L'amour libre*) was published in the journal *L'anarchie* in 1907 and translated into German as late as 1920. A large publication on the topic, Rudolf Quanter's *Die freie Liebe und ihre Bedeutung im Rechtsleben der Jahrhunderte: Eine kulturhistorische Studie* (Free love and its importance for the legal life throughout the centuries: A cultural-historical study) was published in 1906.

The next examples of Freud's radicalism in sexual matters are to be found in the minutes of the Wednesday meetings of the early Viennese psychoanalysts. For instance, Freud, on the occasion of the discussion taking place on 12 February 1908, expressed his view that a large segment of women suffering sexual anaesthesia consisted of 'too well educated young girls' (in

Nunberg and Federn 1962: 310). He meant that in such cases sexual repression had achieved much more than what was intended. And he underlined this interpretation with the remark, 'Charming and attractive women acquire and sustain these qualities only in sexual freedom' (ibid.).

In a number of papers he wrote between 1908 and 1913 he introduced these ideas to a broader public. All these publications focused on the sexually repressive powers of society and their damaging impact on psychic health. The most important publications in this category are:

- *'Civilized' Sexual Morality and Modern Nervous Illness* (1908a)
- *On the Sexual Theories of Children* (1908b)
- *A Special Type Of Choice Of Object Made By Men* (1910)
- *On the Universal Tendency to Debasement in the Sphere of Love* (1912)
- Preface to Bourke's *Scatalogic Rites of All Nations* (1913)

In the powerful paper *'Civilized' sexual morality and modern nervous illness* (1908a), Freud reflected on the repressive hypocrisy of 'civilized sexual morality' and its role in 'modern nervous illness'.

Freud continued to work in this vein. From 1912 to 1922 he deepened his analysis of the cultural environment and intensified his attack on cultural restrictions in his three essays *On the Universal Tendency to Debasement in the Sphere of Love*. In this 1912 paper he wrote that certain peculiarities of the erotic life of women result from sexual repression. Social mores and rules ask them to suspend their desire to explore their somatic sexuality and force them to enrich their fantasy life. A later inability to detach the prohibition from sensuality results in the special importance of 'the forbidden' within female psychic sexuality. For Freud, that special condition seemed to be the counterpart of the importance of the debasement of the sexual object on the part of the male. In this sense cultural sexual repression produce a general debasement of sexual objects and sexuality itself for both sexes.

Especially interesting is the preface to Bourke (1913), where Freud insisted on the necessity of exploring the dark and abjected districts of the mind. It can also serve as an example of Freud having opted for freedom of publication of material with sexual content.

It is also of interest that these publications were produced for journals designed to reach a larger public and to generate a change in the attitude concerning sexual issues. These publication series included:

- *Die neue Generation* (The New Generation)
- *Sexualprobleme* (Sexual Problems)
- *Anthropophyteia* (Origin of Man – founded and edited by Friedrich Salomon Krauss)

The widely read and popular journal *Sexualprobleme*, edited by Max Marcuse, a pioneer of sexology, was involved in matters of sexual reform. *Die neue Generation* was edited by Helene Stöcker, who was well known as an early feminist and pioneer of the issues of fertility, birth control and maternity protection. In her journal issues which seemed of social relevance were discussed on economic, psychological, medical, philosophical and literal levels. Authors included Sigmund Freud, Bertha von Suttner, Rosa Mayreder, Kurt Tucholsky, Alexandra Kollontai, Gerhard Hauptmann, Ricarda Huch, Hedwig Dohm, Lily Braun, Kurt Breysing, Lou Andreas-Salomé, Alexander Forel, Karen Horney and many other authors who were eager to contribute to the reform of social and moral attitudes on erotic and sexual issues.

The papers by Freud mentioned above can therefore be interpreted as contributions to the ongoing discourse on sexual matters with a strong inclination towards change.

In the same time period, only starting a little later, Otto Gross developed his ideas, which led to conclusions regarding the necessity of revolutionary change and a redefining of the function of sexuality and of psychoanalysis within revolutionary approaches.

Otto Gross

Cultural repression

Otto Gross was one of the very first authors to contribute to psychoanalysis and he was the first psychiatrist who tried to develop a synthesis of the then dominating psychiatric theoretical categorisations (neuropathology-brain mythology in the sense of Meynert, Anton and Wernicke, and degeneration theory) and the then radically new Freudian concepts. He was also the only one to develop concepts similar to those Freud had developed in his neuroscientific 'outline of a psychology' contained in his letters to Fliess. Nevertheless he seems totally lost in the historiography of psychoanalysis.

Looking back at the importance of Gross for early Psychoanalysis (Springer, 2008) it seems difficult to understand how it happened that Gross vanished from the official history of Psychoanalysis. How could such 'cultural repression' happen? What were the reasons?

At least partly that process may be understood from certain features of his life and his lifestyle. He was a lifelong dependent drug user, consuming morphine, opium and cocaine. In addition, he had been diagnosed as suffering from schizophrenia by C. G. Jung. He was often transferred to psychiatric wards, mostly because of interventions by his father, the famous criminologist Hans Gross. To keep his son under control, the father used the institutional powers of psychiatry to incapacitate. Being a member of the anarchist community and different bohemian circles all over Europe,

Otto Gross became a partisan of the ideas of the sexual revolution, linking ideas prevailing in these circles with psychoanalytic interpretations. This attitude impacted on the style of his professional behaviour and C. G. Jung accused Gross of demoralising his patients.

Gross's style of analysis seems to have been highly unconventional. In Munich thc treatments took place mostly in the Café Stefanie, better known as '*Café Grössenwahn*' – café of grandiose delusions – a prominent meeting place of members of bohemian society (Mühsam 1929), where they gathered for hours on end. Gross often treated his patients in this, their familial setting. Furthermore he often transgressed professional boundaries and had personal and sexual relations with his patients. These features of his clinical work are passed down anecdotally. But one needs to be cautious and remember that at that time no professional and/or ethical guidelines and rules in respect of the relations between analyst and patient existed. It might well be that Gross did not differ that much in his methods from some of his colleagues. Jung was at that time involved with Sabinea Spielrein. And if we read Anaïs Nin's diaries, we get a glimpse at what even much later on happened in Paris with Rank and Allendy. But it is well documented that the behaviour of Gross led to complications and eventually grave incidents, which were part of the accusations that in the long run helped to justify Gross's incapacitation.

The bohemian

Gross was very interested in the modern arts. Already in 1902, in his monograph on the *Cerebral Secondary Function*, he used the modern Viennese school of art and literature as a point of reference. And he did not restrict himself just to the role of an observer; he personally participated in bohemian circles all over Europe. In this respect he had close ties with Vienna, Munich, Prague, Zurich, Ascona, Berlin and Paris. He befriended many of the leading writers of that period – from J. R. Becher to Franz Kafka – and he had a great influence on German expressionism and on Dadaism as well as on D. H. Lawrence, Robert Musil and Blaise Cendrars. He participated in the intellectual discourses in those circles, representing the psychoanalytic position. One could say that his ideas about psychoanalysis and his interpretations essentially shaped the reception and understanding of that science among the intellectuals and artists of his generation. Freudian psychoanalysis is reflected in the writing of authors such as Thomas Mann and Stefan and Arnold Zweig, while Grossian interpretations are fundamental for the analytic background of the expressionist movement.

Gross figures in many disguises in numerous literary works of the expressionist era (cf. Michaels, Chapter 10; Springer 1987). His whole existence seemed to reflect some of the most important issues of Expressionism: the

Father–Son conflict, the sibling rivalry between Gross and Jung – in a recent interpretation, Heuer (2008) even speculates about psychological 'fratricide' on the part of Jung with Freud as the father figure – the struggle between rational and irrational forces, madness, ecstasy, the search for a 'new man' and a 'new woman', the fight for radically and freely lived sexuality, the fight against power structures and any kind of authority. Some elements of his theories were also compatible with expressionist ideologies, especially his firm conviction of the essentially 'good' nature of the human individual.

The anarchist

Gross also participated in the anarchistic movement and contributed to anarchist journals. His lifestyle, too, seemed to be arranged according to anarchistic principles. In particular, his views regarding sexuality and his relations to women were adapted to anarchist views of free love. He was married but also had many short-lived relationships; some of them bore the burden of common drug addiction and some of them ended tragically – he was accused of having helped at least two young women to commit suicide. In his papers on revolution, free sexuality and the principle of the 'cultic orgy' are issues of great importance. According to the writer Emil Szittya and others, Gross was implementing such ideas among the avant-gardists populating the Monte Verità in Ascona.

These particular features of his life and his work make Gross an 'interesting' and notorious personality. These aspects consequentially have dominated historical research and studies on literature. The promising scientist Gross is not as well documented and studied.

The turning point

1908 was a critical year both for Gross's personal fate, including his relationship to Freud, and also for orthodox psychoanalysis. But it was also a seminal year for certain developments within psychoanalysis itself, which Gross was involved in.

In April of that year, Gross attended the first psychoanalytic congress in Salzburg. Later he reported in the Berlin expressionist journal *Die Aktion* that Freud on that occasion had refuted certain thoughts that he had expressed with respect to the social implications and, indeed, obligations of psychoanalysis – 'We are physicians and physicians we should remain' (Gross 1913b: 506–507) – thus placing psychoanalysis outside of socio-political discourse.

If this incident actually happened that way – there are no other witnesses – it seems rather strange, since Freud himself was involved in that discourse on different levels, as I pointed out earlier, publishing related articles between 1908 and 1913.

Just after the conference, in June 1908, the most decisive turning point in Gross's life took place – Freud referred Gross to Jung for treatment. Freud suspected him of having developed a full-blown cocaine psychosis and Jung diagnosed him to be a case of *Dementia praecox*.

In 1909, one year after having been diagnosed as schizophrenic, Gross published his monograph on *Psychopathische Minderwertigkeiten* (Psychopathic Inferiorities). This work represents his last publication in a well established publishing house. It should perhaps be mentioned that the same publisher also published Weiniger's infamous *Geschlecht und Charakter* (Sex and Character).

In this text Gross took on the basis of Nietzsche's philosophy and, in line with the older French decadent school, reinterpreted the degeneration theory in order to reassess the principle of degeneracy. According to Gross's theory, 'moral or psychopathic degenerates' are necessary stepping stones in the transition to the next phase of evolution. The process of civilisation needs to replace primitive biological necessities with temporarily 'degenerated' forms which nevertheless are the precondition for adaptations to the changing necessities of the evolution processes.

For Freud, the book was 'another outstanding work, full of bold syntheses and overflowing with ideas,' yet, 'I don't know if I shall be able to understand the book. A good deal is too high-flown for me' (Freud and Jung 1974: 227). This book was the last one by Gross that was published by a scientific publishing house. A further comparable scientific book was published only after his death.

Following this, Gross turned away from his academic career to embark on a new and thrilling endeavour: psychoanalysis and radical social change. Nevertheless, he always stood by psychoanalysis. Even in his last paper he named the writings of Freud, Adler, Stekel and Federn as the groundbreaking frame of reference for his clinical and theoretical work. But he wanted to go further, pointing out that classical analysis, feeling at home in society, fails to deduce from its empirical insights socio-political implications and the necessity to implement them in revolutionary action.

Events taking place during the Salzburg conference had shown that Gross was not alone in his ruminations concerning the cultural implications of psychoanalysis. Wilhelm Stekel praised his contribution as having been brilliant and Ferenczi, who was one of the main speakers at the Salzburg congress, proved himself to be a psychoanalytic thinker whose interpretations at that time resembled the theories of Gross. Ferenczi, not unlike Gross, proposed in his paper that any human being – including the so-called normals – suffers from failed repression. He talked about repressed thoughts and tendencies which he perceived to constitute in the unconscious a dangerous complex of anti-social and self-destructive instincts. He also explained the development of controlling institutions: the control of these instincts requires moral, religious and social dogmas. And these again he perceived to be the cause of unnecessary anguish and of a remarkable reduction of the quality of life. Psychoanalysis, Ferenczi proposed, could enable an 'inner revolution' and in this way could become the first revolution that really redeems humankind.

In 1908, therefore, Ferenczi and Gross seem to have had a common belief and a common theory: they both identified the introjection of alien restraints into the developing psychic structure of the child as the most important pathogenic process and they both underlined the pathogenic power of the 'inner conflict between one's own being and alien norms and values'. In this sense both were also forerunners of later developments in psychoanalytic conceptualisations: the structural theory and the theory of super-ego conflict.

An additional outcome of the Salzburg conference was the foundation of the *Yearbook of Psychoanalytic and Psychopathologic Research*. In the foreword to the first edition, Jung pointed out that the decision for this publication had come from the recognition 'that the working out of the problems in question was already beginning to go beyond the bounds of purely medical interest' (Jung 1909: 392).

Later, Otto Gross started to publish a series of papers in which he tried to delineate his view concerning the crippling influence of culture on the 'true essence' of the child and to glorify psychoanalysis as a leading liberating force in freeing that 'essential good' that rests suppressed and distorted in all of us. These essential papers were published from 1909 on, culminating in contributions for political journals (1914–1919).

Psychoanalysis and politics in 1913

In 1913 *Die Aktion* opened a discourse on psychoanalysis. Ludwig Rubiner, a leading force among young left-wing radicals – in addition to his own literary productions he published readers of revolutionary papers and materials – expressed the opinion that Psychoanalysis could not contribute to the revolution and the emancipation of 'the mind'. He could not find any other value in Psychoanalysis – nor in any other psychology – than a technique, arguing that it should remain in that position and accept that its major objective consists in its 'brutal practical advantage; its curative efficiency (treatment success)' (Rubiner 1913: 483).

Otto Gross took part in that discussion. His response to Rubiner focused on his conviction that on the contrary, psychoanalysis represented the psychology of revolution and as such contained a high degree of revolutionary potential. He opined that psychoanalysis as a technique – scorned by Rubiner – knows of no limitations and surely is not restricted to interventions on the individual level. According to Gross, the clinical field of the analyst embraces the whole suffering of mankind and psychoanalysis therefore contains the only hope for an improvement of the human condition.

Gross explored this position in many of his later papers, which were published outside the academic world in political journals. His argument was that since his clinical work had provided evidence that the dominance of authoritarian structures in society condemns all individuals to become sick – and particularly the very best ones in a very special way – revolution had to be redefined as a hygienic necessity for humankind. The basis of such a revolution, he proposed, should be the 'interior liberation of the revolutionary individual'; this liberation could be named 'clinical spade-work' (Gross 1913a: 384; 1919: 25). And Psychoanalysis's objectives – in the view of Gross – certainly include a task like that. This possibility and its relevance for revolutionary projects constituted for Gross the last resort of hope for humanity.

Tirelessly Gross tried to explain that the modern psychology of the unconscious could and should become the mainstay of the necessary changes in all social sciences. Only with the analytic technique, he claimed, would it be possible to recapture the repressed parts of the inner psychic life and to free these from the crippling impact of cultural influences. Such recapture had to include the fight against any kind of adaptation and against authority in any form, especially against the authority that steers family life and interpersonal relationships as well as the relationship to state, capital and its institutions. In this context Gross challenged patriarchy. A vital part of this utopian design was the re-establishment of a matriarchal order that included the social, economical and existential independence of women from men, and as far as motherhood was concerned, the independent social function and responsibility of women. This aspect of his work is crucial to his position as a 'sexual revolutionary'.

Otto Gross's 'sexual revolution'

Gross, not unlike Freud, argued that social regulations and repressive forces impact on the individual's sexual desires, constituting a major component of a '*Konflikt zwischen Eigenem und Fremdem*' (inner conflict between one's own being and alien norms and values) in the unconscious and therefore in the psychic structure of the individual. The conflict between natural individual sexual desires – which, according to Gross, are polygamic/polyandric and bisexual – and social norms and rules leads to psychic catastrophe if the social rules do not conform to individual needs. Such a situation, Gross explained, results from the prevailing patriarchal order, which prescribes monogamy and exclusive heterosexuality.

These ideas were grounded in clinical observations and psychoanalytic interpretations that were similar to the ones we already know from Freud. Not unlike Freud, Gross wrote, in 1913, that the specific vulnerability of women to develop hysteria results not from a gender disposition but from general moralistic ideologies and double standards concerning sexuality

(1913a: 1092). In this context he again criticised Rubiner: 'Ludwig Rubiner is mistaken in contrasting femaleness and free thinking. We believe that such a revolution will be the first one and the real one which brings together woman, freedom and the spirit in one concept' (Gross 1913b: 507).

With such ideas Gross participated in a lively discourse that took place at that time. Using Bachofen's analysis of the development of patriarchy out of a matriarchal matrix, a certain idealisation of assumed ancient matriarchal periods was a common feature of such divergent thought systems as early socialism (Engels, Bebel), the cosmic philosophy of Munich's bohemian borough of Schwabing (Klages, George) and early feminist thinking (Franziska zu Reventlow). Anticipating Freud, Bebel had described that the state of freedom (including erotic liberty) that – according to his interpretation – characterised the woman of matriarchal times, enhanced the beauty, pride, dignity and autonomy of these women.

The cosmic philosophers of Schwabing proposed that women should be freed from the yoke of marriage. They should not be the property of a single man alone. These philosophers idealised the *hetaerae* of ancient times. The cosmics also enthused about the cultic adoration of female fertility represented in the cults of Demeter, Gaia or Astarte. Their desire for 'cosmic sensations' led them to the development of the concept of a 'cosmic eros', a mystery that they thought to be capable of continuously regenerating the world. Accordingly, they proposed that not men but women should occupy the centre of society. Not cold logic and reason, but emotion, passion and the realm of the psyche should be adored, not a 'Super-Father' in heaven, but 'Mother Earth'.

Gross was influenced not only on a theoretical level. His relationships to women who tried to implement these ideas and to fully live out the principle of free love – Frieda Gross, Else Jaffé, Franziska zu Reventlow (the paradigmatic 'modernist *hetaira*') – supported his approach, promising that the dream could become reality. Gross's fantasy world of a 'Revolution in the name of Matriarchy' therefore is a complex system, structured around influences from psychoanalysis, socialism, traditionalistic bourgeois philosophy and religion, as well as his personal experience.

From the fusion of psychoanalysis and theories about a matriarchal past, Gross concluded that 'the revolutionary of today, who with the help of the psychology of the unconscious sees the relations between the sexes in a free and propitious future' (1913c: 387), has to fight against the fathers and against patriarchy, and that 'the next revolution should be a revolution aiming to establish matriarchy' (1919: 21–22).

Gross explicitly expressed these ideas first in 1910 in a response to the anarchist Gustav Landauer which he wanted to be published in the journal *Der Sozialist*. Later, he increasingly aimed for a 'New Humanity', which should arise from the ruins of the patriarchy-based old structures. Otto Gross also believed the matriarchal organisation to be fundamental for the implementation of a primary communistic ideal. In 1913 he mentioned that the primal sin consists in the fact that women are held in slavery because of their having and raising children.

This kind of 'eschatological communist' interpretation and conviction (a type of political thinking that can also be found among other authors of the expressionist generation) culminated in an article he published in the journal *Sowjet* in 1919, where he presented a new interpretation of Genesis and original sin (15–16). According to his new interpretation, original sin is to be found in the loss of 'matriarchal innocence' (ibid.: 19–21). This loss then led to sexual shame and to the interpretation that sexuality is sinful. Gross argued that original sin primarily could not have been targeting sexual activity because of the human being's sexual dimorphism, which in turn imposed sexual activity and fertility. Original sin must have been an act that debased the primary innocent and fertile sexuality. Such an act must have been rape, committed by the male, to establish authoritarian patriarchy, together with its basic concepts: marriage, female submission and dependency, which in turn formed the bourgeois authoritarian family structure. From this perspective, patriarchy stands for a system that is responsible for determining all human relationships as based on the use of power. Gross reinterpreted the biblical prophecy that the woman will 'scrunch the serpent's head', as predicting the destruction of these principles and structures that represent patriarchy in order to re-establish matriarchy.

In a footnote Gross reflected on the cultural background of the encrypted message of Genesis. He thought it probable that the mythical text reflects the struggle between the old Astarte cults and the new monotheism. He believed that the Astarte religion represented all that 'was left of female dignity and female freedom' (1919b: 26–27f.). Together with the romanticisation of ancient cults of mother goddesses Gross undertook a revision of the importance of orgiastic rituals. He interpreted them to have functioned as tradition-keepers for the positive valuation of sexuality inherent in the elder matriarchal value system. Hurwitz believes that in the orgy Gross recognised a model of a communist matriarchy that could come close to a realisation of the possibilities of freedom and joint participation (Hurwitz 1979: 294–295). With Gross's friend Franz Jung I believe that the revitalisation and implementation of orgiastic rituals was intended to re-establish an order that freed sexuality from shame and guilt feelings, separated sexual encounters from sexual appropriation and helped to define the responsibility for children as a duty of society.

Freud, Gross and sexual revolution

On the level of ideas the differences between Freud and Gross seem to be astonishingly marginal. Both authors felt that the moral regulations of sexuality support a cultural system that leads to major disturbances both in the individual as in society. Hence both agreed that such a control system ought to be changed.

Both authors also expressed their conviction that as a result of double moral standards the cultural restrictions of the acting out of sexual needs impact more on women than on men; both drew the conclusion that the special control that is imposed on female sexuality should be abolished.

Conclusions – psychoanalysis and change of cultural norms

It seems to be to Freud's merit that he brought the concept of free love into the discourse of the cultural critiques of his day, and to have given it a sound scientific basis, pointing out that sexual repression leads to major aberrations on the individual as well as on the social level. His major contribution to this development consisted in the clarification that it is not sexuality itself that is dangerous but the way human people handle it. The scientific sexual revolution started when in 1885 the commitment to the 'free love concept' entered academic psychological discourse and was upheld in different forms by eminent psychoanalysts such as Freud himself and Wilhelm Stekel (e.g. 1931).

Otto Gross's thinking came from the same direction. But he, unlike Freud, tried to practise what he preached by living it out. This attitude was facilitated by the fact that he befriended men and women from different walks of life who tried to follow similar directions. These friends and co-operators on their part also structured their lives following the principle of 'free love' in bohemian circles in Ascona, Munich, Vienna and Berlin. They tried to live this experiment differently from the prevailing male-dominated concept of libertinism – even though it was not free from the pitfalls of that model, as we know from some documents of the love lives of Otto Gross and his followers. In particular, the problem of the responsibility for children remains unsolved.

Otto Gross, and later Wilhelm Reich, further tried to integrate the concept of sexual liberation into the context of revolutionary movements. Using his clinical experience and reacting to a cultural atmosphere of double moral standards, Gross proposed that the central issue of any sexual revolution had to be to free women from their slavery and to install a system of erotic equality. He meant that the first step of such a liberalisation needed to be taken in pre-revolutionary times. Psychoanalysis as a method to free individuals from their restrictions – especially their sexual ones – was in that ideational context redefined to become a strategic tool, destined to be 'preparatory work' for the 'anti-bourgeois'/'anti-patriarchic' revolution. With this approach Gross created a dialectic, psychoanalytically based, utopian ideal that actually can only be formulated on the basis of a re-established claim for a better life on the part of individual cultural propositions. These can be constructed only on the basis of the empirically based claim of the individual concerning the liberation of his inner values and norms.

With regard to the importance of sexuality, Gross defined sexual activity as a determining force and major objective for communist or anarchist movements, just as Reich later defined sexual liberation as a crucial aspect of revolutionary attitudes within socialist and communist youth organisations. In this way the issues of sexuality, sexual liberation and psychoanalysis programmatically became introduced into the revolutionary argument.

These ideas were all developed before the Second World War. Since then major changes concerning 'Civilized' Sexual Morality (Freud 1908a) have occurred. It is difficult to assess the importance of the different developments in our cultural landscape that contributed to these changes and to separate the impact of psychoanalysis from other mechanisms and processes. Ironically the 'soft revolution' of Freudian origin, avoiding any revolutionary rhetoric, but relentlessly and soberly revealing society's shortcomings regarding the undesired outcome of moral regulations, probably proved to be highly efficient concerning profound changes in sexual attitudes and behaviours. But otherwise, the process of social change took place without challenging the ideological fundaments of the social system and the distribution of power. Thus the new sexual order could easily be incorporated and brought under the control of the traditionally prevailing regulations of authoritarian patriarchal society and eventually became adapted to the rules of consumer society. This kind of sexual liberation and gender equality definitively has not transformed living conditions to become an earthly paradise. Therefore the Freudian revolution might have contributed to a situation in which some needs can be satisfied, but even more fundamental ones possibly remain repressed. They may eventually determine certain aspects of juvenile anti-authoritarian unrest and of gender politics in popular culture, youth culture and the postmodern feminist approach. Probably these movements uphold and continue the Grossian approach by advancing similar basic ideas adapted to a changed cultural landscape and to a different ideological frame of reference.

Bibliography

Breuer, J. and Freud, S. (1895) *Studies on Hysteria. SE*, Vol. II. London: Hogarth.

Freud, S. (1908a) *'Civilized' Sexual Morality and Modern Nervous Illness. SE*, Vol. IX. London: Hogarth.

Freud, S. (1908b) *On the Sexual Theories of Children. SE*, Vol. IX. London: Hogarth.

Freud, S. (1910) *A Special Type of Choice of Object Made by Men. SE*, Vol. XI. London: Hogarth.

Freud, S. (1912) *On the Universal Tendency to Debasement in the Sphere of Love. SE*, Vol. XI. London: Hogarth.
Freud, S. (1913) Preface to Bourke's *Scatalogic Rites Of All Nations. SE*, Vol. XII. London: Hogarth.
Freud, S. and Jung, C. G. (1974) *The Freud/Jung Letters*. London: Hogarth Press and Routledge & Kegan Paul.
Gross, O. (1902) *Die cerebrale Sekundärfunction*. Leipzig: Vogel.
Gross, O. (1909) *Über psychopathische Minderwertigkeiten*. Wien & Leipzig: Braumüller.
Gross, O. (1913a) Die Einwirkung der Allgemeinheit auf das Individuum. *Die Aktion, 3*, 1091–1095.
Gross, O. (1913b) Ludwig Rubiner's 'Psychoanalyse', *Die Aktion, 3*, 506–507.
Gross, O. (1913c) Zur Ueberwindung der kulturellen Krise. *Die Aktion, 3*(14), 384–387.
Gross, O. (1919) Die kommunistische Grundidee in der Paradiessymbolik. *Sowjet, 1*, 12–27.
Heuer, G. (2003) *The Devil Underneath the Couch: The Secret Story of Jung's Twin Brother*. Retrieved from www.iisg.nl/womhist/heuer
Heuer, G. (2005) Otto Gross: Leben, Werk und Wirkung. In G. Dienes, A. Götz von Olenhusen, G. Heuer and G. Kocher (eds.), *Gross gegen Gross*. Marur: LiteraturWissenschaft.de (p. 39).
Heuer, G. (2008) Brudermord auf der Couch: Otto Gross und C. G. Jung. In R. Dehmlow, R. Rother and A. Springer (eds.), *Die Rebellion des Otto Gross*. Marburg: LiterturWissenschaft.de (pp. 136–149).
Hurwitz, E. (1979) *Otto Gross: Paradies-Sucher zwischen Freud und Jung*. Zürich: Suhrkamp.
Jung, C. G. (1909) Editorial Preface to the *Jahrbuch. CW* 18. London: Routledge & Kegan Paul.
Mühsam, E. (1929) Liebe, Treue, Eifersucht: Die Ansichten der Gräfin Franziska von Reventlow. *Die Aufklärung, 1*(10), 315.
Nunberg, H. and Federn, E. (1962) *Minutes of the Vienna Psychoanalytic Society, Vol. I, 1906–1908*. New York, NY: International Universities Press.
Nunberg, H. and Federn, E. (1977) *Protokolle der Wiener Psychoanalytischen Vereinigung Band II: 1908–1910*. Frankfurt: Fischer.
Rubiner, L. (1913) Psychoanalyse. *Die Aktion, 3*(19), 483.
Springer, A. (1987) Psicoanalisi e espressionismo. In: A. M. Accerboni (Ed.) *La cultura psicoanalitica: atti del convegno, Trieste 5–8 dic. 1985* (*Collezione Biblioteca*). Studio Tesi (pp. 589–595).
Springer, A. (2008) Otto Gross als Wissenschaftler. In R. Dehmlow, R. Rother and A. Springer (eds.), *Die Rebellion des Otto Gross*. Marburg: LiteraturWissenschaft.de (pp. 51–78).
Stekel, W. (1931) *Die moderne Ehe*. Basel/Leipzig/Wien: Wendepunkt.
Werfel, F. (1990) *Barbara oder Die Frömmigkeit*. Frankfurt/M: Fischer.

Chapter 8

The birth of intersubjectivity

Otto Gross and the development of psychoanalytic theory and clinical practice

Gottfried M. Heuer

The psychology of the unconscious is the philosophy of the revolution.
(Otto Gross 1913a)

'I have only mixed with anarchists and declare myself to be an anarchist,' Otto Gross told psychiatrists (Berze and Stelzer 1999/2000: 24) who examined him in 1913. He continued, 'I am a psychoanalyst and from my experience I have gained the insight that the existing order [. . .] is a bad one [. . . A]nd since I want everything changed, I am an anarchist' (ibid.). The psychiatrists in 1913 promptly noted Gross's political views as one of the symptoms of mental disorder.

Although the Austrian psychoanalyst and anarchist Otto Gross (1877–1920) played a pivotal role in the birth of what today we are calling modernity, with wide-ranging influences in psychiatry, analysis, politics, philosophy, sociology, literature and ethics, he has remained virtually unknown to this day. To a large extent, this is the result of an analytic historiography that Erich Fromm, in 1958, somewhat provocatively called 'Stalinistic' (1989: 195): dissidents become non-persons and vanish from the records. Today, when we think of the origins of analysis, immediately the names of Freud and Jung spring to mind. But there was someone else who stood between these two, in direct contact with both – who, in a way, has been pushed into their shadow. Otto Gross's first biographer called him a 'Seeker of Paradise' (Hurwitz 1979). In this search he was radical and without compromise. In the historiography of psychoanalysis that was sufficient for making him a non-person. Of course, I do not mean to claim that Gross was on a par with Freud and Jung. But I do hope to show that he significantly influenced the development of analytical theory and clinical practice.

I have divided this chapter into two parts, which cover Otto Gross's life history, and his contributions to psychoanalytic theory and clinical practice, respectively.

Life history

Otto Hans Adolf Gross was born on 17 March 1877 in the small village of Gniebing near Feldbach in Styria, Austria. His father was Professor Hans Gross, world authority and founder of the science of criminology.

Otto Gross was educated mainly by private tutors and in private schools. After qualifying in medicine in 1900, he travelled as a naval doctor to South America. In 1902 he became an assistant lecturer at Graz University and gave seminars on Freud's psychoanalysis. In the same year he married and went to the world-famous psychiatric clinic of the Burghölzli in Zürich for his first treatment for drug addiction. It is assumed that it was here that he met Jung for the first time.

In 1906 Gross became an assistant psychiatrist with Emil Kraepelin in Munich and began to thrive in the Bohemian circles of Munich. On and off he lived in Ascona in Switzerland, where he had an important impact on many expressionist writers (cf. Michaels, Chapter 10) and artists as well as anarchist radicals. He was not only preaching the sexual revolution – a term he is said to have coined (Werfel 1990: 349) – but was also living it: in 1907 he fathered three children with three different women who not only knew of each other but were and remained – friends. His son Peter was born that year by his wife Frieda. He had another son, also called Peter, born in December 1907, with his wife's friend Else Jaffé. And a daughter, Camilla, was born in the summer of 1908 to the Swiss writer Regina Ullmann. In 1907 Gross also had a passionate relationship with Else Jaffé's sister, Frieda Weekley, neé von Richthofen. Later she became the wife of D. H. Lawrence. Through her Gross's ideas on sexuality and sexual liberation had an important influence on D. H. Lawrence (cf. Turner, Chapter 11) and Anglo-American literature.

In 1907 Otto Gross submitted a paper to the *Archiv für Sozialwissenschaft und Sozialpolitik*, edited by Max Weber, the founder of modern sociology: '*Der Psychologismus seit Nietzsche und Freud*' (The Psychologism since Nietzsche and Freud). Weber wrote a scathing rejection, but Gross's ideas of the sexual revolution nevertheless had a strong impact on him (cf. Chapter 6 and Chapter 12).

In the autumn of 1907 Gross took part in the International Congress for Neuro-Psychiatry in Amsterdam, where he met Jung again and vigorously defended Freud's theory of the neuroses. In the following year he gave a talk at the First International Psychoanlytic Congress in Salzburg. Wilhelm Stekel later remembered: 'Attending the meeting was also the highly gifted Otto Gross. In his inspiring speech he compared Freud to Nietzsche and hailed him as a destroyer of old prejudices, an enlarger of psychological horizons, and a scientific revolutionary' (1950: 122).

Shortly after this congress, Gross had further treatment for drug addiction at the Burghölzli, where he was analysed by C. G. Jung – and, in turn, analysed Jung. Initially, Jung was enthusiastic and wrote to Freud, 'in Gross I discovered many aspects of my own nature, so that he often seemed like my twin brother' (Freud and Jung 1974: 156). Ernest Jones was suspicious from the start. In May 1908, in the first letter that he wrote to Freud, which is almost entirely about Otto Gross, he worried, 'I hear that Jung is going to treat [Gross] psychically, and naturally I feel a little uneasy about that for Jung [. . .] has a pretty strong dislike for Gross (Freud and Jones 1993: 1).

Forty years later, though, in his autobiography, Ernest Jones writes, 'Jung did his best to help [Gross]; [. . .] he told me that one day he worked unceasingly with Gross for twelve hours, until they were almost reduced to the condition of nodding automata' (Jones 1990: p. 164).

Gross broke off this treatment by escaping over the wall of the psychiatric clinic – although, since he had admitted himself voluntarily, he could just as well have walked out through the front door. Rather than admitting failure, Jung diagnosed Gross an incurable schizophrenic in what might seem more like an act of revenge (Hurwitz 2001). He was deeply resentful. In an as yet unpublished letter of the following year Jung wrote to Ernest Jones: 'I believe that by openly advocating certain things one cuts off the branch on which culture rests [. . .] In any case the extreme which Gross preaches is definitely wrong and dangerous for the whole cause' (1909a).

One-sidedly, Jung seems to have blamed Gross for the failure of their analysis. Even almost 30 years later, Jung's negative feelings continue to be rather strong. In a letter to the psychoanalyst Fritz Wittels in New York he wrote, early in 1936:

> Indeed, I have known Dr. Otto Gross well. I have met him [. . .] when he was interned at the Zürich clinic for cocainism and morphinism. One cannot really say that he actually possessed the qualities of a genius, but rather an ingenious instability which deceived many people. He practiced psychoanalysis in the most notorious bars [. . .] He delighted in an unlimited megalomania and always thought that he himself was treating the doctors psychically, myself included. By then already he was socially completely derelict. [. . .] I have not observed any other indications of a genius in him unless one sees wisecracking and incessant chatter about problems as a creative symptom. He was morally and socially totally derelict and physically run-down, too, as a consequence of the excesses [. . .] He mainly hung out with artists, writers, political dreamers and degenerates of any description.
>
> (in Heuer 2001: 670)

Gross thus became the first in the history of psychoanalysis to be branded with the label of mental illness. In the years to come so many of the best analysts were labeled similarly by their colleagues – Jung himself, Ferenczi, Rank, Reich, to name but a few – that it can almost be seen as an order of merit: the – psychoanalytic – revolution devouring its children.

Recently the psychiatrist Emanuel Hurwitz (2001), who for years held Jung's former post as chief physician at the Burghölzli Clinic, studied all the available evidence including Jung's case notes and all the other psychiatric diagnoses and reports on Gross. Taking also into account the criteria for schizophrenia in those times, he found no evidence for that diagnosis.

Gross turned his back on bourgeois society, gave up his chair at the university and lived in the Bohemian world of Munich and Ascona where he planned to found a school for anarchists. He was in contact with the leading German anarchists of his time: the Jewish writer Erich Mühsam, whom he analysed in 1907, was a close friend. Mühsam enthusiastically wrote to Freud, thanking him for the wonderful cure from a severe neurosis that Gross had achieved, using Freud's method. (Mühsam was murdered in 1934 by the Gestapo in Oranienburg Concentration Camp.) Otto Gross had a strong influence on the whole generation of expressionist writers, who were his friends: Max Brod, Leonhard Frank, Franz Jung, Franz Kafka and Franz Werfel (Michaels 1983). What united them all was the revolution of the new against all that was tradition – the rebellion of the sons against the generation of their fathers. Gross supplied this insurrection with a foundation of psychoanalytic theory.

In 1913 Gross lived in Berlin where he had a considerable influence on the emerging Dada movement. C. G. Jung's diagnosis and Gross's radical political activities served as a basis for his father to have him arrested as a dangerous anarchist and abducted for internment in a psychiatric institution in Austria. Gross's friends organised an international press campaign and he eventually was set free after six months. But his father did manage to have Otto declared of diminished legal responsibility and even had him placed under his own guardianship.

With Franz Kafka, Gross planned to publish a journal, and another – also unrealised – plan was to publish a 'Journal against the Will to Power', together with the writers Anton Kuh and Franz Werfel. But in 1916, with a group of radical writers and artists in Berlin, Gross edited the journal *Die freie Straße* (The Free Road) as a 'preparatory work for the revolution'. During the war, Gross worked as a military doctor in Eastern Europe. He had begun a relationship with a nurse, Marianne Kuh, and in 1916 their daughter Sophie was born, who today lives in Berlin and is the Honorary President of the International Otto Gross Society. She is the baby Kafka mentioned in a letter (cf. below), after Gross and Kafka had met again in the summer of 1917, on the night train from Vienna to Prague. Gross was travelling with Marianne Kuh, their young daughter Sophie and Marianne's brother, the writer Anton Kuh. Later, Kafka wrote:

Figure 8.1 Otto Gross (second from left).

> I have hardly known Otto Gross; but I realised that there was something essential here that at least with its hand reached out of the 'ridiculous' [*aus dem 'Lächerlichen'*]. The perplexed frame of mind of his friends and relatives (wife, brother-in-law, even the enigmatically silent baby amongst the travelling bags [. . .]) was somewhat reminiscent of the mood of the followers of Christ as they stood below him who was nailed to the cross [. . .] I was then going to Prague and towards haemorrhaging.
>
> (1983: 78)

Gross's final writings were published during the time of the failing German revolution after the war. He died on 13 February 1920 in Berlin, having been found half starved and frozen in a doorway two days previously. The cause of death was stated as 'pneumonia', but, in fact, this would have been exacerbated by the decades of having been addicted to cocaine. Gross's friend Franz Jung wrote: 'The star of a great fighter against the social order – the star has exploded, is extinguished, has gone down. The time has not been ripe' (1921: 91).

In one of the few eulogies that were published after his death Otto Kaus wrote in the Vienna journal *Sowjet* about Gross:

> Germany's best revolutionary minds have been educated and directly inspired by him. In a whole series of creations by the younger generation one can find his ideas elaborated with that specific clarity and far-reaching consistency that he gave them.
>
> (1920: 55)

Contributions to psychoanalytic theory and clinical practice

> The soul cannot exist without its other side which is always found in a you.
>
> (C. G. Jung 1944: para. 454)

Today, most analysts have never heard of Otto Gross, and if they have, their knowledge is often confined to, 'Isn't that the one who was schizophrenic?' Yet there was a time, in the first decade of this century, when the greatest minds in analysis were full of the highest praise for Otto Gross. In 1908 Freud wrote to Jung: 'You are really the only one capable of making an original contribution; except perhaps O. Gross's (Freud and Jung 1974: 126). In 1910 Ferenczi wrote about Gross to Freud: 'There is no doubt that, among those who have followed you up to now, he is the most significant' (Freud and Ferenczi 1996: 154). In 1912, Alfred Adler referred to Gross as 'brilliant' (1997: 58). Both Karl Abraham (1905) and Ferenczi (1920) repeatedly reviewed Gross's works. Wilhelm Stekel spoke of 'the highly gifted Otto Gross' (1925: 552). And in the autobiography Ernest Jones was working on at the end of his life, he wrote that, Gross 'was my first instructor in the technique of psychoanalysis' (1990: 173–174), calling him 'the nearest approach to the romantic ideal of a genius I have ever met' (ibid.).

One generation before Wilhelm Reich, Otto Gross was the first analyst to propose a dialectical interdependence between individual inner change on the one hand and collective political change on the other. Gross had a lasting impact on Freud, Jung and other leading analysts. The Hungarian writer Emil Szittya (1886–1964), who knew Gross well, in an unpublished fragment of a novel even went as far as calling Gross 'a friend of Dr. Freud and the intellectual father of Professor Jung' (n.d.: 211). Jung wrote '*The Significance of the Father in the Destiny of the Individual*' (1909b) together with Gross – although in later editions he deleted all reference to Gross (ibid.: para. 659, n. 8). Jung also based his differentiation of the extraverted and the introverted character types on concepts that Gross had first formulated 20 years earlier (1920: paras 461–467, 470–480, 693n., 879).

'Anarchy and therapy are not mutually compatible,' Irvin Yalom (1999: 172) recently claimed. I, however, want to argue that Gross combined anarchist thinking with psychoanalytic theory and practice in a way that impacts on current theory and practice. I shall show that Gross played a role in changing psychoanalytic practice from the way it started as a traditional hierarchical doctor–patient power relationship to the contemporary perspective where both participants are seen as being in a mutual relationship.

When psychoanalysis was created some 120 years ago, Freud worked within the traditional hierarchical relationship of the medical model. Freud soon discovered that his patients developed feelings towards him that seemed to belong to their experience outside the consulting room. Since they were transferred from other relationships, he called them 'transference'. Freud believed them to be detrimental to the analytic work and only gradually came to understand them as important. Initially, Freud was confident that he himself was free of such feelings – after all, he had completed his self-analysis.

It was only in 1908 when Jung – encouraged by his then patient Otto Gross – started a passionate relationship with his patient Sabina Spielrein and wrote about this to Freud that the latter started to realise that an analyst, too, might develop feelings originating in his own life experience, at least in *response* to feelings from the patient. The concept of 'countertransference' was born. It took decades before analysts discovered that countertransference, too, could be used as an important tool in the 'talking cure'. Gradually thus, the analysis of the neurotic patient changed into an analysis of the relationship between analyst and patient and this relationship came to be understood as mutual, dialectic. It was Jung who first formulated this in 1944 in a radical diagram in which both partners of the analytical couple appear as equals (ibid.: para. 422) – I have replaced here Jung's original terms of *adept* and *soror*, derived from alchemy, with those of the clinical practice:

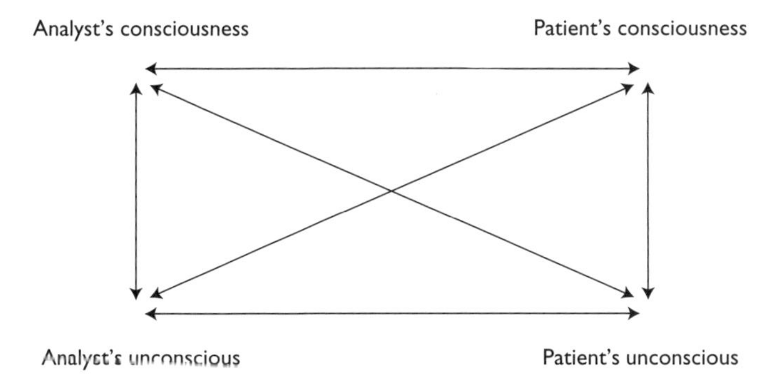

Figure 8.2 Jung's radical 1944 formulation of the mutual interrelationship between analyst and patient. From his The Psychology of the Transference (1944: para. 422).

Jung postulates that the consciousness and the unconscious of both analyst and patient are in continuous conscious and unconscious contact and exchange, *intra*personally as well as *inter*personally. Jung wrote: 'The meeting of two personalities is like the contact of two chemical substances: if there is any reaction, both are transformed' (in Russell 1992: 20).

For Freudians, divorced from Jungian thought since 1913, it took nearly a further 50 years before they formulated corresponding concepts – without any mention of Jung (Dunn 1995) – of what they now call 'intersubjectivity' or 'interpersonal analysis' (cf. Heuer 1996).

Now, what does all this have to with Otto Gross? A lot. In 1914 he wrote: 'In the depths of the human psyche we find a conflict that rents asunder the harmony of the soul and we find that this conflict is in every human being and that this disruption of the psyche pervades all of humanity' (529). It is the 'conflict between that which is one's own and that which is the other's' – der '*Konflikt des Eigenen und Fremden*', as Gross first called it in 1909 (cf. also Gross 1915). This concept describes the core of each relationship, the interrelationship of self and other. Gross focussed on these issues at a time when no one else in the field did.

In this regard Gross can be seen as a pioneer of what today we call object relations theory, particularly as it was formulated in Anglo-American analytic theory in the 1930s by Suttie (1935) and later by Fairbairn (1952). This is a development that culminated in Winnicott's famous statement:

'There is no such thing as a baby' (1952: 99). We become and are what we are only in and through relating.

Gross perceived the individual within the dynamics of the nuclear family and was the first to empathise deeply with the child in this conflict. And he recognised the way in which family structures that violate the individual reflect those of patriarchal society. In 1914 he wrote:

> In the existing family the child, with his beginning capacity to experience, experiences that his inborn character, his inborn will towards his own, his desire to love in the way that is inborn, is neither understood nor wanted by anyone. There is no response to his longing to be redeemed: to keep his own individuality and to be allowed to love according to his own inner laws. Nobody replies to this longing but his own realization to be rejected and suppressed without defense, the realization of the immense loneliness all around. And to this infinite fear of the child in his loneliness, the family, as it exists today, has only one response: be lonely or become the way we are. No human can live without love already as a child. That is impossible [. . .] In the existing family the child has to become like those who surround him [. . .] The fear of loneliness [. . .] forces the child to adapt.
>
> (Gross 1914: 530)

In a way Gross anticipated here what Freud was to call more than 20 years later the narcissistic wound – as well as what Anna Freud would call the 'identification with the aggressor'. Nobody else at that time spoke as compassionately about the situation of the child in the family. These sentences were written some 65 years before Alice Miller's *The Drama of Being a Child* (1995).

The capacity to relate thus became the goal of Gross's therapeutic efforts. Fairbairn would later suggest that 'there was an ego (primitive) present at birth which was libidinally oriented towards an external object' (Clarke 2001). Gross saw this not only in an interpersonal sense, but also – one generation before Wilhelm Reich – in the collective realm of revolutionary politics: the capacity to freely relate as equals:

> The will to relate in contrast to the will to power has to be [. . .] shown as the highest and true goal of revolutions [. . .] It will have to be demonstrated that human nature as it is conceived and inborn in everyone strives towards the two great values of freedom and relationship.
>
> (1919c)

His lifelong concern with ethical issues culminated for Gross in the concept of an 'inborn "i n s t i n c t o f m u t u a l a i d"' (1919b: 682) which he described as the 'basic ethical instinct' (1914: 529). In this Gross was explicitly referring to Kropotkin and his discovery of the principle of mutual aid in the field of biology. Mutuality is a core concept of anarchist thought. Some 150 years previously Proudhon had used the term 'mutualism' for the free relationships of groups of equals that exist through mutual exchange. Kropotkin elaborated this concept in his book *Mutual Aid, a Factor of Evolution*, first published in England in 1902. Contemporary researchers in neurobiology, anthropology and genetics seem to confirm this theory (cf. Chapter 17). According to an article in the *Guardian* newspaper, where Natalie Angier writes about 'Why we can't help helping each other': 'It's not simply noble to be nice to our fellow man – it's hardwired into our genes' (2001: 3). Gross was the first analyst to introduce this ethical concept into psychoanalytic theory and practice.

> [I]nnate among man's most powerful strivings towards his fellow men, beginning in the earliest years and even months of life, is an essentially psychotherapeutic striving. The tiny percentage of human beings who devote their professional careers to the practice of psychoanalysis [. . .] are only giving explicit expression to a therapeutic devotion which all human beings share.

This is neither Kropotkin nor Gross, but Harold Searles writing in 1975 on 'The Patient as Therapist to His Analyst' (1979: 380).

In May 1908 C. G. Jung wrote to Freud about his treatment of Gross at the Burghölzli:

> I have let everything drop and have spent all my available time, day and night, on Gross, to best further his analysis [. . .] Whenever I got stuck, he analyzed me. In this way my own health has benefited.
>
> (Freud and Jung 1974: 153; translation modified)

This is the first testimony of a mutual analysis in which – at least periodically – both partners worked with each other as equals – something Gross had already previously practised with his friends. I believe that C. G. Jung and Otto Gross's mutual analysis can be understood as a key experience that profoundly influenced the formation of Jung's theory which later found ultimate expression in the diagram of dialectic relating (cf. Figure 8.1).

Otto Gross extended this concept of a dialectic relationship from the analytic couple to the way we relate as individuals to the outside world in its political dimension. An important result of his thinking concerns the interrelatedness of the personal, even the profoundly intimate, with the political, as the term 'Sexual Revolution' suggests ideas that only became more widely popular some 50 years later. At the Salzburg Congress of 1908, Freud had responded defensively to Gross: 'We are physicians, and physicians we should remain' (Gross 1913b: 506–507). This echoed the conclusion Freud had reached earlier in the same year at the end of his own tentative critique of society from a psychoanalytic perspective: one of the final sentences of *'Civilized' Sexual Morality and Modern Nervousness* is: 'It is certainly not a physician's business to come forward with proposals for reform' (1908: 204). It was to take more than 20 years before Freud ventured again into the realm of social critique in *Civilization and its Discontents* (1930). Freud's rejection of one of the central notions of his thought, the application of psychoanalytic thinking to culture and society, deeply troubled Gross. In the last of his works published during his lifetime, just weeks before his death, Gross mourns the 'repression of final revolutionary conclusions [. . .] by the ingenious discoverer of the exploratory method' (1920c: 319). Gross held that

> None of the revolutions in the course of history succeeded in establishing freedom for the individual. They all fell flat, each the forerunner of a new bourgeoisie, they ended in a hurried desire to conform to general norms. They all failed because the revolutionary of yesterday carried within himself the authority . . . that puts any individuality in chains.
>
> (1913a: 386)

Psychoanalysis seemed to offer itself as the ideal tool in the revolutionary struggle. With the help of psychoanalysis it would be possible, so Gross hoped, to unchain the psyche. From this perspective

> The psychology of the unconscious is the philosophy of the revolution, i.e. it is qualified to become that as the ferment of revolt within the psyche, as the liberation of the individuality bound by its own unconscious. It is qualified to prepare internally for freedom, qualified as the preparatory work for the revolution.
>
> (ibid.: 384)

Thus, within the development of theory about the essence of the analytic relationship, there are lines that unmistakably spring from Gross's mutual analysis with Jung. These lines, linked, in Gross's case, to the anarchist concept of mutual aid (Kropotkin 1905), lead to what is now called intersubjectivity by some psychoanalysts (Dunn 1995).

I believe that the experience of his mutual analysis with Gross also played an important role in Jung's break with Freud. In his memoirs, Jung recalls as a turning point in his relationship with Freud the moment when, just over a year after his experience of the mutual analysis with Gross, Freud refuses just such a mutuality (Jung 1963: 181–182).

The influence of Gross's ideas on mutuality is not confined to the realm of analysis. I have discovered that Martin Buber knew Gross's work. A fierce dispute with Gustav Landauer, another leading German anarchist, about traditional family values, which the latter wanted to uphold, had brought Gross into indirect contact with the then burgeoning philosopher Martin Buber, a close friend of Landauer's. In 1911, Buber supported Landauer in his decision not to publish Gross's response to Landauer's attacks in his journal *Der Sozialist* (Buber 1911, in Landauer 1929: 383, n. 1) because both agreed that it was 'rubbish'. Nevertheless, in the text in question Buber also encountered Gross's concept of the basic conflict between that which is one's own and that which is the other's – in conjunction with Gross's emphasis on relating, a pre-formulation, one might venture to say, of Buber's own dialogic concept of the 'I–Thou' relationship, which the latter published nearly a decade later (Heuer 2003b). There is also an obvious connection to Jürgen Habermas's 'ideal speech situation' that has not been acknowledged before.

There are a number of other cornerstones of Analytical Psychology of which we can find initial traces and formulations in Gross's work. That they had a direct influence on Jung is not provable in the sense that there is no acknowledgement of Gross by Jung in relation to these thoughts. But can that be expected, if, as I have mentioned, Jung even later removed the reference to Gross that acknowledged his co-authorship in the ideas expressed in *The Influence of the Father*, thus intentionally falsifying the record? And, of course, these traces and first formulations that I point out are just that and not fully worked out concepts as in Jung's later works. Until full and free access to all of Jung's papers is permitted, all that may be stated here is a similarity in a number of key areas that predate Jung's later formulations.

Gross took his ideas about relationship towards a realm that Jung much later would call the *unus mundus*, or the *mundus imaginalis* (Samuels 1989: 161–172), the underlying interconnectednes of all beings, that Samuels, referring to Winnicott, calls 'the third area' (ibid.: 167). This term, also 'the analytic third', is used to describe the area of experience between those who constitute the relationship. Given the influence Gross had on Buber, it is interesting to note that Samuels refers to Buber, too, in this context (ibid.). Like Buber after him, Gross made no distinction between interpersonal relating and relating in the religious realm. In fact, he spoke of relating as constituting the numinous. In 1913 Gross wrote of 'relationship as a third, taken as religion' (1913c: col. 1180). Gross was the first to link analysis with the religious and spiritual realm. He continues to say that, understood in this way, relationship contains the obligation [almost compulsion] towards individualising. This obligation is an automatic showing up of all possibilities of experience, the capacities to maintain all psychical warmth that strives towards general, all-embracing psychical warmth (ibid). In the same year, Gross had stated that sexuality was 'not identical with the individual, but the pure great third' (Gross 1913a: 1142; cf. also Chapter 17).

Jung's responding to Freud's concept of positing a duality of life and death instincts – Eros and Thanatos – by suggesting to replace the latter with the (Nietzschean) 'will to power' (Jung 1917/42: 53) closely corresponds to Gross's much earlier concept of also contrasting 'the will to relating' with 'the will to power'. And when Jung, in his diagrammatic depiction of the psyche in the form of concentric circles where the outer ones stand for the surface layers and the central one for the innermost core, surprisingly understands the latter to be equal with the collective unconscious (Jung 1935: 44), we may understand this as echoing Gross's concept of the personal being the political, i.e. the collective.

A further important influence of Gross in the area of psychoanalysis has only recently come to light, with the discovery of what so far can be assumed to be Gross's final writings (Gross 1920a, 1920b) in the Dorian Feigenbaum bequest kept at the New York Psychoanalytic Institute. Unlike Freud, Ferenczi, Reich and Jung, Dorian Feigenbaum (1887–1937) is no longer a well-known name in psychoanalysis. He met Gross during the First World War in the army and was subsequently analysed by him. For six years he worked as a psychiatrist in Switzerland, then as psychiatric adviser to the government in Palestine, and later emigrated to New York to settle there as a psychoanalyst. In his application to the New York Psychoanalytic Society he gave Gross's name as that of his training analyst. In 1930 Feigenbaum edited a special issue on psychopathology of *The Medical Review of Reviews*, for which Freud wrote an introduction that ended with the words 'It is to be hoped that works of the kind that Dr. Feigenbaum intends to publish in his Review will be a powerful encouragement to the interest in psycho-analysis in America' (Freud 1930b: 255). Feigenbaum was the co-founder in 1932 and editor in chief until his death of the third-oldest psychoanalytic journal, *The Psychoanalytic Quarterly*. In the words of his obituary, 'Dr. Feigenbaum achieved the position he held as one of the outstanding representatives of psychoanalysis in the United States' (Lewin and Zilboorg 1937: 2).

For the assessment of Gross's position in the history of psychoanalysis, this means that one of the leading American psychoanalysts of the Twenties and Thirties had the core of his psychoanalytic training – that always is the training analysis – with Gross.

Some of Gross's ideas on the role of language were later taken up by Lacanian analysts. But his influence was not confined to psychoanalysis. From his psychiatric writings links have been made to Laing and Cooper's Anti-Psychiatry – Gross himself has been called an Anti-Psychiatrist (Hurwitz 1979: 111; Dvorak 1978: 53) – to Foucault's work and to Judith Butler's gender theories (Choluj 2000).

Figure 8.3 Dorian Feigenbaum, 1887–1937, with Otto Gross, at the end of the First World War.

Conclusion

I have argued that Gross significantly influenced the course of analytic theory and clinical practice to the present day. Otto Gross was an 'enthusiast for life-experiment' (Green 1999: xx). He took Freud at his words that 'every psycho-analytic treatment is an attempt at liberating repressed love' (1907: 90) and he tried to live his revolutionary ideas in both his private and his professional life – which he refused to separate. Thus he became unacceptable to those trying to establish the credibility of analysis as a science in the eyes of society and academe in the early years of the last century. Already in 1921, less than a year after his death, Gross's brother-in-law-to-be, the writer Anton Kuh, wrote of him as

> a man known only to very few by name – apart from a handful of psychiatrists and secret policemen – and among those few only to those who plucked his feathers to adorn their own posteriors.
>
> (1921: 161–162)

Perhaps it is only now that we can allow the repressed to return.

Bibliography

Abels, N. (1990) *Franz Werfel*. Reinbek: Rowohlt.

Abraham, K. (1905) Otto Gross: Zur Biologie des Sprachapparates. *Münchner Medizinische Wochenschrift*, *1*, 38–39.

Adler, A. (1997) Über den nervösen Charakter. Grundzüge einer vergleichenden Individualpsychologie und Psychotherapie. In K. H. Witte, A. Bruder-Bezzel and R. Kühn (eds.), *Kommentierte textkritische Ausgabe*. Göttingen: Vandenhoek & Ruprecht.

Angier, N. (2001, 22 September) Why we can't help but help each other, *The Guardian*, *Saturday Review*, p. 3.

Berze, J. and Stelzer, D. K. (1999/2000) Befund und Gutachten (A. Hansen, ed.). *Gegner*, *3*, 24–36.

Clarke, G. (2001, 5 April) Letter to the author.

Choluj, B. (2000) Psychoanalyse und ihre politischen Implikationen nach Otto Gross. In Erich-Mühsam-Gesellschaft (ed.), *Anarchismus und Psychoanalyse zu Beginn des 20. Jahrhunderts. Der Kreis um Erich Mühsam und Otto Gross 19*. Lübeck: Erich-Mühsam-Gesellschaft (pp. 125–134).

Cremerius, J. (1986) Vorwort. In A. Carotenuto (ed.), *Sabina Spielrein. Tagebuch einer heimlichen Symmetrie*. Freiburg: Kore (pp. 9–28).

Dunn, J. (1995) Intersubjectivity in psychoanalysis. *International Journal of Psycho-Analysis*, *76*, 723–738.

Dvorak, J. (1978) Kokain und Mutterrecht. Die Wiederentdeckung von Otto Gross. *Neues Forum, 25*(295/96), 52–64.

Erich-Mühsam-Gesellschaft (ed.) (2000) *Anarchismus und Psychoanalyse zu Beginn des 20. Jahrhunderts. Der Kreis um Erich Mühsam und Otto Gross 19*. Lübeck: Erich-Mühsam-Gesellschaft.

Fairbairn, W. R. D. (1952) *Psychoanalytic Studies of the Personality*. London: Routledge & Kegan Paul.

Ferenczi, S. (1920) Otto Gross: Drei Aufsätze über den inneren Konflikt. *Internationale Zeitschrift für Psychoanalyse, VI*, 364ff.

Frank, L. (1976) *Links wo das Herz ist*. Frankfurt/M: Fischer.

Freud, S. (1907) *Delusions and Dreams in Jensen's* Gradiva. *SE*, Vol. IX. London: Hogarth.

Freud, S. (1908) *'Civilized' Sexual Morality and Modern Nervous Illness*. *SE*, Vol. IX. London: Hogarth.

Freud, S. (1930) *Civilization and its Discontents*. *SE*, Vol. XXI. London: Hogarth.

Freud, S. (1930b) Introduction to the Special Psychopathology Number of *The Medical Review of Reviews*. *SE*, Vol. XXI. London: Hogarth.

Freud, S. and Jung, C. G. (1974) *The Correspondence of Sigmund Freud and C. G. Jung*. London: Hogarth, Routledge & Kegan Paul.

Freud, S. and Ferenczi, S. (1996) *The Correspondence of Sigmund Freud and Sándor Ferenczi. Vol II*. Cambridge, MA and London: Belknap Press of Harvard University.

Freud, S. and Jones, E. (1993) *The Complete Correspondence of Sigmund Freud and Ernest Jones 1908–1939*. Cambridge, MA and London: Belknap Press of Harvard University.

Fromm, E. (1989) Vom Parteigeist der psychoanalytischen Bewegung und ihren Opfern. In *Schriften über Sigmund Freud*. Stuttgart: Deutsche Verlagsanstalt (pp. 195–204).

Green, M. (1999) *Otto Gross. Freudian Psychoanalyst 1877–1920. Literature and Ideas*. Lewiston, NY: Mellen.

Gross, O. (1909) *Über psychopathische Minderwertigkeiten*. Wien and Leipzig: Braumüller.

Gross, O. (1913a) Zur Ueberwindung der kulturellen Krise. *Die Aktion, III*(14), 384–387.

Gross, O. (1913b) Ludwig Rubiner's 'Psychoanalyse'. *Die Aktion, III*(20), 506–507.

Gross, O. (1913c) Notiz über Beziehungen. *Die Aktion*, Vol. 3(51), col. 1180–81.

Gross, O. (1914) Über Destruktionssymbolik. *Zentralblatt für Psychoanalyse und Psychotherapie, IV*(11/12), 525–534.

Gross, O. (1915) Vom Konflikt des Eigenen und Fremden. *Die freie Straße*, 4, 3–5.

Gross, O. (1919a) Die kommunistische Grundidee in der Paradiessymbolik. *Sowjet, 1*(2), 12–27.

Gross, O. (1919b) Protest und Moral im Unbewußten, *Die Erde, 1*(24), 681–685.

Gross, O. (1919c) Zur funktionellen Geistesbildung des Revolutionärs. *Räte-Zeitung, 1*(52), Beilage.

Gross, O. (1920a) Themen der revolutionären Psychologie. In A. Götz von Olenhusen and G. Heuer (eds.), *Die Gesetze des Vaters. 4. Internationaler Otto Gross Kongress, Graz 2003*. Marburg: LiteraturWissenschaft.de (pp. 421–423).

Gross, O. (1920b) Zum Solidaritätsproblem im Klassenkampf. In A. Götz von Olenhusen and G. Heuer (eds.), *Die Gesetze des Vaters. 4. Internationaler Otto Gross Kongress, Graz 2003*. Marburg: LiteraturWissenschaft.de 2005 (pp. 415–421).

Gross, O. (1920c) Zur neuerlichen Vorarbeit: vom Unterricht. *Das Forum*, *4*(4), 315–320.

Gross, O. (1990) The Otto Gross–Frieda Weekley Correspondence. In J. Turner with C. Rumpf-Worthen and R. Jenkins (eds.), *The D. H. Lawrence Review*, *22*(2), 137–227.

Heuer, G. (1996) Letter to the Editor. *International Journal of Psycho-Analysis*, *77*, 395–396.

Heuer, G. (2000) Auf verwehten Spuren verschollener Texte.Verlorene, wiedergefundene und neu entdeckte Schriften von Otto Gross. In R. Dehmlow and G. Heuer (eds.), *1. Internationaler Otto Gross Kongress Berlin*. Marburg/Hannover: LiteraturWissenschaft de./Laurentius (pp. 164–205).

Heuer, G. (2001) Jung's twin brother. Otto Gross and Carl Gustav Jung. *Journal of Analytical Psychology*, *46*(4), 655–688.

Heuer, G. (2003a) Der Außenseiter der Außenseiter. Neues über einen Unbekannten. Entdeckungen zu Johannes Nohl (1882–1963): Leben und Werk. *Juni*, *36/37*, 108–137.

Heuer, G. (2003b) 'Ganz Wien in die Luft sprengen? . . . Das wäre ja wunderbar!' Otto Gross und der Anarchismus. In G. Dienes and R. Rother (eds.), *Die Gesetze des Vaters. Hans und Otto Gross, Sigmund Freud und Franz Kafka*. Wien: Böhlau (pp. 114–125).

Hurwitz, E. (1979) *Otto Gross. Paradies-Sucher zwischen Freud und Jung*. Zürich: Suhrkamp.

Hurwitz, E. (2001) Otto Gross' 'Schizophrenie'. In G. Heuer (ed.), *2. Internationaler Otto Gross Kongress, Burghölzli, Zürich*. Marburg: LiteraturWissenschaft.de.

Jones, E. (1974) *Sigmund Freud. Life and Work. Vol. 2*. London: Hogarth.

Jones, E. (1990) *Free Associations*. New Brunswick, NJ and London: Transaction.

Jung, C. G. (1909a) Letter to Ernest Jones, 25 February 1909. Sigmund Freud Copyrights.

Jung, C. G. (1909b) *The Significance of the Father in the Destiny of the Individual*. CW4.

Jung, C. G. (1917/42) *On the Psychology of the Unconscious*. CW7. London: Routledge & Kegan Paul.

Jung, C. G. (1920) *Psychological Types*. CW6. London: Routledge & Kegan Paul.

Jung, C. G. (1934) *A Rejoinder to Dr. Bally*. CW10. London: Routledge & Kegan Paul.

Jung, C. G. (1935) *The Tavistock Lectures*. CW18. London: Routledge & Kegan Paul.

Jung, C. G. (1936[?]) Letter to Fritz Wittels, 4 January. In Heuer, G. (2001) Jung's twin brother. Otto Gross and Carl Gustav Jung. *Journal of Analytical Psychology*, *46*(4), 670.

Jung, C. G. (1944) *The Psychology of the Transference*. CW16. London: Routledge & Kegan Paul.

Jung, C. G. (1952) *Synchronicity. An Acausal Connecting Principle*. CW8. London: Routledge & Kegan Paul.

Jung, C. G. (1963) *Memories, Dreams, Reflections*. London: Fontana.
Jung, F. (1921) Von geschlechtlicher Not zur sozialen Katastrophe von Dr. med. Otto Gross, nebst einer Einleitung, Biographischem und einer grundlegenden Darstellung psychoanalytischer Ethik als Lebensform und Lebensglaube des Dr. Gross. In J. Michaels (1983) *Anarchy and Eros: Otto Gross' Impact on German Expressionist Writers*. New York, NY: Peter Lang (pp. 183–219).
Jung, F. (1991) *Der Weg nach unten*. Leipzig: Reclam.
Jung, F. (1996) *Briefe 1913–1963. Werke 9/1*. Hamburg: Nautilus.
Kafka, F. (1983) *Briefe an Milena*. Frankfurt: Fischer.
Kaus, O. (1920) Mitteilungen. *Sowjet*, *8/9*, 53–57.
Kropotkin, P. (1905) Anarchism. In R. N. Baldwin (ed.), *Kropotkin's Revolutionary Pamphlets. A Collection of Writings by Peter Kropotkin*. New York, NY: Dover, 1970 (pp. 283–300).
Kuh, A. (1921) *Juden und Deutsche*. Berlin: Reiss.
Landauer, G. (1929) *Ein Lebensgang in Briefen. 1*. (M. Buber, ed.). Frankfurt/M: Rütten & Loening.
Lawrence, F. (1961) *The Memoirs and Correspondence*. London: Heinemann.
Lewin, B. and Zilboorg, G.[1] (1932) In Memoriam. Dorian Feigenbaum, MD, 1887 1937. *The Psychoanalytic Quarterly*, Vol. VI(1), 1–3.
Michaels, J. (1983) *Anarchy and Eros. Otto Gross' Impact on German Expressionist Writers*. New York, NY: Peter Lang.
Miller, A. (1995) *The Drama of Being a Child*. London: Virago.
Russell, R. with Laing, R. D. (1992) *R. D. Laing and Me: Lessons in Love*. Lake Placid, NY: Hillgarth Press.
Samuels, A. (1989) *The Plural Psyche*. London and New York, NY: Routledge.
Searles, H. F. (1979) The Patient as Therapist to his Analyst. In *Countertransference and Related Subjects. Selected Papers*. Madison, WI: International Universities.
Stekel, W. (1925) Zur Geschichte der analytischen Bewegung. *Fortschritte der Sexualwissenschaft und Psychoanalyse*, *2*, 539–575.
Stekel, W. (1950) *The Autobiography of Wilhelm Stekel*. New York, NY: Liveright.
Suttie, I. (1935) *The Origins of Love and Hate*. London: Kegan Paul.
Szittya, E. (1998) *Die Internationale der Aussenseiter*. Freudenstein: Deutsches Monte Verità Archiv.
Szittya, E. (n.d.) *Er sucht einen Namen für seine 80 Jahre*. [Fragment, manuscript] Deutsches Literaturarchiv: Marbach.
Werfel, F. (1990) *Barbara oder Die Frömmigkeit*. Frankfurt, M: Fischer.
Werfel, F. (1992) *Die schwarze Messe. Romanfragment*. Frankfurt, M: Fischer (pp. 159–213).
Whimster, S. with Heuer G. (1998) Otto Gross and Else Jaffé and Max Weber. *Theory, Culture and Society. Special Issue on Love and Eroticism*, *15*(3–4), 129–160.
Winnicott, D. W. (1952) Anxiety associated with insecurity. In *Through Paediatrics to Psycho-Analysis*. London: Hogarth, 1987 (pp. 97–100).
Yalom, I. D. (1999) *Momma and the Meaning of Life*. London: Piatkus.

Note

1 The text is unsigned, but it is clear from the content that the authors are Feigenbaum's two co-editors.

Chapter 9

Wilhelm Reich's theory of sexuality

Nick Totton

Introduction

It has been said more than once that Wilhelm Reich's work recapitulates the earlier theories of Otto Gross. In fact the German radical writer Franz Jung described Reich in easy-to-understand German as 'eine direkte Kopie von Otto Gross's (Jung 1996: 491; quoted in Sheppard 1997: 242). In what follows I will explore the ways in which this is partially true, and the important ways in which it is not. My main focus will be on identifying what is radical and interesting in Reich's ideas about sexuality, and separating this out from what is surprisingly conservative and banal.

At first glance the similarities between Reich and Gross are eerie; it is not hard to produce an identikit account which could be applied equally to either man – a psychoanalyst with a strong personal relationship to Freud, but who fell out with him because of his concrete view of the importance of sexuality and his insistence on drawing radical social conclusions from psychoanalytic theory; a charismatic and authoritative figure who both practised and preached sexual freedom; joined the Communist Party but was closer to anarchism in his approach; was accused of insanity and was imprisoned for his views. Nearly a generation apart in age, the two men seem strikingly similar in their attitudes and activities; they even each had a son called Peter.

Strangely, however, there is little or no reference to Gross in Reich's published writings, even in his letters and diaries. Each of the three great sexual rebels of early psychoanalysis – Gross (1877–1920), Georg Groddeck (1866–1934) and Reich (1897–1957) – seems oddly isolated from the other two, with only occasional and apparently unimportant links between them. This may be because the scholarship on all three is relatively undeveloped (many of Reich's manuscripts, for example, are still unpublished); and perhaps also because the later two, Groddeck and Reich, were both, like many gifted thinkers, somewhat narrowly focused on their own theories and uninterested in other people's ideas.

Reich's sexual theories

Unlike either Gross or Groddeck, who despite their formal links with analysis were both essentially independent, Reich was for years an earnest student of Freudian psychoanalysis and always saw his work unambiguously as carrying forward the implications of Freud's thinking – which in Reich's view Freud himself abandoned (Reich 1972a). 'For seven years I thought that I was working in complete accordance with the Freudian school of thought. No one divined that this line of questioning would lead to a fatal clash' (Reich 1983a: 95). Reich in fact stayed closer to Freud's theory than Freud himself, which was what created the clash: he took up Freud's concept of the so-called 'actual neurosis' (*aktualneurose*, or 'current neurosis'), the here-and-now sexual issue which in Freud's earlier view (Freud 1916–17: 390f) locks a person into a psychoneurosis. Hence two elements are needed for someone to develop neurotic symptoms: a current sexual block caused by external factors, and a sexual conflict deriving from infancy.

In Freud's theory, the here-and-now sexual block – which, significantly for Reich, is understood to give rise primarily to somatic symptoms (Laplanche and Pontalis 1988: 11) – although never repudiated, becomes de-emphasised and fades out of discussion. For Reich almost the opposite happens: the here-and-now block becomes his primary focus, and the infantile conflict is in a sense significant mainly because it helps to create the here-and-now block. Reich believes that 'those who are psychically ill need but one thing – complete and repeated genital gratification'(1983a: 96). Hence the logically central question is: how can this be achieved? How can all obstacles be removed?

A considerable part of Reich's answer lies in a reorganisation of societal rules. Reich was active in campaigning for free access to contraception, abortion and sexual information, beginning with educational sessions for women, men and children held in Viennese parks (Sharaf 1984: 130), and culminating in an entire political mass movement, the German Association for Proletarian Sex Politics or Sex-Pol (Sharaf 1984: 160ff). As part of the Sex-Pol movement Reich also campaigned for young people to be given opportunities for private and hygienic sexual encounters.

But access to sexual intercourse was in Reich's view by no means enough on its own to meet his criteria for '*complete* . . . genital gratification'. By 'complete', Reich meant something a good deal more than male ejaculation, or even simple sexual climax. He coined the term and concept of 'orgastic potency', defined as 'the capacity to surrender to the flow of biological energy, free of any inhibitions; the capacity to discharge completely the dammed-up sexual excitation through involuntary, pleasurable convulsions of the body'(Reich 1983a: 102).

A lot of Reich's thinking can be grasped through unpacking this definition. It clearly draws deeply on Freud's energetic model of the bodymind, often rather confusingly termed the 'economic model', and these days frequently dismissed as an outdated nineteenth-century hydraulic metaphor (e.g. Meissner 1995). However, any theory and practice which is genuinely psycho*somatic*, rather than focused on mental processes in isolation from their embodiment, will necessarily have to take energetic aspects seriously, since for all living organisms their energy economy is a core aspect of their existence. And psychoanalysis is in its origins, as I have argued at length elsewhere, 'centrally the study of how the human mind confronts the impulses of the body – how it denies, represses, ablates, compromises with, permits into split and partial representation those impulses' (Totton 1998: 10). Mainstream psychoanalysis has gone on to emphasise the *mental* effects of this confrontation; Reich, in a perfectly logical reading of Freud's original work, emphasised its *psychophysical* effects.

However, Reich's almost unique strength is that he never splits the physical from the psychological, or indeed, as we shall see, from the psychosocial. His theories highlight the 'functional identity' (e.g. Reich 1983a: 270–1) between a person's psychological character and their embodiment. When Reich speaks of 'surrender' as the key condition for orgastic potency, he takes full account of all its many dimensions, in particular of the way in which most people's character structure is organised to *defend against* surrender, which, as a word and as an experience, has ambivalent implications of both defeat and release. He also notes its gender coding: 'Men who feel that surrender is "feminine" are always orgastically disturbed' (Reich 1983a: 105).

Unfortunately this is pretty much the full extent of Reich's contribution to the deconstruction of gender. Although there is little or nothing in his work which depreciates women (the same is unfortunately not true as regards homosexuality, as we shall see) and although, long before Lacanian feminism, he introduced the term 'patriarchy' into analytic discussion (see for example Reich 1983a: 7–8), Reich seems profoundly uninterested in anything other than a narrowly social egalitarianism of genders. It is hard not to connect this with his obsessive focus on genitality.

Only at the genital stage, in the classic Freudian account of sexual development, are male and female clearly differentiated; and it seems that for whatever reasons, connected or not with his personal history, Reich is deeply uncomfortable with any more ambiguous state of affairs, which he defines repeatedly as 'unnatural', and purely a side effect of the external or internal repression of genitality. 'By and large, pregenital sexuality is antisocial and is at variance with natural feelings' (Reich 1983a: 188) – and by 'pregenital sexuality' Reich basically means anything other than heterosexual penetrative intercourse:

> Now, when the *natural* streaming of the bioenergy is dammed up, it also spills over, resulting in irrationality, perversions, neuroses, and so

> on. What do you have to do to correct this? You must get the stream back into its *normal* bed and let it flow *naturally* again.
>
> (Reich 1967: 43–4, my italics)

And what is 'natural' and 'normal', in Reich's view, is heterosexual penetrative intercourse, preferably in the context of serial monogamy. Thus, although he militantly opposes anti-homosexual legislation, this is on the grounds that 'homosexuality is . . . the result of a very early inhibition of sexual love' (Reich 1969: 209) and therefore an inevitable side effect of life in an anti-sexual society: homosexuals should be helped, not punished.

Reich's position on homosexuality is, in fact, rather similar to Freud's – both men being extremely liberal for their day and age – but it contrasts sharply with Freud's insistence (1905: 144n.) that *all* forms of sexuality *equally* require explanation. Reich parts company with Freud in privileging heterosexual penetration as the one form of sexuality which needs only nature as its explanation. Oddly, he seems quite unaware of this divergence, and does not defend it in the way that he robustly defends other differences from his teacher – another factor which leads one to think that Reich's genital supremacism was not fully available for conscious consideration.

Of course, the theory could still be valid whatever its personal derivation. But Reich's concept of genitality is highly simplistic, and has several unfortunate consequences for his thinking. These include a naive naturalism which identifies a preordained developmental pattern through libidinal stages culminating in the formation of 'decent', 'healthy', 'genital characters' (Reich 1972b: 181–2); and a total blind spot about child sexual abuse, about how children can be damaged by sexual *invasion* as well as by sexual *repression*. Reich of course never anywhere condones the sexual exploitation of children by adults (an absurd projection which has repeatedly been made onto him), but he simply ignores it. This is particularly strange given Reich's extreme sensitivity to other forms of childhood suffering, for example around birth or circumcision (e.g. Reich 1983b: 3–4).

There certainly are features of Reich's early life which provide a context for this aspect of his theory. Reich experienced childhood sexual abuse, which he never acknowledged to *be* abuse, portraying himself rather as an exemplar of healthy childhood sexuality. He was one of many middle class children at this period to be drawn into sexual activity by their nursemaids and other servants, starting for Reich, by his own account, at the age of four (Reich 1990: 6); by the age of ten and a half Reich was in a condition he himself describes as 'sexual hyperesthesia' (ibid: 21–2). At 11, Reich says, he began to have intercourse 'almost every day for years' with a cook. His way of dealing with these experiences was through a theoretical position which normalised them, generalising from his own experiences – an understandable and inevitable feature of any psychological theory; but any theory, to be useful, has to encompass other people's *differences* from oneself.

This, then, is the conservative side of Reich's sexual theories; and it has had a damaging effect on the whole body psychotherapy tradition, so that body psychotherapy has actually tended to be more reactionary around sexuality than therapy as a whole. I am thinking in particular about homophobia: what was progressive in the 1920s was not so in the 1960s, when the prominent Reichian Elsworth Baker announced that 'the basic cause of homosexuality is fear of heterosexuality. Extensive therapy is usually required to cure this condition' (Baker 1967: 89). The founder of bioenergetics, Alexander Lowen, similarly strongly affirms 'normal' heterosexual activity but equally strongly pathologises homosexuality: 'Despite the protestations of some confirmed homosexuals that homosexuality is a "normal" way of life, the average invert is aware that his propensity amounts to an emotional illness' (Lowen 1965: 74).

Perhaps paradoxically, I would argue that Reich's work is actually greatly strengthened if we discount what he himself regarded as its absolute core, his claim that 'orgastic potency' is a necessary and sufficient condition of human decency, productivity and happiness. Reich seems to have no sense of the force of Freud's deconstruction of human sexuality; and little sense, one sometimes feels, of the subtleties, complexities and ambivalences of human desire in general. Although he talks of the need for 'a much deeper grasp of desire', his reduction of desire to genitality is actually *superficial*, and seems to relate to an implicit essentialism of the body, a tendency to privilege unthinking physicality over and against the mental: his genital supremacism is founded on what one might call somatic chauvinism. It is also founded on – or gives rise to – the surprising claim that only penetrative heterosexual intercourse leads to fully satisfying orgasms: a view with which very many people would disagree, some of them – especially women – in fact taking the opposite position (so to speak).

Leaving this on one side, though, enables us fully to recognise the radical side of Reich's position. I suggest that this has three important aspects to it: the first, his campaign for freedom of sexual information and activity, is now commonplace and a part of everyday life in most of the West, but Reich deserves great credit for his pioneering role. The other two are still much less widely accepted or understood: the link between sexual repression, psychological character and muscular tension; and the link between 'orgastic potency' and anti-authoritarianism. I shall look at each of these in turn.

Sex and character

Reich develops the analytic concept of character further than any other theorist before him, making it the cornerstone of his mature analytic technique. He does this because of repeated experiences (common to all the early analysts and many later ones) of analyses which were formally successful but in actuality failures: convincing interpretations back to the oedipal crisis were delivered, but nothing actually got better for the analysand. Many modern analysts might consider that what was often missing was an interpretation of pre-oedipal attachment issues. Reich concluded – and this may ultimately amount to the same thing – that these analyses failed to address *character resistance*: that is, to interpret the *way in which* the analysand speaks, moves, looks, relates, rather than the content as such.

> In addition to the known resistances which are mobilized against each new piece of unconscious material, there is a constant resistance factor which has its roots in the unconscious and pertains not to content but to form. . . . [W]e call this constant resistance factor 'character resistance'.
>
> (Reich 1972b: 51)

In Reich's view, the character structure is available for the purpose of analytic resistance because its whole original function was in fact resistance: the ego's simultaneous defence against both external attack and internal libidinous impulses (which are themselves forbidden expression by external forces). Because the function of character is to ward off threats to the ego, Reich speaks of 'character armour', which we can imagine as plates of hard, dead psychic substance blocking the entry to consciousness of external or internal energies that threaten the stability of the ego. These protective plates, in Reich's imagery, are constructed from bound anxiety. Character armour

> serves on the one hand as a defense against external stimuli; on the other hand, it proves to be a means of gaining mastery over the libido, which is constantly pushing forward from the id . . . Anxiety is constantly being bound in the processes which are at the bottom of the formation and preservation of this armour.
>
> (Reich 1972b: 48)

Hence, the deepest function of character armour is to maintain the repression of sexual impulses, which (in Freud's first theory of anxiety, which Reich continued to maintain), when repressed, transform directly into anxiety. Upthrusting libidinal energy is visualised being blocked by armour which is itself constructed out of previously blocked libido, so that character is constructed like a symptom – is in fact a particular kind of symptom – so as to covertly express both desire and its repression. (There are clinical examples throughout Reich 1972b.)

Reich's rather brilliant next move – and part of what ultimately led to his exclusion from the International Psychoanalytic Association – was to suggest that character armour, along with its associated language of rigidity and defense, is more than a metaphor. Character armour, Reich argues, is 'functionally identical' to 'muscular armour'. There are patterns of defensive rigidity in the body which precisely parallel those in the psyche, each creating and created by, supporting and supported by, the other.

> Muscular attitudes and character attitudes have the same function in the psychic mechanism: they can replace one another and be replaced by one another. Basically, they cannot be separated. They are identical in their function.
>
> (Reich 1983a: 270–1)

Reich's realisation that character is grounded in the musculature is a synthesis of several earlier ideas. One of these is his emphasis, which I have already discussed, on the 'actual neurosis':

> Suddenly it was clear where the problem of quantity [the amount of libido] was to be sought: it could be nothing other than the organic groundwork, the 'somatic core of the neurosis', the actual neurosis which results from dammed-up libido. And, therefore, the economic problem of the neurosis as well as its cure lay, to a large extent, in the somatic sphere, i.e. was accessible only by way of the somatic content of the libido concept.
>
> (Reich 1972b: 14)

Another strand was a question which Reich had long pursued: What, in fact, is resistance? *How* do we resist?

> Until now, analytical psychology has merely concerned itself with *what* the child suppresses and what the motives are which cause him to learn to control his emotions. It does not enquire into the *way* in which children habitually fight against impulses. *It is precisely the physiological process of repression* that deserves our keenest attention.
>
> (Reich 1972b: 300, italics in original)

These 'physiological processes' Reich identifies as primarily techniques of controlling the breathing by tightening the diaphragm and abdominal and chest muscles; this control of the breath eventually draws in all the expressive musculature which would be used to cry, to yell, to hit out and so on. In this idea Reich draws on Freud's famous characterisation of the ego as 'first and foremost a bodily ego' (Freud 1923: 364). However, Reich identifies the ego not with the skin, as Freud does, but with the musculature that lies beneath the skin, and that tenses up to bind anxiety and to inhibit the impulses and expressions that make us anxious.

The ultimate implication of Reich's work, in fact, is that the ego as we usually experience it is functionally identical with muscular tension. I have written elsewhere (Totton and Edmondson 2009) of the 'spastic ego', the characterologically armoured, defended ego which is embodied in and given stability through the patterns of muscular armour in the body. Reich's great achievement is to *bring metapsychology back to the musculature*, at last creating a proper place for energetics within analytic theory, making it possible for the 'information' and 'energy' approaches to psychoanalysis to be brought into coherent relation with each other (Totton 1998).

We can now perhaps offer a clarified and less genitally focused version of Reich's theory of sexuality and biopsychic economy, which emerges most clearly in his critique of the death drive (Totton 1998: Chapter 6; Totton 2006). Human psychosexual economics are organised around the enormous difficulty we have in surrendering to extreme pleasure, which throws the ego 'off guard' and appears to threaten our bodily and psychic integrity, dissolving us into death. Learning to welcome deeply exciting sexual experience is thus a complex and gradual process, bound up with the whole process of maturation, the development of a sense of security which is internal rather than external, and the ability to tolerate a degree of physical and psychic 'violence'. But orgasmic surrender is as important to our well-being as, say, surrender to sleep (although in both cases, some individuals can find alternative means of relaxation).

However, while it will always be *difficult* for the ego to surrender to orgasm, this can become *impossible* through traumatic childhood experiences which reinforce the association between surrender and defeat, and hence the sense that surrender is a threat to survival. (Many of these will be attachment traumas, which is why I suggested above that Reich's theory implicitly gives an important role to pre-oedipal material.) Masochism is one response to this impossibility – 'conserving and warding off' traumatic experience (Reich 1972b: 305), taking up the trauma within the sexual act, and bundling together punishment, death and orgasm (Totton 2006). Unlike Freud, Reich radically separates from these ambivalent attitudes to death the whole question of aggression, which he sees as a natural human function, 'the life expression of the musculature, of the system of movement' (Reich 1983a: 156).

Reich traces the fear of death which emerges in some analysands back to genital anxiety:

> Fear of death and dying is identical with unconscious orgasm anxiety, and the alleged death drive, the longing for disintegration, for nothingness, is the unconscious longing for the orgastic resolution of tension.
> (Reich 1983a: 155)

Freud's revised theory of anxiety (Freud 1926), which treats it no longer as a direct transformation of repressed sexual libido but rather as a 'signal' of the (perceived) danger which leads to that repression – essentially, the threat of castration – is for Reich yet another abandonment of the 'actual neurosis', the direct relationship between sexual frustration and emotional disturbance; Reich tends to see castration anxiety as itself a transformation of orgasm anxiety ('surrender' of the erect penis). He stresses 'a functional antithesis between sexuality and anxiety' (Reich 1972b: 263) – a single bodily energy which turns from one to the other depending on the level of frustration. Freud's abandonment of this view means that 'there is no longer any psychoanalytic theory of anxiety that satisfies the clinical needs' (Reich 1983a: 137).

Reich's picture of the human subject, then, is of a bodymind struggling with the conflict between its drive for self-preservation and its drive for satisfaction – the stability of the spastic ego and its dissolution ('To be or not to be', in fact). The balance swings to and fro between satisfaction and pleasure on the one side (which Reich sees as the foundation for all other life achievements), and frustration and anxiety on the other. Character instantiates an often heroic compromise between these forces, a permanent ego-syntonic symptom, a way of being in the world which expresses both desire and its repression. 'A person's character conserves and at the same time wards off the function of certain childhood situations' (Reich 1972b: 305).

Orgastic potency and anti-authoritarianism

Reich contrasts what he sees as ordinary neurotic character structure with his ideal of the 'genital character', who has reliably achieved orgastic potency. I have already spelt out why I do not believe that the 'genital character' is our salvation, and indicated how it might be that Reich went down this blind alley: effectively, the theory of the genital character is how Reich himself 'conserves and at the same time wards off the function of certain childhood situations' which he himself experienced.

What does seem to me significant and valuable, though, is how Reich sees the 'genital character', what qualities he ascribes to it. They key concept here is *self-regulation*: another of Reich's terms which stitch together the bodily, the psychological and the sociopolitical realms. Self-regulation in the first instance is a bodily state of free pulsation, not inhibited by muscular contraction. According to the principle of functional identity, a person who is somatically self-regulated will also be self-regulated on a psychological level – that is, autonomous, self-motivated and appropriate – and vice versa. Reich opposes self-regulation to external morality:

> Morality functions as an obligation. It is incompatible with the natural gratification of instincts. Self-regulation follows the natural laws of pleasure and is not only compatible with natural instincts; it is, in fact,

> functionally identical with them. . . . Steadily alternating between tension and relaxation, it is consistent with all natural functions. . . . *The person with a healthy, self-regulated structure does not adapt himself to the irrational part of the world; he insists on the fulfilment of his natural rights.*
>
> (Reich 1983a: 181–2, my italics)

This also works the other way around: a person who is able to live a self-regulated life, without interference from others, is likely to be able to sustain somatic self-regulation as well. As one of Reich's most important students puts it:

> The most important condition for enabling the child to keep its free biological pulsation is self-regulation and the opportunity for alive contact with other people who are themselves tolerably free from anxiety and inhibitions.
>
> (Raknes 1971: 171)

However, children's natural, autonomous rhythm of life is very generally interfered with by the distress patterns of the adults around them. Reich points out that 'free, self-regulated behavior fills people with enthusiasm but at the same time terrifies them' (Reich 1983a: 183); and when terrified, people tend to become aggressive and controlling, with the result that the self-regulated pursuit of pleasure begins to feel too dangerous, and the child (or adult) begins to bind anxiety into armouring.

In *The Function of the Orgasm* (1983a), Reich reports drastic changes in his analysands' view of the world following on from the relaxation of their muscular armour and their enhanced capacity for surrender:

> Quite spontaneously, the patients began to experience the moralistic attitudes of the world around them as something alien and peculiar. . . . Their attitude toward their work changed. If, until then, they . . . had considered their work a necessary evil which one takes upon oneself without giving it much thought, now they became discriminating . . . It became an almost intolerable burden. . . . The change in the sexual sphere was just as pronounced. . . . Wives who had patiently endured living with unloving husbands and had submitted to the sexual act out of 'marital obligation' could no longer do so.
>
> (Reich 1983a: 175–7)

Surrender, in other words, is quite the opposite of meek acceptance: if we surrender to our capacity for self-regulation, then we are unable to bear regulation by external forces. Reich may be exaggerating the picture, but I have certainly seen similar changes in my clients and in myself.

The corollary of this, Reich argues, is that character armour is in effect society's way of keeping people obedient to its needs. Sexual energy, which is the source of *all* energy, must be repressed through the mediating mechanism of the family in order to keep workers obedient and docile.

> The family – which is saturated with the ideologies of society, and which, indeed, is the ideological nucleus of society – is . . . the representative of society as a whole . . . The Oedipus complex, like everything else, depends ultimately on the economic structure of society. More, the fact that an Oedipus complex occurs at all must be ascribed to the socially determined structures of the family.
>
> (Reich 1972c: 26)

Hence, 'the character structure is the congealed sociological process of a given epoch' (1972b: xxvi), and each could in principle be deduced from the other.

Reich sees a direct opposition between the family and sexuality expressed in two different relationships between the individual and the outer world. Sexuality (and how much the more true this is if one drops Reich's genitalism!) draws us out into the world to experiment and play, while the family shuts us away from it:

> Sexual desires naturally urge a person to enter into all kinds of relations with the world, to enter into close contact with it in a vast variety of forms. . . . Sexual inhibition is the basis of the familial encapsulation of the individual.
>
> (Reich 1972c: 90)

Reich strongly asserts that external repression precedes and creates internal repression:

> The psychic process reveals itself as the result of a conflict between drive demand and the external frustration of this demand. Only secondarily does an inner conflict between desire and self-denial result . . . The question of why society demands the suppression and repression of drives can no longer be answered psychologically. There are social, more correctly, economic interests that cause such suppressions and repressions in certain eras.
>
> (Reich 1972b: 287)

This leaves some large questions unanswered (how did humans first come to submit to this suppression?) but clears the way for Reich's deeply optimistic view of human nature: at the core, 'under favourable conditions, man is an essentially honest, industrious, cooperative, loving, and if motivated, rationally hating animal' (Reich 1975a: 14). And these 'favourable conditions' are essentially an upbringing which supports the development of our innate tendency to self-regulation.

Conclusion

In my description of Reich's ideas, I have concentrated on his earlier work, up to the mid 1930s. This is emphatically not because I subscribe to the idea once popular in analytic circles that after this Reich went mad (between Parts Two and Three of *Character Analysis* is the usual diagnosis). I find all of Reich's later work interesting and worthwhile, including his investigations of what he names 'orgone energy'. But his important theoretical work on the human psychosexual economy was done in the first half of his career, and that is the subject of this chapter.

In his later work, Reich did lose much of his therapeutic optimism, however; and this optimism about the capacity of therapy to facilitate deep change – including *political* change – is part of what I find attractive about him. The passage quoted above where he describes the (at the time unexpected) changes in his clients' social and political attitudes sums up many of the reasons why I first became a therapist. Everything, of course, turns out to be much more complicated than it looked at first; and Reich's response to this was to invent more and more drastic methods of intervening with – or against – an individual's character structure, methods which eventually could hardly be considered in any sense psychotherapy.

Reich may have come up against the limits of possibility. But in the process he contributed enormously both to psychotherapy and to radical political theory (I first encountered his ideas at the height of the political process kicked off by the May 1968 events, when they were omnipresent). Reich emphasised over and over again that there can be no deep political and social change without a change of character structure: that human beings need to be able to tolerate freedom in order to create it. Reich researched why it is that so many people have a bodily revulsion against freedom; and he found that this revulsion is deeply bound up with what amounts to sexual trauma – not the sexual abuse on which we are so focused today, but the opposite evil of sexual repression, the conditioning of children to fear their own desire. These days sexual repression disguises itself as sexual liberty.

Gross wrote: 'The psychology of the unconscious is the philosophy of the revolution' (Gross 1913: col. 385). This statement is also true from Reich's perspective; but I suspect that he would have meant something very different by it. I see Gross's own intended meaning as paralleling Dada, which later contributed to surrealism: the idea that only through what the surrealists called 'delirium' could bourgeois society be dissolved. Reich's view was much more solidly materialist, and it was from a materialist perspective that he consistently sided, both as a clinician and as a political activist, with the id: the id conceived as the desire of the body. 'The Freudian "unconscious" is present and concretely comprehensible in the form of vegetative organ sensations and impulses' (Reich 1983a: 63).

With this sentence Reich effectively founds body psychotherapy. But he also founds something much more: a concrete politics of the unconscious, which privileges *self-regulation* as the spontaneous state of body, mind, and society. In the social context, self-regulation manifests as what Reich terms 'work democracy' (Reich 1975a: 391ff.): those who do the job determine how it should be done, on every level. But for work democracy and freedom from moralism to be possible, the body and its desires must be self-regulated. Unfortunately, in practice Reich himself sought to regulate other people's sexuality, by instructing them that heterosexual penetrative intercourse was the one true way! Which just underlines how deeply difficult it is for us to pull ourselves up by our own bootstraps:

> *It IS possible to get out of the trap*. However, in order to break out of prison, one must first confess to *being in a prison. The trap is man's* [sic] *emotional structure, his character structure.*
>
> (Reich 1975b: 3, original italics)

References

Baker, E. (1967) *Man in the Trap: The Causes of Blocked Sexual Energy*. New York: Collier.

Freud, S. (1905) *Three Essays on the Theory of Sexuality*, *SE*, Vol. VII. London: Hogarth.

Freud, S. (1916–17) *Introductory Lectures on Psychoanalysis*, *SE*, Vol. XII. London: Hogarth.

Freud, S. (1923) *The Ego and the Id*, *SE*, Vol. XIX. London: Hogarth.

Freud, S. (1926) *Inhibitions, Symptoms and Anxiety*, *SE*, Vol. XX. London: Hogarth.

Gross, O. (1913) Zur Überwindung der sozialen krise. *Die Aktion*, *3*(14), 384–387.

Jung, F. (1996) *Briefe 1913–1963* (S. and F. Mierau, eds.). Hamburg: Nautilus.

Laplanche, J. and Pontalis, J. B. (1988) *The Language of Psychoanalysis*. London: Institute of Psychoanalysis and Karnac.

Lowen, A. (1965) *Love and Orgasm: A Revolutionary Guide to Sexual Fulfilment*. London: Collier Macmillan.

Meissner, W. W. (1995) The economic principle in psychoanalysis: I. Economics and energetics. *Psychoanalysis and Contemporary Thought*, *18*(2), 197–226.

Raknes, O. (1971) Wilhelm Reich and Orgonomy. Harmondsworth: Penguin.

Reich, W. (1967) *Reich Speaks of Freud*. London: Condor.

Reich, W. (1969[1949]) *The Sexual Revolution*. London: Vision.

Reich, W. (1972a[1952]) *Reich Speaks of Freud*. London: Souvenir.

Reich, W. (1972b[1933]) *Character Analysis*. New York: Farrar, Straus and Giroux.
Reich, W. (1972c) *Sex-Pol Essays 1929–34*. New York: Farrar, Straus and Giroux.
Reich, W. (1975a) *The Mass Psychology of Fascism*. Harmondsworth: Penguin.
Reich, W. (1975b) *The Murder of Christ*. London: Souvenir.
Reich, W. (1983a[1942]) *The Function of the Orgasm*. London: Souvenir.
Reich, W. (1983b) *Children of the Future: On the Prevention of Sexual Pathology*. New York: Farrar, Straus and Giroux.
Reich, W. (1990) *Passion of Youth: An Autobiography 1897–1922*. London: Picador.
Sharaf, M. (1984) *Fury on Earth: A Biography of Wilhem Reich*. London: Hutchinson.
Sheppard, R. (1997) Book review. *Journal of European Studies*, *27*(2), 242–3.
Totton, N. (1998) *The Water in the Glass: Body and Mind in Psychoanalysis*. London: Rebus Press/Karnac.
Totton, N. (2006) Birth, death, orgasm and perversion: A Reichian view. In D. Nobus and L. Downing (eds.), *Perversion*. London: Karnac.
Totton, N. and Edmondson, E. (2009) *Reichian Growth Work: Melting the Blocks to Life and Love*. Ross-on-Wye: PCCS Books.

Chapter 10

Otto Gross's influence on German-language writers

Jennifer E. Michaels

Otto Gross's revolutionary psychoanalytical and social theories not only influenced psychoanalysis and radical left-wing and anarchist politics, but also writers. Gross's strong criticism of patriarchal society and his views of a matriarchal utopia where no restraints would hinder individual development seemed to offer solutions to many problems of the times. For some writers, such as Franz Jung and Leonhard Frank, Gross's influence was long lasting, whereas for others, such as Johannes R. Becher and Franz Kafka, it was more fleeting. Still others, such as Max Brod and Oskar Maria Graf, portray Gross figures in their works. This chapter surveys Gross's impact on a variety of creative writers and on one artist, Georg Schrimpf, and highlights aspects of his thinking that they found compelling.

Of the writers in his circle, Gross had the greatest impact on Franz Jung (1888–1963). Jung's social criticism, his views on the social causes of psychological problems and his notion of matriarchy can be traced to Gross. In his 1961 autobiography, *Der Weg nach unten* (The Way Down), Jung gives insights into his relationship with Gross. When Jung and his first wife Margot went to Munich in 1911, where Jung was to continue his studies in economics at the Ludwig-Maximilian University, he joined Erich Mühsam's Tat Gruppe, got to know Gross and became enthusiastic about his theories. Jung criticises Freud and the psychoanalytic movement for discrediting Gross's ideas and blames Freud for not allowing psychoanalysis to develop into a revolutionary movement. After Jung moved to Berlin in 1913, Gross followed. When Gross's father, the criminologist Hans Gross, had his son arrested in 1913 and interned in the psychiatric institute in Tulln, Jung led the campaign to free him. Jung saw the arrest as a misuse of patriarchal authority. He encouraged newspapers to become involved and filled Becher's *Die Revolution* with contributions from writers who protested for the rights of the individual and against patriarchal authority. Jung's successful campaign was a turning point in his life that influenced his later years and gave him greater self-confidence. After Gross's death, Jung reflects that his relationship with Gross was his first experience of a deep friendship and he calls him a great fighter against the prevailing societal order (Jung 1961: 89–92).

Gross's impact on Jung was so strong that Jung planned an edition of Gross's works to be entitled 'Von geschlechtlicher Not zur sozialen Katastrophe' (From Sexual Need to Social Catastrophe) (1921). The edition did not appear, but Jung's long introduction gives insights into Gross's theories and life. Jung focuses on Gross's views on suffering, loneliness and comradeship; his criticism of the patriarchal family, state and religion; and his sexual theories. He likens Gross to Moses, who was allowed to see the Promised Land, but not to enter it. Gross was, in Jung's opinion, a martyr for his ideas (Jung 1921b: 183–219).

Gross provided material and theories for Jung's works. Die Telepathen (1914) and Der Fall Gross (The Case of Gross) (1920) are fictionalised versions of the medical history of Gross's patient, Anton Wenzel Grosz. Gross's affair with the painter Sophie Benz and her suicide provided the plot for Jung's novel *Sophie: Der Kreuzweg der Demut* (Sophie: The Way of Humility) (1915). Jung's focus on tormented relationships, his rejection of the family and authority, his search for community and his advocacy of matriarchy all demonstrate his intellectual debt to Gross. Jung's expressionist novels and stories, such as *Kameraden* (Comrades) (1913), *Sophie* and *Opferung* (Sacrifice) (1916) stress destructive relationships, partly drawn from Jung's own experiences with his wife Margot, but also shaped by Gross's notion of the deformation of relationships between men and women in patriarchal society. In Jung's early works relationships are filled with despair and anguish, and love appears as an illness or madness. Like Gross, Jung believes that the imprisonment of women in patriarchal marriage where they cannot express their sexuality fully leads to their feeling of being violated, and he advocates destroying the patriarchal family and replacing it with a matriarchy. *Sophie*, for example, contains a vision of matriarchy that Jung equates with happiness (Jung 1915: 37–38).

As Jung became increasingly radical (he was one of the founders of the left-wing German Communist Workers' Party) Gross's ideas continued to inform his understanding of revolution and societal change. In his revolutionary works, Jung diagnoses why previous revolutions have failed. Like Gross he believes that for revolution to be successful, the workers and leaders must first free themselves from their repressive upbringings. Of all Jung's works *Die Technik des Glücks* (The Technique of Happiness) (1921a) is closest to Gross's theories in its analysis of the social roots of psychological problems. Jung analyses why people are isolated and afraid of life. In his view, the state forces people to adapt at the expense of their own instincts and destroys their sense of community. For Jung community is essential and like Gross he sees this community as a matriarchy that joins people instead of isolating them and enables them to experience life and love fully. Following Gross Jung argues that society's problems have been caused by the destruction of an earlier matriarchal society by patriarchy, which turned the family into an institution that violates women and children. Because children in such families are forced to adapt, they are destroyed psychologically for life (Jung 1921a: 91–99).

To some extent Gross's theories shaped Dada. Recent scholarship suggests that his ideas informed aspects of Zurich Dada. Unlike Berlin, Zurich Dada was an aesthetic avant-garde movement and rejected politicising art (van den Berg 2002: 243). The Zurich Dadaists, who were aware of Gross's ideas (ibid.: 211), were not interested in his political and matriarchal views, but they were interested in his notions of sexuality. The strongest link to Gross's thinking in Zurich Dada is the concern with erotic misery, the rejection of restrictive bourgeois sexual morality, and the significance of sexuality (ibid.: 251).

Jung conveyed Gross's ideas to the more political Berlin Dada, in which he was active from 1916–1919, and he used his journal, *Die freie Strasse* (The Free Street), to spread Gross's ideas. According to Raoul Hausmann its goal was to disseminate a new psychoanalysis formulated by Gross, and the writers and artists connected to *Die freie Strasse* developed a new attitude to society and art that rejected conventions. In Hausmann's view, Gross's ideas formed the theoretical basis on which the Dada movement in Berlin was built (Hausmann 1965: 232). In its six issues from 1915 to 1917, two of which Jung published, *Die freie Strasse* propagated freedom for the individual, the transformation of relationships between men and women and a new ethic based on psychoanalysis. Most of the journal's contributors – such as Jung, Cläre Otto (later Jung) and Richard Oehring – deal with various aspects of Gross's thought. The fourth issue, published by Gross in 1916, contains his essay Vom Konflikt des Eigenen und Fremden (About the Conflict between the Own and the Strange), an excerpt from Über Destruktionssymbolik (About Symbolism of Destruction) (1914), in which Gross attacks repressive moral values and their harmful effects on children and, drawing on Bachhofen and Engels, argues for a matriarchal society.

The artist Georg Schrimpf (1889–1938), a friend of Oskar Maria Graf's, knew Jung and Gross through Mühsam's Tat Gruppe. Schrimpf, who was drawn to Max Stirner's anarchism, was attracted to Gross's views of the emancipation of women through a matriarchal society. Schrimpf designed a title vignette for five of the six numbers of *Die freie Strasse*, and published the second number himself. The vignette depicts four abstract naked female figures, and his pictures in the second number and his other expressionist works show powerfully built matriarchal earth mother figures, an indication of the strong influence Gross had on him at this time. In his expressionist pictures and woodcuts, such as his oil painting Kameraden (Comrades), Schrimpf often portrays women, marching steadfastly forward into a better future. Schrimpf learned from Gross the importance of knowing oneself. Like Gross Schrimpf believed that only through such knowledge could old ideas be destroyed to make room for a better future. At that time Schrimpf considered such ideas as goals of his art, through which he hoped to communicate a vision of a better world.

Raoul Hausmann (1886–1971), an active member of Berlin Dada, wrote five articles in *Die Erde* (The Earth) in 1919 that show clear signs of Gross's influence. Hausmann was drawn especially to Gross's notion of the conflict between 'das Eigene' (one's own instincts) and 'das Fremde' (pressures from outside). Gross's views changed Hausmann's thinking and he became a missionary for new forms of community and new models of social and sexual relationships, and a propagandist for the destruction of patriarchal family and social structures (Züchner 2000: 89). Between 1916 and 1920 Hausmann was fascinated by Gross's notion of a matriarchal model of happiness (ibid.: 90). Gross was not, however, radical enough for Hausmann, who thought that Gross did not offer solutions to the problems he defined (ibid.: 92). Hausmann came to believe that a communist revolution would destroy patriarchy and bring about a sexual revolution. In his *Erde* articles Hausmann documents the damage caused by patriarchal society and argues for abolishing it. In his view, liberating women will lead to a matriarchy and to promiscuity of which he approves since, in his view, sexual faithfulness in marriage exploits women and reduces them to prostitutes. He believes that all sexual relations – those between men and women, and those between the same sex – should be left solely to the individual. Following Gross, Hausmann defends homosexuality as a natural instinct that should not be repressed.

Leonhard Frank (1882–1961) was impressed with Gross's insights into the devastating effects of society on the individual, a topic that is central to such works as *Die Räuberbande* (The Robber Band) (1914) and *Die Ursache* (The Cause) (1915). In these and other works Frank deals with the conflict of the individual with patriarchal society, with family, school and the law, and he depicts the individual's despairing search for identity. In his autobiographical novel *Links wo das Herz ist* (Left where the Heart is) (1952), Frank looks back from his perspective in 1952 to his years in Schwabing and gives a critical picture of Gross, whom he calls Dr. Otto Kreuz. Frank offers insights into Gross's drug addiction. Overcoming this addiction was difficult for Gross because he felt that without drugs he was unable to work. Although Frank was impressed with Gross's theories, he also warned about the danger of carrying them too far. The fate of Sophie Benz, Frank's former mistress, exemplifies for him Gross's misuse of power over people, and he holds Gross responsible for her suicide. Despite his bitterness about Gross's treatment of Sophie Benz, Frank respected Gross's theories all his life and was grateful for the 'education' he received at the University Café Stefanie (Frank 1952: 49).

Frank was receptive to Gross's theories because they gave him insights into his own repressive upbringing and an understanding of the causes of conflict between the individual and society. In many works, Frank blames the family and society for the problems of his protagonists. Like Gross he believes that the authoritarian patriarchal family enslaves the individual and causes the conflict between 'das Eigene' and 'das Fremde' that leads to psychological illness. In his first novel, *Die Räuberbande* (1914), for example, he depicts a society that mistreats and humiliates young people. There are clear parallels to Frank's own life, but his analysis of the causes of his protagonists' suffering is based on Gross's insights. Frank describes how the repression of children begins in the authoritarian family and continues at school where submission is beaten into them, destroying their sense of self. In Frank's next work, *Die Ursache* (1915), the psychological destruction that leads to the suicide of Michael Vierkant, one of the main characters in *Die Räuberbande*, leads to execution. Frank combines here Gross's psychoanalytical insights with a passionate denouncement of the death penalty. He uses Gross's theories to explain his protagonist, Anton Seiler's, behaviour. Frank depicts the brutal education methods in his family and school that lead to Seiler's inner deformation. Seiler has been so tormented and humiliated by his teacher that he is driven years later to kill him. Like Gross Frank believes that people are inherently good, but society poisons them and transforms them into soulless automatons. In contrast to the constraints of patriarchal society, Frank imagines a community of freedom and love where all live together in peace and where people are free to develop.

Franz Werfel's (1890–1945) confrontation with Gross and his theories in the decade from the end of the First World War was important for the development of his worldview and his works. Werfel got to know Gross in July 1917 at Max Brod's in Prague (Anz 2000: 133). When Werfel moved to Vienna in 1917 his friendship with Gross and his fascination with Gross's ideas deepened. Both were involved in the same artistic and revolutionary circles and took part in preparations for the 1918 revolution in Vienna. In Werfel's novel fragment Die schwarze Messe (The Black Mass) (1920b), the play *Schweiger* (1922) and the novel *Barbara oder Die Frömmigkeit* (The Pure in Heart) (1929), Gross appears as a character, and Gross's ideas feature in Werfel's other works at this time. Gross's concept of a matriarchal prehistoric utopia is central to Die schwarze Messe. His view of the patriarchal family, his rejection of militarism and of patriarchal society, and his ideas on revolution are important in such texts as *Nicht der Mörder, der Ermordete ist schuldig* (Not the Murderer, the Murdered is Guilty) (1920a) and *Barbara*. While Werfel admired Gross, he was also critical of him. This ambivalence became more pronounced as Werfel fell under Alma Mahler's influence and turned to Christianity.

Werfel's ambivalence to Gross is evident in the Gross figures in his works. In Die Schwarze Messe, begun in 1919, the charismatic and demonic Dr. Grauh resembles Gross. Like other Gross figures in Werfel's works, Grauh is addicted to drugs. For Werfel, Grauh's longing for an apocalyptic catastrophe is far too radical. In *Schweiger* Werfel portrays the Gross figure, Dr. Ottokar Grund, as a psychopath and monster (Anz 2000: 134). Kafka, who at this time valued Gross highly, was indignant about what he viewed as Werfel's defamation of Gross (Anz 2000: 133). The most detailed depiction of Gross in Werfel's works is Gebhart in *Barbara*. Werfel describes him as having the eyes of a fanatic and likens him to a bird of prey. The protagonist Ferdinand is both attracted and repelled by Gebhart and his theories. When Ferdinand stays with Gebhart and some of his women disciples he is disgusted by the squalor of the room and its inhabitants. Particularly distressing to him is how Gebhart and the others neglect Lisa's sickly child, the fruit of Gebhart's stress on free love. This and other scenes in the novel show Werfel's scepticism about Gross's notion of free love. In Werfel's opinion free love does not emancipate women, but rather exploits and enslaves them. Ferdinand concludes, however, that Gebhart was the most important person he had ever met (Werfel 1929: 579).

Werfel also examines Gross's views on matriarchy. In the chapter Die Satanische Genesis (The Satanic Genesis) in Die schwarze Messe Grauh talks about the transition from a life-affirming religion based on nature to a life-denying patriarchal monotheism. In Grauh's interpretation, God is the usurper and Lucifer the liberator. Astaroth, the later Greek goddess Astarte, is the fruitful goddess, whereas the prophet Elias is the destroyer who is hostile to life (Puttkamer 1952: 42). In *Barbara* Gebhart similarly views the transition from matriarchy to patriarchy as a catastrophe, and he blames this change for monotheism, monogamy and psychological illness. In his view, Astarte worship was a religion of love that affirmed human instincts in contrast to the will to power of monotheism (Werfel 1929: 348).

Despite Werfel's ambivalence, he agreed in principle with Gross's analysis of patriarchal society. In *Nicht der Mörder, der Ermordete ist schuldig*, Werfel examines the destructiveness of patriarchal society. The protagonist, Karl, is so psychologically damaged by his tyrannical officer father, whose uniform represents the repressive power of the state, that he contemplates killing him. When Karl visits anarchist circles, he learns about the damage patriarchy causes and its destruction of an original free matriarchy. The views Werfel expresses in this novella, the notions of matriarchy and the patriarchal state, and the analysis of the psychological damage caused by patriarchy, are taken almost word for word from Gross. Both Gross and Werfel were convinced that society must be changed. After Werfel's brief involvement in the 1918 revolution in Vienna, he began to disagree with Gross's belief that patriarchal society should be destroyed through revolution. Werfel's attitude was pacifistic and his worldview became increasingly metaphysical and religious. He was sceptical of activism since he believed that in their determination to change the world activists forgot the individual (Werfel 1917: 560–575).

Werfel's familiarity with Gross's ideas was important for his later works. Adolf Klarmann argues that Die schwarze Messe has an important place in Werfel's creative development because it anticipates themes of Werfel's Jeremias novel and his novel *Stern der Ungeborenen* (Star of the Unborn) (1946) (Klarmann 1961: 21). In his view, works such as *Barbara* are important stages in Werfel's development, leading to *Das Lied von Bernadette* (Song of Bernadette) (1941) and to *Stern der Ungeborenen* (Klarmann 1954: 45). Werfel's confrontation with Gross's theories provided a bridge connecting his expressionist works to his later, more conservative and religious ones.

Although there is no direct evidence that Robert Musil (1880–1942) either knew Gross personally or knew of his ideas, he did know people – such as his friend Karl Otten – who were familiar with Gross's theories, and it is possible that he included them in his play *Die Schwärmer* (The Enthusiasts) (1921), begun in 1907 and completed in 1921. Martin Green argues that the play shows 'a more vivid attention to and better sense of Gross than all the other sources' (Green 2005: 68). In his essay about his film of *Die Schwärmer* (1985) the director Hans Neuenfels argues that Musil was inspired, especially in his depiction of Anselm in the play, by the phenomenon of a man like Otto Gross (Neuenfels 1985: 14), and that there are parallels between Anselm and Gross. Neuenfels bases his film of the play on the story of Gross and his father Hans. In Neuenfels' version Anselm is a former lecturer in psychoanalysis, and Josef, Regine's husband, is a professor of law. These professions, which do not appear in Musil's play, underscore the similarities between the guru-like Anselm and Otto Gross, and the representative of patriarchal society Josef and Hans Gross. Neuenfels chose this interpretation because he was convinced that the parallels were too clear to ignore (Neuenfels 1985: 14).

Although there are parallels to Musil's own life in the play, Neuenfels is correct in pointing out similarities to Gross. In the play, Anselm has a relationship with two sisters, Regine and Maria. In 1907 Gross had relationships with two sisters – Else von Richthofen, at that time Else Jaffé, and Frieda von Richthofen, at the time of her affair with Gross Frieda Weekley and later D. H. Lawrence's wife. The situation also calls to mind Gross's relationships in 1915–1916 with the Kuh sisters – Marianne, with whom he had a daughter, Sophie, in 1916, Nina, and perhaps also Margarethe. When Josef threatens Anselm with the police and with a psychiatric institution, his behaviour parallels that of Hans Gross, who had his son arrested and confined to a psychiatric institution, although Josef's words remain only a threat.

People who knew Gross would have seen similarities between Anselm and Gross. Musil's physical description of Anselm is similar to depictions of Gross in works by Werfel and Frank. Musil's themes, such as the relationship between men and women and the sharp criticism of marriage, are also similar to Gross's views. Musil depicts Josef and Regine's marriage as one in which the wife has no possibility to develop. Similarly, the marriage between Thomas and Maria allows no possibilities for growth since Thomas suppresses Maria's spontaneity. Because these marriages lead to desolation, loathing and alienation, Anselm finds it essential to free Maria and Regine so that they can fully develop themselves as individuals, and an important part of this development is that they understand the power of eros. Coetzee observes: 'In asserting the sexual relation as the fundamental cultural relation, and in advocating a sexual revolution as the gateway to a new millennium, Musil is curiously reminiscent of his contemporary, D. H. Lawrence' (Coetzee 1999: 53). Lawrence's depiction of eros was, of course, strongly informed by Gross. Musil was long interested in how people could live more intense lives (Musil 1955: 95). His emphasis in *Die Schwärmer* on becoming, on the role of sexuality in intensifying consciousness and on the emancipation of the individual from a repressive patriarchal society were all concepts dear to Gross.

Karl Otten (1889–1963) belonged to Gross's circle in Schwabing before the First World War. In his autobiographical novel *Wurzeln* (Roots) (1963), Otten recognises the important role that Gross played in his life in his Schwabing years when Gross analysed him. In *Wurzeln* Dr. Othmar, a fictionalised Gross, appears in the chapter in which Otten describes his Munich period. This chapter, Permanente Analyse als Weg zur Freiheit (Permanent Analysis as the Way to Freedom), suggests that Otten valued analysis as a technique to emancipate the individual. Otten employs irony to describe Gross and his disciples. His protagonist, Aage, feels like a laboratory animal when he is analysed, and instead of giving him insights into himself the analysis confuses him. Otten also uses irony to portray the political strategies of the Gross circle. Othmar and his disciples want to destroy the family, emancipate women and abolish marriage, property and the state. Psychoanalysis represents for them the essential preliminary work for revolution because they are convinced that revolutionaries must first free themselves from their own repressions before they can free others. These 'revolutionaries', however, lack the will for action and instead concentrate on writing speeches and manifestoes, whereas Aage wants to begin a revolution immediately. Aage, however, recognises the importance of Othmar's analytical method as a tool to dissect society and he is happy that he was analytically schooled (Otten 1963: 256). Otten's politics were largely formed by his brutal family experiences in his youth and his contacts to revolutionary political and artistic circles before he met Gross. Gross gave him, however, the analytical tools to dissect society. Otten was convinced of the importance of analysis. Permanente Analyse als Weg zur Freiheit thus became integral to his worldview.

During his years in Munich, Gross influenced other writers to some extent. In his autobiographical novel *Abschied* (Farewell) (1940), Johannes R. Becher (1891–1958) relates how his experiences in the Café Stefanie helped him break away from home, change his worldview, and develop his writing. In the café, Becher got to know Dr. Hoch (Gross) and Stefan Sack (Leonhard Frank). Discussions in the Café Stefanie changed his writing. He ignored grammatical rules, no longer rhymed his poetry and put punctuation marks everywhere. Although Becher repudiated his bohemian life when he joined the Communist Party in 1919, it was nevertheless important in helping him form his view of society and his writing style. Like most of Gross's circle, Becher suffered from a patriarchal upbringing, and his understanding of patriarchal society owes much to Gross. In *Abschied* and other works, Becher assaults fathers as representatives of the state and shows their damaging influence on their sons. As *Abschied* also demonstrates, Becher learned from Gross about the importance of the erotic and the need to build a community where people could be free and where there were no conventions to inhibit them, a utopia that Becher later hoped that communism would bring about.

Oskar Maria Graf (1894–1967) was also a member of the Gross circle and of Mühsam's Tat Gruppe, but became critical of bohemian life. In his autobiography *Wir sind Gefangene* (We are Prisoners) (1927) and in the later autobiographical novel *Gelächter von Aussen* (Laughter from Outside) (1966), a title that suggests Graf's individualism, he depicts bohemian life in Munich and Berlin. He soon tired of it since Gross and his circle philosophised, fought or psychoanalysed. Graf was a close friend of Schrimpf and describes other friendships with Otten, Becher, Jung and Frank. The orgies he depicts appealed to his views of sexual liberation and he liked to shout: 'More eroticism! More sexuality!' (Graf 1966: 326). Graf gives an ironic picture of Gross and his disciples, who talked about freedom and were hostile to the state and militarism. Graf was therefore stunned when at the outbreak of the war many of them enthusiastically enlisted. For him this was betrayal. Although Graf knew Gross's ideas, there is little trace of them in his works, except for his depictions of the Gross circle.

In 1917 Max Brod (1884–1968) and Franz Kafka (1883–1924) got to know Gross in Prague. Gross and Brod had common interests in psychology, anarchism and the erotic. In *Das grosse Wagnis* (The Great Venture) (1918), Brod depicts a bohemian community similar to the one in Ascona, and its leader, Dr. Askonas, has traits of Gross. Askonas believes that to live contrary to one's instincts causes irreparable damage to one's inner life and that a healthy society can only be built on healthy relationships. His colony, Liberia, appears to be an ideal, utopian community, but underneath are dissatisfactions. Some stem from Askonas's theory, and particularly his practice, of free love, and others are caused by the colony's lack of freedom. The narrator is fascinated and repelled by Askonas's experiment in forming a colony. He is intrigued with Askonas's ideas of salvation and community, but objects to the colony's restrictive structure, thereby questioning the feasibility of such a community.

Gross and Kafka planned to publish a journal to be called Blätter zur Bekämpfung des Machtwillens (Pages for Fighting Against the Will to Power) (Anz 2000: 133), a plan that did not materialise. Kafka respected Gross, as his outrage at Werfel's depiction of Gross in *Schweiger*, mentioned earlier, indicates. Kafka, who was familiar with Freud's theories, was sceptical of psychoanalysis, yet he often applied psychoanalysis to his own experiences, evident, for example, in *Brief an den Vater* (Letter to the Father) (1919). Kafka expresses his criticism of his father more in Grossian than Freudian terms, since he focuses on the tyranny of authoritarian fathers and their psychological destruction of their sons – a topic that appears in several of his works – rather than on the oedipal complex. Anz also points out similarities between the sudden arrest of Josef K. in the novel *Der Prozess* (The Trial), begun in 1914 but published only in 1925, and Hans Gross's arrest of his son (Anz 2000: 132–133).

Gross may have briefly influenced Walter Hasenclever (1890–1940), particularly in his play *Der Sohn* (The Son), written in 1913–14. Emil Szittya asserts that everything Hasenclever knew about psychoanalysis came from Gross (Szittya 1923: 150). It is unlikely that Hasenclever had personal contact with Gross, but he knew people who knew Gross and his theories. When Hasenclever was in Leipzig from 1909–1914 he was active in expressionist circles where Becher, Brod, Kafka and Werfel played a role. Moreover, Hasenclever's high school friend Otten knew Gross in Schwabing. In *Der Sohn* there is a strong affinity between some of Hasenclever's ideas and those of Gross, in particular the focus on the father–son conflict, the attack on patriarchal authority and the stress on the healing nature of the erotic. In *Der Sohn* the father sends the police after his son, has him handcuffed and threatens to put him in an asylum, an action similar to Hans Gross's arrest of his son. The effect of the son's repressive upbringing, something that Hasenclever experienced himself, is depicted in Grossian terms, since the son, over whom the father has complete power, has no confidence in himself and contemplates suicide. In Gross's view, such death wishes resulted from the psychological damage fathers inflicted on their sons.

Through Margot Jung, Curt Corrinth (1894–1960) was influenced by Gross's notion of sexual freedom. Corrinth's early works focus on brotherhood, harmony and freedom. After he met Margot, Corrinth started to believe that salvation lay in sexual freedom, as the novel *Potsdamer Platz oder die Nachte des neuen Messias* (Potsdam Square or the Nights of the New Messiah) (1919) demonstrates. Its protagonist, Hans Termaden, founds a sexual colony in Berlin and becomes the messiah of the erotic. From all over the world, people stream to Berlin to find sexual fulfilment. The authorities are worried since too many children are born without fathers, and children and wives flee to Berlin, causing the city's population to increase while the rest of the world loses population. The messiah of sexuality defeats the authorities when the armies around Berlin desert after seeing Termaden's female disciples doing a strip tease. The erotic wins and a new age of brotherhood and peace dawns. At the end the messiah rises to heaven on a white cloud. Corrinth's other expressionist novels go even further in dealing with sexual potency, orgies and sexual freedom. Through his exaggerations, in which the whole world becomes a brothel, Corrinth gives a satiric rendering of Gross's beliefs and intends to shock and provoke his readers. His interest in depicting sexual freedom lasted, however, only a few years.

Gross and his theories clearly had an impact on a variety of writers. He had a personal magnetism that was almost hypnotic, at least initially. Gross's attacks on patriarchal society and authoritarianism, his stress on sexual and political freedom and his vision of a free matriarchal society appealed in various degrees to the writers discussed above. Although many were ambivalent to Gross, seeing him as a liberating guru figure but also as one who irresponsibly misused his power over others, most recognised his importance in their development. In their depictions, Gross emerges as a figure of contradictions, as one who wanted to change the world, but could not overcome conflicts within himself, as one who passionately advocated community, but was himself a lonely outsider at the end of his life, as one who hoped to change the world, but was bitterly disappointed before his death that his dream of a matriarchal utopia remained only a dream.

Bibliography

Anz, T. (2000). Früher Verrat an der expressionistischen Generation: Franz Werfels Diffamierung von Otto Gross in der Novelle *Nicht der Mörder, der Ermordete ist schuldig*. In *1. Internationaler Otto Gross Kongress*. (R. Dehmlow and G. Heuer eds.). Marburg: LiteraturWissenschaft.de (pp. 132–137).

Becher, J. R. (1940). *Abschied*. Moscow: Das Internationale Buch.

Brod, M. (1918). *Das grosse Wagnis*. Leipzig: Wolff.

Coetzee, J. M. (1999). The Man with Many Qualities. *New York Review of Books*, *46*(5), 52–55.

Corino, K. (2003). *Robert Musil: Eine Biographie*. Reinbek: Rowohlt.

Corrinth, C. (1919). *Potsdamer Platz oder die Nächte des neuen Messias*. Munich: Georg Müller.

Frank, L. (1914). *Die Räuberbande*. Munich: Nymphenburger, 1951.

Frank, L. (1915). *Die Ursache*. Leipzig: Insel.

Frank, L. (1952). *Links wo das Herz ist*. Munich: Nymphenburger.

Die freie Strasse: Erste bis sechste Folge der Vorarbeit. (1915–1917), rpt. Nendeln: Kraus, 1978.

Graf, O. (1927). *Wir sind Gefangene: Ein Bekenntnis aus diesem Jahrzehnt*. Berlin: Aufbau, 1948.

Graf, O. (1966). *Gelächter von Außen: Aus meinem Leben 1918–1933*. Munich: Desch.

Green, M. (2005). The Dreamers: Otto Gross and Robert Musil. In *Die Gesetze des*

Vaters: 4. Internationaler Otto Gross Kongress. (A. Götz von Olenhusen and G. Heuer eds.). Marburg: LiteraturWissenschaft.de (pp. 63–69).
Gross, O. (1914). Über Destruktionssymbolik. *Zentralblatt für Psychoanalyse und Psychotherapie*, *4*, 525–534.
Hasenclever, W. (1914). *Der Sohn*. Berlin: Propyläen, 1917.
Hausmann, R. (1919a). Der Besitzbegriff in der Familie und das Recht auf den eigenen Körper. *Die Erde*, Vol. 1, No. 8, rpt. Nendeln: Kraus, 1970 (pp. 242–245).
Hausmann, R. (1919b). Der individualistische Anarchist und die Diktatur. *Die Erde*, Vol. 1, No. 9, rpt. Nendeln: Kraus, 1970 (pp. 276–278).
Hausmann, R. (1919c). Zur Weltrevolution. *Die Erde*, Vol. 1, No. 12, rpt. Nendeln: Kraus, 1970 (pp. 368–371).
Hausmann, R. (1919d). Zur Auflösung des bürgerlichen Frauentypus. *Die Erde*, Vol. 1, No. 14–15, rpt. Nendeln: Kraus, 1970 (pp. 461–465).
Hausmann, R. (1919e). Schnitt durch die Zeit. *Die Erde*, Vol. 1, No. 18–19, rpt. Nendeln: Kraus, 1970 (pp. 539–547).
Hausmann, R. (1965). Club Dada. In P. Raabe (ed.), *Expressionismus: Aufzeichnungen und Erinnerungen der Zeitgenossen*. Olten: Walter (pp. 232–234).
Hurwitz, E. (1979). *Otto Gross: Paradies-Sucher zwischen Freud und Jung*. Zurich: Suhrkamp.
Jung, F. (1913). *Kameraden*. Heidelberg: Weissbach.
Jung, F. (1914) Die Telepathen: Eine Novelle. In *Die Aktion*, Vol. 4, 743–749.
Jung, F. (1915). *Sophie: Der Kreuzweg der Demut*. Berlin-Wilmersdorf: Verlag der Wochenschrift *Die Aktion*.
Jung, F. (1916). *Opferung*. Berlin-Wilmersdorf: Verlag der Wochenschrift *Die Aktion*.
Jung, F. (1920). Der Fall Gross. In K. Otten (ed.), *Ego und Eros: Meistererzählungen des Expressionismus*. Stuttgart: Goverts, 1963 (pp. 201–220).
Jung, F. (1921a). *Die Technik des Glücks*. Berlin: Malik.
Jung, F. (1921b). Von geschlechtlicher Not zur sozialen Katasprophe. In Michaels, J. (1983). *Anarchy and Eros: Otto Gross's Impact on German Expressionist Writers*. New York: Peter Lang (pp. 183–219).
Jung, F. (1961). *Der Weg nach unten: Aufzeichnungen aus einer grossen Zeit*. Neuwied: Luchterhand.
Kafka, F. (1919). *Brief an den Vater*. Frankfurt: Fischer, 1994.
Kafka, F. (1925). *Der Prozess*. Berlin: Verlag Die Schmiede. Published in 1937 as *The Trial* (W. and E. Muir, Trans.). New York: Knopf.
Klarmann, A. (1954). Das Weltbild Franz Werfels. *Wissenschaft und Weltbild: Zeitschrift für Grundfragen der Forschung und Weltanschauung*, Vol. 7(1–2), 35–48.
Klarmann, A. (1961). Einleitung. In A. Klarmann (ed.), *Franz Werfel, Das Reich der Mitte*. Graz: Stiasny (pp. 5–41).
Michaels, J. (1983). *Anarchy and Eros: Otto Gross' Impact on German Expressionist Writers*. New York: Peter Lang.
Michaels, J. (2006). Ist Anselm ein Porträt von Otto Gross? Mögliche Kontakte zwischen Otto Gross und Robert Musil. In G. Heuer (ed.), *Utopie und Eros: Der Traum von der Moderne*. Marburg: LiteraturWissenschaft.de (pp. 349–366).

Musil, R. (1921). Die Schwärmer. In A. Frisé (ed.), *Robert Musil, Prosa, Dramen, Späte Briefe*. Hamburg: Rowohlt, 1957 (pp. 303–401).

Musil, R. (1955). *Tagebücher, Aphorismen, Essays und Reden* (Frisé, A., ed.). Hamburg: Rowohlt.

Neuenfels, H. (1985). Die Biographie der Unruhe. In *Robert Musil Die Schwärmer: Ein Film*. Reinbek: Rowohlt (pp. 7–54).

Otten, K. (1963). *Wurzeln*. Neuwied: Luchterhand.

Puttkamer, A. von. (1952). *Franz Werfel: Wort und Antwort*. Würzburg: Werkbund.

Storch, W. (1985). *Georg Schrimpf und Maria Uhden: Leben und Werk*. Berlin: Charlottenpresse.

Szittya, E. (1923). *Das Kuriositäten-Kabinett: Begegnungen mit seltsamen Begebenheiten, Landstreichern, Verbrechern . . . Konstanz*: See, rpt. Nendeln: Kraus, 1973.

van den Berg, H. (2002). '. . . wenn sich der Sexus meldet': Otto Gross und die Imagination und Repräsentation des Sexuellen im Kreis der Zürcher Dadaisten. In G. Heuer (ed.), *2. Internationaler Otto Gross Kongress*. Marburg: LiteraturWissenschaft.de (pp. 207–264).

Wagener, H. (1993). *Understanding Franz Werfel*. Columbia: University of South Carolina Press.

Werfel, F. (1917). Die christliche Sendung. In A. Klarmann (ed.), *Zwischen Oben und Unten: Prosa, Tagebücher, Aphorismen, Literarische Nachträge*. Munich: Langen-Müller, 1975 (pp. 560–575).

Werfel, F. (1920a). Nicht der Mörder, der Ermordete ist schuldig. In *Die schwarze Messe: Erzählungen*. Frankfurt: Fischer, 1989 (pp. 214–335).

Werfel, F. (1920b). Die schwarze Messe: Romanfragment. In *Die schwarze Messe: Erzählungen*. Frankfurt: Fischer, 1989 (pp. 159–213).

Werfel, F. (1922). *Schweiger. Ein Trauerspiel in drei Akten*. Munich: Wolff.

Werfel, F. (1929). *Barbara oder Die Frömmigkeit*. Frankfurt: Fischer, 1988.

Werfel, F. (1941). *Das Lied von Bernadette*. Stockholm: Bermann-Fischer. Published in 1942 as *The Song of Bernadette* (L. Lewisohn, Trans.). New York: Viking.

Werfel, F. (1946). *Stern der Ungeborenen: Ein Reiseroman*. Stockholm: Bermann-Fischer. Published in 1946 as *Star of the Unborn* (G. O. Arlt, Trans.). New York: Viking.

Zeller, B. and Otten, E. (eds.) (1982). *Karl Otten: Werk und Leben: Texte, Berichte, Bibliographie*. Mainz: v. Hase & Koehler.

Züchner, E. (2000). 'Qual zertrennt mich in Feuern'. Die Selbsterziehung Raoul Hausmanns zum Dadasophen. In R. Dehmlow and G. Heuer (eds.), *1. Internationaler Otto Gross Kongress*. Marburg: LiteraturWissenschaft.de (pp. 88–100).

Chapter 11

'Making history'

D. H. Lawrence, Frieda Weekley and Otto Gross

John Turner

'Making history': it was the author and critic Edward Garnett who found the words to describe the hope shared by Frieda Weekley and D. H. Lawrence when they stayed with him in May 1912 on their way to Germany together. Although they had known one another for only two months, and were full of fears and reservations – especially Frieda, who had a husband, three children and a home to lose – there was something in both of them that hoped their love would soon be 'making history'. Garnett's phrase seems to express the affectionate irony of an older man who was himself living unconventionally, at a distance from his wife, but who found in the younger couple a militant desire to change the course of the future that he himself did not feel. Certainly the phrase struck home; Lawrence quoted it wryly on three separate occasions in letters over the next three weeks. Once in Germany, where he had to be kept discreetly out of sight of Frieda's father, he complained to her that making history 'isn't the most comfortable thing on earth' (Lawrence 1979: 390). He quoted it back to Garnett too: 'Making history is no joke', he told him (ibid.: 408), ironically aware that history for the moment was having to wait upon the patriarchal status quo, and that tragedy was only just around the corner. 'I won't die in the attempt, if I can help it' (ibid.), he added, aware that the heroes of Hardy's late fiction, and of his own recently published novel *The Trespasser*, had done just that. Now, in his new life with Frieda, he was determined to escape tragedy. 'Making history': Garnett's phrase, as befitted a publisher's reader, had the ring of the blurb for a novel, even for his own new novel – *Sons and Lovers*, as it would become – and Lawrence surely heard it in this way. 'Oh Lord,' he told Garnett, 'it's easier to write history than to make it, even in such a mild way as mine' (ibid.: 395).

If there is any truth to the exasperated humour of this claim – that Lawrence found it easier to write history than to make it – it is not that he had a novelist's gift to write fictional history but that to write history was only an exercise in imagination, whereas to 'make history' meant to confront the recalcitrant facts of real relationships in the real world. It was his wish to establish a new ethic, a new way of living, a new basis for sexual relationships, and to authenticate them in his own life so that he could then go on to dramatise them in his writing; but to achieve this, he had first to deal with Frieda's family in their social world, he had to deal with Frieda in her world and, not least, he had to deal with the newly revealed truths about his own nature. It is true that all sexual relationships are in a certain sense fiction, in that they take their meaning from narrative, whether written or from the subjective internal narrative, or narratives, that we tell ourselves. The sexual act is nothing in itself, if not woven into a history that gives it meaning and symbolic value. It is true too that those narratives are in an important sense amphibious, inhabiting both the subjectivity of the imagination and the objectivity of the real world. Their business, indeed, is with the relationship between those two realms, making sense of them, establishing connections and easing strains between them. Lawrence's exasperation, however, reminds us that at times the strain can become too great, that these narratives can break down or become illusory. Those people like Frieda and Lawrence who are committed to 'making history' – committed, that is, to sexual revolution – feel this strain particularly since they set themselves against the master-narratives of their age; and their attempt to realise a new future means that not only do they have to cope with the strains caused by the pressures of society, of their partners and of their own inner selves, but with those strains as an expression of the past that they are trying to surpass.

I

In a wonderful passage from the eleventh book of *The Prelude*, Wordsworth looks back upon his youthful revolutionary faith in awe at its presumption:

> Shall I avow that I had hope to see,
> I mean that future times would surely see
> The man to come parted as by a gulph
> From him who had been.
> (Wordsworth 1805/1960, Bk. XI: 56–59)

This avowal is a confession of hubris, understood with the part-appalled, part-amused and part-regretful indulgence of adulthood, and emphasised by the false modesty of that qualifying shift from his own hope for himself to his hope for future generations. His youthful longing had been for what Nietzsche would later call an *Übermensch*, a new, dispassionately rational race of men separated 'as by a gulph' from the men of his own time; and what had now become apparent in the retrospect of adult wisdom was that this 'gulph' was in fact a gap in his own youthful thinking, a flaw in his imagination, a hiatus in the continuity of his historical vision. He had been practising a kind of magical thinking which enabled him to neglect the necessity for a period of transition between the corruption of the old world and the anticipated innocence of that new post-revolutionary age of reason – an age that would bring what Tom Paine had already announced as a 'Regeneration of man' (Paine 1791–2/1969: 136). Now, however, Wordsworth had come to see that his faith in the power of human reason, as it 'promised to abstract the hopes of man / Out of his feelings' (Wordsworth 1805/1960, Bk. X: 808–809), was a hope born of despair. He was putting an idea of man before the reality, creating a false view of the world; and when this false view of the world broke down, he succumbed to a sickness from which, as the last books of *The Prelude* relate, he recovered only by rediscovering those habitual childhood feelings of love and attachment which his revolutionary zeal had led him to betray.

What Wordsworth was examining in *The Prelude* was the moral and intellectual outlook of those revolutionaries – romantic revolutionaries, we might call them – who, like Paine and the young Wordsworth himself, envisaged revolution as a magical transformation not only of the outer political world but also of human nature too. As all the allusions to Shakespearean tragedy in the revolutionary books of *The Prelude* make clear, Wordsworth was examining the tragic potential of revolutionary idealism and concluding that, when it lost its roots in the discipline of feelings of attachment, such idealism produced an alienation within the self that made the desired end of revolutionary change impossible by corrupting the means. The eye was blinded at the point of seeing, so that the harmony of inner and outer regeneration at which the revolutionary aimed was already an illusion. It was this insight that led Wordsworth in his young manhood to try to ground his radical faith in a gradualist politic. He saw that history is not written upon a tabula rasa, that the future does not lie across a gulph from the present, and that the transition between the two must be lived through. The flaw in Wordsworth's imagination had been a tragic flaw, the flaw of hubris; and this tragic vision of one possible fate of idealism, born out of the Terror that followed the French Revolution, was one that lay heavy upon the whole century that followed. It was embodied most famously in the figure of Osvald, in Ibsen's play *Ghosts*, who yearned to enjoy the sexual freedom of Parisian artistic life but finished up in a syphilitic coma in his mother's arms, begging her: 'Mother, give me the sun' (Ibsen 1881/1964: 101). It was a cry that would be echoed some 26 years later by Otto Gross in one of the love letters that he wrote to that 'motherly woman' Frieda Weekley (Gross 1990: 178): 'Let me see the sun!' he begged her (ibid.: 171).

Frieda Weekley had met and fallen in love with the maverick psychoanalyst Otto Gross when on holiday in Munich in the spring of 1907, and the resultant affair, she said, 'revolutionised my life' (F. Lawrence 1961: 351). Until she met Gross, she felt, she had been living 'like a somnambulist in a conventional set life and he awakened the consciousness of my proper self' (F. Lawrence 1935: 1); the things he told her had 'a deep and lasting effect on her conception of herself' (Kinkead-Weekes 1996: 761). It gave her the confidence to identify and rebel against the sexual repressiveness and chauvinism of the early twentieth-century English bourgeois patriarchy into which she had married. There had been much to enjoy in her life with Ernest Weekley, not least her three young children, but increasingly she had found 'her inner life unrelated to the outer one' (F. Lawrence 1961: 92). Such dissociation was not uncommon at the time, and inspired many women to social and political protest; but direct sexual action was quite another matter. The young women whom Lawrence had known before he met Frieda were all in their different ways rebellious; but like many women of their generation, they turned to the education of others to change the world. One of them, Alice Dax, was described by a contemporary as 'a kind of ramrod, forcing the future into their present' (Worthen 1991: 369). But Frieda, with her aristocratic German background, was different; her father kept a mistress; her elder sister, Else, for whom she felt a rivalrous affection, had an open marriage with her husband, and was having an affair with Otto Gross when Frieda met him; and her school-friend Frieda Schloffer, who had married Gross in 1903, was living a life of sexual freedom in the alternative community of Ascona. It was this latter kind of world that Frieda wanted for herself; her life would be important not for the educational work she did for others but for the symbolic meaning that it would carry for them – for had not Otto Gross told her that she was 'the *woman of the future*' (Gross 1990: 165), the woman who possessed 'the wonderful power both to be a real *human being* and *at the same time to live out an idea*' (ibid.: 188). In the sunny sensuous joy of Frieda's erotic self-determination, in her freedom 'from the code of chastity, from Christianity, from democracy and all that accumulated filth', Gross found the embodiment of his ethical ideal – an aristocratic freedom, he thought, achieved through the immunities of 'her laughter and her loving' (ibid.: 165). Doubtless Frieda was secretly gratified too to learn that Gross located the negative side of his ideal – envy, jealousy, asceticism, melancholy, denial – in her sister Else; but Frieda's soul, he told her, had been 'kept pure by its genius for *insisting upon being itself*' (ibid.: 171); she was whole, not 'broken-winged' (ibid.: 186).

Gross, of course, was idealising the holidaying Frieda out of his own deepest needs. 'How strangely,' he wrote, 'in the depths of the soul the future clashes with the past, longing with weakness' (ibid.: 191). He feared that he himself was broken-winged, a victim of morphine addiction and, behind that, of the nineteenth-century patriarchal family that he longed to destroy but whose devastating authority, he knew, '*has penetrated into our own innermost self*' (Gross 1913/2005: 282). His letters to Frieda are the most revealing of all his works to survive, and they show the cycles of joy and despair that he felt as he contemplated the new world that he wanted to build. In the early letters he rejoiced in what Sam Whimster calls his 'Zarathustra moment' (Whimster 1998: 134), glorying in the love shared between himself, his wife, Else and Frieda Weekley; and at such times he was confident that his idealism would rise above the tragedy that threatened it. 'I have spoken face to face with all the ghosts of my evil childhood and all my evil hours, and put away false pride from me, which was indeed nothing but a fear of ghosts – since then I am able to look *everything* in the eye' (Gross 1990: 186). His psychoanalytic mission was to release the repressions of his patients and friends as he believed he had released his own, thereby enabling them to enter upon a life of free love in a spirit of respect for the woman. His hopes for his patients were those that he had for Else:

> that from now on everything from first to last would be pure and beautiful, that all asceticism and jealousy and all denial would disappear before the purity of a good conscience, living in a state of joy and aware of the wealth to be won by saying yes to life.
>
> (ibid.: 175)

Where Paine had trusted to the power of reason to effect the regeneration of man, Gross trusted to erotic power; and thus, when Else turned in love to a man who in Gross's eyes represented 'democracy and all that accumulated filth', he felt betrayed in his deepest trust in life.

It was, he felt, a tragic betrayal, the result of hubris, and he used the language of his classical education to describe it:

> I have had *far too much* of the most wonderful happiness of all – a happiness *too* high for the human condition – I have felt in myself *too much* creative power, too many high intentions – there is a sentence in Heraclitus that is dreadfully true – the sun dare not exceed the bounds of its course – otherwise the spirits of revenge would seize it.
>
> (ibid.: 173)

He had been abandoned by the erotic, 'the one *special* power from which, in the depths of my nature, all the good proceeds that I can experience or do' (ibid.: 179). There was a gulph between the man he wanted to be and the man he was, a gulph between his ideals and the realities of 'the human condition'; and the fact that the '*uncertain realization*' of these ideals caused him recurrent depression, that it raised the 'most paralyzing *doubts* about the future of mankind and the value of my own efforts', suggests a corresponding gulph within his own nature (ibid.: 165). He had not, despite his best belief, succeeded in fully analysing his own repressions.

Wilhelm Stekel, who analysed Gross in 1914, thought that his feminism masked a deep desire for revenge upon women, and that his advocacy of free love was simultaneously a 'flight from love' (Stekel 1925/1953: 152). This was Gross's tragedy – Stekel called his account of the analysis 'The

Tragedy of an Analyst' – that the ends he pursued could not be attained with the means at his disposal. A lover who could not love, an analyst who could not analyse himself, a liberator who could not free himself, Gross was beset by a 'discontinuity and deviousness' (Gross 1990: 179) which meant that his own future could never develop gradually out of his past. Increasingly as he grew older, he turned to political revolution to achieve his ends; but the best of him went into his writings. Their strength lies in the critical account that they give of the psychological damage caused by contemporary society; but, undisciplined by the affections and attachments of childhood, their vision of the future is too theoretical, too idealistic, to be credible. They aim too high for the human condition. As Gross idealised Else and Frieda, so too he idealised his own beliefs, fanatically, as though they themselves were possessed of redemptive power.

Frieda knew, of course, that Otto Gross idealised her. 'It was not true,' she wrote later, 'that she was free and harmonious – far from it. Chaos raged in her soul' (F. Lawrence 1961: 88). She was split within herself, the child of a family which had specialised in the same split living that she was now reproducing in her own married life; and Gross recognised this too. The passionate rhetoric of his letters, inviting her to come to share his life in Munich, is, in part at least, an exhortation against a woman who might at any time lapse back into 'the grey cold *life*' of the English Midlands (Gross 1990: 167), into that endemic pattern of bourgeois conformity and secret adultery that had been tragically illustrated in the destinies of Emma Bovary and Anna Karenina. She must not be cowardly, Gross told her; she might stay with her husband for the sake of the children, but for no other reason. She must avoid cowardly self-deception about her sexual life and hold fast to '*the right to self-determination – the inalienable* right that *never can* be forfeited through any contract or any duty incurred by solemn vows' (ibid.: 192). In fact, Frieda would continue her divided life in Nottingham for another four years until she met Lawrence, taking lovers and even, astonishingly, attempting to set up an erotic community there, a kind of Ascona-on-Trent. 'Fanatically,' she wrote, 'I believed that if only sex were "free" the world would straightaway turn into a paradise' (F. Lawrence 1935: 1). Yet to Frieda herself the truth that underlay her revolutionary views of free love was that 'my real self was frightened and shrank from contact like a wild thing' (ibid.: 5); 'she did not really want a connexion, especially not an emotional one, with others' (F. Lawrence 1961: 94). Her search for sexual connection, like that of Gross, was simultaneously a flight from love; her fanatical attachment to Gross's ideas, and to the idealised image that he gave her of herself, acted as her defence against the division and the inner emptiness of her life.

It also appealed to her vanity, her narcissism, to be cast in the role of a world saviour, especially of the men in it. It was a role for which she had been ready ever since, as a girl, she fancied herself more able than her own mother to manage her father, a man whom at first she thought 'perfection on earth': '"You don't handle him right, I would know better than you how to do it,"' she used to tell herself (ibid.: 49). Like both Gross and Lawrence, she shared the salvationist fantasies that belong to the oedipal situation; all three of them carried this burden as a stigmata of the patriarchal society into which they had been born, a society which in the moment of its dissolution had yielded the theoretical accounts of the Oedipus and Electra complexes. Gross's words spoke to the deepest beliefs that she held about herself. You '*redeem us from all that is past*', he told her (Gross 1990: 174), using the first person plural to indicate not merely one person, one lover, but many people, many lovers. Whilst most people, including Gross himself, were toiling painfully towards the Promised Land, she was already there by right. She had, he wrote in a phrase reminiscent of one that Lawrence would use later, a natural '*genius*' for suffusing the people and things around her with power and warmth (ibid.: 172); she was the golden child who banished evil spirits, and created life perpetually anew out of the magnificence of her own beauty. She was one of those people, Gross thought, who carried the future within herself as 'something inherent' in her own nature (ibid.: 177); with her he heard 'the silver bells of the future ring' (ibid.: 172).

Yet despite this flattering of her vanity, Gross's words also intensified the split within her; his creed of joy and courage, what the Webers called his 'nerve-ethics' (Weber 1926/1975: 377) – his hygienic need to avoid repression by acting out desire – had the cruel effect of increasing her unhappiness as it prompted the surreptitiousness of her sexual life. When Lawrence met her in the spring of 1912, she wrote later, he 'saw through me like glass'; he saw at once 'how hard I was trying to keep up a cheerful front. I thought it was so despicable and unproud and unclean to be miserable, but he saw through my hard bright shell' (F. Lawrence 1935: 4–5). If it was the meeting with Lawrence that finally gave Frieda, not without hesitation, the courage to act out her own desire to escape the claustrophobia of her married life, it was Gross's ideology that gave her the rationale. Gross had written more truly than he knew when he told her: 'You also *can* no longer *think me out of existence* in any future phase of your life' (Gross 1990: 168). Frieda always maintained that it was Otto Gross who had introduced her to her 'proper self' and taught her, as Gottfried Heuer argues elsewhere in these pages, 'the sacredness of love' (Lawrence 1984: 127); but she knew too that it was Lawrence who made that 'proper self' capable of realising 'the sacredness of love' through relationship with other people. It was Lawrence, that is, who had to deal with her narcissism and her fearfulness of commitment.

II

When Lawrence met Frieda in the spring of 1912, he had just passed through one of the great crises of his life. Throughout the previous year he had been working hard at his daytime job as a schoolteacher in Croydon, he had been working late at night on his writing, he had been seriously – and simultaneously – involved with at least four different women, and finally, not surprisingly, he had gone down with an attack of pneumonia that nearly killed him. John Worthen's description of 1911 as Lawrence's 'sick year' is true both physically and psychologically (Worthen 1991: 288). His mother had died in the previous December, and his pursuit of so many different women was an attempt both to recapture the stability that she had always given him and also to discover his masculine identity in a new way of living that was entirely his own. Lawrence, like Gross and Frieda, had grown up in a dysfunctional patriarchal family, a working-class family in which the coal-miner father had been deposed from what he felt was his rightful place as the head of the family by his more educated, socially aspiring wife. The parents were at war, and Lawrence had formed an oedipal attachment to his mother and a hatred of his father which led to a deep disturbance in his sexual life. His mother's love gave him a sense of his own specialness that lent a messianic edge to his character and made the establishment of ordinary friendly relationships difficult; and in addition, he was oppressed by his dependence upon women, haunted by a sense of lost masculinity and disturbed by homosexual leanings.

Before he met Frieda, Lawrence's sexual experiences had been joyless affairs. The most revealing comment on their content was that of Alice Dax, the married woman with whom Lawrence had a brief affair in 1911–12. She claimed, as Frieda had earlier claimed of Otto Gross, that she had been woken up to her true self by Lawrence:

> I thank him always for my life though I know it cost him pains and disappointments. I fear that he never even enjoyed morphia with me – always it carried an irritant – we were never, except for one short memorable hour, whole: it was from that one hour that I began to see the light of life.
>
> (F. Lawrence 1961: 245)

In a period that abounded with euphemisms for the sexual act, 'morphia' is one of the saddest, suggesting as it does that both life and sexuality are illnesses from which even temporary oblivion is to be sought. Like Gross, however, Lawrence believed in sexuality as an instinctual force to be enjoyed, and was angered by its suppression in the puritanical society of his day. Where Gross spoke of repression, Lawrence spoke of denial, a word which recalls both Nietzsche's *Neinsagen* and Peter's denial of the Word of Life in the Bible. To Lawrence, with his religious sense of sexuality as the power of God, it was a sin to deny life; and what he found in Frieda was a woman who was 'direct and free' (ibid.: 246), and similarly committed to the acting out of desire. 'Making history, even in such a mild way as mine' meant for Lawrence an end to the furtive unsatisfactory sexual life that he had hitherto known, and a fierce courage to be honest about his desires, however disturbing they might be.

There must have been much talk about Gross between Lawrence and Frieda in those early days, not least because her husband was writing her long letters blaming Gross for putting 'these "ideas" into her head' (Lawrence 1979: 424). She even told her friends that Lawrence was 'rather like Otto' (Maddox 1994: 136), while apparently telling Lawrence himself what a 'wonderful lover' Gross had been (Lawrence 1984: 126). Amid all their insecurity, so well captured by Lawrence in his play *The Fight for Barbara*, here was yet another reason for him to be anxious. Clearly the absent Gross was a constant presence in their relationship, even in their bed, to such an extent that Lawrence even assumed his identity while walking in Switzerland. As he struggled to find his feet with Frieda, there was much for him to absorb about Gross, and even more to criticise. Certainly Lawrence learned from him, and much of what he learned went into the book that he began soon after meeting Frieda, The Sisters, the book that eventually became *The Rainbow* and *Women in Love*. It was a book that Lawrence would also have discussed with Frieda Schloffer, Gross's wife, whom he met in Fiascherino in 1914, and to whom he sent a copy of *Women in Love* on its publication in 1920.

In their attempt to take the measure of the crisis of the modern world, both *The Rainbow* and *Women in Love* turn upon the two central poles of Gross's thinking, the search of modern woman for sexual self-determination, and the decadent decline of bourgeois patriarchy. Lawrence had told Ernest Weekley, in words reminiscent of Gross: 'Mrs Weekley is afraid of being stunted and not allowed to grow, and so she must live her own life . . . Mrs Weekley must live largely and abundantly. It is her nature' (ibid.: 392). *The Rainbow* was Lawrence's attempt, impelled by his own missionary spirit, to epitomise such growth in modern woman; it was his effort to 'do my work for women, better than the suffrage' (ibid.: 490). *Women in Love* embodies the old decadent world in the figure of Thomas Crich, the dying father whose authority broods over the book with a power that penetrates into his son's '*innermost self*' and drains him of all spontaneity. The picture of Gerald Crich, astride his horse at the level crossing at the start of chapter IX, drawn in all its ravishing effect on Gudrun, symbolises Gross's encapsulation of patriarchal sexual relations as rape, *Vergewaltigung*, or, to use Lawrence's word, violation. Gerald's emptiness, his sense of the unreality of life, his unbelieving conservativism, all show his inability to contact his own inner life. He is an unbeliever, the image of a culture that has grown murderous, lustful and suicidal out of sheer rage and repression.

But while Lawrence learned much from what Frieda told him of Gross and his search for a new way of living, he also found much to criticise; and these criticisms lay at the heart of his struggle with Frieda herself. 'We had so many battles to fight out, so much to get rid of, so much to surpass. We were both good fighters,' Frieda wrote (F. Lawrence 1935: vi–vii). She saw the conflict in terms of gender, class and race; but what lay at the heart of it were the reservations that Lawrence quickly came to feel about the erotic ideas that Frieda had absorbed. Of these we may list three. In the first place, Lawrence objected to the fact that these ideas were just that – ideas about desire rather than desire itself. They were theoretical: Frieda was trying to live life the wrong way round – from the head to the body rather than from the body to the head. What was at stake was what it meant to be a whole human being: Lawrence, with his Schopenhauerian and post-Darwinian sense of the material universe, valued the human animal above its intellect. It was his reaction against the cerebral mother's boy that he had been, his own need to rediscover his old animal self, that led him to create this duality between mind and body. Only by recovering his bodily self could he begin to feel a real person alive in a real world. It is a dualism that sometimes seems valuable and sometimes primitivist in his writings; but it is a position that Lawrence would have argued fiercely as Frieda told him what she had learned from Gross about psychoanalysis. Psychoanalysis, Lawrence thought, gave us more of life in the head, and less of life in the spontaneous body; its stress on the mental life worsened the condition that it sought to cure. Frieda, who already thought she was living by the falsity of an idea herself, was quick to accept Lawrence's view and, as we have seen, to find her own early theories of sexuality fanatical. 'I don't even prance theories or anything else of the sort any longer,' she confessed to Garnett (Lawrence 1979: 439).

Second, Lawrence saw that Frieda's ideas about love were a defence against actual relationship, a self-preoccupation that cut her off from creative contact with a man. Gross described Frieda as a sunny woman; but when Lawrence portrayed Ursula's self-preoccupation in *The Rainbow*, he set her beneath the moon, symbolising a woman's narcissistic absorption in an intellectual idea of herself that reflects the warmth and power of life, but that is not itself that life. Frieda told Garnett she had learned her lesson: 'Yes, my theories have sadly altered, there are two sides to human love, one that wants to be faithful, the other wants to run, my running one was uppermost, but it's going to be faithful now' (ibid.: 498). In fact, of course, she was not faithful, and this fact – omitted, along with much else, from her autobiographical writings – suggests that she never fully lost that narcissistic preoccupation with her own image; indeed, the beauty of her prose rests to a great extent upon its simplifications. The argument with Lawrence crystallised out over the question of marriage. While Frieda was excitedly escaping from marriage and eyeing the free lives lived by her sister and Frieda Gross, Lawrence was adamant that he had found the woman he wanted to marry. 'I know in my heart "here's my marriage",' he told Frieda. 'It feels rather terrible – because it is a great thing in my life' (ibid.: 403).

When later he fictionalised this time in his life, in the unfinished novel *Mr Noon*, his picture was true to what the letters reveal. His hero, Gilbert Noon, satirises the Frieda figure, Johanna, and calls her Panacea because of her belief that 'one should love all men' (Lawrence 1984: 164). Gilbert's protest that he believes only in particular love arouses her fury: 'Just keeping one person all for yourself! Ah, I know the horrors of that. It is all based on jealousy. I think the noblest thing is to overcome jealousy' (ibid.: 165). Lawrence, however, distrusted the simplicity of Gross's ideas of free love, and stated that his goal of releasing 'the profound desires from all mental control' could only be achieved within 'the deep *accustomedness* of marriage' (ibid.: 190). Hence the sacredness of marriage:

> this is perhaps the secret of the English greatness. The English have gone far into the depths of marriage, far down the sensual avenues of the marriage bed, and they have not so easily, like the French or Germans or other nations, given up and turned to prostitution or chastity of some other *pis aller*.
>
> (ibid.: 191)

Marriage had been sentimentalised in Victorian times by the idealisation of women, which was a form of patriarchal disempowerment; it was now up to Gilbert and Johanna to revive it in its full emotional range.

Third, Lawrence had an idea of manliness quite opposite to the matriarchal tenor of Gross's vision, and this was the source of much of his fighting with Frieda. As he told Garnett:

> I shan't let F leave me, if I can help it. I feel I've got a mate and I'll fight tooth and claw to keep her. She says I'm reverting, but I'm not – I'm only coming out wholesome and myself. Say I'm right, and I ought to be always common. I *loathe* Paul Morel.
>
> (Lawrence 1979: 427)

What Lawrence means here is that, since beginning *Sons and Lovers*, he had found another self within himself, grounded in the working-class father whom he had known and loved in childhood. He and Frieda were fighting over what it meant to be 'making history': Frieda thought Lawrence's new self was atavistic, while Lawrence believed he had at last discovered the spontaneous biological animal within him. He was becoming wholesome, he thought, whole, and as a writer he turned his personal dilemma into cultural analysis, searching to imagine and introject the aboriginal masculinity lost to an effeminised culture. Yet it was an enterprise that failed, both personally and artistically. He failed to find within himself the masculinity of which he dreamed; his fullest picture of modern man, struggling to emerge from a declining patriarchy, is that of Rupert Birkin in *Women in Love*, who, like Otto Gross and Lawrence himself, had to grapple with his own bisexuality. The subsequent masculinist phase of Lawrence's career, encompassing novels such as *Aaron's Rod* and *The Plumed Serpent*, is disappointing. Even in *Lady Chatterley's Lover*, with its Wordsworthian return to the landscape, attachments and tenderness of childhood feelings, the pursuit of spontaneous creativity through sexual experience is saddened by the hatred and spleen engendered by the modern world. For all its beauty and revolutionary content, the shock of its language and its heroine's pursuit of a sexual destiny transcending that of Emma Bovary or Anna Karenina, it is not a book that wholly testifies to an author 'coming out wholesome and myself'.

Otto Gross, Frieda Weekley and D. H. Lawrence were all intent on 'making history'; they were each committed to a sexual revolution that would overthrow the patriachal social order whose damaging authority – they would all have agreed with Gross – '*has penetrated into our own innermost self*'. They each had a vision of how life might begin to feel more real by grounding it in the sexual life of the body, and they used their writing to take hold of that vision and bear witness to it. In each case their revolutionary struggle was driven by the sense of the incompleteness of their own lives and of the lives of the people around them. It was not a struggle that brought them wholeness, it was a struggle towards wholeness; and in each case the damage that they had suffered in their early lives shadowed their successes, blinding the eye of their vision and tarnishing their success. Each of them, in contemplating the future, pictured 'the man to come as parted by a gulph / From him who had been'. Gross imagined a matriarchal world free from jealousy, Frieda a world redeemed by erotic love and Lawrence a priesthood of atavistic masculinity; and at such moments their writing flags. Gross's prose becomes theoretical and manic, Frieda's sentimental and naive, Lawrence's repetitive and rhetorical. Yet it is this struggle towards wholeness that gives their writing its life, especially the writings of Gross and Lawrence. Like Wordsworth, they both returned to contemplate their childhood – Gross in his essay On Loneliness (1920), Lawrence in *Psychoanalysis and the Unconscious* (1921/2004) and *Fantasia of the Unconscious* (1922/2004) – in an attempt to understand the powers and the relationships that had been lost to them and that, in a much sexualised age, seemed almost impossible to recover. The rich life of the affections that had sustained Wordsworth, and that had sustained his sexuality as well, was harder for those of a later generation to recover; and in this sense we may say that the revolutionary attempt to recover the spontaneous life of the sexual body, while it was a real cure for the unreality brought about by patriarchal society, was also a symptom of the damage that that society had caused.

References

Gross, O. (1913/2005) On Overcoming the Cultural Crisis (J. Turner, Trans.). In R. Graham (ed.), *Anarchism: A Documentary History of Libertarian Ideas, Vol. 1.* Montreal: Black Rose (pp. 281–284).

—— (1920) On Loneliness (Über Einsamkeit). In A. Marcus and E. Webers (eds.), *Drei Aufsätze über inneren Konflikt*, Bonn: Verlag.

—— (1990) *The Otto Gross–Frieda Weekley Correspondence* (J. Turner with C. Rumpf-Worthen and R. Jenkins, eds.). *The D. H. Lawrence Review*, *22*(2), 137–227.

Ibsen, H. (1881/1964) *Ghosts and Other Plays*. Harmondsworth: Penguin.

Kinkead-Weekes, M. (1996) *D.H. Lawrence: Triumph to Exile 1912–1922*. Cambridge: Cambridge University Press.

Lawrence, D. H. (1921/2004) *Psychoanalysis and the Unconscious*. In B. Steele (ed.), *Psychoanalysis and the Unconscious and Fantasia of the Unconscious*. Cambridge: Cambridge University Press.

Lawrence, D. H. (1922/2004) *Fantasia of the Unconscious*. In B. Steele (ed.), *Psychoanalysis and the Unconscious and Fantasia of the Unconscious*. Cambridge: Cambridge University Press.

Lawrence, D. H. (1979) *The Letters of D. H. Lawrence, Vol. 1, September 1901–May 1913*. Cambridge: Cambridge University.

—— (1984) *Mr Noon* (Lindeth Vasey, ed.). Cambridge: Cambridge University.

Lawrence, F. (1935) *'Not I, But the Wind . . .'*. London: Heinemann.

—— (1961) *Frieda Lawrence: The Memoirs and Correspondence* (E. W. Tedlock, ed.). London: Heinemann.

Maddox, B. (1994) *D. H. Lawrence: The Story of a Marriage*. New York: Simon and Schuster.

Paine, T. (1791–2/1969) *Rights of Man*. Harmondsworth: Pelican.

Stekel, W. (1925/1953) *Sadism and Masochism: The Psychology of Hatred and Cruelty*, Vol. 2. New York: Liveright.

Weber, M. (1926/1975) *Max Weber: A Biography*. New York: Wiley.

Whimster, S. with Heuer, G. (1998) Otto Gross and Else Jaffe and Max Weber. *Theory, Culture and Society*, *15*(3–4), 129–160.

Wordsworth, W. (1805/1960) *The Prelude* (1805 version). Oxford: Oxford University Press.

Worthen, J. (1991) *D. H. Lawrence: The Early Years 1885–1912*. Cambridge: Cambridge University Press.

Chapter 12

No place for a sexual revolutionary

Heidelberg and Otto Gross

Sam Whimster

It was a good period to be a revolutionary in the years between 1900 and 1920 – political, economic, aesthetic, social and lifestyle revolutionaries abounded. Leninism can be taken as the yardstick of what revolution entails: the unity of theory and praxis, absolute commitment to the cause, the relegation of all other personal or ethical concerns as subsidiary, an ever present hatred of the existing regime of things and a boundless contempt for the servants of the existing state of affairs.

It is a bit of a conceit to view Dr. Otto Gross as central to an international sexual revolution. Multifacetted he was: an intelligence able to carve out a non-adaptive Freudianism, a charismatic charm that would pull disciples into his orbit and spread the message of the liberating power of eroticism, and his extraordinary ability to haul himself back (with assistance) from his own self-destructive bouts. He is the bad Lenin of the sexual revolution. Theory and praxis combine in his person. Actions are justified by the oppression of patriarchalism, which on natural law grounds is to be resisted, and theory is underwritten by medical science. Incapacitating drug addictions and socially dysfunctional phobias make for a less than impeccable revolutionary. But with Otto Gross, as well as other revolutionaries, it is not their weaknesses or inconsistencies but the purity of their vision that attracts.

In a proto-revolutionary society a number of revolutionary visions are created, not justifying the correctness of any one vision but testifying to extreme conflict, inequality and dysfunction in the existing society. In Germany in this period, alongside the Marxists, there were on offer syndicalism, anarchism and aesthetic and sexual-emancipatory revolutionary programmes. Each provided a vectored analysis of the unsustainability of the existing society. With Marxism, it was the analysis of class that disclosed the relational basis of inequality, that one class owned the means of production and the proletariat had only its labour to sell on terms not under its control. With Helene Stöcker and her League for Mothercare and Sexual Reform, it was the present organisation of marriage that turned women into prostitutes or chattels of their husbands. With the anarchist

Gustav Landauer, communitarian socialism would resolve the conflicts of capitalism and the authoritarianism of political power. With Otto Gross the vision is the liberation of a patriarchally burdened and damaged psyche through the free acknowledgement of erotic drives and attractions. Nothing is to be suppressed, for this would be to affirm patriarchal authority and its socialising effects on character.

It was in the aftermath of this period – the unfolding train crash that was the Wilhelmine Reich – that Karl Mannheim provided what is still one of the best sociological analyses of revolutionary modes of thought. Mannheim was no ordinary sociologist, which at that time meant being schooled in the dull positivism of evolution and the limited ambition of amelioration. At the age of 19 he read Georg Lukács's *A Modern Drama* (1911) and wrote to the author saying that together they should search for the laws of happiness, which were to be found in Dostoyevsky. Lukács himself, in the first decade of the twentieth century, was fascinated by the plays of Ibsen. He staged a production of Ibsen's *Wild Goose*, which for him encapsulated the collision between the purity of principles and ideals and the conventional reality and hypocrisies of family life (Kadarky 1991: 28–32). Mannheim accompanied Lukács both geographically and imaginatively as Lukács traversed his way from the power of the theatre, to that of aesthetics (studying in Heidelberg) and to that of international workers' revolution. Mannheim left Hungary for good in 1919 after the intelligentsia's short-lived Communist revolution, in which – like Lukács – he was a participant, was suppressed. He settled in Heidelberg working with the sociologist Alfred Weber.

Mannheim, in his sociological reflection on revolution, *Ideology and Utopia* (1960), attuned revolution to the coordinates of time and space. He adopted the terminology of the anarchist revolutionary, Gustav Landauer. The existing social order, which combines a particular economic and political structure with the forms of 'living-together, like love, sociability and conflict, is a situated place – a "*topia*"' (Mannheim 1960: 174). The social order, which for Landauer was authoritarian, has to be transformed by the revolutionary urge to libertarianism into a 'utopia'. With Mannheim the idea of space has more of a cultural inflection. A period will have a cultural style just as the utopian future will represent new cultural ideals. The other coordinate is time, or rather, how time is thought of according to different ideologies. Conservatives like to look back to an idealised time, liberals believe that the future will be progressive, extreme revolutionaries have a chiliastic notion of time. In this last case, the impossibility of the present situation is transformed into the belief that only the present moment counts, indeed the present is absolute. 'For the real Chiliast, the present becomes the breach through which what was previously inward burst out suddenly, takes hold of the outer world and transforms it (Mannheim [1929]1960: 193).

Space and time coordinates provide a conceptual grid in which social movements may be placed. For example, Leninist thought can be placed short of Chiliastic beliefs. Bolsheviks saw revolution as a catalyst to achieving socialism, itself a transitional state towards communism. The revolution, unlike some forms of syndicalism, did not deify the revolutionary deed. Bakunin is a pure Chiliast when he says, 'The will to destroy is a creative will' (quoted in Mannheim 1960: 196). As Mannheim notes, 'he was not fundamentally interested in the realization of a rationally thought-out world' (1960: 223). What was required, to quote Bakunin, was: 'Storm and vitality and a new lawless and consequently free world' (quoted in Mannheim 1960: 196). The anarchist settlers of Ascona can be placed in another part of the map. Theirs was an extreme lifestyle choice and their settlement on the hillside above Lago Maggiore marked it as a utopian space where they could pursue vegetarianism, smallholdings, nudism and fresh air apart from the *topia* of corrupted urban existence. Time, for genuine Asconans, could be happily quotidian with no idea of the moment of revolutionary redemption.

In what follows I will draw attention to expressionistic tendencies in Otto Gross's doctrine. Mannheim, in a very brief passage, does refer to expressionism. It is the fourth (and last) option of intellectuals 'who have thus been cast up by the social process'.

> The fourth group becomes shut off from the world and consciously renounces direct participation in the historical process. We find one symptom of this, for example, in modern expressionistic art, in which objects have lost their original meaning and seem simply to serve as a medium for the communication of the ecstatic.
>
> (Mannheim 1960: 235)

In my view this statement fails to place adequately the significance of expressionist thought and art. By placing Gross's doctrine of a revolution based on a new understanding and practice of eroticism within the coordinates of Mannheim's conceptual grid produces something more significant than Mannheim's own assessment of expressionism. Gross's impact on his contemporaries still reverberates today – and remains something of challenge for our thinking.

Jennifer Michaels has already made the expressionist claim in her *Anarchy and Eros. Otto Gross's Impact on German Expressionist Writers* (1983). In her exposition she itemises the features of Gross's thought and actions that were incorporated by expressionist writers such as Leonard Frank, Franz Jung, Johannes Becher, Walter Hasenclever and others, though without the attribution of expressionism to Gross himself. And in 1913 Gross did in fact join the Berlin expressionist/Dadaist group, which founded the journal *Die freie Strasse*, later one of the leading publications of the Berlin Dadaists.

In the commentaries on expressionism there is a notable reluctance to provide definitions, which to an extent is true to its spirit of being resistant to definition. Expressionism is characterised by an antagonism towards form, structure and style. It is what it chooses to be – a breaker of form, disassociative and inchoate. Other forms of revolution were characterised by rational programmes accompanying utopian hopes. Expressionism was an eschatology without a programme and without a model of achieving change. It represented the revolution of the impossibility of revolution. In many ways it was a unique statement of the irresolvable political, economic and cultural tensions of the Wilhelmine Reich and, despite its modernising surges, the incurable strangeness of that society.

'The sense that the relationship between the experiencing subject and the external, "modern" world has become fractured is fundamental to Expressionism and underlies many of its themes', writes Mary Shields, who does offer an account (1999: 223). The modern world stands for disharmony and 'ego-dissociation' when compared to the rapidly vanishing pre-modern, traditional and harmonious world. Everything is out of sorts in the modern world and expressionism was one movement that searched for the Neue Mensch capable of transforming society. These features take one beyond conventional revolution that germinates within the womb of the old society and the materialist guarantee of a better future. In Marxism the proletariat take control of a capitalistically energised society. 'The Expressionists, then, were characterised by an awareness that the psychic energy that had been lost from traditional social and aesthetic forms could still be tapped at source' (Shields 1999: 223). But, notes Shields, 'tapping it was fraught with danger because these forms could no longer contain it and would be destroyed by it, and also because this energy had so long been repressed that it could erupt in pathological ways' (ibid.). Vietta and Kemper note two antithetical yet co-existing forces: measured social and cultural criticism and 'the messianic path of proclaiming "Seele" and the New Man who will transform society' (ibid.). The search, or rather a yearning, was for a new spiritual truth.

There is nothing mechanistic in this revolutionary vision. While Marxism has been likened to a messianic eschatology it retains strong elements of a rational future, for example its emphasis on economic planning. Expressionism expects no ordered transformation of the old to the new, in which the bourgeoisie are forced to hand over the mechanisms of control to the ascendant proletariat and its vanguard. Through disruption a new universal spiritual truth would be intuited by expressionists but without any guarantee of success or plan of action. Apocalypse was a continuous fear, as in Jakob von Hoddis's poem *End of the World* or Ludwig Meidner's paintings of engulfing catastrophe. Equally, in his play *Transfiguration* Ernst Toller sees the possibility of a new social order and a Neuer Mensch but the process of this transformation is unspecified, fraught, uncertain yet creative in its making (Whimster 1999: 34–5).

Freudianism, to put this in an expressionist context, thought of repression within the family as blocking the full flow of psychic energy, and the pathologies diagnosed in patients could be traced to the displacement from tabooed forms of sexuality into phobias and neuroses. Gross's initial thinking and training led him to argue that healthy neurological development required the lifting of any restraint on children. Emotional freedom allowed a complete neurological development in the child. This he argued in terms of the cellular processes of the brain and nerves. He also took the view that very young children were bisexual and this was forcibly repressed by parents, who socialise children into their proper gender roles. This led to a socialisation of emotional discipline with the possibility of future psychopathologies. Gross wanted to tap into the *Ur*-pyschic energy and release it. He did not want to use psychoanalysis as a technique that enabled patients to adapt themselves and their behaviour to conform with society's expectations.

In Munich Gross developed his doctrine of the erotic. Sexual physical attraction was distorted in many ways within the property-based bourgeois family, as had been pointed out by Friedrich Engels in his *Origin of the Family* (1972[1884]). Women were expected to be married by the age of 20 and men could only marry in their thirties when they had an assured job and income – with all the many attested downsides. Gross's erotic doctrine demanded that people 'live out' the calling of physical attraction, and this paralleled the already established sexual freedom achieved in the artist bohème of Schwabing – one of the first place-based alternative communities. Rebels, most notably Franziska zu Reventlow, had already established their right to their own sexual wishes independently of Freudian insights; indeed Reventlow was highly resistant and sarcastic of psychoanalysis. With Reventlow it was a bold lifestyle choice (Whimster 1999: 12–14). With Gross it was a doctrine that would transform people's behaviour and lead them to unlock a new potentiality within themselves.

When, in April 1907, Otto Gross came to the university town of Heidelberg in the liberal state of Baden, he had added elements of Nietzsche to his doctrine. This is most clearly seen in the love letters he wrote to Frau Dr. Else Jaffé. Gross by this time had married Frieda Schloffer and they had granted each other sexual freedom within marriage. This became a source of conflict, because Otto made the pact according to his theoretical precepts whereas Frieda stood more by the example of Reventlow. Else Jaffé, a school friend of Frieda Schloffer, was born into the minor nobility – a branch of the von Richthofen family. Through considerable determination and intelligence she had entered the world of academia, social policy and social reform and was part of Marianne and Max Weber's circle.

In 1902 she married a fellow Heidelberg doctor Edgar Jaffé. He was in his thirties and had sold up his share in a family business located in Manchester. Edgar had bought the leading academic journal (*Archiv für Sozialwissenschaft und Sozialpolitik*) in the field of social reform, and Werner Sombart and Max Weber became its prestigious editors. Else Jaffé, though married and starting a family, was personally unsettled. She was going through a Madame Bovary phase of her life, having started an illicit love affair with her surgeon, Völcker, who at that point was a bachelor.

Sometime in 1907 Otto wrote the following love letter, probably from Munich, to Else Jaffé in Heidelberg:

> My Else,
> I love you with an insatiable yearning, with a pressing desire to have you by my side now – and to feel myself great and free in your love – Else – I long for the immeasurable fullness of your love – that your love in its engulfing and glowing unfathomableness carries me again to the heights – *as before* – Else, I don't know what would become of me, if it were no longer *so*. Else, what have you given to me – how did you raise me up and make me great with the *yea-saying* of your love? – with the yea-saying of an unfathomable soul, in which I knew myself to be justified – knew myself *blessed*. How have you redeemed all the sources of my best possibilities – given me the fructifying belief in myself in whom you have believed. Only now do I see what you gave to me *at that time*, how *my life has ascended, deepened and developed*. I *knew* I was confirmed by you at that time, if only I went forwards on my own resources and when I moved away from everyone else, you remained for me, who you were.
>
> (Whimster and Heuer 1998: 137)

This is a fairly typical excerpt of one of a series of letters that Else Jaffé kept private and only released towards the end of her life (Roth 2010b: 13). It establishes that their love was indeed an intimate physical relationship and that they were both living out their mutual attraction. This merits comment, because in the Heidelberg of the time there were love relationships that appealed to a transcendent and non-physical love. Gross is a stricken lover and in that mode indulges in semi-scriptural language of the soul and being blessed. But some of the phraseology is less intimate with the references to yea-saying and ascending to the heights. This is a Nietzschean motif of *Übermenschen* who live on a higher plane according to their own values. In another letter Gross, consumed by jealousy because Else has returned to her previous liaison with her surgeon, berates her for indulging in lust with someone of a lower caste. According to the doctrine of the erotic, those who belonged were a freely choosing caste who transcended physical lust in favour of the goodness of a transforming erotic

Figure 12.1 Else Jaffé, 1874–1973.

experience. The erotic was consummated yet retained a purity that for Gross was doctrinal. The erotic revolution for Gross was transfiguring – a motif in expressionism and one notes the imagery in his letter of being engulfed and swept into a world with unfathomable depths.

Gross was the embodiment of a transgressive ethic. Else Jaffé broke with him on a number of grounds. Her younger sister Frieda, then married to the Englishman Ernest Weekley, had come to Munich in April 1907 and started an affair with Otto when Else herself had just conceived a child (Peter) with him. The two sisters for a time fell out badly, 'in the manner of "Brunhild and Krimhild"', as Frieda commented, 'I can laugh now but at the time it cut us both to the quick' (Turner 1990: 196). Else may well have wanted to pull Otto more firmly into academic life and had this worked out he would have been her protégé in Heidelberg. It was Else who submitted an article by Otto Gross directly to Max Weber, co-editor of the *Archiv für Sozialwissenschaft und Sozialpolitik*. The article has been lost, and is mostly remembered through Weber's long and scathing rejection letter (MWG 1990: 393–403). Gross had high hopes for the article, sending it to Else Jaffé with heartfelt love: 'I send you the first part *of that* work which is *for you* – in *this* work I have begun to move out of the great shadows and on my way, to work beyond Nietzsche and Freud. And *that* I was *capable* of this confidence – *have become capable* of this confidence after long, long resignation! – *this was the life energy which I obtained from you*' (Whimster and Heuer: 1998: 137).

For Else Jaffé his drug habit, which she had tried to control, was a factor in her break with him. She writes:

> It seems quite pointless to make any sacrifice for you or your causes, because you are destroying your capacity to achieve anything by your senseless attacks on your own health. We really don't know how much of what makes your ideas so troublesome for us – the lack of discrimination, the need for nuances and the capacity to distinguish individual human beings – is caused in the end by morphine. You already know this makes living with others so difficult.
>
> (Whimster and Heuer 1998: 143)

Her letter also makes the decisive point that Otto acts like a prophet rather than a human being:

> Friedele [Else's sister] was quite right when she said to me in the summer, 'Don't you see that Otto is the prophet of whom it can only be said: He who is not for me is against me.'
>
> Now to a certain extent the prophet has consumed in his fire the last remnants of the human being, Otto, and has taken from him the capacity to love persons individually in their individuality and

> according to their essence. That is an old, old story – and that other prophet said of his brothers: I have no brothers – you (the disciples) are my brothers! For you there are now *only* followers of your teaching (something of this was always there), no longer a particular wife loved for her *essential* self.
>
> (Whimster and Heuer 1998: 143)

This takes her comment towards Max Weber's academic viewpoint. The 'other prophet' is Jesus whose theological status as son of God is declined in favour of the known historical prophet of Palestine. Weber was later to refer to Jesus as a charismatic magician (Weber 1966: 46–7). Otto Gross complained to Frieda Weekley that Else was distancing him through her 'social asceticism', though since she turned to other lovers this is not strictly correct. Gross was being distanced and objectified in Weber's sociological categories. The one courteous note in Weber's rejection letter of Otto Gross's article concerned Otto himself:

> This criticism applies only to this *particular* work – I am very well aware of *how* highly other competent judges rate the level of *other* works by the same author. This criticism in *no way* applies to the *person* and his character, it has to be said. The circumstance that we both will always talk past one another, does not imply – after the brief impression and what your have to say about him – that I would fail to recognize the noble side of his nature, which is certainly among the most endearing one could encounter today. How much purer would the nobility of his personal charisma and that 'Akosmismus' of love, before which I willingly doff my hat, have its effect if it were *not* covered in the dust of specialist jargon and the subject-patriotism of nerve hygiene etc. etc., if he *ventured* to be *what he is* – and that to be sure is something different and better than a follower of Nietzsche. And indeed it is not the enduring part of Nietzsche – the 'morality of superiority' – but simply the *weakest* parts of Nietzsche, the biological padding which he heaps on to the core of his completely moralistic doctrine. Only this moral nobility – *and nothing else* – creates the inner affinity between them both.
>
> (MWG 1990: 402–3)

Weber is dismissive of Gross's doctrine of what he terms 'nerve hygiene' and its naturalistic correlates in psychiatry and in Nietzsche.

In the aetiology of the sexual revolution it has been presumed that Otto Gross brought the doctrine of free love to Heidelberg, and that through the person of Else Jaffé it was transmitted to Max Weber. Else's 'motives, besides the obvious one of bringing into confrontation these two major figures in her life, may have been the hope that Gross – so brilliant as a psychoanalyst – might release Weber from his crippling neurosis' (Green 1974: 56). Just as Else Jaffé might have hoped to have helped Max Weber, so it is also argued that Weber harshly rejected Otto Gross's article out of jealousy of the relationship between Else and Otto; 'he himself [Weber] was in love with Else and felt jealous of her lover,' writes Joachim Radkau (2009: 172). Commentators, following Martin Green, have made a retrospective interpretation: that because Max Weber started an affair with Else Jaffé, the epistolary evidence for which belongs to the much later year of 1919 (Bavarian State Library, Manuscript Dept., Ana 446), it is presumed that Weber was 'really' in love with Else in 1907. Marianne Weber noted in her diary that, during a visit of Max and Marianne Weber and Else and Edgar Jaffé to Grignano on the Trieste coast in September 1909, her husband was in fact courting Else in a way, as she notes with some anguish, that he had never done with her. Else Jaffé had clearly animated Max Weber in a way that had not occurred before. Any subsequent development of Max Weber's suit went no further, for Else accepted the bachelor Alfred Weber as her intimate companion. Here, jealousy does play a part. But it led to Max Weber lecturing Else that while she might enjoy adventures, his brother Alfred was out of bounds. Discord and bad feeling ensued such that no reconciliation occurred between Else Jaffé and Max Weber until 1917. Frieda Gross and Else Jaffé shared between them the most intimate secrets and on 28 November 1909 Else wrote to Frieda of the Grignano holiday, indicating her newfound affection for Max Weber and how this prompted a 'geistig' nostalgia for Otto Gross:

> Being together with the Webers, I means Max W. of course, was a rich experience. But it isn't as you imagine that one would want to submit to him. Not at all, especially when I love and admire him the most, I feel so very clearly *how* differently we look at life. He insists that I am wrong. And I cannot always protest and cry out 'no, no!' He was so movingly kind, full of understanding and warmth, and still is. But I cannot but feel that this relationship, at least as it is now, is like a short-lived tender blossom, which lacks roots in the soil. Strangely enough, since that encounter I keep thinking with increasing longing of the Otto as he once was, in spite perhaps of realizing more and more that *nothing* equals his kind of intellectuality (Geistigkeit). 'His kind of intellectuality' is stupid, I means his very own intellectuality quite apart from the erotic attraction. . . . I am done with Alfred Weber since I have Max, both together doesn't work. Once the Völckers visited me, that too can happen in life.
>
> (Roth 2010a: 44)

A few weeks later Else Jaffé chose Alfred Weber, who then became her lifelong partner, so cementing the break between Else and Max Weber.

Something of the rift that had occurred can be gauged from an incident in Ascona, where Weber was staying in Easter 1914. Else Jaffé came to visit Frieda Gross and Max wrote to Marianne Weber:

> Liebes Mädele,
> I am blockaded in my room today, because yesterday Frieda installed Else in the room directly opposite. On my instructions she has explained that I am away and there is no way she can see me. So I am not allowed to be here. Also I do not wish to see her. Also from what Alfred [Weber] said to Frieda [Gross] in Bellinzona [nearby] the nasty and cowardly absence of chivalrous behaviour of both of these people to me has become only too apparent – there can be nothing more for me than a 'chance meeting'.
>
> (Whimster 1999: 56–7; MWG 2003: 594)

The vehemence of Weber's rejection letter of Otto Gross's article can be accounted for in more prosaic terms. Else Jaffé worked on the *Archiv* with her husband Edgar, co-editor and owner of the journal, and this could be an innocent explanation for why the letter is addressed to Dr. Frau Jaffé. The journal in its opening statement in 1904 said that alongside the investigation of 'the general significance of capitalist evolution for culture (Kultur)', it would also keep in contact with neighbouring disciplines 'the general theory of the state, the philosophy of law, social ethics – and with social psychological inquiry and those inquiries commonly grouped under the name of sociology' (Ghosh 2010: 100). Any author who contravened Weber's own methodological code – that religious, ethical, or political beliefs of an author are quite distinct from scientific analysis and the two should not be conflated – was treated harshly by Weber; for example, the scorn Weber poured over the heads of those who suggested – for example, at meetings of the German Sociological Society – that scientific categories can be substituted for value positions. In an autobiographical note written many years later, Else Jaffé said, 'Otto comes to Heidelberg [in margin, April 1907], Edgar drawn into the new doctrine. Theoretical discussions with the Webers [margin 1907]. The little Peter conceived' (Roth 2010a: 37).

The title of Otto Gross's paper is known only from Marianne Weber pencilling at the top of Max's rejection letter: '*Über psychologistische Herrschaftsordnung. 1. Der Psychologismus seit Nietzsche und Freud*' (The domination of the psychological order. 1. The psychologism since Nietzsche and Freud) (Prussian Secret State Archive, Nr. 92 Nachlass Max Weber, Nr. 30, Bd. 7, B1. 32). The '*theoretischen Auseinandersetzungen*' (theoretical arguments) may well have generated considerable heat, since at that point both Else and Edgar Jaffé were entering the Otto Gross camp while Marianne and Max Weber had not. The interesting theoretical interchange concerns Max Weber's depiction of Otto Gross. Weber sees Otto Gross as capable of the 'Akosmismus' of love and terms him charismatic. This is the first mention of both charisma and 'Akosmismus' in Weber's published writings. 'Akosmismus' of love, the editors of Weber's letters tell us, knows love in an 'unearthly' way and follows the command to love with a disregard for reality (MWG 1990: 402). It is the Christian injunction to love your neighbour irrespective of any circumstance and is found in Dostoyevsky's character of Aloysha in *Brothers Karamazov*. The fictional impact of Aloysha is his heedless saintliness in a world that in fact demands a little more guile if his own life and the lives of others are not to be damaged. Otto Gross, who knew his Dostoyevsky – then a widely read author – would have recognised Weber's description.

To have personal charisma could be reckoned to mean to have the gift of leadership, a divine indwelling spirit that compels others to follow. Weber did not give the term sociological precision and definition until some years later (Weber 1968: 1111–57). But the sense is in line with Else Jaffé's description of Gross as a prophet, who for Weber had some strange gift of compelling people to his views. Weber picks out decisive qualities in Otto Gross and in doing so articulates what was to become a crucial concept in his vocabulary of political sociology. Gross's influence on the most influential social scientist of the twentieth century was, therefore, to conjure up two deeply irrational concepts. Charisma, as Weber came to use it in his sociology, is confined to a pre-modern, non-bureaucratic world. 'Acosmic' found a home within his sociology of religion, as a mystical form of love associated with the preaching of Jesus and Buddhism (Weber 1966: 226). Both concepts have revolutionary capacities. The charismatic leader can erupt from nowhere, overturn the existing order, and just as quickly vanish. An absolute ethic of love has the ability to defy convention and normal reality.

Joachim Radkau has suggested, 'As far as we know, Weber uses the term "charisma" for the first time in a letter to Dora Jellinek of 9 June 1910, referring at that time to Stefan George. From this point on, Weber loves the concept' (Radkau 2009: 581–2). The reference to Gross, I think, has to take precedence. Weber is deploying the term, in his *second* use of it, in relation to the misgivings he has about George's circle creating an aesthetic cult around a 16-year-old boy, Maximilian Kronberger. Weber complains that incarnating this boy into a saviour – with Stefan George as the charismatic leader of this cult – makes no sense to outsiders (MWG 1994: 560–1). This shows that Weber was extending the use of the charisma concept, linking to other ideas in the sociology of religion – sect, cult, salvation. The sense is deeply irrational again, but in a darker and more inward-looking sense than the original Grossian inspiration. Radkau also argues that Weber's erotic awakening through Else Jaffé inaugurates a new intuitive and instinctual phase of his life. This argument underpins Part III of Radkau's biography (2009: 345), which he entitles *Erlösung und*

Erleuchtung (Salvation and Illumination). A Weber back in touch with his natural side, due to the acceptance of the power of eros, opens the floodgates to a highly productive phase of his career, it is argued. One of these productive concepts is 'charisma' and Radkau has not held back in pointing up some of its more bizarre and irrational manifestations. However one wishes to analyse the irrational dimensions of charisma – a not inconsiderable undertaking – the Grossian inspiration, independently of Else Jaffé, is enough to establish its arrival. The common feature of the 1907 letter and Weber's later sociology of charisma is that Weber's attitude to both is governed by methodological strictures. Otto Gross was 'anthropologically strange' to Weber and suggested to him the concept of charisma. Radkau's idea that Weber's burgeoning comparative studies was floated on Else Jaffé's erotic nimbus is an argument that must remain open to question.

To summarise the Weber–Gross encounter: Else Jaffé played the role of go-between but perhaps in not the affectually 'loaded' sense as has previously been assumed. It is Otto Gross, the man, who becomes the object of Weber's conceptual attention, calling forth two more esoteric terms from Weber's encyclopaedic brain. There is, however, a tribute to expressionism here, in that Gross represented the revolutionary and the irrational whose impact could produce the unexpected.

Otto Gross clearly did have an impact within the closed circles of academic Heidelberg. Frieda Gross started an affair with the philosopher Emil Lask, whose letters to her showed a mixture of the besotted and the philosophical. He, he wrote to her, was merely a receptacle for philosophical problems whereas she is 'too apart, much too great and beautiful and mature and so very much more of personality and life for me . . . I am worse in my Sachlichkeitspathos', and her remarks about him show a disparaging impatience with his mannerisms (Heidelberg University Library, Manscript Section, H. HS. 3820). Emil Lask then went on to start other affairs, for example with Lina Radbruch, the wife of Gustav Radbruch. Edgar Jaffé took advantage of what had become an open marriage. Else Jaffé reverted, as noted, to her previous lover, Völcker, as well as other lovers, aside from her liaison with Alfred Weber. But what did occur in Heidelberg remained private and was mediated through a very particular academic sensibility, so defeating one of Otto Gross's public aims of an open sexual morality.

In terms of Mannheim's coordinates, Heidelberg's 'sexual revolution' occurred within a private space and had few chiliastic moments. For the few brave and bold women involved, public exposure could leave them vulnerable to the legal rights enjoyed by husbands as well as themselves becoming the objects of scandal. Else Jaffé had to deploy considerable deftness as well as reliance on friends and her family to ensure stability for herself and her children. The arrangements with her husband and Alfred Weber were elaborate, tried the patience of many involved, including Max and Marianne Weber, and, to note, remain closed to the outside world (Roth 2010a: 35–47).

Frieda Gross did not fare as well as her friend, and she became very dependent on the support of Max and Marianne Weber and others. Writing from Ascona to Marianne in April 1913, Max Weber provided a detailed account of Frieda Gross's predicament:

> I sat with Frieda yesterday by her fireplace for a few hours. She has a great need to talk things out. Her life is completely wrecked. *How so* can be quickly told. Dementia praecox was already diagnosed before her marriage to Otto Gross. The parents had *concealed* this from her. Then it went as Jaspers predicted of Bloch: she became dreadfully overtaxed, completely and wretchedly eaten up and on top of this – which she confesses – the terrible drain of emotions owing to her polygamy. It's of no consequence who started this: mentally she *couldn't* meet the demands of her husband, she has become a complete nervous wreck, and *must* have 'the other' (for opposite reasons as Else!).
>
> (Whimster 1999: 47; MWG 2003: 182)

Sexual revolution in the age of bourgeois patriarchy had a price, as the Webers were very much aware. The open marriage pact of Frieda and Otto Gross did not alter the fact that Frieda still remained dependent on her husband for income. She did not have an occupation though did some training in nursing. Else Jaffé was very exceptional both in obtaining her university degree and in becoming a factory inspector in Baden. Even she, though, was forced to accept that she would have to give up her post were she to have children. Otto Gross was able to hold down the post of hospital doctor only for relatively short periods due to his instability, and he was dependent on his successful father, Professor Hans Gross, for money. Hans Gross paid Frieda Gross an allowance but solely for the upbringing of Peter Gross. When Frieda Gross took up with the anarchist Ernst Frick and had a child, Eva Verena Gross, Hans Gross applied to the Austrian courts to have Eva declared illegitimate, and for Otto to be placed under his guardianship, a move which made Frieda vulnerable to having her son taken away from her. This is part of Frieda Gross's psychological desperation, as described by Weber. From this point onwards Max Weber acts as her unofficial legal counsel in fighting Hans Gross. And to the extent that her material existence was salvaged, it was due to the power and influence of people like the Webers and, in particular, a Zurich high court judge, Otto Lang (Whimster 1999: 66; Goetz von Olenhusen 2002: 183–206).

Weber's comment on the sexual conduct of Frieda Gross and Else Jaffé shows their different routes of achieving their own autonomy. Jaffé pursued her physical desires in contravention of marital norms. Frieda Gross liked the public spectacle and excitement of affairs. A few days later Max Weber describes her behaviour in public:

> We sat in the café when shockingly all of a sudden this refined and elegant being began to play the *complete coquette* – only to show up the 'middle class' ladies who were there. I don't know what it was – whether in the hasty and dishevelled appearance (within *ten minutes* of having got out of *bed*, she had suddenly made a decision and had dashed on to the boat [to Locarno]), the cigarettes, the loud voice, the way of holding her head and gestures, and how she unconsciously reacted to that! Defiance against 'society'. The feeding of self-esteem through 'the pathos of distance' against society and all such feelings were at once there. I can imagine her in Munich's Schwabing but *not* in Heidelberg, she doesn't fit into the ensemble: Gruhle thinks she could be integrated again, but I do not. She should move to *Zurich*. There was even a law proposed to permit *concubinage* for *foreigners* who are not able to divorce [Otto and Frieda had a Catholic marriage]. . ., but it was rejected after a referendum.
>
> (Whimster 1999: 49; MWG 2003: 189–90)

Frieda Gross's quandary as described by Weber illustrates a law of uneven development. Otto Gross, the anarchists and the Berlin expressionists/dadaists thought and acted in terms of spontaneous acts of revolt as a way of undermining patriarchalism from within. But the social forms of the family and the local environment and milieu of place operated according to deeply ingrained expectations and attitudes that were slow to move. Else Jaffé knew the difference between Heidelberg – progressive in a political sense but still conservative in matters of social decorum – and the artistic and bohemian Schwabing. Frieda Gross, by choosing to live with the anarchist Ernst Frick, who had served a two-year jail sentence for an anarchist deed, would probably not have been allowed by the authorities to return to Schwabing and Munich. Ascona became her 'utopia' but more in the sense of being nowhere. But for Frieda Gross's anarchist associations, she should have belonged to the demi-monde within a cosmopolitan city.

Weber's letters from Ascona muse over these dilemmas. In 1913 he was reading Lukács's *Die Seele und die Formen* (1974[1911]). Lukács deliberately passed up the consummation of physical love (with the artist Irma Seidler) for the literary exploration of the existential moment of love. He asked how avant-garde writers, while introducing the figure of the New Woman, who knew her own desires and demanded autonomy in her life, could pass beyond the conventions entrenched in bourgeois capitalist society. Lukács only solved this dilemma for himself, and very much to the chagrin of Max Weber, by making an existential leap of faith into revolutionary Marxism and by taking the proletariat to be the new Hegelian –

and ethical – subject in historical dialectic. Lenin became his new idol, 'Lenin always saw the problems of the age as a whole: the onset of the last phase of capitalism and the possibilities of turning the now inevitable final struggle between bourgeoisie and proletariat in favour of the proletariat – *of human salvation* (Lukács [1924]1970: 10–11; Kardaky 1991: 280–1).

Weber's musings led him to consider that the erotic had its own forms, just as the aesthetic had its own forms, a point he questioned Lukács about in March 1913 (MWG 2003: 117). It was pointless to ask, in respect to the aesthetic, how these were derived or to be justified, they just were – a given. The roots of eroticism were *unterirdisch*; the point, however, was to give the erotic form. In his essay Intermediate Reflections (1948: 323–359), Weber elaborated this into a theory of sublimation, in the sense of refinement. The civilised form of sexuality is the refinement and the intensification of the erotic in contradistinction to the mere physicality of sexual intercourse (Whimster 1995: 451). Weber in this respect was rejecting Kantian morality. The erotic had its own scale of values apart from the moral – universal ought – rules of marriage. He condoned Else Jaffé's extra-marital excursions in terms of the exceptionality of her person – her transgression, being the person she was, added more to the world than it subtracted. Weber recognised that one of the implications of sexual sublimation is that the erotic is likely to occur outside marriage, and on a biographical note it was probably Frieda Gross who offered him attractions, perhaps more the courtesan than the mistress. A letter from 2 March 1920 shows he always wanted to return to Ascona or for Frieda Gross to come to Munich (Prussian Secret State Archive, Rep. 92 Nachlass Max Weber, Nr. 30, Bd. 8, B1. 72–3).

Sublimated eroticism as a practice would seem to presume a new development within the forms of the bourgeois family and a degree of sophistication by all involved – in some ways a shift towards the looser conventions of court society. Weber never really envisaged the ending of the civilisational form of the *haute bourgeoisie*. By Otto Gross's standards Weber was a counter-revolutionary and it is hard to see the sustainability of the latter's version of eroticism in a more democratic society.

The successful sexual revolutionaries were Frieda and D. H. Lawrence. The story has been told many times and does not need to be retold here (Green 1974; Worthen 1992). But it is worth briefly reflecting just how long the message of sexual emancipation took to become an almost majority view, and what difficulties it underwent. Else's younger sister Frieda, then married to Weekley, did not deny Otto Gross's sexual evangelism. She went on to take lovers who had working-class backgrounds – Frick and then Lawrence – introducing a democratic element in what was otherwise an 'aristocratic' doctrine for *entgleiste* bourgeoisie. Under English patriarchally oriented divorce law, she had to abandon her children to live with D. H. Lawrence, and as a couple they were forced out of England, eventually to the artist colony of Taos in New Mexico. Lawrence reprised in his novels many of the characters drawn into the orbit of Otto Gross's charismatic force, and their consequent dilemmas. Or as Frieda's mother ('die Baronin') proudly complained to her: 'But it's always you in Lorenzo's books, all his women are you' (Byrne 1996: 234). At the time, 1920, her mother was an avid reader of Lawrence but hid the fact from friends lest she be thought to be reading the output of a pornographer. The first review of *Women in Love* was entitled 'A Book the Police should Ban' (ibid.: 251).

In fact, the whole of the Richthofen family and the anecdotes and episodes of their lives appear almost as a secret family history camouflaged in the narrative of Lawrence's prose – and most of all biographically in *Mr Noon* and *Twilight in Italy* (Turner 1990: 155–8). The connections to the Richthofen family history came to light late in the day. Guenther Roth has pointed out that Else Jaffé did not want to be forgotten next to her sister. As she wrote to E.W. Tedlock in 1960:

> [Frieda lived] in the inner turmoil caused by the impact of what we called Freudian theories on our feelings and thoughts. (About 1907) I say *our*, because it was through me that Frieda knew that 'remarkable disciple of Freud' she mentions at the beginning of her book *Not I but the Wind* . . . We shared the happenings of that period.
>
> (F. Lawrence 1961: 426)

It was only when a general sexual revolution had started at the end of the 1960s that Else Jaffé thought it safe to release some of her correspondence to Martin Green in 1973. Any hint of these matters during the collapse of so many revolutionary movements after 1920 would have been not only extremely embarrassing but also dangerous. Edgar Jaffé had become finance minister in Eisner's revolutionary government in Bavaria in 1919. When it collapsed, in bloodshed, the Jaffé family was ostracised and this was intensified by a vicious current of anti-semitism, which attached to Edgar Jaffé. In the 1930s, likewise, when academics such as Alfred Weber lost their posts because of their liberal views, any hint of the halcyon world of old Heidelberg before the war would have been highly dangerous. In the early 1930s Else Jaffé was trying to obtain US and English sponsors for the emigration of her children, Hans and Friedel Jaffé, from Germany (Roth 2010b: 9–14).

Though D. H. Lawrence is regarded as a modernist – with a prose that delves for authenticity and truth, unsparing descriptions of all aspects of living, and being as a new ontological topic – Martin Green has made the acute observation that Lawrence belongs in the tradition of the English family novel (Green 1999: 265 ff.). If we take *Women in Love* as an example of this, Lawrence works through the generational confrontations, which, to remind ourselves, can be extremely brutal, just as he works through the changes in class structure – think of Gerald Crich as the modernising owner of a coal mine. Changes in the primary social relationships in the family take time to work through. The ethical anarchist Gustav Landauer was highly critical of Otto Gross's anarchist friend Erich Mühsam's ideology of sexual liberation and open marriage. The anarchist historian Ulrich Linse writes:

> Landauer's Federation disagreed completely with Mühsam's 'sexual politics' (if such a pompous term may be used). The central question for organised labour was the abortion issue (the struggle against Paragraph 218 of the Penal Code) and free access to contraception.
> (Linse 1999: 135)

To introduce a legal and materialist note, it was only in the 1960s in Great Britain that these issues were finally resolved. Abortion was legalised, as was homosexuality; the obscenity laws were reformed; after a famous trial Lawrence's *Lady Chatterley's Lover* was published by Penguin books; and women in around 1968 could obtain contraception by prescription through the National Health Service. The two Richthofen sisers, Else and Frieda, were in part (Frieda more so) fictionalised as Gudrun and Ursula in *Women in Love* (Lawrence 2007[1920]: 532). The effective revolutionaries were embedded in Lawrence's novels and did not occupy the chiliastic/public space part of Mannheim's grid. As we watch Ken Russell's film *Women in Love* when Alan Bates and Oliver Reed wrestle naked are we looking at the delayed echo of Otto Gross's theory that to love a woman is to empathise as a man, what it is to love another man (Gross 1920: 10ff.)?

References

Byrne, J. (1996) *A Genius for Living. A Biography of Frieda Lawrence*. London: Bloomsbury.

Engels, F. (1972[1884]) *The Origin of the Family and Private Property*. London: Lawrence and Wishart.

Ghosh, P. (2010) Max Weber, Werner Sombart and the *Archiv für Sozialwissenschaft*: The authorship of the 'Geleitwort' (1904). *History of European Ideas*, *36*, 71–100.

Goetz von Olenhusen, A. (2002) Die Sorge des Hausvaters. Die Prozesse von Hans Gross gegen Otto und Frieda Gross. In G. Heuer (ed.), *2. Internationaler Otto Gross Kongress*. Marburg an der Lahn: LiteraturWissenschaft.de.

Green, M. (1974) *The von Richthofen Sisters: The Triumphant and the Tragic Modes of Love. Else and Frieda von Richthofen, Otto Gross, Max Weber, and D. H. Lawrence, in the years 1870–1970*. London: Weidenfeld and Nicolson.

Green, M. (1999) *Otto Gross. Freudian Psychoanalyst 1877–1920*. New York: Mellen.

Gross, O. (1920) Über Konflikt und Beziehung. In *Drei Aufsätze über den inneren Konflikt*. Bonn: Marcus & Weber Verlag.
Kardarky, A. (1991) *Georg Lukács. Life, Thought and Politics*. Oxford: Blackwell.
Lawrence, D. H. (2007[1920]) *Women in Love*. London: Penguin.
Lawrence, F. (1961) *Memoirs and Correspondence* (E. W. Tedlock, ed.). London: Heinemann.
Linse, U. (1999) Sexual Revolution and Anarchism: Erich Mühsam. In S. Whimster (ed.), *Max Weber and the Culture of Anarchy*. Basingstoke: Macmillan.
Lukács, G. (1911) *A Modern Drama*. Budapest: Franklin.
Lukács, G. (1970) *Lenin: A Study on the Unity of his Thought*. London: NLB.
Lukács, G. (1974[1911]) *Soul and Form*. Cambridge, MA: MIT Press.
Mannheim, K. (1960) *Ideology and Utopia*. London: Routledge.
Mannheim, K. (1960) *Ideology and Utopia* (L. Wirth and E. Shils, trans.). London: Routledge & Kegan Paul.
MWG (1990) *Max Weber Briefe 1906–1908*. M. R. Lepsius and W. J. Mommsen with B. Rudhard and M. Schön (eds.). Tübingen: J. C. B. Mohr.
MWG (1994) *Max Weber Briefe 1908–1910*. M. R. Lepsius and W. J. Mommsen with B. Rudhard and M. Schön (eds.). Tübingen: J. C. B. Mohr.
MWG (2003) *Max Weber Briefe 1913–1914*. M. R. Lepsius and W. J. Mommsen with B. Rudhard and M. Schön (eds.). Tübingen: J. C. B. Mohr.
Michaels, J. (1983) *Anarchy and Eros. Otto Gross' Impact on German Expressionist Writers*. New York: Peter Lang.
Radkau, J. (2009) *Max Weber: A Biography*. Cambridge: Polity.
Roth, G. (2010a) Edgar Jaffé (May 14, 1866–April 29, 1921) and Else von Richthofen (October 8, 1874–December 22, 1973): A biographical essay based on the family archive of Christopher Jeffrey. Unpublished manuscript.
Roth, G. (2010b) Else von Richthofen, Edgar Jaffé und ihre Kinder im Kontext ihrer Zeit (forthcoming). *Festschrift für Hubert Treiber*.
Shields, M. (1999) Max Weber and German Expressionism. In S. Whimster (ed.), *Max Weber and the Culture of Anarchy*. Basingstoke: Macmillan.
Turner, J. (1990) The Otto Gross–Frieda Weekley Correspondence (transcribed, translated and annotated by J. Turner with C. Rumpf-Worthen and R. Jenkins). *D. H. Lawrence Review*, *22*(2), 136–225.
Weber, M. (1948) *From Max Weber* (H. H. Gerth and C. W. Mills, eds). London: Routledge & Kegan Paul.
Weber, M. (1966) *The Sociology of Religion*. London: Methuen.
Weber, M. (1968) *Economy and Society*. New York, NY: Bedminster Press.
Whimster, S. (1995) Max Weber on the erotic and some comparisons with the work of Foucault. *International Sociology*, *10*(4), 447–462.
Whimster, S. (1999) Introduction to Weber, Ascona and Anarchism. In S. Whimster (ed.), *Max Weber and the Culture of Anarchism*. Basingstoke: Macmillan.
Whimster, S. and Heuer, G. (1998) Otto Gross and Else Jaffé and Max Weber. *Theory, Culture and Society*, *15*(3–4), 129–160.
Worthen, J. (1992) *D. H. Lawrence: The Early Years. 1885–1912*. Cambridge: Cambridge University Press.

Part IV

Sexual revolutions

Chapter 13

Sexual liberation: Where have we got to?

Psychoanalysis and the engagement with sexual liberation[1]

Susie Orbach in conversation with Brett Kahr

The following is a revised version of the conversation held between Susie Orbach and Brett Kahr at the 'Sexual Revolutions' symposium in January 2009 of the 'Laws of the Father: Freud/Gross/Kafka' exhibition at the Freud Museum, London, upon which this book is based (cf. 'The Continuing Life of an Exhibition', pp. 29–30).

Brett Kahr: Good morning ladies and gentlemen. I am very honoured to be able to have a conversation with Professor Susie Orbach, because, as you know, conversation is something that Susie does extremely well. And, in a way, I think conversation may well lie at the heart of Susie's definition of the art of psychotherapy and psychoanalysis, because she regards the psychological encounter as a very special kind of conversation in which people may be seen, and heard, and met, and understood, and ultimately healed. I am particularly pleased to have this conversation only two days after the publication of Susie Orbach's new book *Bodies* (2009), which appears in the wonderful 'Big Ideas' book series, edited by Lisa Appignanesi – who is here with us today – published by Profile Books. This series serves as a potent reminder that 'Big Ideas' have not died, and that people still crave this kind of reading and thinking, which I find very gratifying. I regard *Bodies* as a seminal work, one which represents a beautiful line of intellectual and clinical thought which began back in the 1970s, specifically in 1978, with the publication of *Fat is a Feminist Issue* (Orbach 1978), or '*FiFi*', as we know it. We might describe Susie Orbach's *Bodies* as not only the apotheosis of the development of her thinking, but also as a resting point, as I know that there will be more books from Susie in the future, particularly about the real pain with which each individual struggles, over the challenges of inhabiting a body across the life cycle.

So, Susie and I will have a conversation, and we do have a plan. We hope to talk together for approximately 40 minutes, and then we will open the conversation up for discussion, and hope to pick up on the threads and themes which have emerged already in the discussions this morning. We shall try to focus our conversation on three areas. First, we will explore the

Sexual Revolution/Sexual Liberation of the 1960s, especially from Susie's viewpoint as a participant-observer. Susie will, I trust, tell us about her experiences on the front lines. Second, we will investigate some Otto Grossian themes to see how far the Sexual Revolution/Sexual Liberation movement has progressed since that time. Third, and finally, we hope to examine the role that psychoanalysis has played both in the development of Sexual Liberation and in its inhibition, because I think that psychoanalysis occupies a very complex position in relation to sexuality, and not always an obvious one, and certainly not the position which we see lampooned by the general public, namely, that of the sex-obsessed psychoanalyst.

Well, let us start at the beginning, back in the 1960s. I remember that wonderful poem by Philip Larkin (1974), *Annus Mirabilis*, where he writes that sexual intercourse started in 1963, at the time of the end of the ban on Lady Chatterley and the first Beatles LP. He regarded himself as a bit too old to have enjoyed it, and, I have to confess, I was a bit too young in 1963 to have known about it, but you were there, on the front lines.
[General laughter]

Susie Orbach: I was on my back . . .
[General laughter]

Brett Kahr: I believe that after your time as a university student, you had begun to train as a clinician. And if I recall, you began working with forensic patients in a penal institution.

Susie Orbach: New York City was quite enlightened at that time, and people who were too vulnerable because of what would now be called sexual dysmorphia, or gender dysmorphia, men who wished to present themselves as women, transsexuals or transvestites who got into terrible trouble with the law, were put on probation rather than sent to prison, and were seen as outpatients. That was my first clinical setting, but it was in the early 1970s.

Brett Kahr: Ah, so you had not yet started clinical work. Well, let us backtrack then, because I want to situate you in the period before you wrote '*FiFi*'.

Susie Orbach: But before that, in the 1960s, for me and for many other of the women of my generation, the position from which we attempted to engage in the Sexual Revolution, which indeed struck us as very liberatory, was not from the position of being able to identify a sexuality for ourselves particularly, it was very much from the position that feminists would *later* describe as male-identified. If one wanted to be *active* sexually, there was not the notion of bringing forward a kind of active female sexuality, because there was no real understanding of it. It meant being free from the strictures of monogamy, it meant smashing the State and smashing the monogamous relationship, but I don't think we had a notion of what might constitute sexual pleasure. We knew what desire was, but I don't think we knew what pleasure was. In the first phase of Pre-Feminism and Feminism it was, 'Get yourself on the pill, or whatever, and DO IT!' We needed to 'do it' to prove something to ourselves about the potential for liberation. I don't think it was actually terribly erotic, frankly. In today's terms it would be considered, in my words, very masculine, which is not to blame the men. It is to say, we did not have a vocabulary of an erotic at that particular moment. And, what David [Bennett] (cf. chapter 2) was talking about, from my own days in a political commune, where we did have – I don't think we called it a fuck-list – but the determination to break down sexual ownership, having read our Reich and our Engels, did mean that one was required to engage in sexual practices with multiple partners, and to try. When we were not out in the streets doing whatever we were meant to be doing politically, sexual experimentation was an absolute accompaniment. And it took quite a while for the women to even know the word 'feminism' and what it meant, [i.e.] to be thinking about this from the perspective of femininity or women's experience, and a very long time before women's desire could get on the table. It was before *Our Bodies, Ourselves* (Boston Women's Health Book Collective 1973) had been written. We'd had Masters and Johnson (1966) talking about female anatomy and how, actually, women did work, and we had *The Joy of Sex* (Comfort 1972), but we needed to revise for ourselves something about what really constituted the 'Sexual Revolution'. Actually, I think for an awful lot of women it meant getting themselves on the page rather than *The Story of O* (Réage 1954), or those kinds of sexual fantasies.

Brett Kahr: Did you have a sense of being right in the middle of something important at that time? I mean, did you and your colleagues in the commune recognise yourselves as being in the midst of a revolution, or did you simply regard yourself as 'hanging out' with some unusually racy, progressive people?

Susie Orbach: The main import was to put together these two phenomena: something that was happening among hippies, who were doing it, who were relaxed about sex, and exploratory, and a bit San Francisco-ish, with a bit of Marcuse and a political thrust to destroy capitalism and imperialism. We saw ourselves as young pioneers for the New World, and we would look back to people – we didn't know about [Otto] Gross, of course, since Gottfried [Heuer] hadn't yet brought him to our attention, but we did know about [Wilhelm] Reich, and we studied Reich, and we knew about [Anatoly] Lunacharsky, we knew about Alexandra Kollontai, we knew about the Bolshevik revolutionaries, and we knew all about sexual practices that went along in that revolution. We were owning ourselves sexually in a different kind of way, just as David [Bennett] said, in a kind of militant, anti-monogamist stand, which was extremely problematic and took a long time for people to recover from and to think through, and ask: 'Actually, what is this thing called sexual liberation?' I don't think we used a word like 'promiscuous' at all, because I think we would have had a critique of that notion. It took feminism to bring to the fore questions like, 'But what is this thing attachment?' 'And what about the idea of relationship?' 'What about the idea of caring?' rather than sex as mechanical or ecstatic, which I think were the two positions that were posed.

Brett Kahr: Your remarks remind me of that wonderful chapter in Volume 2 of Ernest Jones's (1955) biography of Sigmund Freud, the chapter called Opposition, in which Jones talked about the vile comments which greeted the early psychoanalysts when they had first begun to present papers at conferences. Jones reported that at a Congress of German Neurologists and Psychiatrists in 1910, the noted psychiatrist Professor Wilhelm Weygant denounced Freud's theories, exclaiming: 'This is not a topic for discussion at a scientific meeting; it is a matter for the police' (quoted in Jones 1955: 109). I find myself wondering, therefore, what sort of resistances you might have encountered at that time, especially as you and your colleagues had steeped yourselves in very 'subversive' texts, such as the writings of Wilhelm Reich and so forth.

Susie Orbach: It is an interesting question. I think we were a very arrogant generation who came of age at a particular moment in history, and thought we were going to change the world, and I don't think that we in any sense gave two damns about the opposition. In fact, the opposition was our fight. So that was no problem to us, and paradoxically psychoanalysis was part of what we opposed. I was living in the States at the time, even though I was English, and psychoanalysis, in the 1950s, had been *totally* recruited to be a kind of normalising, moralistic force, designed to support the post-Second World War government incantation, 'give us back our wives and sweethearts'. So psychoanalysis was anti-sexual in a way that Andrew [Samuels] has described. We weren't engaged in taking on psychoanalysis at the time; we were engaged with a previous political generation and we were engaged with that which we identified as complacent in the all too desperate suburban America. They were the inheritors of the post-war settlement – 'give us back our wives and sweethearts' – who we (arrogantly) felt terribly sorry for as they were so bereft of the chance to express themselves. Pete Seeger's song *Little Boxes* – and I was very moved that Barack Obama had Pete Seeger at his inauguration concert – was really what we were fighting against, which was corporation man, the military-industrial complex, cookie-cutter people who were capable of consuming, and we were what we thought was liberation. We were flamboyant, angry, but our main impulse was to fight capitalism. There you could get a lot of opposition. You could get arrested as often as you needed to. You know, it was that kind of feeling.

Brett Kahr: You experienced such wonderful fervour, such wonderful passion. And I very much like what you say about the arrogance that may be necessary in order to confront the opposition. Perhaps unlike the early Freudian psychoanalysts, all busy dodging the bullets, you and your comrades tried to engage in a more active way – proactively rather than reactively.

Susie Orbach: Well, we were actively engaged with the notion that there shouldn't be shame. I wasn't a therapist at that time, and therefore, I wasn't aware of the need to take into account the intrapsychic processes of change.

Brett Kahr: Did it surprise you, ultimately, that you did become a psychotherapist and a psychoanalyst, in view of the 1950s legacy that you have described, imprisoning the wives and sweethearts, and in view of the fact that American psychoanalysis completely obliterated radical sexologists and psychoanalysts such as Wilhelm Reich from their discourse, and perhaps still do?

Susie Orbach: Well, there is a real continuity between the methods, the process of the accumulation of knowledge, I suppose you would say, in today's vernacular, that happened in the women's liberation movement – which was consciousness-raising, where you spoke and were listened to, and you listened to each other – and the processes of therapy. So, those continuities are quite significant. [Herbert] Marcuse, despite the fact that one might have thought he was very deterministic and far too Freudian for most of us, raised the issue for us of the conscious, or unconscious processes, I probably would say; and we could observe in the struggles of feminism the inhibitions that women had – and I focus on sexuality rather than all the other inhibitions – to experience something that felt like an erotic experience for them. We were interested in the question 'What are the structures that exist inside of us?' – the material structures in our minds, if you like. And, actually, you can't go much further *without* thinking about psychoanalysis. So, in a way, it doesn't surprise me, but one can only tell one's story retrospectively.

Brett Kahr: And, did you have any comfort from, or did you feel that you had good maternal role models in figures such as Marie Bonaparte, whose book on female sexuality appeared in English in 1953, or Helene Deutsch (1925), or Karen Horney (1967)? I suppose you engaged with those texts, but did Freud's women prove at all useful to you?

Susie Orbach: No. I think what was interesting for us of that generation was that Helene Deutsch's work could be read as a very skilled and accurate account of the psychic effects of the oppression of women. Bonaparte was not an attractive figure to us, because she had tried to have her clitoris moved. We were fighting to shift the dominance of the vagina–penis construct. We felt enormous sorrow for Bonaparte, but our struggle was to redefine sexuality for women. So the text around what this woman's/girl's tortuous journey was in order to give up an infantile or immature sexuality was just a source of outrage! And Dora (Freud 1905) was a source of outrage because we saw Freud as pimping for *Herrn* K. So, I don't think initially we could read the texts of psychoanalysis in a way that was of use to us. It wasn't the *specific* interpretations that Freud offered us, it was more the forms of contact that could allow for a different kind of reflection/speaking/listening. Does that make sense?

Brett Kahr: Yes, yes, absolutely. I think that you have a really important point, and we may wish to pick up on that in the discussion. Certainly, the position of the mothers of psychoanalysis has shifted over the decades.

Susie Orbach: We read Clara Thompson (1964), Karen Horney (1967), Jean Strouse (1974) and Ethel Person (1983). These were women writing in the States, and we felt very enthusiastic about them. But, largely, when we went into psychoanalysis, we couldn't find the things we wanted to find.

Brett Kahr: You made quite a breakthrough in terms of theory-construction in your 1978 book '*FiFi*' by repositioning the whole question of the woman's body. It has occurred to me that so many of the early psychoanalytical writings involved the analysis of a single body part, such as a paralysed arm, or an anaesthetised thigh, or a study of the vagina, or of the clitoris. But you took the *entire* female body into consideration in a most comprehensive way, identifying the so-called 'compulsive slims' who became the anorexics of the next decade.

Susie Orbach: That's a very interesting thought. I never actually thought about it in that way. I don't think I was aware of attempting to talk about the body. In my current book, *Bodies* (2009), I'm talking about bodies that don't exist for the individual in a sustainable way but have to be constructed. Psychically, many girls and women feel bodiless or that they are not living in their bodies. That's to say that they suffer agony and anguish and are not able to feel they have a body. Rather, they feel a need to produce a body. It's quite interesting that in '*FiFi*' I was trying to bring attention to the whole body as a hurt, rebellious, angry agent. I think you are absolutely right, compulsive eating was linked to agency of the whole body.

Brett Kahr: I think it might be far too crude to hypothesise that Freud treated his female patients in the 1890s solely as part-objects. That would be too crude and too unfair. But I do think that we can identify key moments in the history of psychoanalysis when practitioners progressed from the analysis of *symptoms* to the analysis of *character* (e.g. Reich 1933). And I believe that you have done something similar, introducing a very important type of body-analysis – a sort of integrated, totalistic body-and-psyche analysis.

Susie Orbach: That's very interesting. I need to think about this, and I need to think about this in relation to the last 15 years, and to the spate of cutting, especially teenage cutting, because I think that's a kind of reinstatement of 'one has an overall symptom which is the body', as the whole body thing is a mess. I need to think about this. Why didn't you discuss this with me before I wrote this book, for God's sake?!

[General laughter]

Brett Kahr: Did the 1960s work? Did the sexual liberation movement work?

Susie Orbach: What do you mean by that question?

Brett Kahr: Well, do you feel that you succeeded in what you had set out to do, and do you believe that people now enjoy a more conflict-free sexuality in the nineties and noughties, as compared with the fifties and sixties?

Susie Orbach: I don't think we set out – we weren't programmatic in that sense. In so far as we were programmatic, we were questioning and challenging the conformist manner in which we had been constructed. So, I don't know – did we set out? Certainly we set out to try to enjoy sex. I think we also set out to think about what the hell it was. Or, at least, people like me were very interested in the question 'what on earth is sex?' If you don't take sex as a given, what is it? And I'm still pondering that (Orbach 2000), I still am intrigued by that question. I'm sure most people are confused if you dare to ask the question, 'What is sex? What is the erotic?' So, the fact that it is part of public discourse is one thing, the fact that we have a highly sexualised culture, but a deeply, I think, unerotic culture, is another. The fact of your own work, where you detail what for an awful lot of people is very, very shocking material, the fact that, when we read your books (Kahr 2007, 2008), we realise it is the experience of so many people in sexual fantasy, that I am not sure 'achieve' is really a word that I would use at all. But I'm not sure that I want to use the word 'achieve' because that sounds too much like the business of energy having to be let off in some kind of way. I certainly think that if I look at material of women of my own generation, they had access to different erotic formulations for themselves than most of their mothers. That's pretty significant. *The Vagina Monologues* (Ensler 2001) is a wonderful play which has gone all around the world and has anecdotes from women of every decade, and it's about the difficulty of their genitalia. And it's really a fantastic account of sex, and the impossibility of it. And I do think that my friends' generation have been allowed or have fought for a kind of access to an erotic life that is radically different for us and for our children. If you want to discuss how successful that is, then I think that is a different question.

Brett Kahr: I'm thinking of your most recent work, such as your paper in the American psychoanalytic journal *Studies in Gender and Sexuality* (Orbach 2008), which I regard as really excellent, especially your work on 'merged attachment' in the mother–daughter relationship. In this paper, and in your *Bodies* book, you present some descriptions of horrific cases, quoting shocking figures about how many young girls wish to have plastic surgery such as face lifts and nose jobs, even at the ages of 12 and 13! Quite apart from the high incidence and prevalence of eating disorders among young girls, I wonder what kind of legacy the mothers of the 1960s have bequeathed to their daughters in the wake of sexual liberation. The daughters of 1960s mothers have now reached sexual maturity. What do we know about their experience?

Susie Orbach: The paper that you are referring to is not about my generation. I'm a terribly late mother, and so I'm really writing about the generation of girls raised by mothers who are the in-between generation. And part of the difficulty, I think, lies in the fact that those mothers weren't actively part of feminism, but they were meant to be its inheritors. And they were inheritors of a version of feminism that was nothing to do with a feminism which understood the political, economic, social, and psychological conditions of women's experience, and thus could collectivise women's issues. They were inheritors, instead, of that terrible notion, I think proposed by Shirley Conran, that 'You can have it all!' and be a 'superwoman'. Superwoman was about the production of a self that was about being post-feminist(!). This had absolutely nothing to do with conflict, and struggle, and fellowship, which are all completely central to notions of feminism. So, I don't think I'm writing about daughters of my generation at all, because I do think that's a different story. It's a kind of skip situation. But, what I thought you were going to refer to, something that I found very disturbing – and it's not the hooking-up and all of that kind of thing, friends with benefits, that's going on, because that seems to me ordinary adolescent exploration – is the account I give of nine-, ten-, eleven-year-olds on school buses, giving oral sex to boys before they get to school, and perceiving this as an essential part of their identity because of insecurities that rest inside of them in relation to themselves, but also to their body, sense of self, and their own recognition. And that sexuality, or the giving of sexual favours to boys who don't want them, and end up in the counsellor's office in these schools, at 11, saying, you know, 'This is – I haven't had a wet dream yet!', feeling very perplexed, and really trying to understand, 'what is it that's happened?' That this commodity called 'sexual practice' is now something that girls are using as a way of establishing some form of recognition and visibility when they don't feel it. So, I'm more disturbed about that aspect, or as disturbed about that aspect as I am about the creation of a body sense that is so disturbed that it only exists by being related to. In other words, when I'm writing about the plastic surgery statistics or the desire for body change, I am making an argument that there are not bodies there, that the only way psychically the person is relating to the body is by thinking of it in transformative terms as a way of instituting processes which might create a body, so one becomes the creator of one's own body, because it hasn't been there. And I would rest that at the generation between me and the other '68ers' who are sitting in the room, and the mothers who grew up in the Thatcherite, post-feminist moment where women were actually seriously in competition with each other and with men, and were supposed to have it all without any of the benefits of emotional connection, and in which the notion of independence, which was a totally Thatcherite notion, was promulgated so that people didn't need each other. You were an acquiring and a consuming and a producing individual, and there wasn't a hell of a lot to give to your daughter, except to project onto her the desire you had for your own self achievement – but perhaps without the emotional equipment in place, because you hadn't got it any better than the generation of my mum's had, if that makes sense.

Brett Kahr: Yes, you have explained this really beautifully. Last weekend, just round the corner from the Freud Museum, at the Tavistock Centre, we had a conference, sponsored jointly by Confer and by the Society of Couple Psychoanalytic Psychotherapists, called 'Taking Our Time'. This was not a conference about making love slowly [General laughter]. In fact, the full title of the conference, 'Taking Our Time: How Long Does it Take for Psychological Change to Occur?', gives an indication of what we addressed. In the conference, my colleagues and I explored the art of long-term, open-ended psychoanalytical treatment, and we investigated what role long-term treatment plays in an era of short-term, quick-fix email culture, in which cognitive behavioural therapies predominate. We had, as one of our speakers, the wonderful cultural commentator Carl Honoré (2004), who has written a book about the art of moving slowly, which proved very popular upon publication a few years ago. Honoré has collected a whole dossier of newspaper articles of really violent episodes that take place in bed between a husband and wife, when, for example, the wife finds out that the husband answers his emails on his Blackberry in the middle of the lovemaking act.

Susie Orbach: That is a new one! I'm sorry, that is new. That is new!
[General laughter]

Brett Kahr: Well, it is, and it isn't. In the course of my research project on sexual fantasies (Kahr 2007, 2008), I identified a phenomenon which I refer to as the 'intra-marital affair', namely, the indulgence in complex sexual fantasies about a person other than one's spouse or partner during the act of lovemaking. I think that we see a certain numbing which occurs during the so-called intimate relationship between two long-term sexual partners. It seems to me that there might be some merit in thinking about whether the Sexual Revolution of the 1960s has produced a generation of post-Revolution offspring for whom ordinary sex becomes so tame, and so uninteresting, that they must resort to fantasy more frequently. Carl Honoré told us that the best-selling pornographic video at the moment is that of the American socialite Paris Hilton. The video does not teach us any new sexual techniques, but it has become famous because in the middle of performing the sexual act, Paris Hilton actually answers her mobile telephone and then proceeds to have a conversation with a third party. Now, of course, this provides us with a glimpse into this young woman's psychology, but it also serves as a cultural trope. I do wonder about women of this generation, those women born in the wake of the sexual battlefront. What sort of numbness have we inherited?

Susie Orbach: I'd love to talk to you about numbness and fantasy, because I probably am alone among psychoanalysts in not really 'getting' sexual fantasies. And I wouldn't mind putting that on the table, just to be completely 100 per cent honest. But, John Berger said a long time ago, 'women look at themselves from the outside' – and I paraphrase this – 'and that is an aspect of their relation to themselves. It is to be the voyeur of their own experience.' He was talking about bourgeois women from many centuries ago. But I think that relation has become the relation that I observe in the consulting room. Hanging out with my daughter's friends, hanging out with young people, which I tend to do, perhaps rather more than is seemly for my age, my experience of their accounts of sexuality is that they are looking at themselves, that their way into sex is imagining themselves in a position that has been structured for them as an erotic, or that they have been invited to structure, being made into an erotic. Now, it may involve Paris Hilton's millions and the clothing she's wearing, for all I care, but it doesn't surprise me that the phone is there, because it is about . . . I suppose the 50s and 60s equivalent, would it have been a mirror on the top of the bedroom, or the bordello? So, I think that phenomenon has now extended so that one is outside of oneself. And I know that at a conference in which you and I were talking some time ago, about sex and pornography, for the Tavistock Centre for Couple Relationships, I was talking about how women are using pornography in a slightly different way in long-term relationships than men do, because they are using it to learn and bring that learning back into the relationship: 'I'd like to do this', or 'Can we try this?' Not maybe as crudely as that, but it was not simply about having an orgasm, but it was about, 'I want to do, I want to learn things', whereas for men, it had a different flavour. Who the hell is Paris Hilton's pornography selling to? I'm intrigued. Has anybody here looked at it? It intrigues me because it seems to me that she is a figure who represents something, so let's try not to be moralistic – highly problematic in terms of yourself as a consumerable construction of God-knows-what, right?

Brett Kahr: I think we may be much too old to be libidinally cathected to Paris Hilton [General laughter], but young people aged 20 to 30 all have very passionate views about her. Paris Hilton has become such a reference point, and such a focus of projections for all sorts of issues. But let us move on, because I have many other topics that I wish to discuss with you today. I would love to think with you about psychoanalysis, and about what role psychoanalysis has had in the sexual revolution, and in sexual liberation. Has psychoanalysis caused the liberation, and helped it to progress, or has psychoanalysis inhibited liberation quite profoundly?

Susie Orbach: When you said that, the thought that came to my mind – and I'm sure you don't want a personal account – but when sex came up in my own analysis it was from a male perspective. I had a lovely woman analyst, a Freudian, and my sexuality was not on the table, whether it was to do with reproduction, or whether it was to do with sexuality, and so she might comment, 'So, you would refuse to give your husband a baby', as though a baby were about a husband rather than about something either about me or in the relationship. Now, that's very recent, and I don't think it's atypical. The continual referencing by Kleinians of the idealised couple in the patient's mind is something I've rarely understood. I've never ever understood the force of that particular formulation. It always seemed to me to be a contradiction. Child development does have something to do with how a person is and their fantasy life and that does not always produce a picture of a perfect reproductive intercourse. I've always found that a very odd formulation. So, what has psychoanalysis done for the sexual revolution? I don't know what to say to you. I do think that I, and Luise [Eichenbaum], we have been accused of leaving the father out of psychological development, as though talking about mother, and the social context in which we essentially had single-parent rearing, is to leave out the father (Eichenbaum and Orbach 1984). I think the father has often been left out of his own option to be engaged in the family, so I'm not sure I could say that. But I think psychoanalysis is addressing that more now. And I think Andrew [Samuels] is quite right – we valorise long-term relationships, we do not look at celibacy; we do not look at its prevalence in long-term relationships (Orbach 2000). Psychoanalysis looks at what sex is; it just accepts it as being 'a thing'. And I don't think it trains psychotherapists – let's leave the theory out for the moment – on how to actually talk dirty. Since, let's face it, Woody Allen is right, for most of us sex is still dirty, and I know that when I say 'fuck' or 'cunt', or those kinds of words in a session, because that is the vernacular of the patient that I am working with, I have to enter into a part of myself that is quite a surprise to myself, because it isn't my normal vocabulary, let alone my normal clinical vocabulary. I sometimes wonder whether it's my job to correct old or young men's impressions that they don't need to go on forever for it to be a good sexual encounter. I don't have a way of talking about sex in practice. So, it would be useful if we could discuss how one invites conversations about sex that don't impinge on privacy but invite the individual to be able to find a language. This means we ourselves need to find a way to create a language that makes it possible to have this kind of dialogue. We seem to have no kind of problem impinging on people's psychic development or their defensive structure, but we do seem to be totally reticent when it comes to sexual practice and sexual activity and the erotic. All these things are very unpacked for a profession that got its start by looking at sexual damming up, so to speak.

Brett Kahr: I always struggle as to whether I should say this in public, but I *will* say this in public. When I trained in couple psychoanalytic psychotherapy at the Tavistock Marital Studies Institute – I do regard it as the most profound training that one can undertake in couple work, and we do provide a deeply effective form of treatment that saves about 95 per cent of marriages – during my training, my teachers insisted that one must *never* ask a couple about their sexual life, not unless the couple themselves bring it up in conversation as a problem. In my bones, I knew this to be quite mistaken. Indeed, I had always found a way to ask couples about their sexual relationship, in a diplomatic way. I might say to a couple in the first assessment session, 'I notice that you haven't mentioned your physical relationship, and I wonder, in view of what you told me . . .'

Susie Orbach: And they don't think you were talking about skiing.
[General laughter]

Brett Kahr: Exactly, exactly – and the psychological relief that couples experience when one can talk with them about sexuality, well, it can be enormous. But we still have a reticence over what I call the 'sexual interviewing skin' (Kahr 2009: 7), about our professional capacity to deal with intimate details of sexuality. I think that we often have a fear of being voyeuristic by wondering about the couple's sexual life, or about the individual patient's sexual life. And yet, when patients do not have an experience of sharing some aspect of their sexual history or sexual anxiety, they very often feel misunderstood, and in my experience, they will then be much more prone to sexual enactments. When my book *Sex and Psyche* (2007) appeared, I became quite surprised by how many of my colleagues took the trouble to tell me that they had read the theoretical and clinical sections of the book, but that they had skipped over the texts of the actual sexual fantasies reported by my research participants. This data is in fact primary data from the human mind, and yet many colleagues, especially the older ones, took pride, as if it were a badge of honour, in informing me that they had no desire to immerse themselves in the visceral language of sexual fantasies.

Susie Orbach: Don't you think they were just lying?
[General laughter]

Brett Kahr: I have no idea. Perhaps yes, some of them may have lied, but I cannot be certain. I suspect that some really did recoil from reading actual sexual fantasies.

Susie Orbach: I know, I don't think they were lying.

Brett Kahr: You know, it did not occur to me! I find that very interesting.

Susie Orbach: When I published *The Impossibility of Sex* (2000), I was hauled over the coals for talking about erotic countertransference. I was brutalised for it, as though anybody who had these kinds of thoughts was unethical. The lack of conversation or discourse about either the absence or presence of an erotic countertransference and content about sex in the session is dire. Now, in relation to your book, I thought what was so striking was how unremittingly hurtful those fantasies were. And that they didn't feel connected to the people. They were about a disconnect, and that's what interests me. Any maybe what you're trying to theorise, Brett, is that they were a way of dealing with hurt. You're saying that sexual fantasy is not something that we can understand outside of a theory which doesn't recognise hurt bodies.

Brett Kahr: Yes. I agree that the fantasies in my research sample contain a great deal of hurt and sadism. In fact, I propose that the fantasy constellation becomes the primary arena in which much of human sadism finds expression. But I do find it striking that so many of our very experienced colleagues still struggle when discussing sexuality.

Susie Orbach: Despite sexuality being a piece of Freud's legacy, we haven't breathed air into it. The commercial sector has, but we haven't. Perhaps you could say a little bit about what, a year on, has stayed with you about your exploration of sexual fantasies.

Brett Kahr: Well, I will, just for a few minutes, because I do want to open up the conversation to colleagues in the audience. I could say a great deal about what I have learned from the five-year research project which culminated in the book, and from the reactions of readers. But in this context, I find myself still quite struck by the responses of mental health professionals. I received lots of reviews, and lots of letters and emails from ordinary people (e.g. lawyers, doctors, househusbands, business women, students, etc.), most of whom *engaged* with the book, but without doubt, the group that struggled most happens to be our colleagues. Ordinary people who found their way to the book did not seem to have the same problem reading the work. Sometimes they found some of the fantasies shocking, sometimes revolting, sometimes titillating, but they read the book straight through. But colleagues struggled. Regardless, the book has changed my clinical practice in many ways, because I now have patients who come to me because they have read my work on sexual fantasies, and they tell me that they have grappled with their fantasies for decades, but have never discussed their anxieties around sexuality with another living soul. Many had undergone psychotherapy or psychoanalysis previously, and quite a few have told me that they experienced their analysts as too old or too stuffy to talk about sexuality in a straightforward manner. Now, of course, part of this complaint might be based on a transferential situation, or on projection, but part of the complaint might be based in truth. Perhaps some younger patients found it difficult to speak of sexuality with older analysts, rather akin to the inhibition of talking about sexuality in front of one's parents.

Susie Orbach: Well, I was going to ask you about that.

Brett Kahr: I think that we have not theorised this whole area sufficiently. Consider the relationship between a younger person lying prone on a couch, with an older person sitting behind in a chair, who probably does have grey hair, and who might well be the age of the patient's parents. As we all get longer in the tooth, our patients do become younger and younger. So we have to consider how this chronological, hierarchical situation inhibits sexual discussion in the consulting room.

Susie Orbach: Well, I think that you are right about the architecture of the room. As you know, and because I'm so interested in bodies, I can't have somebody lying down with me being behind them, it just doesn't work for me, it never has. But I am interested in whether you've been able to develop a vocabulary that can enable other people to talk. Because, certainly, I'm sure I can do it with the people that I know, but have I taught the next generation of therapists? I'm not sure. And, maybe, you have learned how to do that.

Brett Kahr: I do try. I think my colleagues in the couple psychoanalysis field now do feel more authorised to speak about sexual fantasy. In fact, within the Society of Couple Psychoanalytic Psychotherapists [now the British Society of Couple Psychotherapists and Counsellors], we have had quite a few conferences on sexuality, pornography, etc. in the last two years at the Tavistock Centre. We do have a lot of couples presenting because of pornography-related matters. Of course, we still have the extramarital affair, and the birth of the first baby, as very common presenting complaints, as well as loneliness in marriage; but concerns about pornography usage now feature quite frequently in first interviews. In individual psychotherapy or psychoanalysis, one can speak frankly about sexual matters, but one can also hide a great deal; but in marital work, it becomes impossible to hide the difficulties in the sexual arena, because the spouse will have direct evidence of the struggles, often quite concrete evidence. I do feel hopeful that we have now opened up the subject much more fully. I also had my first experience of facilitating a training seminar with a fairly conservative, middle-class group of psychoanalytic trainees. We had about 12 people in the seminar. To my great surprise, amid a discussion on pornography, one of the trainees – a female trainee – actually spoke up and told us, 'I just want you all to know that I use pornography, and I find it enjoyable.' Goodness, in 25 years of teaching, I have never come across such a candid communication from someone on a psychoanalytical course.

Susie Orbach: That is interesting. But I think if you go back to the 70s, I think it was Lonnie Barbach (1975) who started writing erotic stories for educated women, and invited lots of people to put them in, everybody from Erica Jong to . . . So I'm not surprised that it's in the visual, given that there was this precursor to it when women decided that they had an entitlement to sexuality, even if they didn't quite know how to do it.

Brett Kahr: Well, we shall have to pause our conversation here. Susie, thank you for speaking in such a frank and intelligent way. And thank you for your enormous contribution to the improvement of psychological thought, especially in the areas of gender and sexuality. Thank you.

References

Barbach, L. G. (1975) *For Yourself: The Fulfillment of Female Sexuality. A Guide to Orgasmic Response*. Garden City, NY: Doubleday.

Bonaparte, M. (1953) *Female Sexuality* (first published in 1951, in French). London: Imago.

Boston Women's Health Book Collective (1973) *Our Bodies, Ourselves: A Book by and for Women*. New York, NY: Simon and Schuster.

Comfort, A. (1972) *The Joy of Sex: A Gourmet Guide to Lovemaking*. New York, NY: Crown.

Deutsch, H. (1925) *Psychoanalyse der weiblichen Sexualfunktionen*. Vienna: Internationaler Psychoanalytischer Verlag.

Eichenbaum, L. and Orbach, S. (1984) *What Do Women Want?* London: Fontana.

Ensler, E. (2001) *The Vagina Monologues*. London: Virago.

Freud, S. (1905) Fragment of an Analysis of a Case of Hysteria. *SE*, Vol. VII, 7–122.

Honoré, C. (2004) *In Praise of Slow: How a Worldwide Movement is Challenging the Cult of Speed*. London: Orion.

Horney, K. (1967) *Feminine Psychology*. New York, NY: Norton.

Jones, E. (1955) *The Life and Work of Sigmund Freud: Volume 2. Years of Maturity. 1901–1919*. New York, NY: Basic Books.

Kahr, B. (2007) *Sex and the Psyche*. London: Allen Lane/Penguin.

Kahr, B. (2008) *Who's Been Sleeping in Your Head? The Secret World of Sexual Fantasies*. New York, NY: Basic Books.

Kahr, B. (2009) Psychoanalysis and Sexpertise. In C. Clulow (ed.), *Sex, Attachment, and Couple Psychotherapy: Psychoanalytic Perspectives*. London: Karnac (pp. 1–23).

Larkin, P. (1974) *High Windows*. London: Faber and Faber.

Masters, W. H. and Johnson, V. E. (1966) *Human Sexual Response*. Boston, MA: Little, Brown.

Orbach, S. (1978) *Fat is a Feminist Issue*. London: Paddington.

Orbach, S. (2000) *The Impossibility of Sex*. London: Penguin.

Orbach, S. (2008) Chinks in the merged attachment: Generational bequests to contemporary teenage girls. *Studies in Gender and Sexuality*, *9*, 215–232.

Orbach, S. (2009) *Bodies*. London: Profile.

Person, E. S. (1983) Women in Therapy: Therapist Gender as a Variable. *International Review of Psycho-Analysis*, *10*, 193–204.

Réage, P. (1954) *The Story of O*. London: Corgi (1994).

Reich, W. (1933) *Character Analysis*. New York, NY: Farrar, Straus & Giroux (1961).

Thompson, C. (1964) *Interpersonal Psychoanalysis: The Selected Papers of Clara M. Thompson*. New York, NY: Basic Books.

Strouse, J. (1974) *Women and Analysis: Dialogues on Psychoanalytic Views of Femininity*. New York, NY: Grossman.

Note

1 Revised by the discussants, based on the transcription by Gottfried Heuer from recordings that he made, as well as from recordings made by a crew of the Swedish film company Vilda Bomben, Göteborg, who filmed and recorded most of the symposia. These recordings are available for study at the Otto Gross Archive, London (gottfried.heuer@virgin.net).

Chapter 14

Carnal critiques

Promiscuity, politics, imagination, spirituality and hypocrisy[1]

Andrew Samuels

Personal dimensions

You'd better find somebody to love, sang Jefferson Airplane in 1967. May 1968 followed soon after. An opportunity to speak at a conference to mark the fortieth anniversary of those events enabled all of us who were around then to reflect on the personal and political trajectories of our lives and to discuss it all with younger colleagues. I chose to present on Promiscuity – Then and Now and used the moment to work up reflections on sexuality and social critique in a historical framework. In the event, the paper itself was less confessional and personal than it might have seemed – but the responses it evoked were highly charged as memories, many of them doubtless held in the body, played into the current positions and preoccupations of the audience.

In 1968 I had just dropped out of Oxford. There was, as you'll recall, a revolution supposed to be going on and no one would need degrees in the society that would emerge. As part of involvement in anti-apartheid politics, I had been briefly imprisoned in South Africa and beaten up so the student movement seemed a really safe place to be. My main interest was in politically engaged experimental theatre and members of the company I founded lived communally and engaged in considered and considerable sexual experimentation. There were joys to this, but also a good deal of pain as jealousy, arising out of the very training for monogamy we were contesting, was rife. At the time, such experimentation was almost an ideological requirement.

I moved into youth work with 'unclubbable' teenagers, still using drama. Here, I encountered equally non-traditional sexual behaviours but apparently devoid of ideology. I still reflect on the class divide wherein youthful Oxford dropouts behaved sexually in much the same way as disadvantaged kids in an impoverished South Wales new town – but the associations and cultural referents could not have been more different.

Then I slipped into encounter groups, psychiatric social work, and Jungian analysis. I started analytical training in 1974 and qualified in 1977.

Hence I fit the story told by the psychotherapist organisers of the conference: 'many radicals found their way into psychotherapy trainings.' The story is a bit more complicated than this. Some radicals stayed radical even as therapists. After all, there were in the 1970s several politically progressive therapy projects, such as Red Therapy and the Women's Therapy Centre, that demonstrated the viability of a hybrid organisation. But some radicals took a much more conservative and Establishment direction in terms of psychotherapy and, especially, psychoanalysis.

I am one of those who became devoted to the idea that there could be a hybrid of politics and psychotherapy and this led, among other things, to the founding of Psychotherapists and Counsellors for Social Responsibility, Antidote (a campaign for emotional literacy in the public sphere), political consultancy with politicians and groups, and professional work in the areas known variously as inclusivity, diversity and equal opportunities. I was active in the campaign to remove discrimination against lesbians and gay men who were seeking psychoanalytic training.

More recently, I added a third side to the coin, welcoming both the political and psychological relevance to psychotherapy of spiritual and transpersonal ideas. All may be considered 'more-than-personal'. In my writing, I have introduced the idea of a 'resacralisation of culture' (Samuels 1993: 3–23) and developed a contemporary and progressive 'anatomy of spirituality' (Samuels 2001: 122–134; 2004: 201–211). I return to these ideas later.

The problem with promiscuity

In the 1960s, reference was to 'non-possessive relating' or 'alternative families' or 'free love'. No one used the word 'promiscuity'. I have decided to retain this word for political and intellectual as well as shock reasons. I do not want to end up merely complementing non-monogamy by writing about a kind of serial non-monogamy. For many (not all) more recent polyamorous discourses seem to assume that such relationships will be long-term (or at least not terribly short-term). I'll return to the crucial value-judgement role played by elapsed time later but for now will indicate that I am trying to explore the implications of a divorce between sex and relationship. This is an explosive and paradox-ridden topic. At the conference, I was taken for an idiot for apparently assuming that there could be sex outside of relationship. The point was (correctly) made that any interpersonal encounter involves a relationship. Therefore my critic had made it clear that, for her, no matter how lustful and transient a physical encounter, there is really (in the sense of implicitly) a relationship present. Yet, at the same time, she evinced a marked hostility to and contempt for promiscuity which, she said, could not involve a real (in the sense of authentic) relationship. This led to some participants questioning the value-laden relational category difference 'committed/uncommitted' in terms of sexual behaviours.

On reflection, I can see that the various territories mapped out under 'monogamy', 'non-monogamy', 'polyamory' and 'promiscuity' overlap and that there are frictions between them. Polyamory may seek to differentiate itself from promiscuity, but, from the standpoint of monogamy, will not succeed. Non-monogamy includes both polyamory and promiscuity. Monogamy, as we know, often conceals a polyamory that is known to the partners or their circle but not beyond; this can be contrasted with wholly overt polyamory. And we know that promiscuity is completely reconcilable with monogamy. The two stalk each other. Each is the shadow of the other: the uxorious lust in their heart while libertines yearn for peace and quiet.

The problem I am worrying away at may be exacerbated by the different habits of thought of psychotherapy/psychoanalysis and the social sciences. I come from a tradition that, despite the stress on listening, attunement and accurate feedback, tends to be less impressed by what people state their position to be in survey or focus group.

I don't think we can leave it there, in a kind of fourfold parallelism: monogamy, non-monagamy, polyamory and promiscuity each being a path pointing in more or less the same direction to more or less the same ends. I see a lot of competition and bargaining between these relational tropes; in terms of both academic writing and personal experience, people want to justify the choices they have made. All relationships, regardless of composition, involve power issues and carry the potential for the abuse of power. But the inherent antagonism of monogamy and non-monogamy is useful heuristically, performing a function of gluing together the discourse without arching over it. They are linked by their defensiveness against the other: monogamy defending a weak ego and low self-esteem, promiscuity a defence against the dangers of intimacy. Of course, the defensive properties of promiscuity are much more extensively theorised by therapists than those of monogamy, and I return to this problem later.

Another way to manage this question is to see that each of the four (that I selected) yearns to have what the others have – but can do no more than mourn and maybe rage for the lost hypothetical opportunity. I find it hard to say which of monogamy and non-monogamy is the foundational relational state that has been lost. It means that the mourning cannot be wished away by saying that, in one's life, one may have periods of monogamy and periods of non-monogamy. It isn't a logical mutual exclusiveness, but a *psycho*logical one.

Returning to the conference, I had thought there would be many presentations on sex or sexuality but there was only one mention in all the abstracts and that was a quote from Lacan that 'there is no sexual ratio' (1958: 280). It seems that, until the recent flowering of writing about polyamory and related matters (e.g. Barker 2004), there has been a collapse of ideology into psychopathology.

It is still hard to find much contemporary discussion of promiscuity in a Western context that does not take a negative line. The OED defines promiscuity as: 'consisting of members or elements of different kinds massed together and without order; of mixed and disorderly composition or character. Without discrimination or method; confusedly mingled; indiscriminate. Making no distinctions. Casual, carelessly irregular'. The word that appears over and over again in the context of sex is 'casual'. Casual sex is the term with which we are now most familiar.

If, thinking deconstructively, we look for antonyms of 'casual', we get to words like formal, deliberate, ceremonial, ritualistic. There is a history of promiscuity that is formal, deliberate, ceremonial and ritualistic – usually in a religious or spiritual context (see Qualls-Corbett 1987) or as part of pagan and Wiccan practice. This forms the background for my later excursion into spiritual and transpersonal promiscuous phenomena.

Let me say at this point, in anticipation of objections, that I think we should hold back from trying to clean this up by making an overprecise distinction between the erotic and the sexual or between fantasies and acts. That kind of precision can be spurious and defensive. Nor do I care to be undermined by being typed or smeared as advocating rather than investigating promiscuity.

Promiscuity and politics

Promiscuity is the background phenomenon that since the late nineteenth century has underpinned numerous discussions that couple politics and sexuality. Conventional accounts of intimate relations praise them when they radiate constancy, longevity, and fidelity. But more radical accounts suggest that ownership and control of the other are also critically important. The best known of these was Friedrich Engels' *Origin of the Family, Private Property and the State* (1884) in which he states that the first class opposition that appears in history coincides with 'the development of the antagonism between man and woman in monogamous marriage' especially in 'the possessing classes' (34–35).

The background formulation with which we are more familiar today is that you cannot have social change without deep personal change (e.g. in the pattern of relationships and hence in the play of emotions) – and no personal change is possible if society remains the same. This point, first made explicitly by Otto Gross nearly a hundred years ago (1913a), both anticipates and slightly differs from 'the personal is political' in Gross's utopic and trans-rational forcefulness. (See Eichenbaum and Orbach 1982 for a nuanced discussion.) It was actually Gross who coined the term 'sexual revolution' (see Heuer 2001: 663), stating that 'smashing monogamy, and its even sicker form, polygamy, means not only the liberation of women, but still more that of man' (1913b: 1142, translated by Gottfried Heuer).

Today's monogamy may be seen as chiming and co-symbolising with market economics and with implicit and explicit claims by powerful Western countries and corporations to 'possess' planetary resources. Monogamy, it can be argued, is therefore implicated in a wide range of injustices – environmental, economic and ethical. Now, this point can be made with greater or lesser passion, for monogamy certainly has its merits and cannot only be reduced to the level of political tyranny.

The corollary – that non-monogamy is correlated with sustainability, equality and social justice – remains, perforce, untested though hugely suggestive. Ownership is a tendentious perspective on relationships and geopolitics alike; public strategies for sustainability, such as the principle of 'global commons' can be seen to co-symbolise with non-monogamy in the private sphere (see Samuels 2001: 115–126).

Notwithstanding these arguments, I think it is too easy to see the sexual as merely reflecting the power dynamics of the wider society. Sex is also a matter of power in and of itself and so, at the very least, there is a feedback loop in which sexual behaviours and the fantasies that both drive them and are produced by them have an impossible-to-quantify impact on the political. I have written of the ways in which the practice of 'flipping' or 'switching' in consensual submission–domination sexual behaviours could be seen as a metaphor for the capacity to be powerful in one sphere of life and much less powerful in another, to rule and to be ruled. Switches don't get the idea from politics or the internalisation of social organisations and relations; they are not thinking first of a political way to behave sexually and then doing it. Do we have to say where switches get the idea from outside of the sexual? Do we really know where they got it from, if 'from' anywhere? Similarly, we can note switching between registers – as when the powerful businessman dons nappies during his regular Friday afternoon visit to a dominatrix. (The political variant of switching is best expressed in Michael Walzer's *Spheres of Justice* [1983].)

If we consider, for example, the Midrashic story of Lilith we can understand the possible relations between politics and sexual behaviour a bit more fluidly. Lilith was Adam's first consort who was created from the earth at the same time as Adam. She was unwilling to give up her equality and argued with Adam over the position in which they should have intercourse – Lilith insisting on being on top. 'Why should I lie beneath you,' she argued, 'when I am your equal since both of us were created from dust?' Adam was determined and began to rape Lilith who called out the magic name of God, rose into the air, and flew away. Eve was then created. Lilith's later career as an evil she-demon who comes secretly to men in the night (hence being responsible for nocturnal emissions), and as a murderer of newborns, culminated, after the destruction of the Temple, in a relationship with God as a sort of mistress.

My point is that this kind of material can be taken as much as an expression of the influence of the sexual on the political as the other way around. The experience people have of the sexual is also a motor of their politicality, political style and political values. Sexual experience and its associated imagery express an individual's psychological approach to political functioning (see Samuels 1993: 167–170; Samuels 2001: 47–53).

Concluding this section on promiscuity and politics, it is interesting to reflect on the micro-politics of non-monogamous relating, using this term to include promiscuity. The politics of relationality in these contexts includes whether or not the agreement of members or officially recognised partners is to be sought and, if agreement is reached, what the meaning of such agreement might be. All relationships are political.

Historical considerations

Was there a 'sexual revolution' in the 1960s that could be seen as a precursor to today's array of non-monogamous relation styles? This is an important background question to our discussions. Did attitudes to sex, sex education, the sexuality of women, to marriage and to same-sex relations change in a way that was a major disjunct with what had come before? Or was it simply a technological shift, based on the pill? Perhaps it was something that affected so few people that it could not be called a 'revolution'. Some have suggested that the sexual revolution was simply an extension of market capitalism into the sexual area leading to the creation of a sexual marketplace occupied by sexual producers and consumers.

Nevertheless, many believe there was a sexual revolution and base that on their experience or their observations of the behaviour of others. I think there are more interesting questions than the 'was there or wasn't there?' kind. Belief that there was sexual revolution is a complicated thing to understand. It could be seen as the supreme triumph of nurture and culture over nature and the innate – or the reverse. Or the dominance of ego consciousness over the drives – or vice versa. Even scepticism about the sexual revolution may mean more than it seems. Perhaps there is a relief in such scepticism because then the status quo is protected. After all, Reich, one of the sources for mid twentieth-century shifts in the sexual, became too much for Freud as much for his sexual ideas as for his political ones. I am sure Reich was right to suggest Freud wrote *Civilization and its Discontents* (1930) specifically contra himself – and, let us add, as Heuer has suggested (personal communication 2008), against Gross as well.

There is a contemporary temptation to indulge in a knee-jerk rejection of what Wilhelm Reich said in 1927 in the Introduction to *The Function of the*

Orgasm: 'Psychic health depends upon . . . the degree to which one can surrender to and experience the climax of excitation in the natural sexual act' (Reich 1927: 62). What Reich (and others such as Roheim and Marcuse) were doing was to elaborate, with great ingenuity, some implications of Freud's theories of psychosexuality that supported the idea that politics and sexuality were 'intimately bound together', in Fisher's felicitous phrase (2007: 238). Hence, Fisher goes on, we tend to forget that, alongside his championing of sexual expressiveness, Reich (with varying degrees of support from Freud) advocated the rights of children and mothers, supporting legalised abortions and contraception.

Many sceptics adopt a reactionary approach. Family breakdown, teenage pregnancy, sexually transmitted diseases – these are held up as the inevitable and disastrous sequelae of the departure from traditional mores. But not all sceptics are so Burkean. Sheila Jeffrey's radical political lesbian point (1990) was that the so-called sexual revolution was just a further subtle oppression of women by men.

A note on non-monogamy in conventional politics and in psychoanalysis

As one who has written on political leadership (Samuels 2001: 75–100), I am interested in historical shifts concerning collective evaluations of promiscuous behaviour on the part of (usually male) politicians. The old assumption that, whatever goes on in the United States, Europeans are far too sophisticated to care about the sexual lives of their political leaders, does seem to have shifted in the twenty-first century. Even in Europe, it seems that Western political leaders must *appear* faithful to their spouses. Nothing guarantees the slippage from idealisation of a leader to denigration more than the discovery of promiscuous behaviour.

There is an interesting parallel with the history of psychoanalysis. Jung admitted to Freud that he suffered from 'polygamous tendencies' and this gave the older man powerful character-assassinating ammunition. It was no surprise that, when evidence emerged that Freud had a physical relationship with his sister-in-law, the psychoanalytic establishment went into overdrive to smear the researchers. In intellectual life, as in politics, it's the zipper, stupid.

Promiscuity and spirituality

Having reviewed some of the problems with the idea of promiscuity, and placed my ideas in a historical context, I want further to deepen and complexify the discussion by positioning promiscuity as a spiritual phenomenon. It is generally accepted that 'spirituality' can be distinguished from religion but, for some, religious and non-religious, it is the 'S' word and they hate it; for others this is the *sine qua non* of today's progressive politics – the so-called 'rise of the religious left' and the emergence of networks of spiritual progressives. (The best-known network clusters around the Jewish idea of *Tikkun*, meaning repair and restoration of the world; there are equally inspiring Islamic concepts – the one that interests me is the Qur'anic proposition of *Ta'Aruf*, in which the deeper and transformative aspects of conflict are recognised.)

It is hard to define 'spiritual', but it involves something 'more-than-personal' that lies over or under or beneath or behind the everyday. Often there is a sense of being confronted with something awesome and 'bigger' than oneself – more-than-personal. But this is a spirituality that is ubiquitous, hidden in the open, waiting to be discovered, not a result of a 'sell' by anyone with ambitions for their religion, sect or cult.

My anatomy of spirituality suggests that there are different kinds of spiritual deficits or lacks that contemporary Western citizens suffer from. A defect in social spirituality means that the individual has little or no experience of the incredible togetherness that ensues when a group of committed individuals pursue a social or political goal. A defect in craft spirituality means that work is not only without meaning but is also soulless and spiritually damaging. Democratic spirituality is a reworking of the notion of 'equality in the eyes of the Lord' – and who can doubt that today's polities have resolutely turned their back on paying anything more than lip service to egalitarian goals and ideals?

The focus here is on the fourth element in the anatomy – profane spirituality: sex, drugs and rock and roll (or popular culture). The thinking here comes from Jung's insight, conveyed to the founders of Alcoholics Anonymous, that alcohol abuse is not only about seeking spirituous drafts but is also a spiritual quest. Herein, I am talking, not only about addictions (and sexual activity can certainly become addictive and compulsive, even statistical), but specifically of the spiritual quest carried by lust and by promiscuity, about sex as force and not sex as relation, to use Muriel Dimen's phrase (personal communication 2007).

This kind of sexual behaviour may be understood in terms of mystical experience. There's something numinous about promiscuous experience as many readers will know. Overwhelming physical attraction produces feelings of awe and wonderment and trembling. There is a sort of God aroused, a primitive, chthonic, early, elemental God. There is an unfettered experience of the divine.

The idea of a mysticism between people is one by which contemporary theology is captivated. 'There is no point at all in blinking at the fact that the raptures of the theistic mystic are closely akin to the transports of sexual union,' wrote Richard Zaehner in *Mysticism – Sacred and Profane* (1957). In literature, D. H. Lawrence (1913: 167) fashions a creation myth out of sexual intercourse in *Sons and Lovers*: 'His hands were like creatures, living; his limbs, his body, were all life and consciousness, subject to no will of his, but living in themselves'.

In Chassidic mysticism, reference is made to a quality known as *Hitlahabut*, or ecstasy. Buber held that this quality transforms ordinary knowledge into a knowledge of the meaning of life. For the Chassids, Hitlahabut expresses itself bodily in dance, during which, according to Buber, the whole body becomes subservient to the ecstatic soul. Similarly, William Blake sang that 'man has no body distinct from his soul'.

In a series of works (for example 2004: 59), Robert Goss has been suggesting that, behind non-monogamous relating, we find the presence of a 'promiscuous God', one who loves indiscriminately (if hardly casually). Although Goss is primarily concerned with the reclamation of the bible for LGBT and queer people, his remarkable phrase is a suitable note on which to end this discussion of spirituality and promiscuity.

Promiscuities

Promiscuity is not a monolith – there are often perplexing differences to do with gender, sexual diversity, class and ethnicity. For reasons of space, I will consider only gender and sexual diversity.

It is sometimes argued that promiscuity as a discourse is written by and for males (this is what Sheila Jeffreys means). But it is interesting to see how much of the non-monogamy literature is written by lesbians. Are we to take this as indicating that it is only where heterosexual relating is concerned that promiscuity is a male game? Surely not. And I had thought that feminism made it clear that most advantages in marriage lay with the husbands who are 'obeyed'. Yet, at the May 1968 conference, enraged women turned on male members of the audience as much as on the speaker in a moralising frenzy. One said in response to my positing promiscuity as a political as much as a sexual phenomenon: 'I cannot believe I've heard you say what I think you've said.'

Sexual desire generates an anxiety that calls forth a certitude that is really not at all grounded. I am sure that my thinking about promiscuity suffers from this – and that what might be said against it will suffer from an element of dogmatism as well. I have discussed elsewhere (Samuels 2009) that the promise of an end to sexual anxiety is what gives religious fundamentalism its appeal to adherents and its fascination for those who do not see themselves as fundamentalist. We are too quick to theorise why people become fundamentalists without pausing to ask why we are so keen to offer such theorising. My point, succinctly, is that even the critics of fundamentalism are caught up by the seductiveness of its promise of an end to sexual anxiety.

In connection with gender and promiscuity, one of the most interesting documents we have is Catherine Millet's *The Sexual Life of Catherine M* (2001). One of the most explicit books on sex written by a woman, it recounts Millet's sexual experiences over 30 years. It is an incisive and destabilising work that makes generalising about gender differences in connection with sexuality seem impoverished. Millet tells us that she 'exercises complete free will in my chosen sexual life . . . a freedom expressed once and for all' (2001: 34). She explains how special is the excitement of an encounter with a new lover: 'my pleasure was never more intense . . . not the first time that I made love with someone, but the first time we kissed; even the first embrace was enough' (ibid.: 22). She is no stranger to jealousy: 'I personally have experienced my confrontations with these passionate epressions of jealousy' (ibid.: 22), saying that jealousy is an 'injustice'.

One passage I found interesting is a reflective memory from Millet's childhood. As a girl, she ran numbers over and over in her mind, and now she is numbering her future husbands:

> Could a woman have several husbands at the same time, or only one after the other? In which case, how long did she have to stay married to each one before she could change? What would be an 'acceptable' number of husbands: a few, say five or six, or many more than that, countless husbands?'
>
> (ibid.: 58)

Questions of time and duration pepper the promiscuity field, no matter the gender of the subject, and I return to time when I come to discuss hypocrisy.

Continuing to look at the plurality of promiscuities, this time with sexual diversity rather than gender in mind, it is interesting to note how often discussions about promiscuity, even in quite liberal professional circles of psychotherapists, collapse into discussions about promiscuous cottaging (or cruising) on the part of gay men. I have been arguing for many years that therapists have been unconsciously influenced by the media and collective cultural discourses as much as by their own theories concerning the general psychopathology of homosexuality. They have got caught up in a moral panic concerning cottaging and haven't noticed that they've allowed heterosexual promiscuity to fall out of the conversation. Hence, it is well-nigh impossible to manage a reasoned conversation about either promiscuity or cottaging.

Can we make something positive out of this homophobic moral panic? Flip it around? Yes, I think we can if we revisit Leo Bersani's contention in 'Is the rectum a grave?' (1987) that the great lesson and gift of gay men to the rest is the massive individualism of promiscuous sex. It is a very specific and powerful form of resistance precisely because there is no political agenda. Bob Dylan made much the same point: 'I've never written a political song. Songs can't save the world. I've gone through all that.'

Finally, a note on bisexuality and promiscuity. Bisexuals as a group experience specific pressures in relation to promiscuity. I agree with those who insist – for political and psychological reasons – that bisexuality is not a cover for something else and wish to retain the term. They are up against strong opposition. Some will say that bisexuality is but a cover for disavowed homosexuality (if the critic is psychoanalytic), or for politically unacceptable heterosexuality (if the critic is lesbian or gay). As a phenomenon, bisexuality adds a further layer of complexity and paradox to our thinking about monogamy and non-monogamy and the connections between them. As far as psychoanalysis is concerned, Freud's insight of a fundamental bisexuality all too easily gets overlooked (similarly, Jung wrote of a 'polyvalent germinal disposition' [in McGuire 1974: 99] in the sexual realm).

Promiscuity and imagination

Up to now, we have been discussing historical, political and spiritual aspects of the promiscuities. But, as a therapist, I know that promiscuity is not only a literal matter. It is also implicated in a whole array of imaginative and metaphorical discourses. For, in addition to the political symbolism, we have to think of promiscuity as symbolising boundary-breaking creativity in both an artistic and a general sense (one could be politically promiscuous, for example).

From a psychological point of view, promiscuity calls up symbolic or metaphorical dimensions of issues of freedom, differentiation from parental and family background, and a new relation to the primal scene – meaning the image we have in our mind of the intimate life or lack of it of our parent(s). Kleinian psychoanalysis refers to 'the couple state of mind', the parents in the mind engaged in fertile and creative intercourse. The intent is to propose a universal symbol of fecundity and mental health generally: 'the basis or the fount of personal creativity: sexual, intellectual and aesthetic' (Hinshelwood 1989: 241). But the result is very often a distressingly literal application of the idea. Hence, we must ask: is the couple state of mind, the couple in the mind, always a stable 'married' or committed couple? We could also ask: is it always a heterosexual couple? Always a couple of the same ethnicity? Not only is this particular Kleinian theory – widely utilised in British object relations psychoanalysis even beyond the Kleinian group – unquestioningly heteronormative (see Samuels 2001: 49–51), it is also ferociously conventional.

Re-visioned imaginatively, promiscuity holds up the promise – and the threat – of an internal pluralism (Samuels 1989) always on the brink of collapsing into undifferentiatedness but, somehow, never quite doing so. On a personal level, we are faced with what could be called the promiscuous task of reconciling our many internal voices and images of ourselves with our wish and need to be able to feel, when we desire it so, integrated and able to speak with one voice.

Returning to bodies for a moment, there is also a metaphorical aspect to promiscuous sex. Promiscuous traces and shadows may be present in constant sexual relationships via the operation of fantasy; and there as a constant element in apparently promiscuous behaviour, if the image of the sexual Other remains psychically constant. This takes us back to the Freud–Jung schism over sexuality. Freud spoke for the literal, the instinctual, the causative; Jung for the metaphorical and the teleological, asking 'what is sex really for?' Sexual imagery is not only a desire for physical enactment. It is also a symbolic expression of an emotional longing for some kind of personal regeneration through contact with the body of an Other.

Support for the idea that there is a promiscuous element in sexual constancy can be found in an unlikely place – Rabbinic Judaism of the early part of the Christian era. In his book *Carnal Israel: Reading Sex in Talmudic Culture* (1993), Daniel Boyarin explains how the tension between procreative and non-procreative sex operates as a kind of in-house promiscuity. Non-procreative sex is exclusively for pleasure, and pleasure, whether to do with sex or with eating, is regarded by the Rabbis as a Good Thing. Among other revelatory ideas, he shows quite clearly how Judaism strives to heal, as well as force, the split from the body with which it is too easily associated.

In Philip Roth's novel *The Dying Animal* (2001), made into the film *Elegy* in 2008, David Kepesh, academic superstar (and Jew), lives a sexual life of studied promiscuity. But: 'No matter how much you know, no matter how much you think, no matter how much you plot and you connive and you plan, you're not superior to sex' (2001: 41). Kepesh falls in love with a much younger woman, who will eventually be diagnosed with breast cancer and undergo a mastectomy (he had 'worshipped' her breasts). Roth is not making a moral or (pseudo)mature point about the collapse of the promiscuous ideal (nor was the book ever in praise of the promiscuous life). He is underscoring how sexual relating is all about struggle, indeterminacy and – above all – anxiety. As I said earlier, when considering monogamy, non-monogamy, polyamory and promiscuity, you can't have it all – not even in fantasy! Nevertheless, Roth's aperçu in connection with promiscuous sex is worth repeating: 'The great biological joke on people is that you are intimate before you know anything about the other person' (ibid.: 41–42).

Promiscuity and hypocrisy

Hypocrisy is the act of opposing a belief or behaviour while holding the same beliefs or performing the same behaviours at the same time. Hypocrisy is frequently invoked as an accusation in politics and in life in general. Noam Chomsky argued that the key feature of hypocrisy is the refusal to apply to ourselves the same standards we apply to others. So hypocrisy is one of the central evils of our society, promoting injustices such as war and social inequalities in a framework of self-deception.

With these thoughts in mind, I want to turn to my own profession of psychotherapy, both in and of itself and as representative of the wider culture. My accusation is that, when it comes to promiscuity, psychotherapy as an institution and many (but not all) psychotherapists as individuals are hypocritical. In terms of the etymology of the word hypocrisy, they are play acting or feigning something. As well as scoring points, I am interested in probing this phenomenon.

It is significant that sex outside of relationship is largely untheorised by analysts and therapists – or, if there is a theoretical position taken, it is invariably in terms of psychopathology, an alleged fear of intimacy, problems in attachment ('ambivalent attachment') and relationship, perversion and so on. There is an absence of consideration of what I referred to earlier as sex-as-force (but see Kahr 2007). Actually, with some notable exceptions, there is very little contemporary psychoanalytic writing on bodily experience at all (but see Orbach 2009). When Lyndsey Moon (personal communication 2008) was undertaking research focusing on the needs of bisexual clients, during which she interviewed 40 therapists (lesbian, gay male, heterosexual, queer and bisexual), only three (including the present writer) 'actually went anywhere near "sex" as having a meaning that needs to be talked about or talked through with clients.' Moon speculates that the bulk of the therapists were experiencing 'much fear of the sexual body and sexual behaviour.'

I think it is interesting to ask whether there might be something in the fundamental thinking or set-up of psychotherapy that leads to a carnality-averse conservatism. Certainly, the proliferation of schools in psychotherapy is a gorgeous metaphor for this whole topic: on the one hand, historically, most therapists have been monogamously wedded to one school, yet the field itself is – or so it could be argued – becoming ever more, and ever more threateningly, promiscuous.

We have learned that, for every majority discourse, there is likely to be a subjugated minority discourse. In psychotherapy – as in society – the majority discourse is relational. Hence, the subjugated minority discourse will be the opposite of relational; in the language of this chapter, promiscuous. I have wondered if the silence of psychotherapists on the topic of promiscuity reflects a kind of sexual horror – so they translate everything into a discourse of relationality in which 'persons' get split off from 'sex'.

Putting these ideas – of hypocrisy and a subjugated non-relational discourse – together exposes the secret moral conservatism of numerous psychotherapeutic clinicians compared with their often very different sexual behaviour as persons. We could begin to understand this more deeply by seeing it as envy on the part of the therapist of the sexual experimentation and out-of-order behaviour related to them by their clients. Many psychotherapists are not overtly judgemental about promiscuous behaviour but tell us that it is a stage or phase of psychosexual development – usually adolescent. As such, the client should grow out of it because it cannot be sustained into middle or old age. It is not hard to see that, aside from whether it is true or part of a general cultural denial about the sexuality of older people, this is far from non-judgemental accepting and rules out any possibility that promiscuity might function as one template (in classical Jungian terminology, 'archetypal structure') for lifelong relational individuation. We don't talk much about the need to hold the tensions between the one and the many when it comes to relationships.

The matter comes to a head when psychotherapists engage with infidelity ('cheating') on the part of their clients. While not denying that some therapists, particularly couple therapists, understand cheating as a systemic phenomenon, the overall psychotherapeutic take on the matter is that it is a symptom of something else, some problem in the cheat, usually of a narcissistic kind. The cheated upon usually feels immense pain and the cheat often feels great guilt. These are strong affects for the therapist to engage with. Hence, unsurprisingly perhaps, what we see in the majority of instances is a counter-resistant valorisation of relational longevity and an utterly literal understanding of 'object constancy' at the expense of relational quality. Provided you are in a longstanding relationship, you are, to all intents and purposes, OK. (I take up this point in relation to persons seeking to train as psychotherapists in Samuels 2006.)

However, when it comes to sexual desire, time doesn't have all that much to do with it. When I was a schoolboy, there was a joke about the theory of relativity: if you kiss a sexy girl for five minutes it feels like ten seconds; if you stick your hand in a flame for ten seconds it feels like five minutes. In the unconscious, time doesn't work the way it does at the conscious level.

The same is true in relation to sexual desire. One of the most compelling accounts of this is in Ernest Hemingway's *For Whom the Bell Tolls* (1941). Mortally wounded, the Spanish Civil War volunteer, Robert Jordan, is going to cover the escape of his comrades. Lying on the ground, weapon at the ready, he reflects on how he has lived a lifetime of sexual intimacy and a kind of 'marriage' with Maria, a girl living with the partisan band who has been raped by Franco's soldiers. He tries to recall: 'Well, we had all our luck in four days. Not four days. It was afternoon when I first got there and it will not be noon today. That makes not quite three days and three nights. Keep it accurate, he said. Quite accurate' (1941: 262). And earlier, in passion, '. . . there is no other now but thou now and now is thy prophet. Now and forever now . . . there is no now but now' (ibid.: 176). And later, reflectively, 'I wish I was going to live a long time instead of going to die today because I have learned much about life in these four days; more I think than in all the other time' (ibid.: 264).

Erotic time is no truer than any other form of time.

Concluding thoughts

My hope in this chapter was to be able to think outside the box in relation to the role of psychotherapy in cultural critique, fashioning that critique this time out of the carnality that we find in promiscuity. Lessons from May 1968 and observations from today suggest that, in the West, understandings of the manifold connections, including symbolic connections, between relationality, sexuality and politics are hindered by negativity and hypocrisy on the part of many psychotherapists, mental health professionals, academics and critics. Psychotherapists who seek to impact the political need to pay attention to the limits placed upon their laudable ambition by retrogressive attitudes to promiscuity and sex outside of conventional relational structures of a monogamous nature.

But there was also an additional goal stemming directly from the shift in consciousness I mentioned earlier, whereby personal and social change are understood as inseparable. The exploration of the sexual is indeed just that. But as we move onto the social level, and then onto the spiritual level, we are challenged to find out more about suffering, pain, dislocation and alienation, and to see how promiscuity might function as a secret spiritual and social passage to the fullest possible healing engagement with a suffering world.

Acknowledgements

I am grateful for the challenging and stimulating feedback on earlier drafts of the paper from Aaron Balick, Gottfried Heuer, Jean Kirsch, Lynne Layton, Lyndsey Moon, Susie Orbach, Rosie Parker, Anna Price, Bernard Ratigan, Tom Singer, Nick Totton, and Paul Zeal.

References

Barker, M. (2004) This is my partner and this is my . . . partner's partner: Constructing a polyamorous identity in a monogamous world. *Journal of Constructivist Psychology*, *18*, 75–88.

Bersani, L. (1987) Is the rectum a grave? In D. Crimp (ed.), AIDS: Cultural Analysis/Cultural Activism. Cambridge: MIT Press (pp. 197–223).

Boyarin, D. (1993) *Carnal Israel: Reading Sex in Talmudic Culture*. Berkeley, CA: University of California.

Eichenbaum L. and Orbach, S. (1982) *Outside in . . . Inside Out: Women's Psychology: A Feminist psychoanalytic Approach*. Penguin: Harmondsworth.

Engels, F. (1884/1972) *Origin of the Family, Private Property and the State*. New York, NY: International Publishers Company.

Fisher, D. (2007) Classical psychoanalysis, politics and social engagement in the era between the wars: Reflections on the free clinics. *Psychoanalysis and History*, *9*(2), 237–250.

Freud, S. (1930) *Civilization and its Discontents*. *SE*, Vol. 21. London: Hogarth.
Goss, R. (2004) Proleptic sexual love: God's promiscuity reflected in Christian polyamory. *Theology and Sexuality*, *11*(1), 52–63.
Gross, O. (1913a) Zur Ueberwinding der kulturellen Krise. *Die Aktion*, III, 384–387.
Gross, O. (1913b) Anmerkungen zu einer meuen Ethik. *Die Aktion*, III, 1141–1143.
Hemingway, E. (1941/1994) *For Whom the Bell Tolls*. London: Arrow.
Heuer, G. (2001) Jung's twin brother: Otto Gross and Carl Gustav Jung. *Journal of Analytical Psychology*, *46*(4), 655–688.
Hinshelwood, R. D. (1989) *A Dictionary of Kleinian Thought*. London: Free Association.
Jeffreys, S. (1990) *Anticlimax: A Feminist Perspective on the Sexual Revolution*. New York, NY: New York University.
Kahr, B. (2007) *Sex and the Psyche*. London: Allen Lane.
Lacan, J. (1958) The significance of the phallus. In *Ecrits* (1977) (A. Sheridan, Trans.). London: Tavistock.
Lawrence, D. H. (1913/1992) *Sons and Lovers*. Cambridge: Cambridge University Press.
McGuire, W. (1974) *The Freud/Jung Letters*. London: Hogarth; Routledge & Kegan Paul. Princeton, NJ: Princeton University Press.
Millet, C. (2001/2003) *The Sexual Life of Catherine M*. London: Corgi.
Orbach, S. (2009) *Bodies*. London: Profile.
Qualls-Corbett, N. (1987) *The Sacred Prostitute: Eternal Aspects of the Feminine*. Toronto: Inner City.
Reich, W. (1927/43) *The Function of the Orgasm*. New York, NY: Orgone Institute.
Roth, P. (2001/2006) *The Dying Animal*. London: Vintage.
Samuels, A. (1989) *The Plural Psyche. Personality, Morality and the Father*. London and New York, NY: Routledge.
Samuels, A. (1993) *The Political Psyche*. London and New York, NY: Routledge.
Samuels, A. (2001) *Politics on the Couch: Citizenship and the Internal Life*. London, New York, NY: Karnac.
Samuels, A. (2004) A new anatomy of spirituality: Clinical and political demands the psychotherapist cannot ignore. *Psychotherapy and Politics International*, *2*(3), 201–211.
Samuels, A. (2006) Socially responsible roles of professional ethics: Inclusivity, psychotherapy and 'the protection of the public'. *International Review of Sociology*, *16*(2), 175–190.
Samuels, A. (2009) The fascinations of fundamentalism: Political and personal perspectives. Manuscript submitted for publication.
Walzer, M. (1983) *Spheres of Justice*. Oxford: Blackwell.
Zaehner, R. (1957) *Mysticism – Sacred and Profane*. Oxford: Oxford University Press.

Note

1 Previous versions of this chapter were presented at the conference 'Psychotherapy and Liberation: The Legacy of May 68' at the Institute of group Analysis, London, 2–4 May 2008, and published in 2009 in *Psychotherapy and Politics International*, *7*(1), 4–17.

Chapter 15

Rethinking virginity

A post-Jungian reframing[1]

Amanda Hon

Introduction

Virginity is an ambiguous concept, defined as much by its absence or loss as by its presence, as exemplified in the widely acknowledged Madonna/whore dichotomy (Bernau 2007; Douglas 1990; Harding 1990; Qualls-Corbett 1988; Rowland 1999; Warner 1976, 1995; Welldon 1992; Woodman 1985). It has been valued or despised for one or the other aspect throughout human history (Yates 1930, in Holtzman and Kulish 1997: 36). Whether virginity has any intrinsic significance or meaning as a state of being has not been clearly debated. I will explore what has been and is understood by 'virginity', where and how the concept itself is unclear and unhelpful and how it might be rethought.

Jungian literature has focused on the symbolism of virginity, relating it to its imagistic representations in mythology, literature, religion/theology and art (Cater 2003; Harding 1990; Jung and Kerényi 1993; Layard 1982; Shearer 1998; Stroud and Thomas 1982; Warner 1976), leaving a gap for a reassessment of its embodied, relational, sexual aspect to fill. It is an area untouched in post-Jungian writing. With reference to historical, sociocultural, medical and religious constructions of virginity, I hope to start to bridge this gap by bringing together the physical and imaginal. I will briefly review some of the myths of virginity originating in the body and look at how virginity has been understood historically in Western Europe, culminating in a review of its manifestation in modern-day Britain and America. I propose a new deliteralisation of virginity, freeing it from heterosexist assumptions (hooks 1987: 150; Medley-Rath 2007) and relating it to autonomy of the self. I will argue that virginity, and how one engages with it, has a pivotal role in the psyche and is central to how one engages with life, and has long been misrepresented, misunderstood and mistakenly attached to 'Misses'.

Finally, I will look at the darker, less acknowledged aspects of the Virgin archetype, which have profound implications for the individual and for the collective (Hillman 1982; Moore 1982, 2005; Papadopoulos 1992), and will argue that it is crucial that we bring this element into awareness and seek out a 'fulcrumatic' point of balance between wildness and the social/civilised. The importance of this balance is vital both with regard to enabling creative living and, more portentously, in preventing the perpetration of unconscious acts of brutality. I will consider how, by rethinking and reframing the concept of virginity, this patriarchal, disempowering construct might be newly embraced in such a way that it becomes a helpful, enabling concept for society as a whole.

What is virginity?

It is easier to say what virginity is not than what it is. It is not a passive state, defined by its negative relationship with an Other, and, despite insistence upon defining it in carnal terms, it is not an objective condition inextricably bound up with the body. The Cartesian presumption of a split between the mind/body has long been debated, but to date, this central area of virginity retains a sacred aura even in secular arenas where it frequently manifests in its profane aspect, despite the fact that this is where the two meet. 'True' virginity requires a passionate, connected, *erotic* engagement with life. For anyone who aspires to psychological, spiritual and physical well-being, it is imperative to retain contact with a *perceptually perpetual* virginal aspect within, regardless of one's sexual activity or inactivity, of one's sex, gender, age or sexual orientation. This deliteralised virginity has value in many domains. The way in which one connects with virginity impacts profoundly on how one perceives oneself and how one engages with the Other. It is of value, too, with regard to how we perceive and inhabit our roles, power, and sense of agency within wider society. It has bearing on one's engagement with politics, domestic and foreign, and so has the potential to touch the lives of many. This concept is sufficiently elastic to extend its value to having a role in facilitating a conscious embracing of plurality and complexity and so contribute to a reduction in inter-communal and inter-racial tensions, sexual abuse, rape, 'gay-bashing', and the panoply of other ills that result from unconscious acting out. It is also important in the cultural domain, as creativity is nurtured or stifled largely according to the connection we have with our virginity, and in the domain of social progress, where, after more than a century characterised by so many human-generated horrors, it can help to restore what has been broken or lost. One might wonder whether it is naïve to think in terms of social progress, which might arguably seem defunct as a notion after decades in which countless acts of unspeakable cruelty, aggression, and destruction have taken place. Has too much happened, resulting in the lights having gone out for good? I think not, and part of what I am attempting in rethinking virginity is in service of this view.

I question the widely held assumption that actual, physical loss of virginity should necessarily be defined as a male defloration of the female and propose that this is an insufficiently examined and unsustainable hangover from more endemically patriarchal times and that it is, furthermore, an expression of the modernist assumption of the pre-eminence of male/female pairings as something essential, which is no longer tenable in postmodern or post-postmodern (Epstein 1997) consciousness. In line with the depth psychological view of body states I will argue that it is in virginity's embodied 'loss' that we find our connection with beginnings, newness, life. Following penetration, however one experiences oneself to have been penetrated, for both men and women a psychoid hymen might be said to re-form, enabling one to re-experience its loss anew, each time differently, as one's consciousness moves in a spiraling journey throughout life.

I will investigate how physical and spiritual virginity coexist and interact and the extent to which engagement with one's physical virginity, whether through vowing to retain it until marriage or for all time, or by losing it as quickly as possible, or any of the multitude of other possibilities between those poles, is intimately bound up with core, libidinal energy driving the individual life journey.

Since childhood, I have puzzled over the question of what it means to be female. Following Douglas's explorations (1990), I want to find out whether the tools of analytical psychology, a system with a masculine language and symbology, developed by Jung, described by Rowland as a 'powerful male misogynist myth maker' (1999: 36), can be helpful in this task. Approaching virginity from the starting point of embodied realities and moving from there to an examination of the social, archetypal and spiritual dimensions, the nature of my undertaking is distinctive from Jung's approach, which takes the archetypal as a point of departure. This divergence is due, in part, to our being of different genders, living in different times and cultures, and having different sets of biases and prejudices or, using Gadamer's term, different 'horizons' (in Kulkarni 1997: 23–59).

In revisiting, rethinking virginity, I am also attempting a 're-writing [of] the patriarchal text' (Heilbrun 1988: 20, in Douglas 1990: xii) or, in starker, more corporeal terms, to grapple with the infibulation of the text, to loosen the patriarchal bonds that have made it so difficult for women to speak their truths.

Myths of the body

> We tend to think of the body as a thing, a fact, a given. But the body is always an imagined body. A physician, an anatomist, an artist, and a lover will imagine a particular body differently. Varied meanings and emotions will inform a person's experience of the body depending upon the imagination. Throughout history the body has been treated allegorically: the eye as judgment, the heart as feeling, and the head as intelligence. [. . .] But the body is also a collection of images less

> definitely related to specific symbols. A body part can suggest a great world of metaphoric significance.
>
> (Moore 2005: 56)

Historically, the hymen has been widely regarded as the 'anatomical representative of virginity' (Holtzman and Kulish 1997: x), although its existence is conjectural. Virginity had been written about as a physical state long before the hymen began to be discussed in medical literature in the sixteenth and seventeenth centuries, though the gynaecological treatises of neither Aristotle (384–322 BC) nor Galen (AD 129–200/17), two of the ancient Greek theorists who retained an authoritative position with regard to medical theory in Europe from the Middle Ages far into the seventeenth century, refer to it (Bernau 2007: 4).

Galen's four humours theory held that choler, phlegm, bile and blood, each with its corresponding element of fire, water, earth and air, had to be kept in balance to ensure healthy functioning of the body. Women's bodies were considered to be cooler, moister, more susceptible to physical and mental illness and lecherousness, which was understood to be driven by women's seeking of sexual contact with men to compensate for their own integral lack of heat (ibid.: 10). Jung was echoing this idea of the complementarity of the sexes in his concept of the anima and animus, which has been frequently misunderstood to mean the contrasexual counterpart to maleness and femaleness, an interpretation which has prompted Butler to criticise this theory as heteronormative (Samuels 2009). However, although Jung seems to have been unaware of the impact of his own 'horizons' (Gadamer, in Kulkarni 1997: 23–59) on the gender-boundedness of his thinking (Samuels 1999: 216), *anima* and *animus* in fact communicate ungendered otherness: the contrasexual emphasis has arisen simply because each sex images that which 'is "other" [. . .] [as] a being with an-other anatomy. The contrasexuality is truly something "contrapsychological"; sexuality is a metaphor for this' (ibid.: 212). *Animus* and *anima* provide a considerable extension of the gender narrative: the theory equalises the psychological range of the sexes (Samuels 2009).

In the Middle Ages, the female's body, particularly the virginal body, was viewed as toxic to herself and others. Myths of 'Venomous Virgins' and 'Pest-Maidens' (Bernau 2007: 12) anticipated Freud's *The Taboo of Virginity* (1918) in which he refers to woman carrying a 'hostile bitterness against the man, which never completely disappears in the relations between the sexes, and which is clearly indicated in the strivings and in the literary productions of "emancipated" women' (ibid.: 205). Between these periods, the seventeenth century had seen 'the beginning of an age of repression [. . .], an age which perhaps we still have not completely left behind' (Foucault 1998: 17). 'Masculo-femininity' (Bernau 2007: 20) was despised: 'Christian tradition held the virtues of silence, obedience and discretion as especially, even essentially, feminine, [. . .] The Silent Woman was an accepted ideal' (Warner 1995: 29). In the latter part of the following century, Sade (1740–1814) held up a mirror to reveal the unacknowledged shadow of the society in which he lived, exposing male disgust and fear of women and abuses inherent in the dynamics of the interplay of the powerful vis-à-vis the powerless as being all too apparent (Carter 2000: 2; Moore 2005). In the eighteenth and nineteenth centuries, anxieties about female sexuality deepened, as a result of which the necessity of confining female sexuality to heterosexual intercourse within marriage and for the purposes of reproduction began to firmly assert themselves (Bernau 2007: 18–20). A steady desexualisation of women occurred, culminating in the assertion by Victorian medical authorities 'that sex went against a woman's nature, and that only depraved or corrupted women could enjoy it' (ibid.: 20). Biological essentialism came to the fore, bringing a fixedness to ideas of racial and gender attributes (ibid.). In 1906, seeking to challenge essentialist definitions of gender and thus anticipating the work of third-wave feminist writers of the 1990s, Emma Goldman wrote:

> Indeed, if partial emancipation is to become a complete and true emancipation of woman, [. . .] [i]t will have to do away with the absurd notion of the dualism of the sexes, or that man and woman represent two antagonistic worlds.
>
> (in Carter 2000: 151).

Virginity in the twenty-first century

Virginity is elusive. It quickly becomes apparent that there are two intertwining aspects to consider: the physical and the spiritual. How might one orient oneself when considering virginity in the twenty-first century?

In 1950s Britain, the average age for a woman's first experience of sexual intercourse was 20, and for a man it was 21. By 2000, the average age had dropped to 16 for women. This shift was ushered in by the sexual revolution of the 1960s, which dramatically altered attitudes to sex and relationships, together with contemporaneous improvements in contraception (Harris 2007). A 2008 UK survey of the reported sexual behaviour of 14 to 17-year-olds revealed that 40 per cent of this group are sexually active: 22 per cent reported having had had full intercourse and 17 per cent of 16-year-olds had already had more than one sexual partner; 63 per cent of those who had had sex had it under the age of consent. Only six per cent of teenagers who took part in the survey said they would wait until marriage before having sex (YouGov 2008).

American research in 2007 analysed teen magazine *Seventeen*'s health and sexuality advice columns between 1982 and 2001 and found that for girls, loss of virginity was defined as occurring when they have intercourse, while for boys there was some flexibility, allowing them to choose whether to base their virginity status on their achievement of orgasm rather than penile penetration of a vagina, thus perpetuating sexual double standards (Medley-Rath 2007: 35) and reinforcing a heteronormative script (ibid.: 24 and 30). Carpenter notes that, for those who identify as lesbian, gay or bisexual, sex is marginalised, pathologised or rendered invisible by the widely held acceptance of the definition of virginity loss in terms of heterosexual vaginal sex (2005: 6–7).

The chastity movement

An area in which virginity features strongly in twenty-first-century discourse is the chastity movement. 'Chastity, said Aldous Huxley in 1939, was "the most unnatural of sexual perversions", but today it is one of the most hotly debated issues' (Harris 2007). Huxley's words anticipated the sexual revolution to come. The centuries-long influence of the church in shaping how virginity is understood, with its emphasis on the importance of remaining virginal until marriage and practising self-control, persists (Bernau 2007: 58). The present conservative evangelical Protestant debate, particularly in the USA, continues to maintain the Puritan emphasis on virginity until marriage and a 2002 article in the *Observer* newspaper cited chastity as the fastest growing youth movement in America (Bernau 2004: 97). Reporting on the British government's campaign to tackle high rates of teenage pregnancy, a July 2009 article in the *Guardian* newspaper stated: 'Unexpectedly, [. . .] participants more commonly reported teenage pregnancies, early heterosexual sex and expectation of becoming a teenage parent . . .' (Boseley 2009). The government has subsequently changed tack by providing a £25.5 million package providing teenagers with better access to contraception and information on the risks of unprotected sex (O'Hara 2009).

Yet the chastity movement continues to maintain a growing presence. Within it there are those who argue that 'revirginisation' is achievable through becoming a 'born-again' virgin by adjusting one's social life and habits, renouncing drugs, alcohol and masturbation, and finding new friends who share these values. (Bernau 2004: 103). Organisations such as the 1996 American-founded 'Silver Ring Thing' 'offer a message of forgiveness and new beginnings [. . .] to those who have become sexually active and [. . .] an opportunity to embrace a "second virginity"' (Silver Ring Thing 2009). But for those women not of an evangelical bent who are otherwise motivated to seek to 'restore' that which they have 'lost', there are quicker ways, if they can afford to pay.

Surgical virginity

In the twenty-first-century liberal capitalist West, virginity has become a consumer item (Bernau 2004: 105). Recent years have seen a growth in popularity of surgery to 'restore' the hymen to its 'original' state, reflecting a persisting belief in this elusive body-part as a physical marker of virginity (Bernau 2004: 98; Harris 2007), unhelpfully perpetuating the myth of provable virginity (Bernau 2007: 27). The current popularity of vaginal surgery, which is often purely cosmetic and designed to remodel the vagina in such a way that it resembles that of a young girl, is underpinned by the ongoing fetishisation of virginity and youth in Western – and other – cultures, with clinics often preying on female insecurities about their body (ibid.: 28–29). In 2008, the British Association of Aesthetic Plastic Surgeons' audit reported more than triple the amount of cosmetic procedures than in 2003 (Cosmetic Price 2009). Such procedures reflect the dominance of the puer/puella within society today and since the mid 1960s. This archetype drives the culture's obsession with newness and consuming and it is what lies beneath the difficulty it has in accommodating – and indeed its denial of – aging and death. Attempts at renewal-by-surgery, exemplified most literally by revirginalisation procedures, reveal the power of the drive, the longing for something deeper . . .

This something, these deeper aspects of experience . . . this virginity . . . is unattainable in this way. We are not just of the body.

From representations in the fallen Eve and the Virgin Mary to medieval adolescents imperilled by auto-toxification, through to evangelised and surgically modified (post)moderns, virginity has maintained an active presence in the collective psyche, simultaneously identified by its bodily and/or cultural forms, the two conflated categories twining helix-like through the generations. This conflation renders sharply visible other binomial categories where certainty has been assumed, including the very central one of gender (Bernau 2004: 105). Recognising the illusoriness and problematic inherent in gender certainty, Samuels writes: 'Humanity is not just divided into women and men but also into those who are certain about gender and those who are confused about gender' (1989: 94). I suggest that it might also be divided into those who are attuned to a particular kind of perceptual, perpetual virginity and those who, like Baum's Tin Man (1900), unquestioningly accepting of the charlatan wizard's gift of a red silk heart stuffed with sawdust, vainly seek to find virginity in metaphors of the flesh and worn-out cultural constructs.

Rethinking virginity

Rethinking virginity requires the addressing of both strands: spiritual/philosophical and physical. I will first discuss the spiritual/philosophical.

At the end of the nineteenth century, Nietzsche famously announced that 'God is dead' (1997: 5), while Freud had rejected Him before that (Rizzuto 1998). Jung, disillusioned with his father's Protestantism, wrote:

> The Gods have become diseases; Zeus no longer rules Olympus but rather the solar plexus, and produces curious specimens for the doctor's consulting room, or disorders the brains of politicians and journalists who unwittingly let loose psychic epidemics on the world.
>
> (1929 par. 54)

In secular Western societies, God/the gods have been incorporated into late Modern postholocaustal humans' bodies and psyches, the original birthplace of all gods, a reintrojection that can lead either to freedom, or to alienation from society or from oneself. How this enormity is grappled with plays out in myriad ways: some choose, for example, the collective path of organised religion, projecting God right back out again; others find meaning and solace in the Arts, work, prescribed family roles, or in substances, materialism, gang-membership, or perhaps symbiotic clinging to partners, whether love is there or not, bringing to mind Harlow's excruciating experiments with baby rhesus monkeys in the late 1950s (Harlow 1958). So much in human experience speaks of despair, there are so many failed attempts at connecting with depth and meaning that one senses are there if only the way can be found. There is neither a single path nor one destination.

Writing of the alienation experienced in modern society, Zoja cites consumer-driven advertising as addressing 'one of the human being's most ancient spiritual needs: the need for change or self-transformation' (1997: 53). This same need is expressed in drug-induced regeneration experiences and the danger and death-seeking behaviours of adolescents, who hunger for 'self-transformation at a truly instinctual level [. . .] because something inside them delivers the message that a life untouched by initiation is worse than no life at all' (ibid.). It is this need that leads to the seduction of the call to a one-sided, patriarchal ideal of duty for some young people, drawn by the 'purity' of a cause, not recognising that whether they kill or are themselves killed, either way they are sacrifices for an abstract Other. This is true of many who join the armed forces as well as other lost boys and girls who seek transformation and identity within clandestine terrorist organisations. It is the same need that leads to unwanted pregnancy, teenage or otherwise. Jung was one of the first to recognise neurotic conflicts as attempts to grow (Jung 1935: par. 389), and to trace their origin to a sense of emptiness and meaninglessness in life (Jung 1939: par. 627). Symbols, for Jung, are experiential manifestations of archetypes. They define one's humanity and ability to conceptualise that which is unknown or unknowable; they connect the conscious mind with the unconscious. Though arising in the body (Jung 1940 par. 291) it is through symbols that the material realm is transcended and relationship with a supraordinate, transpersonal reality reached (Hopcke 1999: 29–30). By rethinking virginity, freeing it from the snaggling nets of Christianity and science, neither of which speak of a virginity that can be clearly identified or which enriches lives in any meaningful way, conversely, indeed, serving to exacerbate alienation, it is possible to connect with profound depths, to live symbolically, and with more aspects of oneself in relationship with others.

Virginity, as I conceive of it, is inseparable from autonomy. The acquiring of autonomy, individuality, is widely represented in myths as involving curiosity-motivated transgression, usually a theft, such as Prometheus stealing the fire of the gods, Psyche stealing Persephone's beauty secret, Pandora opening the box, or Adam and Eve eating the forbidden fruit and so gaining knowledge of good and evil. (Warner 1992: 68; Harding 1975: 203). The sexual interpretation of the latter myth has profoundly impacted Western psyches for centuries and continues to be propounded by fundamentalist preachers who, in so doing, perpetuate the essentialist patriarchal disempowerment of the female and the feminine. Heinberg notes a connection between this and the psychoanalytical attribution of a sexual aetiology to humanity's psychological distress (1995: 192), and Duncan cites Irigaray's suggestion that 'psychoanalysing a woman is tantamount to adapting her to a society of a masculine type' (in Adams and Duncan 2003: 74).

Paradoxically, virginity only comes into existence as a concept when relationship is constellated, recalling Winnicott's statement, 'there is no such thing as a baby – only a nursing couple' (1965): as soon as it enters the discourse, virginity is already lost. But the Self[2] perpetually contains virginity, and by its very nature, virginity is erotic in that it only exists in relation to an Other. Though not synonymous with sex, Eros cannot be completely separated from it. Freud identified Eros with the Life Instinct, the other basic instinct of his model being the Death Instinct. Jung shared his view with regard to Eros but departed from Freud in identifying its opposite as the will to power (in Samuels, Shorter and Plaut 2003: 55). Sade's work, replete with images of virgins and libertines, the inseparable pair, dual poles of a single archetype, reveals the connection of Eros with soul (Moore 2005: 28) and abounds with illustrations lending support to Jung's connecting of Eros with power.

The popular fascination with horror stories, abductions, murders, rapes, and accidents (Guggenbühl-Craig, in Moore 2005: xi) expresses widespread repressed Eros, part of our shadow, disowned and projected onto the Other. '*In-nocere* in Latin can mean either not to hurt, or not to be hurt. Both are present in the [. . .] compelling need to see oneself and to be seen as beyond reproach' (Moore 2005: 34). Sade would not tolerate feigned innocence, and perhaps this was why his society would not tolerate him.

Citing the virgin as the archetype of purity, like Sade, Papadopoulos also sees it as constellating intolerance, sharing connections with monotheism in its exclusivity. He notes its dark shadow, pointing a finger at its presence in the atrocity of the Holocaust, which saw the mass murder of 'God's Chosen People' by 'the pure Aryan race'; two clashing virginal psychologies,

'Victims and victimizers, victimizers and victims, dancing together in a hellish ballet of death' (1992: 73–76).

Virginity, as I rethink it, does not hold the virgin irredeemably fixed at one end of an archetypal polarity. It engages with the Other in passionate, symbolic embrace and so holds the tension between wild, red in tooth and claw (Tennyson 2007/1850) aggression – in Jungian and Nietzschean terms what might be called the Dionysian – and the social/civilised, the Apollonian. This balance is vital with regard to its role in enabling creative life and to precluding the unconscious eruption of repressed shadow. Autonomous to the core, it rejects all essentialism and embraces fluidity. Its nature is dynamic. It comes into existence at the point of its constellation, like the universe at the moment that it exploded into being, though moments had not yet begun as this point was beyond time, as Calvino expresses so beautifully (1993: 43–47). This virginity does not project its matter outward, neither does it hold itself apart. Its nature is erotic: it creates and connects. It does not deny: 'all' shadow aspects are known to its consciousness. Heuer refers to a shift in consciousness and integration of shadow that has occurred, as yet barely perceived, with the publication of *The Gospel of Judas* (Kasser, Meyer and Wurst 2006); he describes the wholeness formed in the union of Jesus and Judas therein, comparing it to the Eastern yin/yang symbol in which light and shadow symbolically embrace (Heuer 2009a). Judas's role as betrayer of Jesus is *crucial* to the unfolding of the story. Without Judas there could be no redemption: he is Jesus's essential counterpart. Together, they are virginal.

Kant understood the Fall and humanity's acquiring of free will and reason as mankind's coming of age (Heinberg 1995: 195). Could it be that, following the rupturing of the collective symbolic hymen by horrors such as the two World Wars, Vietnam, Bosnia, Rwanda, and all the other tragedies that belong on this list, we have reached a metaphorical menarche and are now able to integrate more of our own darkness and so enlarge, deepen our consciousness? At this time when, on a global level, we are facing irrevocable climate change, economic collapse and ongoing battles for territory and resources, and struggling with questions of demographics and immigration, this re-storied virginity offers a way of remaining engaged without falling into simplified polarised arguments of right and wrong. It not only provides a sense of agency for the individual, it renders the voice powerfully multi-tonal.

To fully rethink and reframe virginity, this plurality must be extended to its physical, embodied aspect. The research cited above reveals the inadequacy of the 'traditional' definitions: that is all they are. The heterosexual matrix really *is* an *imaginary* logic (Butler, in Kulkarni 1997: 75). Rejection of the patriarchal legacy of the heteronormative essentialism of Christianity and scientific rationalism and the embracing of a more complex view of sexuality and of what defines virginity and its loss together constitute an assertion of individual autonomy and authority of the self. This reclaiming of the body is particularly liberating for those marginalised, pathologised or rendered invisible by the lenses habitually used to view sexuality and sexual behaviour. With people openly inhabiting diverse sexualities at younger ages than before (Carpenter 2005: 7), a reassessment of what constitutes virginity is timely, if not overdue.

I assert that, in accordance with Carpenter's findings (2005: 44–56), virginity is a subjective state that can be defined neither by the condition/presence/absence of a body-part nor by the participation, or not, in the singular, nominated act of heterosexual intercourse. Kinsey's research has shown 'that sexual orientation is actually a *range* of behaviours and identities rather than a *condition*, that homosexuality is one of a number of normal variations in human sexual behavior' (Hopcke 1989: 4). Given this diversity of normal human experience, unless one is willing to be monomaniacally fascistic, it must be acknowledged that 'loss' of virginity occurs at whatever point an individual experiences it as having occurred. Furthermore, men and women of all ages and experience describe feelings of newness and excitement at the start of a new relationship or upon entering a new phase in an existing relationship: having opportunities to do things differently from how one might have done them before, moving in spirals not circles, psychological growth occurs, which, in turn, feeds back into the relationship. With this sense of virginity, one can access that energy at any time: it does not get 'lost' in any concrete way. Its ability to overcome the polarised positioning that sometimes arises between partners, to enable them to reconnect passionately and erotically, in the sense of relating fully and truly meeting, can mean the difference between remaining in relationship and separating. For people with children, this is very significant.

Revirginalisation and the 'forgiveness' proffered by *ersatz* symbols such as the Silver Ring Thing can only have meaning within an infibulating, outdated discourse which construes sex outside narrowly defined boundaries as something 'wrong', to be corrected or defended against. To participate in such a discourse is an abnegation of the authority and autonomy of the self. I do not advocate abandoned engagement in *free love*, however. The sexual revolution of the 1960s was a reaction against residual Victorian sexual repressiveness and as such served to wake society up out of a deep sleep that had gone on for too long. But, despite initial appearances, it also perpetuated the patriarchal positioning of women in a new guise before ending in a sexual counter-revolution, the revolutionary having 'been carrying [. . . the authoritarian structure] within himself' (Gross, in Heuer 2009b: 73). Having in mind Mühsam's understanding of 'sexuality as the relating of people to the individual, sociability as the interpersonal relationship, and religiosity as the relationship of the individual to the cosmos' (in Heuer 2009b: 70), I regard sexuality as fundamental. It does not preclude passionate engagement with celibacy: virginity can accommodate this, too. The virginal is located wherever the energy is most intensely present with the Other within or without. Virginity is about renewal; of energy, of pace, of view, of possibilities, of sense of self. If one inhabits it, or allows it to inhabit one, it opens up the world and bestows psychological and physical well-being. I share Harding's view that:

> To take life solely on the pleasure principle leads inevitably to satiety and boredom. Man [*sic*] [. . .] is also a living spirit and can find satisfaction in life only through the devotion of all his powers to some end beyond his own personal pleasure. This end beyond [him] is [. . .] to be found through taking [. . .] love more, not less, seriously.
>
> (1975: 214)

Thomas calls for a radical return to a metaphor of the virgin as 'whole within itself' with 'an undeniable inner authority, an integrity, a being complete within oneself' (in Stroud and Thomas 1982: 141). This is what is constellated when one embraces virginity.

Conclusion

In rethinking virginity I have reframed it in post-Jungian terms. I have discussed the ambiguities inherent in the concept of virginity as both a sociocultural-medical and a philosophical construct and have unveiled its patriarchal underpinnings. Does virginity continue to have any intrinsic meaning as a state of being? Certainly not as it had in pre-sexual-revolutionary times: the veil has been ripped from the collective persona by wars and the Holocaust, that monolith of man's brutality to man. The torn veil has exposed the bare humanity beneath, the softness and vulnerability of skin, its tendency to coarsen in hostile environments, to erupt in furious acne, to tingle at the touch of another's skin, to sag, to shine, and to blush. . . male and female alike. Out of the dishevelment of the twentieth century, analytical psychology continues to provide useful tools to understand the human psyche, enabling a critical deconstruction of the self. One of its central concepts, that of the anima/animus syzygy, has emerged altered but intact: detached from gender, it allows an understanding of otherness based on difference rather than 'opposites' (Samuels 1999: 223). It is at such thresholds of otherness that virginity is most at home. Giegerich writes: 'To talk about gender issues in psychology is psychological baby talk' (1999: 29). But why just talk when there are so many more erotic ways to connect and to become?

Bibliography

Adams, T. and Duncan, A. (eds.) (2003) *The Feminine Case*. London and New York, NY: Karnac.

Baum, F. E. (1900) *The Wonderful Wizard of Oz*. Chicago, IL: George M. Hill.
Bernau, A. (2004) Girls on film: Medieval virginity in the cinema. In M. W. Driver and S. Ray (eds.), *The Medieval Hero on Screen: Representations from Beowulf to Buffy*. Jefferson, NC and London: McFarland & Co.
Bernau, A. (2007) *Virgins: A Cultural History*. London: Granta.
Boseley, S. (2009) Teenage pregnancies rise despite £6m government campaign. *The Guardian*, 8 July. Retrieved from http://www.guardian.co.uk/lifeandstyle/2009/jul/08/teenage-pregnancies-rise-despite-campaign
Calvino, I. (1993) *Cosmicomics*. London and Basingstoke: Picador/Cape.
Carpenter L. (2005) *Virginity Lost*. New York, NY and London: New York University.
Carter, A. (2000) *The Sadeian Woman*. London: Virago.
Cater, N. (2003) *Electra Tracing a Feminine Myth through the Western Imagination*. New Orleans, LA: Spring.
Cosmetic Price (2009) Retrieved from http://www.cosmeticprice.co.uk/in.asp?catalogid=107
Douglas, C. (1990) *The Woman in the Mirror*. Boston, MA: Sigo.
Duncan, A. (2003) Individuation and necessity. In T. Adams and A. Duncan (eds.), *The Feminine Case: Jung, Aesthetics and Creative Process*. London: Karnac.
Epstein, M. (1997) The place of postmodernism in postmodernity. *Russian Postmodernism: New Perspectives on Late Soviet and Post-Soviet Culture*. Retrieved from http://www.focusing.org/apm_papers/epstein.html
Foucault, M. (1998) *The Will to Knowledge. The History of Sexuality: Volume One*. London: Penguin.
Freud, S. (1918) *The Taboo of Virginity*. *SE*, Vol. XI. London: Hogarth.
Giegerich, W. (1999) The patriarchal neglect of the feminine principle: A psychological fallacy in Jungian theory. *Harvest*, *45*(1), 7–30.
Harding, M. E. (1975) *The Way of All Women*. New York, NY: Harper & Row.
Harding, M. E. (1990) *Woman's Mysteries Ancient and Modern*. Boston, MA and Shaftesbury, Dorset: Shambhala.
Harlow, H. F. (1958) The Nature of Love. *American Psychologist*, *13*, 673–685.
Harris, S. (2007) Whatever happened to virginity? In *The Independent*, 22 April. Retrieved from http://www.independent.co.uk/news/uk/home-news/news-review-whatever-happened-to-virginity-445682.html
Heilbrun, C. G. (1988) *Writing a Woman's Life*. New York, NY: Norton.
Heinberg, R. (1995) *Memories and Visions of Paradise*. Wheaton, IL: Quest.
Heuer, G. (2009a) For 'a new heaven and a new earth'. *The Gospel of Judas* – An emerging potential for world peace? A Jungian perspective. *Spring*, *81*, 265–290.
Heuer, G. (2009b) The sacral revolution: The synthesis of analysis, religion and radical politics. Origins and reception. Appendix: On overcoming the cultural crisis, by Otto Gross. *International Journal of Jungian Studies*, *1*(1), 68–80.
Hillman, J. (1982) Salt: A chapter in alchemical psychology. In J. Stroud and G. Thomas (eds.) (1982), *Images of the Untouched: Virginity in Psyche, Myth and Community*. Dallas, TX: Spring.
Holtzman, D. and Kulish, N. (1997) *Nevermore: The Hymen and the Loss of Virginity*. Northvale, NJ and London: Jason Aronson.
hooks, b. (1987) *Feminist Theory From Margin to Center*. Boston, IL: South End.

Hopcke, R. H. (1989) Why Jung, Jungians and homosexuality?: A brief introduction. *Jung, Jungians and Homosexuality*. Boston, MA: Shambhala.

Hopcke, R. H. (1999) *A Guided Tour of the Collected Works of C. G. Jung*. Boston, MA and London: Shambhala.

Jung, C. G. (1929) Commentary on *The Secret of the Golden Flower*. *CW* 13. London: Routledge & Kegan Paul.

Jung, C. G. (1935) The Tavistock Lectures: Lecture V. *CW* 18. London: Routledge & Kegan Paul.

Jung, C. G. (1939) The symbolic life. *CW* 18. London: Routledge & Kegan Paul.

Jung, C. G. (1940) The psychology of the child archetype. *CW* 9i. London: Routledge & Kegan Paul.

Jung, C. G. and Kerényi, C. (1993[1949]) *Essays on a Science of Mythology*. Princeton, NJ and Chichester: Princeton University.

Kasser, R., Meyer, M. and Wurst, G. (eds.) (2006) *The Gospel of Judas from Codex Tchacos*. Washington, DC: National Geographic.

Kulkarni, C. (1997) *Lesbians and Lesbianisms*. London and New York, NY: Routledge.

Layard, J. (1982) The incest taboo and the virgin archetype. In J. Stroud and G. Thomas (eds.), *Images of the Untouched: Virginity in Psyche, Myth and Community*. Dallas, TX: Spring.

Medley-Rath, S. R. (2007) 'Am I still a virgin?': What counts as sex in 20 years of *Seventeen*. *Sexuality and Culture*, *11*(2), 24–38.

Moore, T. (1982) The virgin and the unicorn. In J. Stroud and G. Thomas (eds.), *Images of the Untouched: Virginity in Psyche, Myth and Community*. Dallas, TX: Spring.

Moore, T. (2005) *Dark Eros*. Putnam, CT: Spring.

Nietzsche, F. (1997) *Thus Spake Zarathustra*. Ware: Wordsworth.

O'Hara, M. (2009) Teenage pregnancy rates rise. In *The Guardian*, 26 February. Retrieved from http://www.guardian.co.uk/society/2009/feb/26/teenage-pregnancy-rise

Papadopoulos, R. (1992) *Carl Gustav Jung: Critical Assessments*. London and New York, NY: Routledge.

Qualls-Corbett, N. (1988) *The Sacred Prostitute: Eternal Aspects of the Feminine*. Toronto: Inner City.

Rizzuto, A.-M. (1998) *Why Did Freud Reject God?* New Haven, CT and London: Yale University.

Rowland, S. (1999) Michele Roberts' Virgins: Contesting gender in fictions, re-writing Jungian theory and Christian myth. *Journal of Gender Studies*, *8*(1), 35–42.

Samuels, A. (1989) *The Plural Psyche*. London and New York, NY: Routledge.

Samuels, A. (1993) *The Political Psyche*. London and New York, NY: Routledge.

Samuels, A. (1999) *Jung and the Post-Jungians*. London and New York, NY: Routledge.

Samuels, A. (2009) Homosexuality. Seminar at the Centre for Psychoanalytic Studies, University of Essex, Colchester, 4 March. Personal notes.

Samuels, A., Shorter, B. and Plaut, F. (2003) *A Critical Dictionary of Jungian Analysis*. Hove and New York, NY: Brunner-Routledge.

Shearer, A. (1998) *Athene: Image and Energy*. London: Arkana Penguin Books.

Silver Ring Thing (2009) Retrieved from http://www.silverringthing.org.uk/aboutus_vision.asp

Stroud, J. and Thomas, G. (eds.) (1982) *Images of the Untouched: Virginity in Psyche, Myth and Community*. Dallas, TX: Spring.

Tennyson, A. L. (2007) In Memoriam A.H.H. In *Selected Poems: Tennyson*. London: Penguin.

Warner, M. (1976) *Alone of All Her Sex*. New York, NY: Vintage.

Warner, M. (1992) Women against women in the old wives' tale. In D. Petrie (ed.) (1993), *Cinema and the Realms of Enchantment: Lectures, Seminars and Essays*. London: BFI Publishing.

Warner, M. (1995) *From the Beast to the Blonde*. London: Vintage.

Welldon, E. (1992) *Mother, Madonna, Whore: The Idealization and Denegration of Motherhood*. New York, NY and London: Guilford.

Winnicott, D. W. (1965) The theory of the parent-infant relationship. In *The Maturational Processes and the Facilitating Environment*. London: Hogarth. Retrieved from http://thepsychoanalyticfield.com/?s=no+such+thing+as+a+baby

Woodman, M. (1985) *The Pregnant Virgin*. Toronto: Inner City.

YouGov (2008) Highlights from YouGov's Sex Education survey. Retrieved from http://sexperienceuk.channel4.com/teen-sex-survey

Zoja, E. P. (1997) *Abortion: Loss and Renewal in the Search for Identity*. London and New York, NY: Routledge.

Notes

1 This essay is a shortened, revised version of a longer, unpublished paper by the author.

2 Samuels, Shorter and Plaut's definition of 'Self': 'An archetypal image of man's fullest potential and the unity of the personality as a whole' (2003: 135).

Chapter 16

The colour of rainbows

The advent of post-postmodernity and the notion of forgiveness

Birgit Heuer

Introduction

Among the early psychoanalysts at the beginning of the last century, Otto Gross stands out as the originator of the idea that sexual revolutions are a psychoanalytic concern. At the same time, he endeavoured to live a life that was to sexually liberate himself and his partners. Towards the end of his days, however, he was expressing a need for forgiveness. I quote from an undated letter to his wife Frieda:

> Frieda, (I know now that) I have always concentrated *on others*, on what *they* were lacking and how to help *them*, but *I never focused on myself*. Only the awareness of my own irredeemable guilt (towards you) and the experience of complete powerlessness in this regard, has led me now to look at myself (and my effect on others) . . . You have suffered so much, Frieda, through me and I had never thought to look within *myself* for the reasons.
>
> (in G. Heuer 2000: 201; my translation)

It seems that Gross, having lived a version of sexual revolutions according to his time, in the end felt the need for forgiveness. Gross had introduced the socio-political dimension to psychoanalytic discourse; did it now occur to him that sexual revolutions as a political and psychoanalytic programme needed a relational counterpart in the form of forgiveness? In this context, then, forgiveness becomes a notion that is located at the interface of the personal and the political as a bridging medium and has a linking, relational function. In this chapter, I would like to suggest this particular idea of forgiveness as a keynote melody to which I shall add other harmonies.

My central theme will thus be regarded as multifaceted and explored in a variety of ways. Forgiveness can seem extremely personal and intimately bound up with one's own psycho-biography. At the same time, the ramifications of forgiveness are often highly public and political. Traditionally speaking, forgiveness has been regarded as a subject of religion

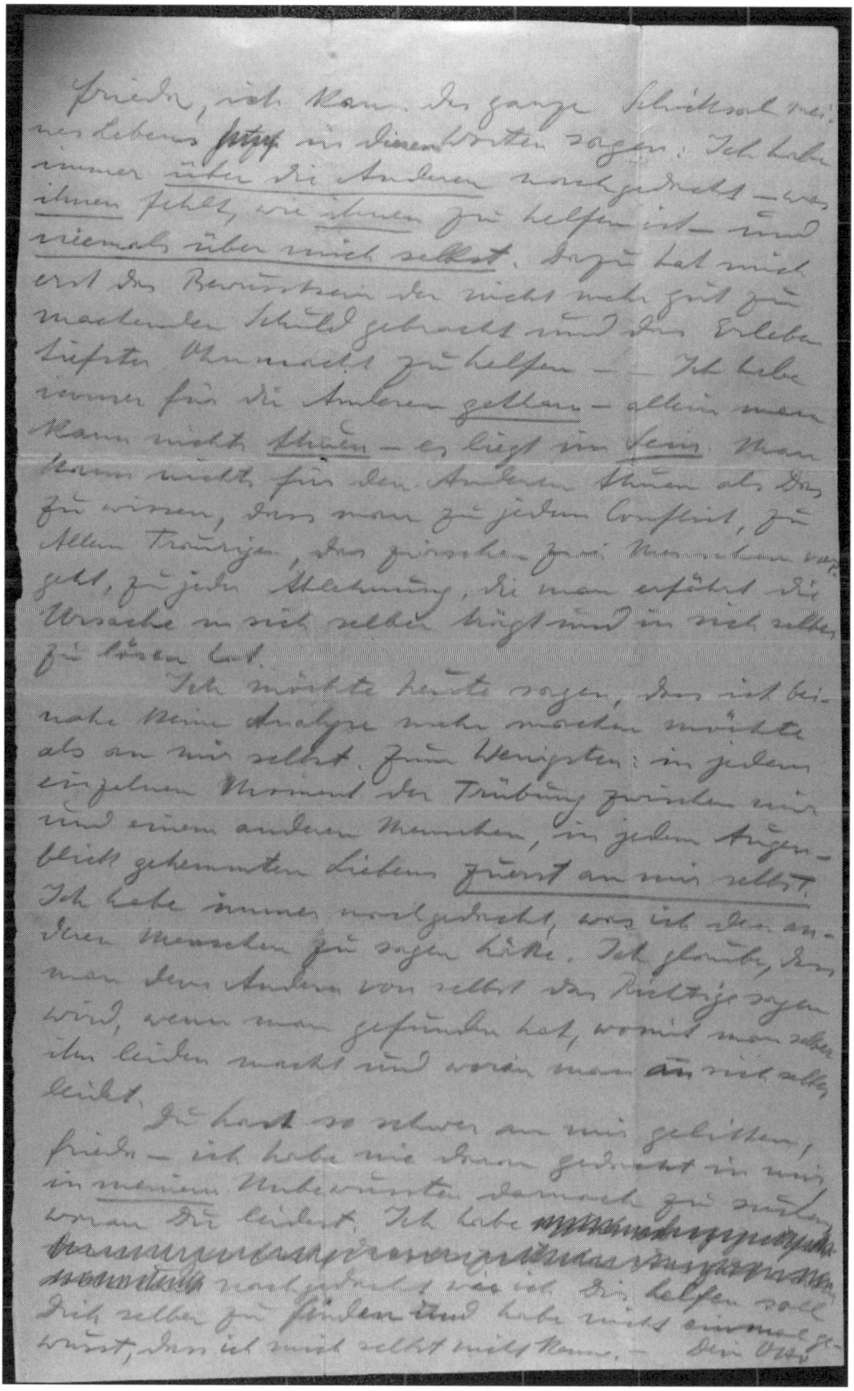

Frieda, ich kann das ganze Schicksal meines Lebens in diesen Worten sagen: Ich habe immer *über die Anderen* nachgedacht — was *ihnen* fehlt, wie *ihnen* zu helfen ist — und *niemals über mich selbst*. Dazu hat mich erst das Bewusstsein der nicht mehr gut zu machenden Schuld gebracht und das Erleben tiefster Ohnmacht zu helfen — Ich habe immer für die Anderen *gelebt* — allein man kann nichts *thun* — es liegt im *Sein*. Man kann nichts für den Anderen thun als das zu wissen, dass man zu jedem Conflict, zu allem Traurigen, das zwischen zwei Menschen vorgeht, zu jeder Ablehnung, die man erfährt die Ursache in sich selber trägt und in sich selber zu lösen hat.

Ich möchte heute sagen, dass ich beinahe keine Analyse mehr machen möchte als an mir selbst. Zum Wenigsten: in jedem einzelnen Moment der Trübung zwischen mir und einem anderen Menschen, in jedem Augenblick gehemmten Lebens *zuerst an mir selbst*. Ich habe immer nachgedacht, was ich den anderen Menschen zu sagen hätte. Ich glaube, dass man dem Andern von selbst das Richtige sagen wird, wenn man gefunden hat, womit man selber ihn leiden macht und woran man an sich selber leidet.

Du hast so schwer an mir gelitten, Frieda — ich habe nie daran gedacht in mir, in *meinem* Unbewussten danach zu suchen woran Du leidest. Ich habe nachgedacht was ich Dir helfen soll Dich selber zu finden und habe nicht einmal gewusst, dass ich mich selbst nicht kenne. — Dein Otto

Figure 16.1 Otto Gross's letter to his wife, Frieda, undated.

and spirituality. Forgiveness has also been called an 'art and a science' (Worthington Jr. 2005) and its many aspects have also been studied empirically for the past 25 years. Here, I shall attempt to convey a flavour of this diversity of approaches.

Returning to the notion of forgiveness as a bridgeing medium, I shall also introduce the concept of an essence of forgiveness that permeates its many facets in a subtle way. I have traced the connection between the mystical experience of grace and what contemporary physicists now term quantum-reality in a previous paper (B. Heuer 2008). From this perspective 'ordinary reality', including scientific empirical reality, subtly interweaves with a view of reality that is traditionally only accessible through faith. It is in the paradigmatic context of this revised view of reality that the idea of an essence of forgiveness emerges and thrives. Forgiveness might then involve a mystical place, located in a flow of grace that is accessible both scientifically and through inner experience.

The wider paradigmatic setting of the notion of forgiveness thus involves a complex fastening of science and spirituality that, crucially, can be traced from within empirical science. This, in turn, heralds a shift in weltanschauung which I propose to call post-postmodernism, a term first used by Epstein (1997). I have further developed this term, however, both from a philosophical and a psychological angle and brought it to life as an emerging view of reality that supersedes the postmodern analytic one while retaining the latter's achievements. As a Jungian analyst, I have come to call analytic work informed by this evolving weltanschauung a post-post-Jungian approach for which I propose the term sanatology (B. Heuer 2008). My concept of post-postmodernity moves on from Aristotelian binarity – which underpins all postmodern analysis – to a deeper pre-unity, hailing from quantum information theory, that revolves around connection rather than division and utilises channels other than causality and determinism. As a consequence, stark opposition recedes and a softened sensibility pertains to this world view. Thus post-postmodernism has no need to 'go for the gap', as it were, nor focus on what is wrong or missing, and is able to fully conceive of positives, such as goodness, love and forgiveness instead. In other words, post-postmodernism is conceptually equipped to fill out and metaphorically colour in all the hues of the rainbow.

A further section of this chapter concerns clinical aspects of forgiveness. For this purpose, I shall look into practical, emotional and bodily instances of forgiveness, including its shadow aspects. I shall also bring my thoughts on the essence of forgiveness into the clinic.

Finally, I shall address specific socio-political aspects of forgiveness and their relation to the essence of forgiveness. Here I shall explore relationally oriented ways of resolving conflict. In particular, I shall mention the work of the Truth and Reconciliation Commission and the socio-political possibilities of forgiveness that restorative justice might enable.

This chapter then enquires into the notion of forgiveness as a bridging medium encompassing the personal and the collective/political as well as the scientific and the mystical. Approached in this way, paradoxically the notion of forgiveness is de-mystified and becomes more accessible. My overall intention, though, is more illustrative and evocative than critical and I hope to bring depth and texture to the theme of forgiveness.

Empirical science and forgiveness

The empirical exploration of forgiveness started in the mid eighties and forgiveness is now the subject of a science. No unified definition has come forward, however, as forgiveness has been studied in a multi-faceted way. Thus a multitude of aspects has emerged:

Forgiveness has been studied in relation to conciliatory group behaviour in primates. It has also been examined as individual human behaviour and as related to spirituality/religion, as related to physical health, as related to emotional health, as based on character, vengeful or forgiving; it has been considered from the angle of the victim's experience and their behaviour and/or psychology. There are fewer studies concentrating on the perpetrator. Forgiveness has also been considered in relation to couples, families and larger social groups and from the point of view of social intervention.

Enright and Fitzgibbons (2000) explore forgiveness as a process involving behaviour, cognition and affect that move through twenty steps in naturally occurring settings, thus contributing hypotheses about the natural occurrence of forgiveness. McCollough, Fincham and Tsang (2003) conceptualise forgiveness as a redirection of conscious motivation that can change and be measured, with a two-component approach to forgiving, reducing negative motivations and increasing positive ones. Sandage and Williamson (2005) have studied forgiveness in the context of culture, while Mahoney, Rye and Pargament (2005) have addressed forgiveness and the sacred and the particular challenge of forgiving desecration. There is research into 'anger towards god' by Exline and Martin (2005). Tagney, Boone and Dearing (2005) have written on forgiving the Self. Farrow and Woodruff (2005) have published a paper on the neuro-imaging of forgivability. Wade (2002) has examined group interventions to promote forgiveness and Armour and Umbreit (2005) have studied the paradox of forgiveness in restorative justice.

The notion of an essence of forgiveness

As empirical research highlights the manifold facets of forgiveness, might there be an alternative approach, involving what I shall term the essence of forgiveness? This implies an epistemological discussion about the creative tension between an empirical approach and a paradigm that is informed by the findings of contemporary quantum research. Moreover, it implies a metaphysical shift in what is regarded as the very nature of reality. In a previous paper (B. Heuer 2008) I have explored how a quantum-scientific and a mystical view of the world interweave in what might be called an integration of reality and eternity. The 'result' is a logical hybrid where two opposing views of reality coexist simultaneously. From a meta-paradigmatic angle, one might say that mystical experience requires 'making real' in the Winnicottian developmental sense. A similar process is currently unfolding via the socio-cultural reception of contemporary quantum physics. I would like to propose these considerations as a frame for exploring the essence of forgiveness.

The essence of forgiveness emerging from this is best articulated in poetic/mystical language, inviting resonance to its manifold facets, such as a song. Such a song might sing of forgiveness as an act of grace, created by the Divine on our behalf, and of forgiveness as inspired by the love of the beauty and goodness of human beings. It reverberates with the essence of forgiveness as the transformative power of the Divine and with human forgiveness as a highly creative and imaginative act. It might sing of forgiveness as the capacity to imagine something better, more wholesome. Another stance might sing of the mystical Divine that is constant in complete forgiveness, at all times, unconditionally. Silently and imperceptibly, continues the song, the mystical Divine always transforms badness into goodness, into grace. Suffering ensues where this flow is seemingly interrupted. Forgiveness is to do with the secret, invisible point at which transformation occurs. Might it flow into us at all times unconsciously and create a capacity, which like any creative talent can be honed? Is forgiveness a transformation that has already happened, akin to Jones's (2002) view of Jung's teleology? If future forgiveness is already constellated, does it then need 'making real' in the Winnicottian sense?

Forgiveness also links with the Buddhist view of the wheel of karma. The essence of forgiveness brought to the notion of karma means that the wheel is 'halted' and karma voided. If all karma has been transmuted, we are then challenged to 'realise' this, i.e. by softening and unlearning the concept of crime and punishment, the talion law. If we ourselves are forgiven, the talion law ceases to make sense psychologically. As we learn emotionally about Divine forgiveness, we are inspired by its gentle, yet extremely powerful ways, enabled by Divine generosity to be generous ourselves. The essence of forgiveness then involves a transformative, generous creative act, inspired by the flow of Divine grace. It involves the unfolding of the holy heart in the human heart, perhaps the development of a heart-mind.

Biochemical empirical research (Pert 1997) now holds that we think and feel with all of our bodies, so that a forgiving heart might be located anywhere in the body or extend to the whole of the body. Broadly speaking, one might consider all instances of non-linearity as a transformation of the talion law, which leads to an abundance of instances of forgiveness. In this way, nature seems designed to be forgiving, as are our bodies. The earth, Gaia, might be called extremely forgiving in her profound non-linear ability to regenerate in the face of abuse or lack of care and this includes the seasons, the daily rising and setting of the sun, our bodies' ability to rejuvenate and all healing of physical ailments.

Towards post-postmodernity

The notion of an essence of forgiveness can also be accessed through setting it in a wider paradigmatic landscape which I refer to as post-postmodern. Using Epstein's (1997) term, I have developed this into a conceptual amalgam that extends from a paradigmatic view of reality based on quantum logic to a non-bivalent style of academic discourse that I call soft argument and a corresponding clinical approach, a post-post-Jungian sanatology (B. Heuer 2008).

The metaphoric landscape for this emerging weltanschauung induces a particular optimistic mood that springs from an orientation towards the whole rather than the part or the positive rather than the negative. Metaphorically speaking, it might be imagined as a panorama subtly wreathed in rainbows. In some contrast, the postmodern vista evidences the flowering, to fullest capacity, of analytical thought accompanied by a particular mood, which Wilber (1998) refers to as flat, that is, denuded of interiority and meaning. Which factors, then, suggest and enable such a manner of shifting paradigmatic scenery? First, its scientific collateral comes from contemporary quantum science, particularly quantum information theory. It is noteworthy that quantum information theory rests on Bell's (1964) famous inequality which effectively imbues all reality with quantum dynamics. Goernitz and Goernitz (2006), a quantum physicist and a Freudian analyst respectively, have introduced a particular world view, which they call 'henadic', that is based in empirical science. The term stems from the Greek *hen*, meaning one, so that henadic implies a complex yet fundamental unity. The term was selected to signify a specific unity that is not quite accessible via the more familiar vernacular of holism. This is best illustrated by putting henadism into the context of quantum logic.

Quantum logic has evolved out of its bivalent Aristotelian cousin. The latter rests on a complete, sharp delineation of yes and no or of logical attributes, leading to a black and white division, with a *tertium non datur*, an injunction against any overlap. Quantum logic, however, mainly provides a yes, and any negation is only ever 66 per cent accurate (ibid.). This means that according to quantum logic, anything that is taken to be the case – and thus conventionally speaking excludes its opposite – must still be assumed to be trailing 33 per cent of quantum-potential which cannot be made to disappear. The reason for this lies with the deeper, yet complex, henadic unity of subject and object which can only be artificially separated by means such as Aristotelian axioms. Quantum logic thus brings to mind descriptions such as positive, generous or abundant and this, in turn, evidences qualia of experience emerging in empirical science in a hitherto inconceivable way. The latter, combined with a tendency towards the positive, are, in my reading, important features of post-postmodernity. In addition, the henadic unity of subject and object implies a non-causal and non-deterministic pre-connection between researcher and subject which, strikingly, recalls the particular type of reason used in mysticism. According to Ferrer (2002), mystical reason is concerned with knowledge *in* rather than knowledge of, which, in quantum terms, involves a henadic identity of human and Divine. In my view, such knowledge *in* might be arrived at via quantum resonance and coherent wave patterns. In any case, a convergence of empirical science and spirituality can be seen to emerge here – another hallmark of post-postmodernity. In conclusion, post-postmodernism then is able to reconnect spirit and science as well as researcher and subject, minimise opposition, which leads to softer sensibilities, and, finally, introduce generosity of thought in the form of a full – non-reductive – conceivability of positives such as love or faith. It is this subtly rainbow-hued paradigmatic landscape that offers the most fitting setting for the notion of forgiveness.

Some clinical aspects of forgiveness

In my view, the most important clinical aspect of the essence of forgiveness lies in its potential power of transformation. Conceptually, Jung's transcendent function is closely related to this, as is his idea of an archetypally patterned morality. Clinical instances of forgiveness can be mental, emotional, bodily or spiritual. I consider the most basic – and at the same time profound – instance of forgiveness clinically to lie in the fact of sheer survival of extreme trauma. The fact that the patient who has survived extreme trauma has not killed herself/himself or anybody else seems to me to express forgiveness, in that the talion law is already transcended and continues to be so with every day of survival. Another instance of forgiveness is the release of bodily symptoms related to trauma as in the physical symptoms of post-traumatic stress syndrome, or the release of bodily symptoms that relate to other painful psychic experience. Here it is the body that potentially forgives first. A different example from couple therapy would be the warring couple who have managed to find a degree of peace – without any formal acts of forgiveness – where the forgiveness lies in learning a better way of living together. These are all instances of forgiveness where transformation occurs on a day-to-day level through the way life is lived, rather than any formal acts of forgiveness. It is noticeable that, on this level, there is an abundance of forgiveness everywhere as part of ordinary life. There are untold numbers of everyday ordinary gestures of forgiveness. Yet they link with the deeper, mystical essence of forgiveness and thus have a transcendent numinous aspect in the midst of seemingly ordinary experience. There is something like perception through the eyes of forgiveness that makes them visible, so that instances of forgiveness seem abundant. When this is realised, particularly clinically, it may create a positive cycle, increasing the potential for forgiveness.

There are, of course, shadow aspects of forgiveness. According to Murphy (2005), these occur when forgiveness becomes 'cheap grace', where it allows an unacceptable situation to continue and constitutes a form of masochistic rage, or where forgiveness is given as a form of manipulation; where forgiveness is an attempt at moral superiority; or where it is given too quickly to defend against resentment, rage or the realisation of trauma. Another shadow aspect of forgiveness arises when we 'play God', by individually attempting to forget and forgive the collectively 'unforgivable', rather than addressing it through socio-political processes of restorative justice.

Forgiveness can also be seen as a creative act. Here its essence inspires the ability to imagine something better and to participate in bringing it about. Unforgiveness, in my view, imprisons a person or an experience in the past. There is usually a traumatic element that serves as an unconscious trigger. This area then becomes split off from the psychic blood supply of embracing emotional reality. Here the ordinary work of recovering the repressed is needed, as well as creativity and imagination. Forgiveness can thus be highly individual like a fingerprint and include creatively dreaming up, as well as receiving from the essence of forgiveness, an individual way forward that is transformative. As such it needs to be authentically desired (consciously or unconsciously) and then creatively received and brought about. The act of forgiving then is co-terminus with the creative act.

Clinical instances of forgiveness thus range from sheer survival of trauma or the release of bodily symptoms to rituals of forgiveness, from unconscious to conscious expression, and include unilateral or bilateral ways of forgiving. Sometimes it needs atonement from the perpetrator; sometimes this is not possible, yet forgiveness can still be creatively arrived at. Returning to the song of forgiveness, clinical instances of forgiveness are then inspired by the flow of grace from the essence of forgiveness and 'made real' by a creative act.

Social and political aspects of forgiveness

A recent development in the socio-political sphere is the emergence of restorative rather than retributive justice. The concept of restorative justice involves a relational element, as perpetrator and victim are implicitly acknowledged to belong to the same dynamic. This relates to a systemic view (Armour and Umbreit 2005), and also to Jung's idea of the *unus mundus* (Williams 2007). Examples of restorative justice are to be found in the mediation movement and in the Truth and Reconciliation Commission in South Africa. Both approaches transcend talion law, which links them to the essence of forgiveness. Bishop Tutu writes:

> Here the central concern is not retribution or punishment, but [. . .] the healing of breaches, the redressing of imbalances, and the restoration of broken relationships. This kind of justice seeks to rehabilitate both the victim and the perpetrator who should be given the opportunity to be re-integrated back into the community he or she has injured by his or her offence as something that has happened to people and whose consequence is a rupture in relationships.
>
> (Tutu 1999)

Human interconnectedness and the essence of forgiveness come together in the African concept of *ubuntu*. Bishop Tutu explains:

> *Ubuntu* is very difficult to render into a Western language. It speaks of the very essence of being human. [. . .] We say, 'a person is a person through other people.' It is not 'I think therefore I am'. It says rather: 'I am human because I belong.' I participate, I share. A person with *ubuntu* [. . .] is diminished when others are humiliated or diminished, when others are tortured or oppressed [. . .] *Ubuntu* means that in a real sense even the supporters of apartheid were victims of the vicious system which they implemented. [. . .] The humanity of the perpetrator of apartheid's atrocities was caught up and bound up in that of his victim whether he liked it or not. In the process of dehumanising another, in inflicting untold harm and suffering, the perpetrator was inexorably being de-humanised as much, if not more than the oppressed.
>
> (Tutu 1999: 34)

In moving beyond talion law, *ubuntu* brings the essence of forgiveness into the socio-political sphere by connecting it with the very essence of humanity.

Bishop Tutu headed the South African Truth and Reconciliation Commission and gives a moving account of this in his book *No Future without Forgiveness* (1999). The members of the commission were empowered to grant amnesty to perpetrators of crimes against humanity under apartheid. Several features stand out in this example of restorative justice. Perpetrators could only gain amnesty if they came forward to give full and truthful accounts of their deeds. They had to 'plead guilty' as amnesty would not be granted if they tried to defend their actions. Thus amnesty was given in exchange for the truth. Wherever possible, perpetrators and victims or their relatives were to be present together. Perpetrators were not required to show remorse or a wish to atone and equally no expectation was made of victims to forgive.

Bishop Tutu's account seems imbued with the spirit of *ubuntu*. He describes occasions where the perpetration of hellish atrocities transforms, as forgiveness is either spontaneously asked for or given and a step is made to restore the humanity of both victim and perpetrator. Armour and Umbreit (2005) define forgiveness as a change in the victim's as well as the perpetrator's attitude, when both are brought together in a restorative justice process. They describe the psychological changes thus: In the victim's eyes, the perpetrator may turn from an inhuman monster into a human being who can be empathised with, and equally, for the perpetrator the victim might become a human being with feelings, rather than a thing that can be abused. While the deed is still completely unacceptable, it becomes subtly differentiated out and neither victim nor perpetrator is completely defined by it any longer. It then seems that with these relational processes which are promoted by the frame of restorative justice, the element of forgiveness lies in re-establishing the humanity of both victim and perpetrator, and in restoring empathy. The restorative justice movement thus carries the essence of forgiveness, adding a particular note, that of humanity shared by us all and that of the basic human right to empathy.

Conclusion

In this chapter, I have inquired into the manifold facets of the notion of forgiveness as a bridging medium, ranging from empirical study to personal-clinical and socio-political aspects. Metaphorically, I have set this in the emerging panorama of post-postmodernism which I have developed in the context of quantum logic and the ratio of mysticism. My inquiry has been in the spirit of exploration, inviting resonance rather than argument. Some emphasis has been given to the idea of an essence of forgiveness which for me, like a song that subtly sounds at all times, is potentially always available, but needs 'making real' creatively. When the perception of what might constitute forgiveness is opened up, it appears more abundantly available and, when set in a relational context, it becomes intertwined with the essence of our humanity. In the words of Bishop Tutu:

> When we had listened to the testimony of people who had suffered grievously, and it all worked itself out to the point where they were able to forgive and embrace the perpetrators, I would frequently say: 'I think we ought to keep quiet now. We are in the presence of something holy. We ought metaphorically to take off our shoes because we are standing on "holy ground".'
>
> (Tutu 2004: 3)

Bibliography

Armour, M. and Umbreit, M. S. (2005) The paradox of forgiveness in restorative justice. In E. L. Worthington Jr. (ed.), *Handbook of Forgiveness*. New York, NY and Hove: Routledge.

Bell, J. S. (1964) On the Einstein-Podolsky-Rosen paradox. *Physics*, *1*, 195.

Enright, R. D. and Fitzgibbons, R. P. (2000) *Helping Clients Forgive: An Empirical Guide for Resolving Anger and Restoring Hope*. Washington, DC: American Psychological Association.

Epstein, M. (1997) The place of postmodernism in postmodernity. *Russian Postmodernism: New Perspectives on Late Soviet and Post-Soviet Culture*. Retrieved from http://www.focusing.org/apm_papers/epstein.html

Exline, J. J. and Martin, A. (2005) Anger toward god: A new frontier in forgiveness research. In E. L. Worthington Jr. (ed.), *Handbook of Forgiveness*. New York, NY and Hove: Routledge.

Farrow, T. F. D. and Woodruff, P. W. R. (2005) Neuroimaging of forgivability. In E. L. Worthington Jr. (ed.), *Handbook of Forgiveness*. New York, NY and Hove: Routledge.

Ferrer, J. N. (2002) *Revisioning Transpersonal Theory: A Participatory Vision of Human Spirituality*. Albany, NY: State University of New York.

Goernitz, T. and Goernitz, B. (2006) Das Unbewusste aus der Sicht einer Quanten-Psycho-Physik. In M. B. Buchholz and G. Goedde (eds.), *Das Unbewusste In Aktuellen Diskursen*. Giessen: Psychosozial.

Heuer, B. (2004) Buddha in the depressive position. On the healing paradigm. *Proceedings of the XVIth IAAP Congress, Barcelona*. Einsiedeln: Daimon (on CDROM).

Heuer, B. (2008) Discourse of illness or discourse of health: Towards a paradigm-shift in post-Jungian theory. In L. Huskinson (ed.), *Dreaming the Myth Onwards: New Directions in Jungian Therapy and Thought*. New York, NY and Hove: Routledge.

Heuer, G. (2000) Auf verwehten Spuren verschollener Texte. Verlorene, wiedergefundene und neu entdeckte Schriften von Otto Gross. In R. Dehmlow and G. Heuer (eds.), *1. Internationaler Otto Gross Kongress, Berlin*. Marburg/Hannover: LiteraturWissenschaft.de/Laurentius.

Jones, A. M. (2002) Teleology and the hermeneutics of hope: Jungian interpretation in the light of the work of Paul Ricoeur. *Journal of Jungian Theory and Practice*, *4*(20), 45–55.

McCollough, M. E. and Root, L. M. (2005) Forgiveness as change. In E. L. Worthington Jr. (ed.), *Handbook of Forgiveness*. New York, NY and Hove: Routledge.

McCollough, M. E., Fincham, F. D. and Tsang, J. (2003) Forgiveness, forbearance and time: The temporal unfolding of transgression-related interpersonal motivations. *Journal of Personality and Social Psychology*, *84*, 540–557.

Mahoney, A., Rye, M. S. and Pargament, K. I. (2005) When the sacred is violated: Desecration as a unique challenge to forgiveness. In E. L. Worthington Jr (ed.), *Handbook of Forgiveness*. New York, NY and Hove: Routledge

Murphy, J. G. (2005) Forgiveness, self-respect and the value of resentment. In E. L.

Worthington Jr. (ed.), *Handbook of Forgiveness*. New York, NY and Hove: Routledge.
Noll, J. G. (2005) Forgiveness in people experiencing trauma. In E. L. Worthington Jr. (ed.), *Handbook of Forgiveness*. New York, NY and Hove: Routledge.
Pert, C. (1997) *Molecules of Emotion*. New York, NY: Scribner.
Sandage, S. J. and Williamson, I. (2005) Forgiveness in cultural context. In E. L. Worthington Jr. (ed.), *Handbook of Forgiveness*. New York, NY and Hove: Routledge.
Tangney, J. P., Boone, A. L. and Dearing, R. (2005) Forgiving the self: Conceptual issues and empirical findings. In E. L. Worthington Jr. (ed.), *Handbook of Forgiveness*. New York, NY and Hove: Routledge.
Tutu, D. (1999) *No Future without Forgiveness*. London: Rider.
Tutu, D. (2004) Heaven can Wait. Interview with Desmond Tutu by P. Stanford. *The Independent*, 26 January, pp. 2–3.
van Oyen Witvliet, C. (2005) Unforgiveness, forgiveness and justice: Scientific findings on feelings and physiology. In E. L. Worthington Jr. (ed.), *Handbook of Forgiveness*. New York, NY and Hove: Routledge.
Wade, N. G. (2002) Understanding REACH. A component analysis of a group intervention to promote forgiveness. *Dissertation Abstracts International*: Section B: Sciences and Engineering, 63, 2611.
Wilber, K. (1998) *The Marriage of Sense and Soul*. New York, NY: Random House.
Williams, R. (2007) *Atonement*. MSc. Thesis. Colchester: University of Essex.
Worthington Jr., E. L. (2005) Initial questions about the art and science of forgiving. In E. L. Worthington Jr. (ed.), *Handbook of Forgiveness*. New York, NY and Hove: Routledge.

Chapter 17

'The sacredness of love'[1] or 'Relationship as third, as religion'[2]

Otto Gross's concepts of relationship today[3]

Gottfried M. Heuer

Introduction

> No man is an *Iland*, intire of it selfe; every man is a peece of the *Continent*, a part of the *maine*.
>
> John Donne

In this chapter, I want to focus on three different themes to demonstrate the continuing relevance of the early psychoanalyst Otto Gross (1877–1920) that reverberates through a number of disciplines. Some 90 years after his death, his ideas prove to be topical in a way that continues to point way beyond present-day concerns towards an as-yet-to-be-realised future. I shall start from thoughts that constitute the central core of his work: his concept of relationship. Already in 1929 the writer Franz Werfel, one of Gross's close friends, had written of Gross that, '"relationship" was the central focus of his teachings for renewing the world' (Werfel 1990: 347). It is indeed particularly in this area that Gross goes way beyond modernity and post-modernity towards revolutionising both individual as well as collective – political – ways of understanding relating. I shall link these ideas of Gross to cutting-edge discoveries in three realms: first, neurobiology and research into human behavioural as well as maturational processes; second, an unusual understanding – albeit not entirely new – of political justice; and third, philosophical-analytical theories of relating. Around the time of the recent Millennium completely new concepts and ideas were formulated which both fundamentally verify some of Gross's concepts, and, of course, take them further. Although in each instance this has happened without any direct reference to Gross, there exist nevertheless important links, as I shall demonstrate – just as there are rivers that, for stretches, flow underground before unexpectedly emerging again above ground and nevertheless may be sharing the same source.

These current ideas are also further linked with regard to a possible aim: in each instance, they focus on what Otto Gross some hundred years ago first described as the transformation of the will to power between self and other – with the aim of freeing a capacity to love, a capacity to relate which Gross always understood simultaneously as *inter*personal as well as *intra*personal *and* intrapsychic.

Following a brief outline of the ideas central to Gross's work, which I take as the starting point of my considerations, I shall present some of the cutting-edge findings in the areas mentioned in each of the following three parts of this chapter. In this, I proceed from the common bases of biology and the behavioural sciences via the collective realms of politics and law towards the personal in individual relationships, before concluding with a summary.

'Relationship as third, as religion'[4]

As Werfel stated, for the whole of his life, relationship/relating was probably Otto Gross's main concern. It forms the red thread that leads through everything he wrote about '*das Eigene und das Fremde*' – that which is one's own and that which is the other's – in short: self and other. At the same time, Gross perceived the 'will to relating in contrast to the will to power [. . .] as the highest, essential goal of revolutions' (Gross 1919b). He sees this as being closely linked with an 'inborn "instinct of mutual help"' (Gross 1919a: 682), for him the 'fundamental ethical instinct' (Gross 1914: 529): 'This is [. . .] a congenital, *Ur*-instinct, characteristic of the human species, that aims simultaneously at preserving one's own individuality as well as a loving-ethical relationship with the individuality of others' (ibid.).

Here, Gross explicitly refers to Peter Kropotkin, who had published *Mutual Aid: A Factor in Evolution* (1902) – his response to the rise of Social-Darwinism – just after the previous turn of the century. Gross's focus on what he called the 'inner conflict' between self and other should not be understood as being in contrast to the 'will to relating', but rather as its dialectical completion. Gross himself knew very well that the solution of this 'inner conflict' did not lie in a simplistic either/or: he seems to have clearly expressed this in writing, in 1919, 'that human nature, as it is designed and inborn in all, is striving towards the two great values, freedom and relationship' (Gross 1919b). At least implicitly I understand Gross here as expressing the necessity of an inner balance in which each may dialectically enhance the other.

Gross speaks of 'relationship as third, as religion' (Gross 1913b: 1180). He calls it 'the pure, great third' (Gross 1913a: 1142), which he equates with 'faith'. In his known writings, he does not give any further explanation as to what exactly he means by that. Only from some of his love letters which have survived do we know a bit more of the religious depths of his personal experience. In 1907 he writes to Frieda Weekley – who was to become D. H. Lawrence's wife: 'You see, these have been the two great transformations that love has wrought for me: through Frieda I have [. . .] learnt to have faith in the world' (in Turner *et al.* 1990: 167; translation modified). Gross here underlines 'transformations', 'love' and to 'have faith': might they be identical for him? Could it be that the experience of the mystery of transformation in his love relationship awakens his religious feelings, his faith? In another letter he writes of the 'miracle' (ibid.: 165; translation modified) of their relationship. Later, in one of his novels, D. H. Lawrence has the woman who stands for Frieda say about her lover: 'He made me believe in love – in the sacredness of love' (Lawrence 1984: 127).

When Gross in another instance in emotional language speaks of his love relationship – in this instance with Frieda's sister, Else Jaffé – as 'the *first* blossoming of a new *world*-spring' (in Whimster and Heuer 1998: 142), he also expresses something else that is relevant for our considerations: that the personal-intimate is identical with the collective. Later Gross speaks of the identity of the personal and the political in saying, 'The psychology of the unconscious is the philosophy of the revolution' (Gross 1913c: 384). Lawrence scholar John Turner comments on Gross's 'erotic creed [. . .] – his faith in the power of love to transcend the individual ego [. . .] and thus to transform the cultural history of the many' (Turner *et al.* 1990: 157–158).

Otto Gross formulates an idea of the relationship between two creating a third that constitutes the numinous. From this basis he develops the concept of a dialectic relationship between a psycho-philosophical theory of relating, religion and radical politics respectively. With this analytic understanding of the personal as being simultaneously the political and with a re-sacralisation of this linkage, Gross sets off one of the most important socio-political and intellectual trends of the last 100 years. Already in 1909, Gross's anarchist friend Erich Mühsam described the essence of his theory:

> In an individual, nothing happens independently of these equally important aspects of the psyche: religion and sociability. The argument that sexuality embraces both, is correct, but in the same vein religiosity embraces sex and sociability, just as the latter includes sexuality and the religious. They are three coordinated and mutually inclusive aspects. We might understand sexuality as the relating of people to the individual, sociability as the interpersonal relationship, and religiosity as the relationship of the individual to the cosmos. The fact that each of these flows into the other, that there are no boundaries, and that each of these aspects embraces the other two, is self-understood. [. . .] It should be our task to heal not only the sexual 'complexes' but maybe even more the social and the religious ones, to help the individual develop a sense of community and to re-experience the buried beauty of the world.
>
> (Mühsam 2000: 15–16)

The elegant ease with which Mühsam was able to connect here the different dimensions of relating is highly topical, as only now, a hundred years later, similar ideas are just beginning to be formulated again.

Neurobiology and behavioural science: Darwin's error – or 'the principle of humaneness'?[5]

Let us start with the biological basis: Already in 1902, in one of his first publications on 'the phylogenesis of ethics', the neuropsychiatrist and psychoanalyst Otto Gross had tried to give ethics a basis in the natural sciences: 'Based on the preformed linkages of associations, the perception of suffering in an other [. . . leads] to the emotional state of compassion as the root of all ethics' (Gross 1902: 103). When we read how Gross, at the end of the First World War, elevated the thesis of mutual aid, proposed by the non-biologist Kropotkin, to the rank of an instinct, we may well take this to be hardly more than an enthusing utopianism.

In his recently published book *Prinzip Menschlichkeit* (The Principle of Humaneness) (2006a), the German neurobiologist Joachim Bauer also engages critically with Darwin's work. All too often Darwin's theory of evolution is presented in such a way as to suggest that it is so closely linked to his behavioural-biological concepts of the struggle for survival and the survival of the fittest that any doubt about the latter can easily be dismissed as questioning the former. By contrast, Bauer sees Darwin's theory of evolution as completely separate from the theories of what came to be called Social-Darwinism. What Kropotkin was able to present some hundred years ago as *Mutual Aid in the Human and Animal Realm* (Kropotkin 1993: re-translation of the title of the German popular edition of 1908; Ritter 1975: 7), could, due to the technology of his time, only be a theory based on observations of human and animal behaviour. Today, thanks to technical developments, Bauer, as a neurobiologist, is able to confirm these theories with cutting-edge discoveries in cell-research.

Bauer describes the disastrous effects of Darwin's seemingly 'logical' conclusions from his theory of evolution about the struggle for survival, especially in the German-speaking countries, where these ideas fell on much more fertile ground than elsewhere. 'One of Darwin's errors,' writes Bauer,

> that have survived to this day, is [. . .] his basic assumption that evolution has turned competition, struggle and selection into the central impetus of living organisms. [. . .] This basic assumption rests on an inadmissable transference onto living nature of an economic thinking that is based on competitive struggle and the maximisation of profit.
>
> (2006a: 123)

Whereas Bauer directly blames Darwin for this development, other scientists have a more differenciated view. The psychologist and primatologist Frans de Waal, for example, observes that Darwin, too, speaks of a 'moral sense or conscience' in animals (Darwin 1982: 71–72).

Darwin firmly believed his theory capable of accommodating the origins of morality and did not see any conflict between the harshness of the evolutionary process and the gentleness of some of its products. Rather than presenting the human species as falling outside of the laws of biology, Darwin emphasised continuity with animals even in the moral domain (de Waal 2006: 14).

De Waal sees the origins of Social Darwinism more in Thomas Huxley – at times called 'Darwin's Bulldog'. It was Huxley who 'saw human ethics as a victory over an unruly and nasty evolutionary process. [. . .] Huxley was in effect saying that [. . .] we can become moral only by opposing our own nature' (ibid.: 7).

Bauer describes how Social Darwinism developed ideologically between 1870 and 1930. Already at the beginning of the previous century, the right of the powerful was derived from the evolutionary theories. In 1904 Ernst Haeckel, a 'fanatical convert to Darwinism', whose earlier work had 'really explained Darwinism to the world' (Robinson 2008), advocated 'euthanasia for babies born with physical or mental defects', adding that, 'In considering such important ethical issues like the selection of those unfit for life, "reason" had to come before "emotion".' (Bauer 2006a: 108). Later, concepts such as these led to attempts to form a self-declared 'Master-Race', which would try to improve their race by selection and breeding. Social Darwinist theories thus helped to provide a pseudo-legitimation to efforts of social exclusion (cf. Agamben 2003; Rother 2005; Dienes 2006), selection and, ultimately, genocide. A commentator on a recent BBC documentary on Darwin wrote, 'Darwin was quoted in Berlin when they were planning the genocide of the Jews' (Marr 2009: 21). Many ideas of Otto Gross's father Hans Gross, the founder of modern criminology, about fighting crime and anti-social behaviour, belong into the same context.

Bauer describes simplistic theories about 'selfish genes' or organisms as 'survival machines' as 'socio-biological science-fiction' (Bauer 2006a: 135f.) and compares their popularisation in the last 30 years, predominantly by the non-geneticist Dawkins, to the spreading of Social-Darwinistic ideas 100 years previously.

'Why we naturally co-operate' is the subtitle of Bauer's book (2006a). The fact that as a geneticist he is engaged in cell-research gives special weight to his arguments. In detail Bauer describes not only how life on earth would be impossible without co-operation, but also that it would never have emerged without it:

> Renowned scientists now believe that [. . .] development from simple to complex organisms has only been possible because cooperative processes have played a *central and primary* role.
>
> (ibid.: 140)

> The production of genes as well as the commencement of their functioning is a cooperative enterprise. [. . .] Correspondingly, the origin of individual cells [. . .] can only be conceived of as a highly cooperative process.
>
> (ibid.: 150, 152)

A more direct scientific proof of Kropotkin's thesis is hardly imaginable. Even Gross's understanding of 'relationship as religion' today finds confirmation in the micro-realm of individual cells and their components. The physicist Jean Charon, engaging with the metaphysical implications of subatomic physics, genetics, and cosmology, has discovered that subatomic particles have many extraordinary characteristics that resemble those ascribed to the spiritual and the numinous (Charon 1983). From the perspective of quantum theory, informations of a spiritual content, too, are being exchanged between body-cells in their relation to each other within the space-time continuum. According to Charon, this religious content is continuously on the increase (Monte 2005: 14).

The micro-realm of gene and cell biology can easily be linked in an important way with the macro-realm of mutual relationships from the perspective of human developmental research: 'Infant development researchers such as Colwyn Trevarthen, Daniel Stern and others now say that there is evidence that the infant is born with what *I* would interpret as an *intersubjective instinct*' (Grotstein 2008: ix). Clearly, this confirms the 'will to relating' postulated as an instinct by Gross.

It seems to become ever more evident that maturational processes do not end with childhood or adolescence. The Australian analyst Judith Pickering states:

> Becoming who we are is an inherently relational journey: we uncover our truest nature and become most authentically real through the difficult and fearful, yet transformative intersubjective crucibles of our intimate relationships.
>
> (2008: i)

This has also been confirmed by recent neurobiological discoveries. The Italian physiologist Giacomo Rizzolati succeeded in isolating individual cells that were stimulated by specific stimuli triggered by the behaviour of others. He called these cells mirror neurons. These are the actual receptors that throughout our lives take in the environmental stimuli that they, in turn, pass on to the individual neuronal elements. They can be said to be the very organs that we use to establish relationships. In those processes, gene and cell structures are being transformed. This means that throughout our lives these remain malleable and can be changed (Bauer 2006b, 2007).

Reconciliatory justice and sacral politics: 'No future without forgiveness'[6]

Jungian analysts Pamela Donleavy and Ann Shearer – the former an ex-state attorney – use these discoveries of latest research in the area of justice. Here they differentiate between the talion law predominant in Western culture, with its aims of vengeance and punishments, and a restorative justice characterised by efforts to rebuild a social harmony upset by unlawfulness or crime. The South African former Archbishop and Nobel Peace laureate Desmond Tutu explains:

> Here the central concern is [. . .] in the spirit of *ubuntu*, the healing of breaches, [. . .] the restoration of broken relationships. This kind of justice seeks to rehabilitate both the victim and the perpetrator, who should be given the opportunity to be reintegrated into the community he or she has injured by his or her offence.
>
> (Tutu 1999: 51–52)

'*Ubuntu*' is a religious socio-political concept rooted in African cultural tradition:

> It speaks of the very essence of being human. [. . .] It also means humanity is caught up, inextricably bound up in [that of others]. [. . .] We say, 'a person is a person through other people.' It is not, 'I think therefore I am.' It says rather: 'I am human because I belong.' I participate, I share. A person with *ubuntu* [. . .] belongs in a greater whole and is diminished when others are humiliated or diminished.
>
> (ibid.: 34–35)

Already in one of his first published papers – in the criminology journal founded and edited by his father! – Gross questioned the legal right to punish assumed by society: 'If society carries out punishment [. . .] as justice, is this "punitive justice" not actually an injustice?' (1901: 129). He takes the view that this kind of justice is a 'cruel and unjust emergency measure', a 'terrible brutality' (ibid.: 129f.). Correspondingly today, Donleavy and Shearer state, 'far from bringing transformation, the administration of justice can often reinforce the fear, misunderstanding and hatred between "them", the offenders, and "us", the law-abiding majority' (2008: 100). From a Grossian perspective this would mean to rather sharpen the conflict between self and other, because punitive justice with its talion law is based on the will to power, whereas a restorative justice grows out of a will to relating.

The dire results of efforts to solve the inner conflict between self and other with simplistic either/or decisions become apparent in individual and collective attempts to ostracise and ultimately eliminate the other via shadow projections that are the basis of separating friend from foe in racist and other warlike conflicts. I want to present two examples from the collective realm for the kind of solution suggested by Gross: the first a potential beginning of a radical change in the collective unconscious, the second an effort of a lived practice that has helped to enable the population of a whole nation with its total revolutionary change in such a way that instead of the expected bloodbath, working towards a peaceful solution is now possible. My first example is the publication of *The Gospel of Judas* (Kasser *et al.* 2006) in 2006 (cf. Heuer 2009), the second refers to the work of the South African Truth and Reconciliation Commission, chaired by Desmond Tutu. Both have in common religious aspects of relating and forgiving in the process of reconciliation.

For the publication of *The Gospel of Judas* I would like to use a principle of interpretation C. G. Jung used some 50 years ago for the doctrine of the *Assumptio Mariae* – the assumption of the body of the mother of Christ into heaven – by the then pope. Jung understood this as a cultural event in the sense of the beginning of a revaluation of the feminine in the collective consciousness. The blossoming of feminism shortly afterwards and the degree to which it has changed our world since then may well be taken as confirmation of Jung's interpretation. *The Gospel of Judas* is a recently discovered gnostic text that is only slightly younger than the canonical gospels. The revolutionary significance of this text lies in the complete reversal of the valuation of the role of Judas in Christian myth – one English newspaper spoke of the 'Greatest archaeological discovery of all time' (*Mail on Sunday*, London, 12 March 2006, in Gathercole 2006: 1) and Simon Gathercole, reader of theology at Cambridge University, speaks of it as 'Rewriting Early Christianity' (2006).

Why is such importance being given to *The Gospel of Judas*? Far from being the most despised of the disciples – in many European languages 'Judas' is used as an invective meaning 'traitor' – here Judas is being presented as the disciple closest to Jesus and the only one who most profoundly understands his message. It is for this very reason that Jesus chooses him to play the most difficult role in the fulfilment of his destiny. After two millennia of keeping Jesus and Judas separate as the polar opposites of light and dark, *The Gospel of Judas* suddenly offers the mystery of their union, which Jung termed *mysterium coniunctionis*. The text ends with Jesus's capture. From this new perspective, the infamous 'kiss of Judas' is no longer the epitome of vile treason but a goodbye kiss in intimate and loving friendship. We may well consider what the history of Christianity might have looked like if this kiss in friendship as an expression of a deeply felt will to relating had become the pre-eminent symbol of Christianity instead of the cross, instrument for a slow, torturous and lonely death. (I am grateful to my wife and colleague Birgit Heuer for contributing this particular idea in the course of in-depth discussions.)

In the traditional paradigms of both Christian as well as therapeutic practice, suffering and growth have been seen as inextricably linked – paradigms that have focused on the negative, on pathology. Some cutting-edge Jungians are increasingly questioning this, arguing instead for a "sanatology" (B. Heuer 2008–ongoing), a paradigm focusing on health and healing. Birgit Heuer, for example, writes, 'I wonder what a clinical paradigm might be like that, symbolically speaking, moved from darkness into light, without losing awareness of the darkness' (B. Heuer 2003: 334). '[C]linical change then might also relate to a capacity to unlearn suffering and tolerate and learn reality in the form of innate, but individually specific, goodness' (B. Heuer 2008: 187). Just as Eckhart Tolle writes in 1998, 'The way of the cross [. . .] is the old way to enlightenment', and that 'there is a growing number of humans alive today whose consciousness is sufficiently evolved not to need any more suffering before realizing enlightenment' (1999: 187f.).

It is also remarkable that, for the first time, this text presents us with a *laughing* Christ! It reminds me of the German artist Joseph Beuys's question, 'Can you really imagine a revolution without laughter?!' (Meller, 2008).

Theologian Aaron Saari sees a direct link between the condemnation of Judas and anti-semitism:

> Jesus and the other eleven disciples become Christians, [. . .] and Judas remains the only Jew. When he becomes associated with the Jewish people, we see an unbelievable rise in anti-Jewish violence. Part of this is owed to the idea that Jews are Christ-killers or God-killers. [. . .] Judas is [. . .] the scapegoat.
>
> (in Batty 2008)

In what has been called the 'Scapegoat Complex' (Brinton Perera 1986), unwanted shadow aspects are projected onto a shadow-carrier, originally literally a goat that was then ritually sent into the desert to perish (Leviticus 16: 21–22). It is the psychological mechanism whereby we 'behold the mote that is in' our 'brother's eye', rather than considering 'the beam that is in' our own (Matthew 7: 3). There is no conflict, no war – individually or collectively – without such shadow projection where the other is being demonised in unconscious acting out. Eckart Tolle writes that 'violence would be impossible without deep unconsciousness' (1999: 61). Amazingly, for example, Hitler is supposed to have replied, when asked in 1939,

> whether the removal of Jews from Germany would rid the world of his No.1 enemy, 'We would have to invent them, one needs a visible enemy, one in plain sight. The Jew is always within us, but it is simpler to fight him in bodily form than as an invisible evil.'
>
> (in Hardtmann 1982: 244)

If Hitler really did say this, then it would mean that at least in that moment he was aware of an external splitting that found its internal correspondence. What is the reason for this? With Gross we might say, 'the will to power'. What he had not been able as yet to formulate as succinctly: the greater this will to power, the greater, actually, the unconscious weakness it is designed to conceal. 'Power over others is weakness disguised as strength,' Tolle writes (1999: 36).

We may thus link the will to power with an incapacity to relate. Gross understood the decisive transformative step from the 'will to power' to the 'will to relating [. . .] as the highest, the essential goal of revolutions' (Gross 1919b). In the collective, political sphere I am thinking in this respect first of an event that happened during Gross's lifetime (although it is not known whether he knew of it): the spontaneous Christmas truce in 1914, the first winter of the First World War. It began with the joint singing of carols in the trenches – in which the respectively opposing sides joined! German, British and French troops then left their trenches to swap cigarettes, alcohol and personal mementoes and on Christmas Day played football in No Man's Land (Brown and Seaton 2001).

I would like to take this opportunity to honour the memory of my great grandfather-in-law, Ferdinand Heinrich Eggeling (1877–1954), master blacksmith in the village of Weddingen in the Harz mountains of Germany, who was actively involved in this event as one of the soldiers on the German side. His daughter, Ilse Bauer, from Lübeck, remembers that, as a girl, she would visit with her parents in the evenings, and, though her grandfather Eggeling would not often talk about the war, it would invariably be this Christmas that he would speak of. 'Then his eyes would shine, as he described how the singing started on the German side, to be taken up by the French. And there was a man nearby in a trench who had a mouth-organ . . .'

Taking this a step further: is it possible to communicate this transformation any more convincingly than by taking responsibility for past violence and by kneeling to ask for forgiveness? Recent examples of this are the spontaneous kneeling of the then German Chancellor Willy Brandt in 1970 at the memorial of the infamous Warsaw ghetto, and, early in 2008, the public apology of the Australian Prime Minister Kevin Rudd to the aborigines for the injustice and violence of the past three centuries (Rudd, 2008).

Gross speaking about the religious dimension of relationship makes me wonder whether he might have thought of the numinous aspect of such moments of transformation. Just as Gross's pupil Johannes Nohl supposedly said, 'Wherever one kneels to pray, [. . .] God arises before him' [or her] (Hessel 1913: 140; cf. G. Heuer 2006: 40f.). For Desmond Tutu the sacredness of such a moment seems to be beyond doubt. Frequently he concludes a successful work on reconciliation, as for example between

Figure 17.1 Ferdinand Heinrich Eggeling, 1877–1954.

members of the different sides of the troubles in Northern Ireland, with the words, 'Let's take off our shoes, because we are standing on holy ground' (cf. Genesis 3: 5). Correspondingly, C. G. Jung spoke of the analytic space as a *temenos*, 'a word used by the early Greeks to define a sacred precinct (i.e. a temple) within which a god's presence can be felt' (Samuels *et al.* 1986: 148).

In the very same spirit Tutu also chaired the Truth and Reconciliation Commission between 1995 and 1998, so far the greatest, i.e. nationwide, use of restorative justice. After the end of 'Apartheid' in South Africa, on the basis of 'The Truth Hurts, But Silence Kills' (Tutu 1999: 81), victims of crimes and/or their descendants were invited to meet with the respective perpetrators. In front of the latter, the former had the opportunity to give testimony in public of what they had suffered. Subsequently the perpetrators had the chance to speak from their side about the crimes committed. They received a guarantee of amnesty provided they spoke the full truth and thus publicly took responsibility for what they had done. Well over 20,000 statements were received (ibid.). The work achieved by this commission is seen as a vital contribution to the predominantly non-violent transition in South Africa from the racist 'Apartheid' regime towards a democracy. Thnabo Mbeki, Mandela's successor as president, commented in 1996 that the 'amnesty process [. . .] allow[s] the nation to forgive a past it nevertheless dare not forget' (in ibid.: 79). Of course this does not mean that the goal has been reached. Tutu himself said, 'Reconciliation is a long process. We don't have the kind of race clashes that we thought would happen. [. . .] But maybe you ought to be lenient with us. We've been free for just 12 years' (in Steptoe 2006).

Mutual shadow projecting and its cementation in the vengeful justice based on the talion law is changed in restorative justice into relating with the potential of mutual understanding and reconciliation. For me the project of the Truth and Reconciliation Commission is so far the most magnificent example of a realisation of Gross's vision of a synthesis of mutually embracing and enhancing ideas from the realms of religion, radical politics and relational, i.e. psychodynamic, psychology.

Relational theory: 'Being in love'[7] or 'the art of relating'[8]

Relating is at issue in all the areas touched so far; the totality of the ecological and sociological balance rests on an intricate network of relationships. What about our personal relationships?

Otto Gross assumes the 'inner conflict' between self and other as part of the human condition in which, as mentioned, 'human nature, as it is conditionally inborn, strives towards the two important goals of freedom and relatedness' (Gross 1919b). Only implicitly does he hint at a solution. The analyst Judith Pickering goes a decisive step further: 'The "trick" of successful love is the ability of each mate to remain a separate individual *vis-à-vis* the other, while at the same time being able to remain immersed in an utterly indivisible duality' (Pickering 2008: xi). Explicitly she calls this solution 'the marriage of alterity and altruism' (ibid.: 38). Intentionally, Pickering chooses the term 'alterity' to denote a state of differentiatedness and individuality. She sees this in contrast to an understanding of love in which lack and incompleteness constitute the default position – the platonic concept of being only one half and permanently in search for the other missing half in order to reach completion and fulfillment. Indirectly, this also seems to be the source of the wanting *to own* the other, with all its concomitant aspects of power – in fact, the very opposite of love. In contrast, Pickering in this context quotes the philosopher Edith Wyschogrod commenting on the philosopher Emmanuel Levinas:

> Love represents the paradox of crossing boundaries whilst remaining distinct. We think we overcome alienation by merger, but the implicit denial of difference and autonomy destroys relationships, for there can only be relationship when recognizing the fact of being two, without which relationship is not possible.
>
> (Wyschogrod 2000: 127, in Pickering 2008: 50)

Commenting herself on Levinas, Pickering writes that he

> said that ethics begins in apprehending the face of the Other. The face-to-face encounter is iconic of the primordial reality of a relational context in which ethical responsibility based on doing justice to the otherness of the other person is a metaphysical imperative.
>
> Levinas' description of the face-to-face ethical standpoint is one of standing before the Other as one would approach the holiest of holy.
>
> (Pickering 2008: 50)

This is the concept that Gross first formulated in terms of a respectively dialectic interaction of individuation, relatedness and ethics in a way that he experienced in a numinous way. Pickering observes a similarity

> to the Christian [. . .] paradox of the Trinity: the co-herence of the three-in-one. [. . .] We hover forever between our separateness and interdependence; our bodies and our minds, ourselves and the other, being known and unknowable, becoming one flesh and forever separated in the flesh.
>
> (ibid.: 62)

I said earlier that in terms of what Gross might have meant by 'sacredness of love' (Lawrence 1984: 127), or 'relationship as third, as religion' (Gross 1913b: 1180), we have to rely on speculation. On the one hand his experience of relationship can be understood as underpinning his psychology, yet on the other hand in some of his love letters that have been preserved he directly speaks of the numinousness of these experiences. In one of his letters to Frieda Weekley, Gross quotes Nietzsche's 'will of two people to create *that* which is *higher* than those who created it – it is this will that I call a good marriage' (in Turner *et al.* 1990: 168; translation modified). Gross describes this will as '*higher, infinitely higher upwards, from a belief in the rising and creating anew as that which eternally drives us as the innermost principle of life*' (ibid.; translation modified). It may not be irrelevant for our subject that Nietzsche himself – and Gross is bound to have known of this – writes of the sacredness of such a union (Nietzsche 1902: 104).

When Gross speaks here of 'creating anew', this seems to include that aspect of transformation that our language so clearly expresses with the link between healing, (making) whole and holy. Correspondingly, Freud, some hundred years ago, speaking of the transforming power of his analytic work, wrote to Jung, 'Essentially, one might say, the cure is effected by love' (Freud and Jung 1974: 12f.). We might link this with Jung regarding the analytic space as holy ground (cf. *temenos*, above). For him the success of the analytic work depended, '*Deo concedente*', on God's grace, God's presence (Samuels *et al.* 1986: 211f.). Correspondingly, he had written over the entrance door to his home, '*Vocatus atque non vocatus: deus aderit*' – called or uncalled, God will help/be present – the Latin translation of the motto of the Delphic oracle.

We can easily find in western culture other testimonies of the experience of the numinous in love. From the Christian tradition we know 'God is love' (John 4: 8). 'Liberated from a confined viewpoint of the solitary ego,' writes Pickering, 'we feel an exulted state of being at one not only with our beloved, but also with the whole of creation, the Divine Lover' (Pickering 2008: 23). The ecstasy of love literally gives us experience of being outside of ourselves, which makes us feel divine, thus tasting the numinous. Correspondingly, we experience this connecting force itself, which enables us to transcend the separation from the other, also as divine. The philosopher Martin Buber (1970) was inspired by Gross in perceiving the relatedness between people as being linked to that between humans and God in his 'I–Thou' principle.

Three aspects need to be emphasised here: first, the power of transformation which simultaneously is, second, the capacity to relate, and, third, born of these two, the holy third, the relationship itself. This corresponds to Christ's 'Where two or three are gathered together in my name, there I am in the midst of them' (Matthew 18: 20). For me this links with that mysterious and numinous moment of transformation that Gross refers to when he speaks of converting the will to power – that forever insists on separation and war – into the will to relating, a change that revolutionises us. Barack Obama, in his inauguration address in 2009, spoke of this, too, in terms of 'extending a hand' and 'unclenching your fist'. Did Gross think of this numinous moment when he spoke of 'relationship as third, as religion' (Gross 1913b: 1180)? He adds that this kind of relating contains the 'compulsion to individuation' (ibid.). Are we to understand this as the workings of the life force, as libido, the drive to grow by transformation? This would mean that the deeper we enter into a relationship with our Self, the closer we come in contact with God. 'All transformation includes experiences of transcendence and mystery and involves symbolic death and rebirth' (Samuels *et al.* 1986: 151). This means that change, growth, life itself, possesses the aura of the holy since – all scientific progress notwithstanding – the mystery remains. And if this mystery of creation – that *life* is being created from the interactive relationship of different elements with each other – finds an echo in each transformational step, or is thus being repeated in the creation of something new, and if love does indeed change and heal us, then we get closest to this mystery of creation and its sacredness when being in love.

The islamic poet and mystic Rumi wrote some 750 years ago:

> The subject has no end. If all the seas of the world were ink, and all the trees of all the forests were pens, and all the atoms of the air were

> scribes, still they could not describe the unions and reunions of pure and divine souls and their reciprocal loves.
>
> (1999: 170)

Conclusion

To summarise: starting with Gross's concepts of relationship, I have shown how today his ideas are being confirmed and developed further in various areas of the sciences and the humanities. On an empirical basis, quantum theory and neurobiology have validated the theory of mutual aid that Gross borrowed from Kropotkin to further his own psychoanalytic theory and clinical practice. Cutting-edge observation of human maturational processes has found evidence of an instinct towards relating as postulated by Gross. On a collective level I have spoken of possible indications of a transformation of consciousness in connection with the publication of *The Gospel of Judas*. I have linked this on a political level with the South African Truth and Reconciliation Commission – as one example of what Andrew Samuels calls the 're-sacralisation of politics', a development in the history of ideas that started, in its relationship to analytical theory, at the time of the birth of modernity with Gross's work. At the same time, the commission's work is a practised example of a restorative justice that does not aim at vengeance and punishment but reconciliation and forgiveness. Of these considerations, too, we find initial formulations in Gross's ethical concepts. And finally in the realm of couple relationships I have shown how cutting-edge psycho-philosophical concepts can be directly linked to those of Otto Gross. The solution of what he called the inner conflict between self and other, which he only implied, is now explicitly portrayed in the marriage of alterity and altruism.

'Make love, not war!' or 'Blessed *are* the peacemakers: for they shall be called the children of God'[9]

In 1919, after the failure of the German revolution in the wake of the First World War, for Gross the necessity to replace the will to power with the will to relating became 'the highest, the essential goal of revolutions' (Gross 1919b). The message can hardly be expressed any clearer: 50 years later, Martin Luther King writes,

> Far from being the injunction of a Utopian dreamer, the command to love one's enemy [Matthew 5: 44] is an absolute necessity for our survival. [It . . .] is the key to the solution of the problems of our world. Jesus is not an impractical idealist; he is a practical realist.
>
> (King 1969: 47f.)

King concludes, 'We must live as brothers or perish as fools' (King *et al.* 1994: 224). At the millennium Desmond Tutu proclaims, 'No Future without Forgiveness' (Tutu 1999).

Now – in the words of Nelson Mandela –

> The time for healing the wounds has come. The moment to bridge the chasms that divide us has come. The time to build is upon us. [. . .] We know it well that none of us acting alone can achieve such success. We must therefore act together [. . .] for the birth of a new world. [. . .] Let each know that for each the body, the mind and the soul have been freed to fulfil themselves.
>
> (Mandela 1994)

Bibliography

Agamben, G. (2003). Was ist ein Lager? In G. Dienes and R. Rother (eds.), *Die Gesetze des Vaters: Hans Gross, Otto Gross, Sigmund Freud, Franz Kafka*. Wien: Böhlau (pp. 108–111).

Batty, D. (2008). *The Secrets of the 12 Disciples*. London: Carbon Media for Channel 4 [TV Documentary].

Bauer, J. (2006a). *Prinzip Menschlichkeit. Warum wir von Natur aus kooperieren*. Hamburg: Hoffmann und Campe.

Bauer, J. (2006b). *Warum ich fühle, was du fühlst. Intuitive Kommunikation und das Geheimnis der Spiegelneurone*. München: Heyne.

Bauer, J. (2007). *Das Gedächtnis des Körpers. Wie Beziehungen und Lebensstile unsere Gene steuern*. München: Piper.

Beringer, U. (2006). Die Kunst des Miteinanders. *Buchjournal*, *3*, 62.

Brown, M. and Seaton, S. (2001). *Christmas Truce. The Western Front December 1914*. London: Pan Macmillan.

Buber, M. (1970). *I and Thou*. Edinburgh: T & T Clark.

Charon, J. (1983). *The Unknown Spirit*. London: Coventure.

Darwin, C. (1982). *The Descent of Man, and Selection in Relation to Sex*. Princeton, NY: Princeton University.

de Waal, F. (2006). *Primates and Philosophers. How Morality Evolved*. Princeton, NY and Oxford: Princeton University.

Dienes, G. (2006). Gefängniskunde versus Freikörperkultur. Hans und Otto Gross und das adriatische Küstenland. In G. Heuer (ed.), *Utopie und Eros. Der Traum von der Moderne. 5. Internationaler Otto Gross Kongress, cabaret voltaire/Dada-Haus, Zürich*. Marburg: LiteraturWissenschaft.de (pp. 317–346).

Donleavy, P. and Shearer, A. (2008). *From Ancient Myth to Modern Healing. Themis: Goddess of Heart-Soul, Justice and Reconciliation*. London and New York, NY: Routledge.

Freud, S. and Jung C. G. (1974). *The Freud/Jung Letters*. London: Hogarth and Routledge & Kegan Paul.

Gathercole, S. (2006). *The Gospel of Judas. Rewriting early Christianity*. Oxford: Oxford University.

Gross, O. (1901). Zur Frage der socialen Hemmungsvorstellungen. *Archiv für Kriminal-Anthropologie und Kriminalistik*, *7*(1/2), 123–131.
Gross, O. (1902). Die Phyllogenese der Ethik. *Archiv für Kriminal-Anthropologie und Kriminalistik*, *9*(1), 100–103.
Gross, O. (1909). *Über psychopathische Minderwertigkeiten.*Wien und Leipzig: Wilhelm Braumüller.
Gross, O. (1913a). Anmerkungen zu einer neuen Ethik. *Die Aktion*. *III*(49), 1141–1143.
Gross, O. (1913b.) Notiz über Beziehungen. *Die Aktion*, *III*(51), 1180–1181.
Gross, O. (1913c). Zur Ueberwindung der kulturellen Krise. *Die Aktion*, *III*(14) 384–387.
Gross, O. (1914). Über Destruktionssymbolik. *Zentralblatt für Psychoanalyse und Psychotherapie*, *IV*(7/8), 525–534.
Gross, O. (1919a). Protest und Moral im Unbewußten. *Die Erde*, *1*(24), 681–685.
Gross, O. (1919b). Zur funktionellen Geistesbildung des Revolutionärs. *Räte-Zeitung. Erste Zeitung der Hand-und Kopfarbeiterräte Deutschlands*, *1*(52), Beilage.
Grotstein, J. (2008). What is love? In J. Pickering (2008), *Being in Love. Therapeutic Pathways Through Psychological Obstacles to Love*. Hove and New York, NY: Routledge (pp. ix–xiii).
Hessel, F. (1913/1999). Der Kramladen des Glücks. In *Sämtliche Werke Band I. Romane*. Oldenburg: Igel.
Heuer, B. (2003). Clinical paradigm as analytic third: Reflections on a century of analysis and an emergent paradigm for the new millennium. In E. Christopher and H. McFarland Solomon (eds.), *Contemporary Jungian Clinical Practice*. London: Karnac (pp. 329–339).
Heuer, B. (2008). Discourse of illness or discourse of health: towards a paradigm shift in post-Jungian clinical theory. In L. Huskinson (ed.), *Dreaming the Myth Onwards: New Directions in Jungian Therapy and Thought*. London and New York, NY: Routledge (pp. 181–190).
Heuer, B. (2008–ongoing) *On Clinical Theory, Zero-point Field Theory and Mysticism. Towards Sanatology: A Clinical Theory of Health and Healing*. Colchester: Centre for Psychoanalytic Studies, University of Essex. PhD thesis (in progress).
Heuer, G. (2006). Der Außenseiter der Außenseiter – Neues über einen Unbekannten. Entdeckungen zu Johannes Nohl (1882–1963). Leben, Werk und Wirkung. Mit einem Werkverzeichnis. *Mühsam-magazin*, *11*, 28–85.
Heuer, G. (2009). For 'A new heaven and a new earth': 'The Gospel of Judas' – An emerging potential for world peace? A Jungian perspective. *Spring*, *81*, 265–290.
Kasser, R., Meyer, M. and Wurst, G. (eds.) (2006). *The Gospel of Judas from Codex Tchacos*. Washington, DC: National Geographic.
King, M. L. (1969). *Strength to Love*. London: Fontana.
King, M. L. (1994). Remaining awake through a great revolution. In C. Clayborne, P. C. Holloran, R. Luker and P. A. Russell (eds.), *The Papers of Martin Luther King, Jr.: Vol. II: Rediscovering Precious Values, July 1951–November 1955*. Berkeley, ca: University of California (pp. 220–239).
Kropotkin, P. (1902). *Mutual Aid. A Factor in Evolution*. London: Heinemann.
Kropotkin, P. (1993). *Gegenseitige Hilfe in der Tier-und Menschenwelt* (Trans. G. Landauer). Grafenau: Trotzdem.

Lawrence, D. H. (1984). *Mr. Noon*. Cambridge: Cambridge University.

Mandela, N. (1994). *Statement of the President of the African National Congress Nelson Rohlihlala Mandela at His Inauguration as President of the Democratic Republic of South Africa*. Union Buildings, Pretoria, May 10. Retrieved from http://www.anc.org.za/ancdocs/speeches/inauggpta.html

Marr, A. (2009). Evolution of Evil. *Radio Times*, 28 February–6 March, 21–22.

Meller, M. (2008). Als Jesus lachte. *Frankfurter Allgemeine*, 12–23 March, 31.

Monte, C. (2005). Numen of the Flesh. *Quadrant, XXXV*(2), 11–31.

Mühsam, E. (2000). Erich Mühsam und Otto Gross – Auszüge aus Tagebüchern, Briefen und Publikationen Erich Mühsams. Zusammengestellt von Chris Hirte. *Schriften der Erich-Mühsam Gesellschaft, Lübeck. 19, Anarchismus und Psychoanalyse zu Beginn des 20. Jahrhunderts. Der Kreis um Erich Mühsam und Otto Gross* (pp. 12–35).

Nietzsche, F. (1902). *Also sprach Zarathustra: Ein Buch für Alle und Keinen*. Leipzig: Naumann.

Pickering, J. (2008). *Being in Love: Therapeutic Pathways Through Psychological Obstacles to Love*. Hove and New York, NY: Routledge.

Platon (1983). *Symposion*. In Sämtliche Werke 2. Hamburg: Rowohlt (pp. 203–250).

Rauschning, H. (1973). *Gespräche mit Hitler*. Wien: Europaverlag.

Ritter, H. (1975). Zu dieser Ausgabe. In P. Kropotkin (1993), *Gegenseitige Hilfe in der Tier-und Menschenwelt*. Grafenau: Trotzdem (pp. 7–8).

Robinson, A. (2008). The origin of theories. [Review of R. Richards (2008), *The Tragic Sense of Life: Ernst Haeckel and the Struggle over Evolutionary Thought*. Chicago, IL: University of Chicago Press] *The Financial Times*, 9/10 February, Life and Art, 13.

Rother, R. (2005). Die Damen in der Strafkolonie. Zu Hans Gross und Franz Kafka. In A. Götz von Olenhusen and G. Heuer (eds.), *Die Gesetze des Vaters. 4. Internationaler Otto Gross Kongress, Graz*. Marburg: LiteraturWissenschaft.de (pp. 45–62).

Rudd, K. (2008). Apology to Australia's Indigenous Peoples. Retrieved from http://www.aph.gov.au/house/Rudd_Speech.pdf

Rumi, J. alal-ud-D. (1999). *Teachings of Rumi*. Re-created and edited by A. Harvey. Boston, MA and London: Shambhala.

Samuels, A., Shorter, B. and Plaut, F. (1986). *A Critical Dictionary of Jungian Analysis*. London and New York, NY: Routledge & Kegan Paul.

Schiering, P. (2006). *Beuys & Beuys: Der Jahrhundertkünstler zwischen Fettstuhl und sozialer Skulptur*. Mainz: 3sat, Zweites Deutsches Fernsehen [TV Documentary].

Stanford, P. (2004). Heaven can wait. *The Independent Review*, 26 January, 1–3.

Steptoe, S. (2006). Interview: 10 questions for Desmond Tutu. *Time Magazine*, 23 October, 24.

Tolle, E. (1999). *The Power of Now. A Guide to Spiritual Enlightenment*. Novato, CA: New World.

Turner, J. with Rumpf-Worthen, C. and Jenkins, R. (eds.) (1990). The Otto Gross–Frieda Weekley correspondence. *The D. H. Lawrence Review*, *22*(2), 137–227.

Tutu, D. (1999). *No Future Without Forgiveness*. London: Rider.

Werfel, F. (1990). *Barbara oder Die Frömmigkeit*. Frankfurt, M: Fischer.

Whimster, S. with Heuer, G. (1998). The Otto Gross–Else Jaffé correspondence. In

Otto Gross, Else Jaffé and Max Weber. *Theory, Culture and Society, Special Issue on Love and Eroticism, 15*(3/4), 129–160.
Winnicott, D. W. (1988). *Playing and Reality*. London: Penguin.
Wyschogrod, E. (2000). *Emmanuel Levinas: The Problem of Ethical Metaphysics*. New York, NY: Fordham University Press.

Notes

1 Lawrence 1984: 127.
2 Gross 1913b: 1180.
3 An earlier German version was originally presented at the 7th International Otto Gross Congress, Dresden, Germany, 3–5 October 2008. Different versions of this have been published in *Zeitschrift für Körpertherapie* (2009), Vienna, Vol. 15, No. 51, 5–30 and in W. Felber, A. Götz von Olenhusen, G. Heuer and B. Nitzschke (eds.) (2010) *Psychoanalyse und Expressionismus. 7. Internationaler Otto Gross Kongress*, Dresden 2008. Marburg: LiteraturWissenschaft.de (pp. 109–153). A previous English version has been published in *Psychotherapy and Politics International*, Vol. 8, No.1, 2010, 59–72.
4 Gross 1913b: 1180.
5 Bauer 2006a.
6 Tutu 1999.
7 Pickering 2008.
8 Beringer 2006.
9 Matthew 5: 9.

If not Now, WHEN?

For M.S., teacher and friend.

Nearly always, when I speak of God,
about the sacredness of love,
of hope and joy,
someone is bound to ask —
reproachfully —
"Aren't you forgetting
cruelty and misery,
abuse and hunger, hatred?
Do you not rather look at our world
through rosy-coloured spectacles?!"

How come that
when almost everybody
speaks of nothing but
hunger, hatred and abuse,
misery and cruelty,
I have yet to hear
someone to ask,
"Aren't you forgetting
joy and hope,
the sacredness of love?
And what of God?"

Yes, indeed, God:
How would *you* feel
if you had done your utmost
in preparing for your guests
a feast of abundance,
and all they'd ever do
was bite your hands?

Has ever in the past
staring at the dark
helped to put a single stone
atop another one
to build Jerusalem?!

Has He not given us
all the ingredients
to build another paradise
right here on earth,
where hope turns into joy
for sacred love to reign?!

So what, for *Heaven's* sake
are we *waiting* for?!

Gottfried Maria Heuer
2, 4 October 2010, London

Figure 18.1 Otto Gross and Hans Gross. Psychoanalysis and Criminology – Libido and Power: Eighth International Otto Gross Congress, Graz, 2011.

Index